D1105250

CHRISTIAN THEOLOGY

Volume I

by

H. Orton Wiley, S.T.D.

BEACON HILL PRESS OF KANSAS CITY
Kansas City, Mo.

FIRST PRINTING, 1940

ISBN: 083-410-3346

DEDICATION

To the young men and young women who, feeling the
call of God to the work of the ministry, desire to
"take heed to the doctrine" that they may
be able to direct others in the way that
leads to God and life eternal, this
work is affectionately dedicated.

PRINTED IN THE UNITED STATES OF AMERICA

PREFACE

Nearly twenty years ago I was asked by the Department of Education of the Church of the Nazarene, of which Dr. J. B. Chapman was then chairman, to prepare a work on Systematic Theology for use in the Course of Study for Licensed Ministers. I immediately set myself to the task but my range of vision was too narrow. I was constantly discovering new truth and each new discovery demanded a place in the plan of the work. Now after nearly twenty years of constant study and teaching, I am presenting to the church the result of these efforts in a work entitled *Christian Theology*. It is offered with a prayer that it may find at least some small place in the preparation of young men and women who look forward to the work of the ministry. I have no thought of attempting any new contribution to modern theological science. My purpose and aim has been to review the field of theology in as simple a manner as possible for the use of those who, entering the ministry, desire to be informed concerning the great doctrines of the church.

I wish to acknowledge my obligation to the Rev. Paul Hill of Lynbrook, New York, who has collaborated with me in the preparation of this work and who has made many helpful suggestions and criticisms. To the General Superintendents of the church, Dr. John W. Goodwin, Dr. R. T. Williams and Dr. James B. Chapman, I owe a special debt of gratitude for their constant help and inspiration during the heavy years of preparation. To Dr. Chapman especially I am indebted for the *Introduction* to this work. Dr. Olive M. Winchester has reviewed the references to the Hebrew and Greek texts, and Dr. L. A. Reed has furnished the parallel between the Genesis Account of Creation and Modern Science. To all the above I express my sincere appreciation for the help given to me.

The various publishers have extended me the privilege of making certain quotations from their books, and for this I am deeply grateful. I acknowledge my debt to the following: to Funk and Wagnalls for permission to use a quotation from *The Institutes of the Christian Religion* by Gerhart; to the Pilgrim Press for a selection from their book, *Christ and the Eternal Order* by my former honored professor, John Wright Buckham; to the Cokesbury Press for permission to quote from their work on *Systematic Theology* by Dr. Summers; to the Methodist Book Concern for selections from *Systematic Theology* by Dr. Miley, *System of Christian Doctrine* by Dr. Sheldon, and *Foundations of the Christian Faith* by Dr. Rishell; to Scribners for references to *Present Day Theology* by Dr. Stearns, and *An Outline of Theology* by Dr. William Newton Clarke; to Longmans for a reference to their work entitled *A Theological Introduction to the Thirty-nine Articles* by Dr. Bicknell, and to any others not mentioned above whose works have furnished me inspiration and help in the preparation of this work.

It is to the Nazarene Publishing House that I am specially indebted for the publication of this work now presented to the church. The Manager, Mr. M. Lunn, and the Assistant Manager, Rev. P. H. Lunn, have given the writer every encouragement and been patient with his many shortcomings. Both the writer and the church are indebted to the publishers for the splendid form in which the book is presented.

I would indeed be ungrateful if in this, the publication of my first work, I did not pay rich tribute to her who for the entire period has had an unflagging interest in the preparation of this work, and has ever been a constant stimulus and blessing, my wife, Alice M. Wiley.

H. Orton Wiley,
Pasadena, California.

INTRODUCTION

As far back as 1919 those of us who were serving on the General Department of Education in the Church of the Nazarene felt keenly the need of a work on systematic theology of sufficient scope and thoroughness that it might serve as a standard of doctrine in connection with the development of the literature of our church and movement, and we asked Dr. H. Orton Wiley to undertake to produce such a work. Pressed by many duties as college president, and for a time as editor of the *Herald of Holiness,* Dr. Wiley was unable to give the thought and attention to this subject that was necessary for its speedy completion. Sometimes we felt that he did not make sufficient progress with the task to furnish ground for hope that he would live to complete it. But this delay was useful, for during all this time Dr. Wiley has been gathering material, rearranging his own thought and growing in courage for the stupendous task set before him. And now within recent months he has found it possible to devote more time and thought to the direct task, and he has been able to do better work than otherwise would have been possible. So we are the gainers for waiting.

I am glad to be counted among those who have encouraged Dr. Wiley from the beginning. I have never missed an opportunity to urge him to pursue his task of writing the standard theology for our church, even though he must do it at the expense of neglecting other duties. For I have felt that he would through this channel make the greatest and most lasting contribution of his life. And just now as he is ready to hand over the first volume to the publishers, having myself made a careful examination of it, I am more convinced than ever that he has done a work that few men of this generation are prepared to do, and that he has given us a theology so fundamental and so dependable for scholarship that it will stand as standard with us for many years to come.

Dr. Wiley is a scholar, but he is more than a scholar. He is an unctuous preacher, and an administrator. He has been compelled to try out his theories in the school of life and to test his claims in the furnace of trial and affliction. He is not a speculator nor an inventor. He is at most a discoverer and a judge of sound words. For the space of an average generation he has been before us as a Christian and a leader, and he has everywhere and all the time deserved and received the full commendation of his contemporaries and intimate coadjutors. He is a man of good report among all who know him intimately or distantly. It is a joy to commend him because it is certain none will arise to contradict.

It is not expected that one writing a foreword should enter into an analysis of a book. Especially is this the case when the book is one demanding so much of study and thought as this monumental work which you now have in hand. But you will find the scope adequate, the theses orthodox, the arguments convincing, and the conclusions clear and unequivocal. I really do not see how more could be done with the subject of systematic theology than Dr. Wiley has done.

This work will find its place as a textbook in our schools and in the course of study for ministers. This will probably be its two largest fields. But its style brings it within the scope of the Sunday school worker and layman of the church, and many who are not in the official callings of the church will find pleasure and profit in the study of the great doctrines which lie at the base of our holy religion. I believe the demand for such material is sufficiently great that Dr. Wiley's theology will find a wide field among spontaneous students, as well as among those who must take it in connection with technical preparation for given tasks.

Without the slightest reservation, and with the fullest satisfaction, I commend Dr. Wiley and his work on Systematic Theology to all men everywhere to whom

6

such commendation from me can carry meaning. And my prayer is that God may continue to bless the author and publishers, and that the leaves of this book may serve for healing, even as leaves from the tree of life.

JAMES B. CHAPMAN, *General Superintendent,*

Church of the Nazarene.
Kansas City, Missouri, April 6, 1940.

CONTENTS

PART I. INTRODUCTION: THE PROVINCE OF THEOLOGY

CHRISTIAN THEOLOGY

CHAPTER I

THE IDEA AND RELATIONS OF THEOLOGY

The term "Introduction," when used in a technical sense, is one of extensive application. Every branch of scientific knowledge must be preceded by a preliminary survey, in order to properly determine its boundaries and contents in relation to other fields of investigation. There must be a "recognition of the organic whole of the sciences," says Schelling, and this "must precede the definite pursuit of a specialty. The scholar who devotes himself to a particular study must become acquainted with the position it occupies with respect to this whole, and the particular spirit which pervades it, as well as the mode of development by which it enters into the harmonious union of the whole. Hence the importance of the method by which he is himself to estimate his science, in order that he may not regard it in a slavish spirit, but independently and in the spirit of the whole." The term "Introduction" has in modern times largely superseded the terms "Prolegomena" and "Propædeutic" formerly used in philosophy and theology. The terms "Encyclopedia" and "Methodology" which were frequently used in the sense of a distinct science, must still be considered an important part of the general curriculum. A true "Introduction," however, must embrace (1) formal or systematic Encyclopedia—or a presentation of the information necessary to a study of the several departments of theology; (2) Methodology—or directions as to the best methods of theological study; and to these must be added (3) a History of Theology as systematized in the church. The present chapter (I) will deal with the Idea and Relations of Theology, while the three following chapters will be devoted to (II) Sources and Limitations; (III) Systems and Methods; and (IV) Theology in the Church.

THE NATURE AND SCOPE OF THEOLOGY

Christian Theology, or Dogmatics as the term is often used technically, is that branch of theological science which aims to set forth in a systematic manner the doctrines of the Christian faith. The term *theology* is derived from the Greek words *theos (θεός)* and *logos (λόγος)*, and originally signified a discourse about God. The word was in use before the advent of Christ and the development of the Christian Church. Aristotle in his *Organon* applied the term theology to his highest or first philosophy. The Greeks were accustomed to applying the term *theologoi* to their honored poets and teachers, such as Homer, Hesiod and Orpheus, "who with poetic inspiration sang of the gods and divine things." In its most general sense, therefore, the term theology may be applied to the scientific investigation of real or supposed sacred persons, things or relations. However crude the content of these treatises may be, usage allows it to be called theology if the subject matter is concerned with that which is regarded as sacred. The term is therefore elastic and somewhat vague, and must be made more definite and specific by the use of qualifiying terms as Christian or Ethnic theology.

Definitions of Christian Theology. Christian theology has been defined in various ways by the masters of this science. Perhaps none of these definitions, however, exceeds in adequacy or comprehensiveness that of William Burton Pope who defines it as "the science of God and divine things, based upon the revelation made to mankind in Jesus Christ, and variously systematized within the Christian Church." Others define it as follows: "Christian Theology, or Dogmatics, as it is technically called, is that branch of theological science which aims to give systematic expression to the doctrines of the Christian faith."—WILLIAM ADAMS BROWN. "Dogmatic Theology treats of the doctrines of the Christian faith held by a community of believers, in other words, by the church."—BISHOP MARTENSEN. "Theology is the exhibition of the facts of Scripture in their proper order and relation with the principles or general truths involved in the facts themselves, and which pervade and harmonize the whole."—DR. CHARLES HODGE. "Theology is the science of God and the relations between God and the universe."—DR. AUGUSTUS HOPKINS STRONG. "Systematic Theology is that part of the entire system of theology which has to solve the problem presented by the Christian faith itself—the exhibition of Christianity as truth."—DR. J. A. DORNER. "Christian Theology is the intellectual treatment of the Christian religion."—WILLIAM NEWTON CLARKE. "Theology is a discourse about God as related to moral beings and His created universe."—DR. A. M. HILLS. "Theology may be defined as the systematic exposition and rational justification of the intellectual content of religion."—DEAN ALBERT C. KNUDSON. "Dogmatics deals with the doctrinal teachings of the Christian religion. It is the systematic and scientific presentation of the doctrine of Christianity in harmony with the Scriptures and in consonance with the confessions of the church."—DR. JOSEPH STUMP. "Systematic Theology is the scientific and connected presentation of Christian doctrine in its relation to both faith and morals."—GEORGE R. CROOKS and JOHN F. HURST.

Dr. Wakefield, who edited "Watson's Institutes" and added some valuable material of his own, defines theology as "that science which treats of the existence the character, and the attributes of God; His laws and government; the doctrines which we are to believe, the moral change which we must experience, and the duties which we are required to perform." Closely related to this and to the definition of Dr. Pope, is that of Dr. Alvah Hovey, the great Baptist theologian. "By Christian theology," he says, "is meant the science of the Christian religion, or the science which ascertains, justifies, and systematizes all attainable truth concerning God and His relation, through Jesus Christ, to the universe and especially to mankind."

We may gather up therefore the various phases of truth as set forth in the above definitions and summarize them in a brief but we think equally adequate definition as follows: "Christian Theology is the systematic presentation of the doctrines of the Christian Faith."

The Scope of Theology. The study of Christian Theology must be expanded to comprehend a wide range of investigation, and then systematized according to principles regarded as dominant in the history of Christian thought. If the definition of Dr. Pope be carefully analyzed, and likewise that of Wakefield and Hovey, it will be found that the following subjects are given consideration: *First,* God as the source, subject, and end of all theology. "This gives it its unity, dignity and sanctity. It is the *A Deo, De Deo, In Deum:* from God in its origin, concerning God in its substance, and it leads to God in all its issues." *Second,* Religion as furnishing the basic consciousness in man, without which there could be no capacity in human nature to receive the spiritual revelations of divine truth. *Third,* Revelation as the source of the facts out of which systematic theology is constructed. *Fourth,* the relation of these facts to Jesus Christ, the Personal and Eternal Word in the revelation of God. *Fifth,* the development and systematization of theology in the Church as the expression of its Christian life, under the immediate supervision and control of the Holy Spirit. *Sixth,* Christian Theology must be considered in its relation to contemporaneous thought.

THE RELATIONS OF THEOLOGY

"There is a sense," says Dr. Pope, "in which universal theology is concerned simply with the relation of all things to God: if we carefully guard our meaning we may make this proposition include the converse, the relation of God to all things. Relation, of course, must be mutual: but it is hard in this matter to detach from the notion of relation that of dependence. The Eternal One is the Unconditioned Being. When we study His

nature and perfections and works we must always remember that He is His Perfect Self independent of
every created object and independent of every thought
concerning Him. But there is not a doctrine, nor is
there a branch or development of any doctrine, which
is not purely the expression of some relation of His
creatures to the Supreme First Cause. Hence every
branch of this science is sacred. It is a temple which is
filled with the presence of God. From its hidden sanctuary, into which no high priest taken from among men
can enter, issues a light which leaves no part dark save
where it is dark with excess of glory. Therefore all fit
students are worshipers as well as students" (Pope,
CCT, I, pp. 4-5). But aside from the divine Source of
theology, there are three outstanding and vital relations which it sustains: *first,* to religion; *second,* to
revelation and *third,* to the church.

Theology and Religion. Since theology in a preliminary and general sense is the science of religion, it is
therefore necessary to come immediately to a discussion
of the nature of religion. It may be said that religion
furnishes the basic consciousness in man without which
there could be no capacity in human nature to receive
the revelation of God. It has its roots, therefore, in the
very nature of man. It is the consciousness that he is
made for higher things, and that he has kinship to the
unseen Power upon which he feels himself dependent.
Added to this is a sense of need which expresses itself
negatively in a consciousness of sin, and positively in a
desire for communion with a higher spiritual power. It
is the province of theology to gather up and systematize
these needs and desires, for religion is not merely an
individual but also a social phenomenon. Those who are
brought into communion with God feel that they must
impart this knowledge to others, and thus arise the various religious societies. These crystallize into fixed
institutions with a body of tradition designed to hand
down to posterity the religious insights of the past. Theology and religion are related, therefore, "as effects in
different spheres, of the same cause. As theology is

an effect produced in the sphere of systematic thought
by the facts respecting God and the universe, so religion is an effect which these same facts produce in the
sphere of individual and collective life" (Strong, *Syst.
Th.*, I, p. 19).

Theology and Revelation. Theology bears relation
not only to religious experience in a general way, but
also to that higher type of revealed truth which is found
in Christ and known as the Christian Revelation. Since
the time of Schleiermacher, feeling or the sense of dependence has been given a large place in theological
thought. There are those who fear too great subjectiv-
ity if theology is to be grounded in Christian experience,
but it should ever be borne in mind that the Christian
faith is not something which is self-created. It has its
source in objective revelation. The universe is an external revelation of God. It declares His *eternal power
and Godhead* (Rom. 1: 20). Over against the position
of James Martineau who unwarrantably isolates the
witness of God to the individual soul, Dr. Strong insists
that in many cases where truth has been originally communicated as an internal revelation, the same Spirit
who communicated it has brought about an external
record of it, so that the internal revelation might be
handed down to others than those who first received it.
Both the internal revelations as recorded, and the external revelations as interpreted, furnish objective facts
which may serve as proper material for science.

Theology and the Church. It is to the Church that God
has committed the Scriptures and these have become
its Rule of Faith and Practice. As the early oracle had
its ark, so the Christian Church has become the recep-

The whole creation reveals the Word. In nature God shows His power;
in incarnation His grace and truth. Scripture testifies of these, but Scripture is not the essential Word. The Scripture is truly apprehended and
appropriated when in it and through it we see the living and present
Christ. It does not bind men to itself alone, but it points them to the
Christ of whom it testifies. Christ is the authority. In the Scriptures He
points us to Himself and demands our faith in Him. This faith once begotten, leads us to a new appropriation of Scripture, but also to a new
criticism of Scripture. We find Christ more and more in Scripture, and
yet we judge Scripture more and more by the standard which we find in
Christ.—DORNER, *Hist. Prot. Theology* 1: 231-264.

tacle of the faith which was "once delivered unto the saints" (Jude 3). With the coming of the incarnate Christ, and the gift of the Holy Spirit on the day of Pentecost, the foundations of the Church were laid; and with the enlargement of its mission to include mankind universally, it was necessary, also, that the divine oracles be likewise increased. Becoming the repository of a new dispensational truth, the Church was under obligation from the beginning, both as a teacher and a defender of the faith, to create a theology, by means of which it could systematically present its teachings. This didactic divinity, Dr. Pope insists, was the necessary expansion of what in Scripture is termed the *Apostles' doctrine*. "Its first and simplest form as seen in the writings of the earliest Fathers, was *Expository* or practical, aiming at the edification of the flock; then followed the *Catechetical*, for the preliminary instruction of converts or Catechumens in order to baptism, conducted by pastors as Catechists, and formulated in the permanent Catechism; and thus were laid the foundations of all subsequent biblical theology proper. Defensive assertion of truth was rendered necessary by heresies arising within the community, and by the duty of vindicating the Faith against those without. The latter obligation gave rise to *Apologetics* in all its branches, called in modern times *Evidences:* Apology having reference rather to the position of the Christian society as challenged by the world, Evidences belonging rather to its aggressive missionary character. The former introduced *Dogmatic Theology*, taught first in the Creeds — the Apostles', the Nicene-Constantinopolitan, and the Athanasian; afterward in specific expositions of those creeds, and their individual articles; this as distinguished from Apologetic, is controversial divinity or *Polemics*. In later times, all these branches have been incorporated into the unity of what is called Systematic divinity, or the orderly arrangement of the doctrines of revelation, as they are Dogmas fixed in the decisions of the Church, defended against external assaults, and unfolded in the ethics of human duty. This is the normal development

of the science within Christendom and common to all
its branches. Every Christian community presents in
its own literature more or less systematically all these
various forms of fundamental teaching" (Pope, CCT, I,
pp. 15-16). We have given only in brief outline the
manner in which theology was developed in the Church.

DIVISIONS OF THEOLOGY

The whole field of theology may be broadly divided
into (I) Christian Theology, and (II) Ethnic Theology.
By Ethnic Theology is meant the teachings embraced in
the non-Christian religions as opposed to the revelation
of God in Christ. Non-Christian people, whether crude
or cultured, have their doctrines of God or of the gods,
and of things which they regard as sacred. These must
be classified as theologies. To Christians, the value of
this ethnic theology is chiefly illustrative, setting forth
as it does the outstanding and fundamental differences
between Christianity and paganism. By this contrast,
Christianity is seen to be, not merely a religion which
has attained to a higher scale in natural development,
but one which is unique in that it is a revelation from
God to man, rather than an origination of man in his
state of barbarism. It does, however, have this exegetical
value, for the great doctrines of Christianity will be seen
in a clearer light when placed side by side with the de-
formities of heathenism.

Another division, more popular with the older theologians than at the present time, is that of (I) Natural
Theology, and (II) Revealed Theology. Natural Theology draws its sources from the facts of nature including
the exercise of reason and the illumination of conscience.
Revealed Theology finds its sources in the Holy Scriptures as the authoritative revelation of God to man.
Christian Theology does not regard Revealed Theology
as in opposition to Natural Theology but supplementary
to it. It regards it as gathering up the primary revelation of God through nature and the constitution of man,
into the higher and perfect personal revelation of God
in Christ.

Christian Theology as a didactic or positive science is usually made to conform to the four main divisions of Biblical (or Exegetical), Historical, Systematic and Practical Theology. This fourfold division was generally followed by the earlier encyclopædists, Neosselt, Thym, Staudlin, Schmidt, and Planck. Rabiger and Hagenbach followed the fourfold outline of Schaff—perhaps the arrangement now most commonly employed. Among the more modern theologians, Miley, Pope, Strong, Brown and Clarke follow the fourfold division. There are some of the more prominent theologians, however, who prefer different arrangements. Schleiermacher arranged his material in three divisions, (I) Philosophical; (II) Historical; and (III) Practical—"the root, the trunk, and the crown." Another has a five-fold division, (I) Exegetical; (II) Historical; (III) Apologetic; (IV) Systematic; and (V) Practical. Cave in his *Introduction to Theology* arranges his material in six main divisions, (I) Natural Theology; (II) Ethnic Theology; (III) Biblical Theology; (IV) Ecclesiastical Theology; (V) Comparative Theology; and (VI) Pastoral (or Practical) Theology. Danz attempted still another arrangement making a twofold division (I) that which pertains to Religion, and (II) that which pertains to the Church. With the fresh impetus given to

The arrangement of subjects under the fourfold division which is most commonly followed is that proposed by Schaff in his Theological Propædeutic. (I) Exegetical Theology, including (1) Biblical Philology; (2) Biblical Archæology; (3) Biblical Isagogic, or Historico-Critical Introduction which includes both the lower or textual criticism and the higher or historical criticism; (4) Biblical Hermeneutics. (II) Historical Theology, including Biblical and Ecclesiastical history in the widest sense. (III) Systematic Theology including (1) Apologetics; (2) Biblical Theology; (3) Dogmatic Theology; (4) Symbolics, Polemics, and Irenics; (5) Ethics, Ecclesiastical Geography and Statistics. (IV) Practical Theology including (1) Theory of the Christian Ministry; (2) Church Law and Church Polity; (3) Liturgics; (4) Homiletics; (5) Catechetics; (6) Poimenics; and (7) Evangelistics.

Crooks and Hurst in their *Theological Encyclopedia and Methodology* have the following arrangement of subjects: (I) Exegetical Theology, including Archæology, Philology, Isagogics, Canonics, Criticism, Hermeneutics and Interpretation; (II) Historical Theology, including History of Dogma, Church History, Patristics, Symbolics, and Statistics; (III) Systematic Theology, including Doctrine, Dogmatics, Apologetics, Polemics, Irenics, Theology (in the narrower sense of the term), Anthropology, Christology, Soteriology, Eschatology and Ethics; (IV) Practical Theology, including Catechetics, Liturgics, Homiletics, and Pastoral Theology.

historical studies during the middle and latter part of
the nineteenth century, an attempt was made to place
Historical Theology in advance of the Biblical or Exegetical Theology as formerly accepted. Kienlen and Pelt
adapted a threefold division into (I) Historical Theology,
including exegetical; (II) Systematic Theology and (III)
Practical Theology. Against this, two main objections
may be urged: *First,* since Christian Theology draws its
sources largely from the Scriptures as revealed truth,
its beginnings should coincide with that fact, and therefore be found in a thorough and systematic study of
the documents in which this revelation is recorded. This
is Exegetical Theology. Protestant Theology which is
based so emphatically upon the Bible as the Word of
God, cannot but establish Exegetical Theology as a separate and distinct division, assigning to the Scriptures a
sufficient and unrestricted position in the realm of theological thought. Without this, theology may become
philosophical and barren, never biblical and vital.
Second, we must bear in mind that there is one law
of development which is peculiar to the Scriptures—the
law of progressive revelation, and closely allied to it
another law which governs the systematization of the
truths revealed. Exegetical Theology must take into
account this historical progression, and the recorded
events of sacred history, therefore, become the basis for
the interpretation of all history. The logical arrangement of the revealed truths set forth in sacred history
gives us Biblical Theology. Thus there is given us by

The arrangement of the fourfold division indicated above may be
also justified in the following manner: "The assertion is warranted
that all knowledge is based either on personal (physical or mental)
observation, or on report and tradition, and is, therefore, either theoretical (philosophical) or historical in its nature. Historical knowledge
however, must be obtained by investigation, and for the latter acquaint-
ance with languages and philological criticism is necessary; while
theoretical knowledge leads to its practical application. In like manner
Christianity is, in its positive character, both a history and a doctrine;
but its history is based on the Bible, which must, first of all, be exegetically examined; and its doctrine is not pure knowledge but practical. The truth of revelation is to be applied in the Church and the
various departments of Church activity, to which practical theology has
regard. The two departments of learning are thus confined between two
fields of applied art, the exegetical at the beginning, and the practical at
the end.—Crooks and Hurst, *Encyclopedia and Methodology,* p. 139.

this process a clear idea of the connection which, beginning in Exegetical Theology, traces the progress of historical development down to our own times by means of Historical Theology, combines the truths thus given into a mental picture of orderly arrangement as found in Systematic Theology, and from this makes the necessary deductions which Practical Theology offers for converting theory into practice. Christian Theology, therefore, becomes an Organism of Truth. In our further discussion of the forms of theology we shall observe this fourfold division as indicated. The arrangement of subjects is set forth more fully in the accompanying diagram. (See page 24.)

EXEGETICAL THEOLOGY

Exegetical Theology, or as it is frequently called, Biblical Theology, is a study of the contents of Scripture, exegetically ascertained and classified according to doctrines. Among the Greeks, the term "exegete" referred to one whose office it was to lead out or interpret the oracles to laymen with a view to producing sympathetic understanding. Exegetical Theology covers an extensive field of interpretation, dealing with both the Old and the New Testament Scriptures, and is commonly arranged in two main divisions, (I) Biblical Introduction, and (II) Biblical Exegesis or Interpretation.

1. *Biblical Introduction.* This department includes all the preliminary studies which are introductory to the actual work of exegesis. The older term used to designate this department was Isagogics, and included four branches of study, (a) Biblical Archæology, an auxiliary study of the manners and customs of ancient people; (b) Biblical Canonics, or a discussion of the canon of Scripture as understood by the ancient Jews, the early Christians, the Roman and the Protestant churches; (c) Biblical Criticism, including the lower or textual criticism, with a view to ascertaining the correct reading of the text; and the higher criticism, too often confused with destructive criticism, which deals with the authorship, date and authenticity of the books of the Bible, the

THEOLOGICAL CHART

```
                                                         ┌ Archæology
                                                         │ Philology
                                    ┌ Introduction ──────┤ Isagogics
                 I. EXEGETICAL      │                    │ Canonics
                    THEOLOGY        │                    └ Hermeneutics
                                    └ Exegesis

                                                         ┌ Biblical History
                                    ┌ Sacred ────────────┤ Biblical
                 II. HISTORICAL     │                    └    Dogmatics
                     THEOLOGY       │
                                    │                    ┌ Church History
                                    └ Ecclesiastical ────┤ Patristics
                                                         └ Symbolics

                                    ┌ Apologetics
                                    │                    ┌ Theology
                                    │                    │ Cosmology
                                    │                    │ Anthropology
CHRISTIAN                           │ Dogmatics ─────────┤ Hamartiology
THEOLOGY                            │                    │ Christology
                                    │                    │ Soteriology
                                    │ Irenics            └ Eschatology
                 III. SYSTEMATIC    │
                      THEOLOGY      │ Polemics
                                    │                    ┌ Moral Philosophy
                                    │                    │ Moral Theology
                                    └ Ethics ────────────┤ Casuistry
                                                         └ Ascetics
                                    ┌ Catechetics
                                    │ Liturgics
THEOLOGY                            │ Canonics
   IN            IV. PRACTICAL      │ Homiletics
GENERAL              THEOLOGY       │ Evangelistics
                                    │ Pastoral
                                    └ Theology
                                                         ┌ Brahmanism
                                                         │ Buddhism
                 ┌ History of Religions                  │ Confucianism
                 │                                       │ Taoism
ETHNIC           │                                       │ Shintoism
THEOLOGY         │                                       ┤ Zoroastrianism
                 └ Comparative Religions                 │ Mohammedanism
                                                         │ Barbarian
                                                         │    Religions
                                                         └ Extinct Religions
```

circumstances under which they were written, their occasion and design; and (d) Biblical Hermeneutics, or the science of the laws and principles underlying correct interpretation.

2. *Biblical Exegesis.* Under this division is included, interpretation, exposition and application of the Scriptures. Two things are essential: (a) a knowledge of interpretation as found in sacred and cognate philology, and a proper understanding of oriental archæology. The Bible was originally written in Hebrew, Chaldee and Hellenistic Greek, and a knowledge of these languages is essential to authoritative exegesis. Then there is the Arabic, Assyrian, and Aramaic of the Targums—all related in several ways to the Hebrew language. Oriental archæology is essential as furnishing a knowledge of the social, religious and political life of the peoples associated with the Hebrews at different periods of their national life. (b) The method of exegesis is likewise important. At different periods in church history such methods of interpretation as the Allegorical, the Catenistic, the Dogmatic, the Pietistic, the Rationalistic and the Spiritualistic have all held sway. These will be given a brief description in the History of Exegesis.

3. *History of Exegesis.* Exegetical studies have a history which must be viewed according to the several analyses or plans of interpretation. Prominent among these are: (a) Jewish exegesis, which in its rabbinical form is represented by the Targums, and in its Alexandrian form by the writings of the Hellenistic Jews, particularly Philo of Alexandria. (b) Early Christian exegesis, which made much of quotations from the Old and New Testaments. The allegorical method borrowed from Philo, is found in the writings of pseudo-Barnabas and others. (c) Patristic exegesis, which took three main forms, the literal and realistic interpretations of Tertullian and Cyprian; the historico-grammatical school represented by Jerome and Chrysostom, and the allegorical method which was more or less prevalent in all the forms. (d) Mediæval exegesis, represented by the compilations of the Catenists, consists in expositions selected from

various authors, as the term *catena,* which signifies a chain, would indicate. Along with this was the mystic and scholastic exegesis of many of the schoolmen. (e) Reformation exegesis, which followed the revival of learning, is found in three prevailing forms, that of the German or Lutheran school, that of the Swiss or Reformed school, and that of the Dutch or Arminian school. The work in exegesis done by British and American scholars is abundant and valuable but does not fall into any one distinctive group.

HISTORICAL THEOLOGY

Historical Theology is sometimes enlarged to include the whole range of ecclesiastical history, but in the strictest sense refers only to the historical development of Christian doctrine and its influence upon the life of the Church. It includes two sections: (1) Biblical, which is limited to the historical portions of the sacred Scriptures; and (2) Ecclesiastical, which traces the development of doctrine in the Church from the time of the apostles to the present.

1. *Biblical History.* This subject comprises a study of the historical sections of the Old and New Testaments, and such contemporaneous history as may serve to throw light on the biblical accounts. In the narrower sense of the term, Biblical History has to do primarily with the facts and events related in the Bible in so far as they bear upon the divine plan of human redemption. Biblical Dogmatics, on the other hand, embraces a study of the doctrinal contents of the Scriptures presented in the order of their historical unfolding; for the Bible must ever be viewed as revelation in progress and therefore not complete until the close of the canon. In order to understand the content of Biblical History there must be a proper orientation on the part of the student —such an orientation as enables him to see the point of view of the people to which the Scriptures were addressed, rather than the significance they hold for those of a later day. Once clearly understand this, and it

answers many of the objections offered against the customs and practices of the people under the earlier and less perfect periods of revelation. Christ came not to abrogate the teachings of the Old Testament, but to fulfill them—that is, to bring them to the highest forms of experience and life. There can be no antagonism between the teachings of the Old and New Testaments as such, but the one must be regarded as primary, the other perfect and complete.

2. *Ecclesiastical History.* Here the subject matter is regarded as Church History when dealing with the external events in the Church's struggle with the world, the development of its institutions and its spiritual accomplishments. It is regarded as the History of Doctrine when it takes into account the shaping of the Christian faith into doctrinal statements. Included in this division, also, is the study of the writings of the Fathers commonly known as *Patristics;* and the study of creeds or symbols of the Church generally treated under the head of *Symbolics.*

SYSTEMATIC THEOLOGY

Systematic Theology arranges in logical order, the materials furnished by Exegetical and Historical Theology; and it does this in order to promote fuller study and practical application. It may, therefore, be defined as "the scientific and connected presentation of Christian doctrine in its relation to both faith and morals."

Biblical Theology is the offspring of Protestantism, and in no other than the free and fertile soil of Protestantism can it ever flourish. The history of its origin and rise to a distinct and recognized branch of theological science, is not the least interesting chapter in the internal history of the modern church. But while Protestant freedom and activity have given to the world this and many other phases of biblical and theological study, it would be well for Protestants themselves to hold ever vividly in mind that liberty is not license. . . . . It would be a sad day for the Church, and hence for the world, if Protestantism, in its bounding freedom and eagerness to unveil truth, should swing loose from all historical landmarks, and the word *traditional* should become only a term of reproach, and we should have no more respect for gray hairs of the once mighty past. The middle way is the safest, and if Protestant biblical study, whether in its narrower or more comprehensive sense, would achieve its best results for the Church and the world, in this way it must walk.

"Systematic Theology," says William Adams Brown, "occupies the center of the theological curriculum, midway between the Exegetical and Historical, and the practical disciplines. From the former it receives its materials; to the latter it furnishes their principles. In this it is like philosophy in the curriculum of the university, which stands midway between the sciences and the arts. We may describe it as the philosophy of the Christian life." Systematic Theology, however, is concerned not only with faith but with practice. It insists upon repentance as well as faith. It must therefore include both Dogmatics and Ethics. Lange sums up the relation existing between dogmatics and ethics as follows: "Dogmatics represents life in its transcendent relations to God, the eternal basis of its being; ethics according to its immanent relation to the world of man. Dogmatics regards it in its specifically ecclesiastical character, ethics in its general human character. Dogmatics describes the organ, ethics indicates the tasks that await its energy. Dogmatics teaches how man derives his Christian life from God, ethics how he is to give proof of it in the world of men, by human methods and in that exercise of incarnated power which we call virtue" (LANGE, *Chr. Dogm.*, pp. 46, 47). There appears to be no general agreement as to the divisions of Systematic Theology, but for our purpose we shall treat the subject under the threefold division of (I) Dogmatics; (II) Ethics; and (III) Apologetics.

1. *Dogmatics.* Christian Dogmatics as defined by Martensen, is that branch of theology which "treats of the doctrines of the Christian faith held by a community of believers, in other words, by the Church." It is therefore, "the science which presents and proves the Christian doctrines, regarded as forming a connected system" (MARTENSEN, *Christian Dogmatics*, p. 1). Strong points out the distinction which formerly obtained between Dogmatics and Systematic Theology, insisting that Dogmatic Theology in strict usage, is "the systematizing of the doctrines as expressed in the symbols of the Church, together with the grounding of these

in the Scriptures, and the exhibition, so far as may be, of their rational necessity." Systematic Theology begins, on the other hand, not with the symbols, but with the Scriptures. It asks first, not what the church has believed, but what is the truth of God's revealed word" (STRONG, S. T., I, p. 41). But since Christian Dogmatics forms the central point of all theology, it has come to be identified in present day thought with Systematic Theology itself. This too was the earlier conception for Augusti remarks "that the old and generally adopted usage, which conceives dogmatics and theology as being synonyms, is evidence of the high importance which has always been attached to this first of all the departments of theology" (AUGUSTI, Syst. der Christl Dogmatik, p. 1). The term, however, still connotes a relation to the symbols or dogmatical writings of the Church, in which the particular tenets of a school or denomination are reflected. It is in the words of Lange "in a specific sense the theology of the Church," for dogmatics should bear a direct relation to the Church to which it owes its existence. It is proper, therefore, in this sense, to speak of the dogmatics of Roman Catholicism or of Protestantism, of Lutheran, Reformed or Arminian. Christian Dogmatics must be viewed, not as a philosophy of religion, or a history of doctrine, but as a science including both historical and philosophical elements. It is the science which presents to our notice the material obtained by exegesis and history in an organized and systematic form, representing the sum of the truth of the Christian faith in organic connection

The Reformation seemed to spring primarily from moral, not directly from doctrinal causes. But a change of relations soon took place, which resulted in the attaching of greater weight to the definition of doctrinal points. It might be said that attention was, with entire propriety, directed chiefly to the settling of the truth belonging to the faith, since works spring from faith. But the faulty principles consisted in this fact, that the faith was too little apprehended from the dynamical, and too greatly from the merely theoretical side, the apprehending of the faith being confounded with tendencies of belief, and the understanding of the faith with its power. In this way Christian ethics long failed to receive just treatment. It is not strange, therefore, that Calixtus should fall upon the idea of emancipating ethics from dogmatics, and assigning it to a separate field. The Reformed theologian, Danæus, attempted this even earlier than Calixtus.—CROOKS AND HURST, Encycl. and Meth., pp. 396, 397.

with the facts of religious consciousness. It therefore demands preparatory training in exegesis and history, as well as in philosophy" (CROOKS and HURST, *Encyl. and Meth.*, p. 399).

2. *Ethics.* The second main branch of Systematic Theology is Christian Ethics, formerly known as Moral Philosophy. The term Ethics is from ἦθος or ἔθος and has relation to the home, the seat, posture, habit or internal character of the soul. Morals, on the other hand, comes from the root word *mos* which means custom, and refers more especially to the outward manifestation than to the internal character. The term ethics therefore has largely superseded that of moral philosophy in its application to the Christian life. Christian Ethics may be properly defined as the science of the Christian life. In the evangelical scheme, Dogmatics and Ethics are closely connected. It may be said that Ethics is the crown of Dogmatics, for the manifold truths of revelation find their highest expression in the restoration of man to the divine image. Christian Ethics differs from philosophical ethics in at least three fundamental positions. *First*, philosophical ethics has to do with determining man toward morality considered as a whole and impersonal; while Christian Ethics is purely personal, representing the divinely human life in the person of Christ as constituting the ideal of morality, and therefore requires of every individual that he become like Christ. *Second*, philosophical ethics starts from the moral self-determination of man, while Christian Ethics regards the Spirit of God as the determining power through which the law of God is written within the

Dogmatics is not only a science of faith, but also a knowledge grounded *in* and drawn *from* faith. It is not a mere historical exhibition of what has been, or now is, true for others, without being true for the author; nor is it a philosophical knowledge of Christian truth, obtained from a standpoint outside of faith and the Church. For even supposing—what yet we by no means concede—that a scientific insight into Christian truth is possible, without Christian faith, yet such philosophizing about Christianity, even though its conclusions were ever so favorable to the Church could not be called dogmatics. Theology stands within the pale of Christianity; and only that dogmatic theologian can be esteemed the organ of his science, who is also the organ of his Church—which is not the case with the mere philosopher, whose only aim is to promote the cause of pure science.—MARTENSEN, *Christian Dogmatics*, pp. 1, 2.

hearts of men. *Third,* philosophical ethics treats of the relations which man sustains to the world, while Christian Ethics deals primarily with the relations which he sustains to the kingdom of God. Christian Ethics must not, therefore, be regarded as a catalogue of duties and virtues imposed upon the individual from without; for the positive element does not consist in the authoritative letter of the law, but in a course of life introduced into human conditions, and actualized in Christ. This new life is through the Spirit, continued in the community of believers, and therefore determines its ethical standards.

3. *Apologetics.* It is the task of Christian Apologetics to justify the truth of the Christian religion at the bar of human reason. It has a further task of proving that the Christian religion is the only true and perfect manifestation of God to man in the Person of Jesus Christ. While sometimes regarded as a separate branch of theology, the subject of apologetics is frequently treated in connection with dogmatics. Closely related to apologetics are two similar branches of theology: (1) Polemics or the study of doctrinal differences; and (2) Irenics or the study of doctrinal harmonies with a view to the promotion of Christian unity. Sack in his *Polemik* distinguishes these terms in the following manner: "Dogmatics is Christian doctrine as adapted to Christian thinkers, implying friendliness on their part; apologetics is Christian doctrine in a form adapted to heathen thinkers, and presumes hostility on their part; and polemics adapts the doctrine to the state of heretical Christian thinkers, proceeding on the supposition of dissatisfaction on their part."

PRACTICAL THEOLOGY

Practical Theology is concerned with the application of the truths discovered in the preceding branches of theological study, and with their practical values in the renewing and sanctifying of men. Vinet defines it as "an art which supposes science, or science resolving itself into art. It is the art of applying usefully in the ministry, the knowledge acquired in the three other departments of theology which are purely scientific." Ebrard maintains that Practical Theology "when examined in the light, is not a knowledge but an ability; not a science but an art, in which theological knowledge acquired becomes practical." It embraces churchly activities and functions, whether exercised by the Church as a whole, or by individual members acting in a representative capacity. The arrangement of subjects as classified in this division vary greatly, but the following are generally included: (1) Homiletics treats of the composition and delivery of sermons; (2) Pastoral Theology is concerned with the qualifications of the minister in charge of a church or mission; (3) Catechetics has to do with the instruction of the young, whether in age or Christian experience, as a preparation for church membership; (4) Liturgics deals with the conduct of regular or special services in the church; (5) Evangelistics is a term applied to Home and Foreign Missions, and those forms of local or general work which have to do with the direct spread of the gospel and the salvation of men; and (6) Ecclesiology, more commonly known as Canonics or Church Polity, is a study of the various forms of church organization, including canon law.

A knowledge of the several divisions of theology is of utmost importance—especially to those whom God has called into the ministry. Exegetical Theology furnishes the authoritative sources; Historical Theology gives perspective and balance; Systematic Theology provides the doctrinal standards of the church; and Practical Theology seeks to make effective the knowledge gained in the previous departments. Without this full range of theological science there can be no true perspective, no balanced knowledge, no authoritative standards, and hence no supremely effective ministry.

CHAPTER II

THE SOURCES OF THEOLOGY

The question concerning the sources of theology meets the theologian at the very threshold of his science. It will be profitable, therefore, to give this subject due consideration before entering the temple of truth to survey its inner wealth and magnificence. It is here that we meet the most widely divergent views—the Roman Catholic, the Protestant Evangelical, the Mystical, and the Rationalistic—each of which demands some attention. Not infrequently, also, reason and revelation are regarded as the sources of theology. For our purposes, however, we shall use another classification, arranging the sources in two main divisions: (I) Authoritative Sources; and (II) Subsidiary Sources.

AUTHORITATIVE SOURCES

Christian Theology as the science of the one true and perfect religion is based upon the documentary records of God's revelation of Himself in Jesus Christ. The Bible, therefore, is the Divine Rule of faith and practice, and the only authoritative source of theology. But this statement needs explication if not qualification. In a stricter and deeper sense, Jesus Christ himself as the Personal and Eternal Word is the only true and adequate revelation of the Father. *No man hath seen God at any time; the only begotten Son, which is in the bosom of the Father, he hath declared him.* His testimony is the last word in objective revelation and this testimony is perfected in the Christian Scriptures. "The Oracle and the oracles are one." The Scriptures, therefore, become the perfect disclosure and finished revelation of the will of God in Christ Jesus.

In general, therefore, it may be said that the source of divine knowledge as exemplified in Christian theology is a unity, but a unity which exists in a twofold form with both objective and subjective aspects. Objectively, it is the self-revelation of God in Christ as recorded and presented in Holy Scripture, which "as the archetypal work of the Spirit of inspiration," says Martensen, "the Scriptures include within themselves a world of germs for a continuous development. While every dogmatic system grows old, the Bible remains eternally young" (MARTENSEN, *Chr. Dogm.*, p. 52). Subjectively, the same revealed truth lives in the Christian consciousness of the Church, being begotten and nourished by faith in Jesus Christ. This dual principle has developed through similar processes but with widely divergent results in the two great branches of the Church—the Roman Catholic and the Protestant Evangelical.

The Roman Catholic Church, previous to the Vatican Council, A.D. 1870, held that there were two valid and authoritative sources of theological knowledge — the Bible and tradition. By tradition as here used, is meant religious opinion on matters of faith and practice, which the Church believed to be handed down from apostolic times to succeeding generations by the Holy Spirit. Tradition, therefore, represents the crystallization of the subjective element in Christian consciousness. Lacking the deeper principle of fundamental unity, the rela-

The Roman Catholic position concerning the Bible differs from the Protestant in two important particulars. (1) It has since the time of Augustine included the Apocrypha among the canonical books of the Old Testament and regards them as of inspired and infallible authority. These were declared canonical by the Councils of Hippo (A.D. 393) and Carthage (A.D. 397). Later this action was confirmed by the Council of Trent (1542-1564) with the exception of the two books of Esdras and the Prayer of Manasseh. The Douay Version of the Old Testament (1609) contained forty-six books. (2) It differs from the Protestant position in the matter of inspiration. Protestantism regards only the original Hebrew and Greek texts as inspired, while the Roman Catholic Church by a papal bull holds that the version known as the Latin Vulgate was also inspired. There is also a wide difference in the matter of tradition, the Roman Catholic Church maintaining that tradition was another stream flowing from the same source of Christ who is the fountain of all truth. Thus later there came to be not only a canon of scripture but a canon of tradition, the Council of Trent affirming that the traditions are to be "received with equal piety and veneration with the Scriptures." The Protestant churches rejected tradition entirely as forming an authoritative source of theology.

tion of Scripture and tradition became very early a matter of serious concern. With the increasing authority of the Roman see, the dogmas and customs there received became in effect the criteria for the interpretation of the Scriptures themselves. This current ecclesiastical opinion was made the official position of the Church of Rome, at the Vatican Council in July, 1870, when it adopted the transmontane or Italian theory commonly known as papal infallibility. This was, in effect, a triumph of tradition over the supreme objective authority of the Bible. The Vatican decree had the further effect of changing the principle, originally held by both Eastern and Western Churches, as to the dual source of theological knowledge. Neither the written word nor ecclesiastical tradition is now the authoritative source. Both occupy a subordinate position and find their unity in the supreme authority of the Church. The pope when speaking *ex cathedra* becomes the mouthpiece of the Church, and thereby the source and arbiter of religious knowledge. The Church is thus placed in an abnormal relation to Jesus Christ, its Divine Head, and its decrees and interpretations have superseded the direct and immediate authority of the Holy Scriptures. Whatever honor may be accorded them, they are no longer, for Roman Catholicism, the sole and authoritative source of Christian Dogmatics.

In the Protestant Evangelical Church a similar process took place, though with directly opposite results. The development in Protestantism was perhaps not so conspicuous as that in the Church of Rome, because of the many and varied communions which are embraced in this one general term. It nevertheless had its ill effects in a distorted conception of the nature of the sacred Scriptures, their place in the Church, and their proper relation to Christ the Living Word. The Protestant Evangelical Church, especially during the sixteenth and a portion of the seventeenth centuries, found the dual source of theology, not in the scriptures and tradition, but in the Scriptures and the spiritual illumination of the Church, this latter being known technically as the *testimonium Spiritus Sancti*. These two principles, when rightly construed, find their deeper unity in the glorified Christ, by whom the Holy Spirit is given to the Church. The Spirit then, becomes at once the inspiring source of the Holy Scriptures, and the illuminating, regenerating and sanctifying Presence through whom believers are enabled to perceive and understand the truth as presented in the written Word. This evangelical conception corresponds to the twin principles of the Reformation which found expression in the formula, "Scripture alone, and faith alone."

As the unifying principle grew dim, the dual sources betrayed the same tendency toward severance as was displayed in the case of the Bible and Tradition. There was, however, this important difference. In Roman Catholicism, the material principle of tradition superseded the formal principle of sacred Scripture; while in Protestantism, the formal principle of Holy Scripture superseded the material principle of spiritual consciousness. In the Roman communion, therefore, the Church became the supreme authority and an apostolic succession a necessity; while in the Evangelical communion, the supreme authority was vested in the Scriptures, which being given to the Church by the apostles and prophets became thereby the only true and logical succession. Furthermore, as by undue emphasis upon the material principle, Rome placed the Church in a false sacramental position with respect to her Living Head, and made of it a communion with a priesthood; so also by undue emphasis upon the formal principle, Protestantism placed the Scriptures in a distorted relation to Christ, the Personal Word. The distinction, therefore, so delicately drawn by St. Paul between the letter which kills and the spirit which gives life, soon lost its significance in Christian consciousness. Revelation and the written Word came to be regarded as identical. Intellectual adherence to certain received doctrines was accepted as the standard of orthodoxy. The concept of the Church as at base a spiritual fellowship was not duly emphasized. Legalism superseded spirituality. Further still, the *testimonii Spiritus Sancti* which had been interpreted as a spiritual experience, gradually came to mean nothing more than human reason. Thus there arose a conflict between reason and revelation which finally issued in the rationalistic movement of the nineteenth century. In reaction to this unwarranted emphasis upon reason, there arose various forms of mysticism which attributed no authority to either tradition or reason.

There is but one safe course to follow, in a consideration of the authoritative sources of theology—the Scriptures must be our only rule of faith and practice. Whatever is not contained therein, or may be proved thereby, cannot be enjoined as an article of faith. The Scriptures as we now have them are but a condensation of the teachings of Christ, brought into unity and expanded into their full meaning by the inspiration of the Holy Spirit. No future source, therefore, can rise higher than the source of all truth—the fountainhead opened in Himself. For us, therefore, "the Bible means all revelation, and all revelation means the Bible."

SUBSIDIARY SOURCES

While Protestantism recognizes the Holy Scriptures as under Christ the primary and final authority in the Church, it does take into consideration the fact that there are proximate or subsidiary sources of great value in determining a Christian Dogmatic. Among these secondary and subsidiary sources may be mentioned, *first*, Experience, which is commonly known as the vital source of theology in that it conditions a right apprehension of its truths; *second*, Confessions or Articles of Faith, which are the crystallization of the beliefs of particular periods or groups, generally termed the traditional source; *third*, Philosophy, which is the formal or shaping source of theology; and *fourth*, Nature, as a fundamental and conditioning source.

1. *Experience.* We need to make clear at the outset, that in our use of the term experience, we do not mean

thereby merely human experience of the unregenerate; but Christian experience, in the sense of an impartation of spiritual life through the truth as vitalized by the Holy Spirit. In our previous discussions, we pointed out the sense in which the written Word becomes a true source of theological knowledge, and the subordinate position which it must ever hold in respect to Christ, the Personal and Eternal Word. It now remains for us to show that the formal principle of the Word may through the Personal Word, so coincide with the material principle of faith as to become the *engrafted word* which is able to save the soul. Truth in its ultimate nature is personal. Our Lord made this clear when He said, *I am the truth.* He knocks at the door of men's hearts—not as a proposition to be apprehended, but as a Person to be received and loved. To those who receive Him, He gives the right to become the sons of God. Granting that all personal knowledge must have its root in ethical sympathy, or a likeness in character between the knower and the known, then the knowledge of God involves a filial relationship between the Incarnate Son and the souls of men, a relationship begotten and nourished by the Holy Spirit. This filial relationship is spiritual knowledge, inasmuch as it is an awakening into consciousness of a fellowship with God in Christ. Nor does the New Testament allow that spiritual knowledge of divine things is possible except on the basis of personal contact with God through the Spirit.

Our Lord further emphasized this great truth when He said, *If any man willeth to do his will, he shall know of the teaching, whether it be of God, or whether I speak of myself* (John 7:17). Here Christ asserts that the knowledge of God does not come through scientific investigation or philosophical speculation, but through right ethical and spiritual relationships. Personal knowledge comes not by logical processes but through spiritual contacts. Our Lord further indicates that the pivot of personal knowledge is an obedient will, and that the deepening bond of sympathy makes possible a more intimate communion and an enrichment of personal knowledge. This ethical knowledge growing out of the obedience of faith is, we maintain, a rudimentary but true knowledge of God, and therefore a subsidiary source of Christian theology. We believe with Gerhart, that from it valid conceptions of God may be intellectually constructed, and systematic knowledge may be developed. Then the whole man, personality in all its functions, attains to the possession of divine truth (GERHART, *Institutes*, p. 30).

2. *Confessions and Creeds.* The word "creed," derived from the Latin word *credo,* I believe, signifies a confession of faith or articles of belief. Confessions may be either individual or collective. As collective formulations of a common faith, they are public testimonies concerning the manner in which the doctrines of the Holy Scriptures are understood and taught by the Church. Creeds are not forced upon the Church from without, they grow up from within. Usually they begin as individual convictions, and come gradually to official recognition. Being the outgrowth of experience, such confessions represent a collective or corporate experience, corrected and tested by a wider group of believers. While not authoritative in the sense of a norm of doctrine, they are an outgrowth of the religious life which owes its origin to Jesus Christ through the Spirit, and must therefore be regarded in a subsidiary sense as true sources of theology. They are the conclusions to which the Church has come in its interpretation of the Word of God and its defense against errors. "It is because the great creeds of the Church represent genuine convictions," says William Adams Brown, "and for this reason alone they have a rightful place among the sources of theology." It is true, also, that in the development of the creeds, any lack of balance between the formal and material principles comes clearly to light. When the formal principle dominates and Christian experience is obscured, the creed ceases to be a genuine confession and becomes, instead, a symbol or a rule of faith. This drift from vital spiritual experience to formal statement is always by slow and imperceptible degrees, and in the

transition the creed loses much of its earlier freedom and spontaneity, and becomes increasingly elaborate in character.

According to Henry B. Smith, creeds and confessions have four objects: *first,* to give living testimony to the truth; *second,* to testify against error; *third,* to furnish a bond of union among those of the same belief; and *fourth,* to provide means of continuing the succession of those uniting in the belief, and instructing them and their children. The relation of the creeds to the scriptures is that the former are designed to express scriptural truth in relation to the errors, wants and questions of the times.

The three Ecumenical Creeds may be said to preserve for us the substance of the faith of the undivided Church. These are (a) The Apostles' Creed; (b) The Nicene Creed; and (c) The Athanasian Creed.

(a) *The Apostles' Creed.* Viewed from the standpoint of systematic arrangement, the Apostles' Creed is an expansion of the baptismal formula, its threefold division being that of the names of the Father, the Son, and the Holy Ghost. It is, however, to be regarded as a summary of facts rather than a theological interpretation, and was not written by the apostles, but so named because it represents a summary of their teachings. It appears that in the early Church some form of belief must be confessed in order to admission into the society of believers. The Church had been enjoined by the apostles to hold fast *the form of sound words,* and to guard "the deposit." There were two types of these formulas, (1) the *Kerygma,* which was a condensed record of the life of Christ; and (2) a *Trinitarian* form—these being condensed and combined in our present statement of the creed. In its final form, the Apostles' Creed is the Western baptismal creed. It is variously dated from 100-150 A.D., and in practically the same form as at present. Irenæus and Tertullian state that it had always been the same (Cf. SCHAFF, *Creeds,* II, p. 52ff). It is certain that from the year A.D. 390 it existed in substantially the same form as now. This is shown by Rufin-

ius' commentary. Few additions were made, and Pir-
minius of Frankland gave us the *textus receptus* in about
the eighth century. Since that time it has been cherished
by the Church for more than a thousand years with the
exception of one change, that of *ad inferos* being sub-

The following analysis of the creed will serve to show more definitely
the various ages when the different clauses were added, and also in general, the meaning which has always attached to the various statements of
the creed.

CREDO IN DEUM PATREM OMNIPOTENTEM. Ancient.

(CREATOREM COELI ET TERRAE.) This is found generally in the
Eastern creeds from the earliest times and especially in the writings of
Irenæus. It appears first in the Western creed about A.D. 375. It was
copied from the East without animus and is probably the last article to
be generally adopted. ET IN JESUS CHRISTUM FILIUM EIUS UNI-
CUM DOMINUM NOSTRUM. Ancient. As here used, the word "Jesus"
means Saviour and is the name of the Man, while "Christ" means anointed
and is the representative of God. He is the full representative in that He
is the unique Son, and as "Our Lord" is the object of our religion.

QUI (CONCEPTUS) EST SPIRITU SANCTO, NATUS EX MARIA
VIRGINE. Ancient.

(PASSUS) SUB PONTIO PILATO, CRUCIFIXUS, (MORTUUS) ET
SEPULTUS. Ancient.

(DESCENDIT AD INFERNOS.) Late fourth century, but without
any controversial animus. It is generally understood to connote that
our Lord went into the place of the dead, preached to them, and led
away into Paradise those who would follow Him. This was often mentioned as "the harrowing of hell." Certainly the word "hell" in this
article does not mean the place of torment, but that of departed spirits.
It signifies the realm of the departed.

TERTIA DIE RESURREXIT A MORTIUS. Ancient.

ASCENDIT (AD) COELOS, SEDIT AS DEXTERAM (DEI) PATRIS
(OMNIPOTENTIS). Ancient. It signifies that the humanity of Christ
lives now with God in glory.

(INDE) VENTURUS EST JUDICARE VIVOS ET MORTUOS. An-
cient. The doctrine of the coming of Christ in glory for judgment is
older than that of His coming "in great humility."

(CREDO) IN SPIRITUM SANCTUM. Ancient. To correspond with
the earlier baptismal formula, the Spirit is correlated with the Father and
the Son as a Divine Person.

SANCTAM ECCLESIAM (CATHOLICAM). *Catholicam* is late fourth
or fifth century, the rest ancient. "Catholic" at first meant universal as
opposed to local, but from the third century it meant also and usually, in
harmony with the universal Church as opposed to the heretical and
schismatic.

(SANCTOREM COMMUNIONEM.) This is about contemporary with
Catholicam. There is some doubt about its earlier creedal use. When put
into the creed it meant the unity of life of all the Church, living and
departed.

REMISSIONEM PECCATORUM. Ancient.

CARNIS RESURRECTUIONEM. Ancient. The body will be raised—
the same body by personal continuity, but in a very different condition—
a spiritual body.

(ET VITAM ÆTERNAM.) Late fourth century. "Eternity" here means
superior to mere successiveness in time. Von Hugel defines it as
"simultaneity."

stituted for *ad inferna*. It has been well said that this creed should be treasured in the hearts and minds of all believers and be often upon their lips. The creed is as follows:

I believe in God the Father Almighty, Maker of heaven and earth;

And in Jesus Christ His only Son our Lord; who was conceived by the Holy Ghost, born of the Virgin Mary; suffered under Pontius Pilate; was crucified, dead, and buried; He descended into hell; the third day He rose again from the dead; He ascended into heaven, and sitteth on the right hand of God the Father Almighty; from thence He shall come to judge the quick and the dead.

I believe in the Holy Ghost; the Holy Catholic Church; the communion of saints; the forgiveness of sins; the resurrection of the body; and the life everlasting. Amen.

(b) *The Nicene Creed.* An interesting history attaches to this creed, adopted at the First Ecumenical Council, held at Nicæa in Bithynia during the summer of A.D. 325. The Council was summoned by the Emperor Constantine, who at that time was not a baptized Christian, but who hoped by this measure to restore peace to the Church which was greatly distracted by the Arian controversy. The Council was attended by a great number of bishops from Egypt and Asia Minor, and some from the provinces beyond the Bosphorus. Other countries were ably represented also, and there were in addition a number of missionary bishops present from outside the Roman Empire. The lists of names extant specifies only about two hundred and twenty, but Eusebius, the historian, who was present, speaks of more than two hundred and fifty. Constantine and Athanasius declared that there were over three hundred present. Dr. Dickie suggests that the foundation for the belief in the three hundred was symbolical rather than historical. Since the Greek symbol for three hundred and eighteen is TIH, as early as the Epistle of Barnabas this number, which is that of Abraham's

household in the fight with the kings (Gen. 14), came
to be regarded as the ideal number in the championship of truth against error, T standing for the cross,
and IH being the first two letters in IHSOUS. At the
time of the Nicene Council, however, none of the par-
ticipants seem to have had any realization of its great
importance for the whole future history of Christianity
(Cf. DICKIE, *Organism of Christian Truth*, p. 208).
Even during the life time of Athanasius, it became a
settled belief that there were three hundred and eighteen
present at the Council, and for this reason it is called
"the Council of the three hundred and eighteen holy
fathers." The text of the original creed differs in a few
points from that which came to be used universally in
the Church. We give the text of the latter:

I believe in one God, the Father Almighty, Maker
of heaven and earth, and of all things visible and invisible.

And in one Lord Jesus Christ, the only-begotten
Son of God; begotten of His Father before all worlds,
God of God, Light of light, Very God of very God, begotten, not made; being of one substance with the Father; by whom all things were made; who for us men
and for our salvation came down from heaven, and
was incarnate by the Holy Ghost of the Virgin Mary,
and was made man; and was crucified also for us un-

The text of the original Nicene Creed as adopted in 325 is as follows: "We believe in one God, the Father Almighty, maker of all things
visible and invisible; and in one Lord Jesus Christ, the Son of God, the
only-begotten of the Father—that is of the substance of the Father;
God of God; Light of light; very God of very God; begotten, not made;
of the same substance with the Father; by whom all things were made,
both the things in heaven and the things in earth; who for us men, and
for our salvation, descended and was incarnate, and was made man,
suffered and rose again the third day; he ascended into heaven; and
cometh to judge the living and the dead. And in the Holy Spirit. But
the holy, catholic, and apostolic Church anathemizes those who say there
was a time when the Son was not, or that he was not before he was begotten, or that he was made of things not existing, or who say that the
Son of God was of any other substance or essence, or created, or liable to
change or conversion."
The text of the Nicene-Constantinopolitan Creed of A.D. 381, is essentially as given in the body of the text above, with the exception that
it begins with "We" instead of "I." The clause on Baptism seems to have
been directed against the Novatians, who rebaptized. The Eastern or
Orthodox Church recognized heretical baptism as valid.

der Pontius Pilate; He suffered and was buried; and
the third day He arose again according to the Scriptures; and ascended into heaven; and sitteth on the
right hand of the Father; and He shall come again,
with glory, to judge both the quick and the dead:
whose kingdom shall have no end.

And I believe in the Holy Ghost, the Lord and
Giver of Life, who proceedeth from the Father and
the Son; who with the Father and Son together is worshiped and glorified; who spake by the prophets; and
I believe in one Catholic and Apostolic Church; I acknowledge one baptism for the remission of sins; and
I look for the resurrection of the dead; and the life
of the world to come. Amen.

It will be noted that this creed is but an expansion
of the threefold division of the Apostles' Creed, which
in turn was an expansion of the baptismal formula. The
trinitarian conception seems to have been one of the
earliest principles of systematization. The creed itself
was a growth, having passed through several recensions. In its earlier form, as adopted by the Council of
Nicæa in 325 A.D., it was directed against Arianism and
other forms of error. It was found with the Eusebian

The following notes on the technical terms of the creed drawn from
various sources may prove illuminating and helpful.

GOD OF GOD. Christ is viewed as God derived from God.

LIGHT OF LIGHT. This was a favorite metaphor in the fourth
century.

BEGOTTEN NOT MADE. This is directed against the Arian teaching that Christ was a creature.

BEING OF ONE SUBSTANCE WITH THE FATHER. The divinity
of Christ is here regarded as being the same as that of the Father, because there is but one divinity.

BY WHOM ALL THINGS WERE MADE. This refers to the Son, as
in the pre-Nicene forms. The Logos is the agent of God in creation.
The word *through* Whom is better than that of *by* Whom. The word is
expressive of the meaning of God in nature, and then in man.

CAME DOWN FROM HEAVEN. Metaphorical or mystical in form.

THE HOLY GHOST, THE LORD AND GIVER OF LIFE. The Greek
words for *Lord* and *Life-Maker*, are in the neuter, purely grammatical
gender to agree with the word Spirit.

TOGETHER IS WORSHIPED AND GLORIFIED. More literally, is
co-worshiped and co-glorified.

ONE CATHOLIC AND APOSTOLIC CHURCH. The word *holy* as
in the Apostles' Creed and the earlier text of the Nicene Creed is here
omitted. It belongs, however, before the word Catholic, for *eis* is found
before *mian*, and *hagian* is predicated of the church as well as catholic.

Confession in a letter of Eusebius to his diocese at Cæsaræa, and the closing paragraph contained the anathema. In A.D. 381, at the Council of Constantinople, the creed was revised, some additions and changes made, and the anathema omitted. A paragraph, substantially as now used, was added in order to combat the error concerning the Holy Ghost which Macedonius and his followers had advanced, denying the essential deity of the Spirit. The Nicene-Constantinopolitan Creed is essentially the same as the present creed with the exception that it contained the word holy before the words Catholic and Apostolic Church; and omitted the words "and from the Son" (filioque) as it concerns the procession of the Spirit. The unique feature of the creed is the insertion of the word filioque, which indicates the belief in the procession of the Spirit from the Son as from the Father, but this will be treated more fully under the head of Christology.

(c) *The Athanasian Creed.* The Athanasian Creed is a Latin document of uncertain date. It is frequently assigned to Vincent of Lerins in the fifth century; others assign it to Hilary, Bishop of Arles (A.D. 449), or Vigilius, Bishop of Tapsus in Africa; while Gieseler thinks that it originated in Spain some time during the seventh century. It is a further expansion of the Apostles' Creed, and is far more explicit in its teachings concerning the Trinity and the Incarnation than those which precede it. Dr. Summers characterizes it as "very subtile, metaphysical and minute." It was never adopted by any general council, but was received in the seventh century as one of the ecumenical symbols. The Lutherans placed the Apostles' Creed, the Nicene Creed and the Athanasian Creed in the *Liber Concordiæ;* while the Eighth Article of the Anglican Thirty-nine Articles states that "the three creeds—the Nicene Creed, Athanasian Creed, and that which is commonly called the Apostles' Creed—ought thoroughly to be received and believed, for they may be proved by most certain warrants of Holy Scripture." As to the comparative excellency of the three creeds, it is generally allowed that the Apostles' Creed excels in traditional antiquity the Nicene in formal dogmatic status, and the Athanasian in fullness of explicit statement. The creed is too long for common use and has been omitted from the Liturgy of the Protestant Episcopal Church of America. The following text is from the recension of the creed as inserted in the Anglican Liturgy.

QUICUNQUE VULT

1. Whosoever will be saved, before all things it is necessary that he hold the Catholic Faith.

2. Which Faith, except every one do keep whole and undefiled, without doubt he shall perish everlastingly.

3. And the Catholic Faith is this, that we worship one God in Trinity, and Trinity in Unity.

4. Neither confounding the Persons, nor dividing the Substance.

5. For there is one Person of the Father, another of the Son, and another of the Holy Ghost.

6. But the Godhead of the Father, of the Son, and of the Holy Ghost is all one, the glory equal, the majesty coeternal.

7. Such as the Father is, such is the Son, and such is the Holy Ghost.

8. The Father uncreate, the Son uncreate, and the Holy Ghost uncreate.

9. The Father incomprehensible, the Son incomprehensible, and the Holy Ghost incomprehensible.

10. The Father eternal, the Son eternal, and the Holy Ghost eternal.

11. And yet there are not three eternals, but one eternal.

12. And also there are not three incomprehensibles, nor three uncreated, but one uncreated and one incomprehensible.

13. So likewise the Father is Almighty, the Son Almighty, and the Holy Ghost Almighty.

14. And yet there are not three Almighties, but one Almighty.

15. So the Father is God, the Son is God, and the Holy Ghost is God.

16. And yet there are not three Gods, but one God.

17. So likewise the Father is Lord, the Son is Lord, and the Holy Ghost is Lord.

18. And yet there are not three Lords, but one Lord.

19. For like as we are compelled by Christian verity to acknowledge every person by himself to be God and Lord.

20. So we are forbidden by the Catholic Religion to say there be three Gods, or three Lords.

21. The Father is made of none, neither created nor begotten.

22. The Son is of the Father alone, not made, nor created, but begotten.

23. The Holy Ghost is of the Father, and of the Son, neither made, nor created, nor begotten, but proceeding.

24. So there is one Father, not three Fathers; one Son, not three Sons; one Holy Ghost, not three Holy Ghosts.

25. And in this Trinity none is afore or after another; none is greater or less than another.

26. But the whole three Persons are coeternal together and coequal.

27. So that in all things, as is aforesaid, the Unity in Trinity, and the Trinity in Unity is to be worshiped.

28. He, therefore, that will be saved must thus think of the Trinity.

29. Furthermore, it is necessary to everlasting salvation, that he also believe rightly the Incarnation of our Lord Jesus Christ.

30. For the right faith is, that we believe and confess that our Lord Jesus Christ, the Son of God, is God and Man.

31. God of the substance of the Father, begotten before the worlds, and Man of the substance of his Mother, born in the world;

32. Perfect God, and perfect Man, of a reasonable soul and human flesh subsisting;

33. Equal to the Father as touching his Godhead, and inferior to the Father as touching his Manhood.

34. Who although he be God and Man, yet he is not two, but one Christ;

35. One; not by conversion of the Godhead into flesh, but by taking of the Manhood into God;

36. One altogether; not by confusion of Substance, but by unity of Person.

37. For as the reasonable soul and flesh is one man, so God and man is one Christ.

38. Who suffered for our salvation, descended into hell, rose again the third day from the dead.

39. He ascended into heaven, he sitteth on the right hand of the Father, God Almighty, from whence he shall come to judge the quick and the dead.

40. At whose coming all men shall rise again with their bodies, and shall give account for their works.

41. And they that have done good shall go into life everlasting, and they that have done evil into everlasting fire.

42. This is the Catholic Faith, which except a man believe faithfully, he cannot be saved.

This creed is sometimes called the *Quicunque Vult* from the first Latin word which means *Whosoever*. Dr. Summers says that "the creed itself is a venerable and valuable symbol, and we do not think, with some that its positive and negative propositions are contradictory and puzzling to the understanding. It is not designed for unlearned persons, but as a dialectic development of the dogmas of Christianity, as settled by the most acute and learned theologians of the age in which it was written" (SUMMERS, *Systematic Theology*, p. 35).

Philosophy should be the constant companion of theology, but each is to retain, without interchange or confusion, its own peculiar field. Its work does not consist in the merely logical process of connecting thoughts together (arrangement), nor in the exercise of occasional criticism (reasoning); but rather in combining the great variety of matter into a higher unity for the consciousness. This can be done only after the material has been furnished from without, by experience and history. Philosophy can neither invent the needed material in the exercise of its own authority, nor destroy or make it other than it is through a pretended transformation or idealizing process.—CROOKS AND HURST, *Ency. and Meth.*, p. 74.

3. *Philosophy*. Philosophy is the formal or shaping source of theology. Its claim as a subsidiary source of theology lies solely in the fact that it has the power of systematizing and rationalizing truth, so that it may be presented to the mind in proper form for assimilation. Perhaps the relation of philosophy to theology has never been better stated than by Auberlin in his *Divine Revelation*. "This is the task of all philosophico-theological labors," he says, "to see the actual as it were transparent, as illuminated by the divine idea, the positive as ideal, the real—that which is truly real, that is effected by God—as rational, so that it may lose that external character in which it might seem foreign to our minds."

Christianity was introduced into a world characterized, not only by ancient forms of religion, but also by ancient systems of philosophy. It came into conflict simultaneously with heathen religion and pagan philosophy. As early as the time of St. Paul warnings were offered against the dangers of *philosophy and vain deceit* (Col. 2:8) and *science, falsely so-called* (I Tim. 6:20).

This conflict of theology and philosophy has come down through all Christian history, and so close have been their relations, that the history of one cannot be written without the other. We may classify in a general way, the periods and forms of this conflict in four main divisions: (I) the ancient Greek and Roman philosophy; (II) Scholasticism as a revival of the Greek and Roman philosophy; (III) the period of Rationalism during the 17th and 18th centuries; and (IV) the Absolute or Pantheistic systems of the 19th century.

Christianity came as a system of revealed truth for which it claimed absolute authority as coming from the true God. This revelation is placed over against the pretensions of human reason and was thereby brought into immediate conflict with the philosophy of that time. The conflict reached its heights in the Gnostic and Manichæan controversy of the second and third centuries, and in the Neo-Platonic controversy which extended into the fourth century. Two modes of defense were found in the Church, *first,* that represented by Tertullian who claimed that all philosophy is fiction, and that it is necessary to cling to faith alone; and *second,* the School of Alexandria which maintained that there was a true Christian philosophy, and that on this basis alone the false pagan philosophies must be defeated. Due to this conflict with pagan philosophy and religion, Christian Theology took the form of Apologetics and frequently that of Polemics.

In the scholastic philosophy of the mediæval period we find perhaps the greatest attempt in the history of the Church to reconcile Christianity with traditional philosophy. Scotus Erigena had derived from Platonism a form of theosophic pantheism, which brought on a conflict with those Church Fathers who had adopted the Aristotelian philosophy. Thus was revived the ancient controversy which took the form of Nominalism and Realism. The logic of Aristotle, however, made possible a comprehensive scheme of classification, and of this the Fathers took advantage, using it as a basis for the systematic arrangement of the dogmas of the Church. Thus philosophy shaped the theology of this period into Systematic, or more properly Dogmatic Theology.

In the third, or Rationalistic Period, philosophy is again brought into conflict with theology. Like Hagar, philosophy rendered great service to her mistress, but exalting herself, she was cast out. The Reformation period freed the mind as well as the Church, and made possible the logic of induction which was promptly applied to all spheres of investigation. Philosophy, losing sight of its true mission, attempted to furnish the materials of investigation instead of confining itself to the systematization of the truth derived from nature and revelation. Three tendencies are to be noted, *first,* that of Descartes and the Cartesian School, which appealed to self-consciousness as the ultimate fact; *second,* the appeal to nature, as opposed to revelation. This gave rise to English Deism and German Rationalism; and *third,* a theosophic or mystical tendency which sought truth in pure spiritual vision. As a consequence theology in this period took the twofold form of (I) Natural Theology, and (II) Revealed Theology—the former being largely apologetic. As a consequence also of the false emphasis upon human reason, there arose a number of rationalistic theological systems, all having at base some form of philosophical speculation.

In the fourth period, which covered the nineteenth and the earlier portion of the twentieth century, the rationalistic tendencies of the previous period found expression in Materialism and reactionary Pantheism. The philosophical systems of Kant, Fichte, Schelling, and especially Hegel gave color to much of the theology of the period. The search for the Absolute in philosophy found its counterpart in the theological discussions concerning the Being and Nature of God; while the Synthetic Philosophy of Herbert Spencer, and the investigations of Huxley and Darwin, furnished the impetus for the various forms of theistic evolution which have characterized recent treatises on theology.

4. *Nature as a Fundamental Source of Theology.* The Scriptures recognize the fact that nature reveals God, not only by frequent references to the work of nature but also by direct assertion. *The heavens declare the glory of God; and the firmament sheweth his handiwork. Day unto day uttereth speech, and night unto night sheweth knowledge. There is no speech nor language, where their voice is not heard. Their line is gone out through all the earth, and their words to the end of the world* (Psalm 19: 1-4). The meaning here, according to Dr. Alexander, is that "the idea of perpetual testimony is conveyed by the figures of one day and one night following another as witnesses in unbroken succession. . . . . The absence of articulate language, far from weakening the testimony, makes it stronger. Even without speech or words, the heavens testify of God to all men."

The Apostle Paul in his address at Lystra (Acts 14: 15-17), and also in his Athenian address (Acts 17: 22-34), makes it clear that nature reveals God sufficiently to lead men to seek after Him and worship Him. But

it is in the introduction of his Epistle to the Romans that
he gives us his clearest statement on natural revelation,
and also defines its limitations. *That which may be
known of God is manifest in them; for God hath shewed
it unto them. For the invisible things of him from the
creation of the world are clearly seen, being understood
by the things that are made, even his eternal power and
Godhead; so that they are without excuse, because that
when they knew God, they glorified him not as God,
neither were thankful* (Romans 1: 19-21). From this
it cannot be doubted that God sufficiently reveals Himself through His works, as to lay in nature a sure foundation for Theology. But He limits this revelation in its
scope to a knowledge of "His power and Godhead"—
that is, to His existence and personality. Men may be
led to seek after God by nature, to feel for Him in conscience, but only through the added revelation of His
Word can men find Him in the knowledge of salvation.
Rationalists may assert that the light of nature is sufficient for salvation, but every branch of the historical
Church denies it. No man can tell what is necessary
for salvation, or even that salvation is possible apart
from a supernatural revelation.

CHAPTER III

SYSTEMS AND METHODS

The various systems of theology are scarcely less important as subsidiary sources, than the creeds and confessions. Representing as they do, the various groupings of the great doctrines of Christianity, they are arranged according to some principle of organization which in the mind of the author is regarded as central and comprehensive. Frequently these systems are attempts to relate theology to the philosophy of the times, and so to justify its claims at the bar of reason. Dr. W. B. Pope has given us a paragraph, which sets forth perhaps more clearly than any other, the value of system in theology. "It is of great importance," he says, "that the mind should be imbued at the outset with a sense of the possibility and advantage of a well-articulated system. In the organic unity of Christian truth, every doctrine has its place, while all the lesser systems revolve around their common center, and it is one of the fruits of theological study to enable students to locate every topic at once. But not only so, there are rich and profound harmonies among these truths; and every doctrine having its proper place, has also its relation to almost every other; the quick discernment of these relations is another fruit of devout and earnest inquiry. Putting the two together, the high aim of the proficient in this study should be to discover all the affinities and connections of the truths of the Christian system. Theology, the city of God, is built as it were upon seven hills, which are the great doctrines that may be discerned as fundamental. These several hills of the Lord are not sharply separated from each other, but throw out their spurs in all directions, making it hard to show where one department of truth ends and another begins. To maintain the distinctions without marking them too mechanically is the aim of sound theological science" (Pope, *CCT*, I, p. 26).

The question is sometimes asked by the naive and uninformed, "Why not take the truths of the Bible as God has revealed them, without any attempt to systematize them?" Dr. Charles Hodge answers this question in an argument for systematization which has become classic in theology. "Such, evidently," he says, "is the will of God. He does not teach men astronomy nor chemistry, but gives them facts out of which these sciences are constructed. Neither does he teach us systematic theology, but He gives us in the Bible the truth which, properly understood and arranged, constitute the science of theology. As the facts of nature are all related and determined by physical laws, so the facts of the Bible are all related and determined by the nature of God and His creatures, and as He wills that men should study His works and discover their wonderful organic relation and harmonious combination, so it is His will that we should study His Word, and learn that, like the stars, its truths are not isolated points, but systems, cycles, and epicycles, in unending harmony and grandeur. Besides all this, although the Scriptures do not contain a system of theology as a whole, we have in the Epistles of the New Testament, portions of the system wrought out to our hands. These are our authority and guide." We may say further, that three general arguments are urged in support of the necessity for systematization. *First*, the constitution of the human mind, the nature of which is such that, having gathered factual knowledge, it must of necessity reflect upon these truths and unify them into a harmonious system of knowledge. The mind can never rest satisfied in possession of facts unless these are arranged in an orderly and coherent manner. This is as true in the study of the Scriptures as in any other field of investigation. *Second*, the development of Christian character. Only as truth is thoroughly assimilated does it become conducive to the development of the Christian life. The uniform testimony of the Church is, that the strongest Christians in every age are those who have had a firm grasp upon the great fundamentals of the Christian faith. This is true, not only because of the power of truth itself, but also because of the strength of purpose which leads to patient research, in order that a reason may be given for the hope that is within them. *Third,* the presentation of the truth. Closely related to the fact that the very constitution of the mind demands an orderly system, is the same fact viewed from a different angle. Truth must be presented in an orderly manner if it is to be comprehended by other minds. "If we would discharge our duty as teachers and defendants of the faith," continues Dr. Charles Hodge, "we must endeavor to bring all the facts of revelation into systematic order and mutual relation." According to Dr. A. H. Strong, the object of the Christian teacher must be to replace obscure and erroneous conceptions among his hearers, by those which are correct and vivid. He cannot do this without knowing the facts with regard to their relations—knowing them in short, as parts of a system. With this truth he is put in trust. To mutilate it or misrepresent it, is not only a sin against the Revealer of it, it may prove to be the ruin of men's souls. The best safeguard against such mutilations or misrepresentations, is the diligent study of the several doctrines of the faith in their relation to one another, and especially to the central theme of theology, the Person and work of Jesus Christ (Cf. STRONG, *Syst. Th.,* p. 17).

METHODS OF SYSTEMATIZATION

The various methods of systematization which have been adopted by theologians of the Church, are here presented in brief review as illustrations of systems built upon a central truth, which by its author is regarded as sufficiently comprehensive to express the full range of Christian doctrine.

The Trinitarian Method. We have already indicated in our study of the three ecumenical creeds, that the trinitarian method of systematization seems to have been the earliest method adopted by the Church. This form of systematization has continued even to the present day. Bishop Martensen has worked out his monumental contribution to Christian Dogmatics in a very interesting manner on the three rubrics—the Doctrines of the Father, the Doctrines of the Son, and the Doctrines of the Holy Spirit. Dr. John Dickie, the learned theologian of the Presbyterian Church of New Zealand, follows the same plan in his *Organism of Christian Truth;* and still later, Dr. Joseph Stump, of the Northwestern Lutheran Theological Seminary has adopted the same order. One of the earliest representatives of this system in modern theology is Leydecker (1642-1721) an ardent exponent of the doctrines of the Reformed Church.

The Analytic Method. This was the method of Calixtus (1586-1656), a theologian of the Lutheran Church in Germany, who began with the assumed end of all things as blessedness, and from this works out the means by which blessedness is secured.

The Federal Method. This method grew out of the political science of the sixteenth century, in which federal headship had become the popular theory. As carried over into theology, the method starts with the idea of two covenants, that of works and that of grace, the latter forming the basis for the unfolding of the doctrines of salvation. It was first used by Cocceius (1603-1669), a Dutch theologian from Holland. It was later used by Witsius (1636-1708), another Dutch theologian, and Thomas Boston (1676-1732) a Scottish writer.

The Anthropological Method. Here the central principle of systematization is the idea of man—his sinful condition and his need of redemption. Chalmers (1780-1847) begins with the disease of man and proceeds to set forth the remedy. Rothe (1799-1867) arranges his theology in two main divisions: (a) The Consciousness of sin, and (b) the Consciousness of redemption.

The Christological or Christocentric Method. The central idea here is the incarnation. It is evident to all Bible students that early Christianity was strictly Christ centered. With St. Paul, *To live is Christ and to die is gain.* "Jesus" and the "Resurrection" were the central and dominating themes of early apostolic preaching and teaching. With the rise of the Western Church and the emphasis placed upon divine sovereignty by Augustine, the centrality of Christ was made subservient to the doctrine of the Church. "It almost seems," says Dr. A. V. G. Allen in his *Continuity of Christian Thought,* "as though, if Christ were left out altogether, the scheme of Augustine would still maintain its consistency as a whole and retain its value as a working system." The new movement toward a Christ-centered theology is to be attributed to Friedrich Schleiermacher (1768-1834), a German theologian known as the "father of modern theology." With his background of Moravian mysticism, he reacted against the emptiness and formality of the rationalistic theology of his time, and became the "great revivifier of spiritual theology"; and in the field of dogmatic theology wrought a work comparable to that which John Wesley, his great contemporary, accomplished in revitalizing the formal religion of his day. "His it was to make Christ and His redemption the center of one of the most skillfully developed systems of theology which the Christian Church has known," writes Henry B. Smith, who himself was to become the apostle of the movement in this country. Others who have adopted this method are Hase (1800-1890), Thomasius (1802-1875), Andrew Fuller (1754-1815), Gerhart (1817-1904), while his outline would seem to indicate otherwise, his theology is essentially Christocentric, especially as it concerns the knowledge of God; and Dr. Olin A. Curtis is by some writers also placed in this class. Dr. A. H. Strong, and William Newton Clarke are generally classified otherwise, but give large attention to the Person and Work of Christ in their theological treatises. To Principal Fairbairn of England is usually attributed the most constructive and far-reaching contribution to the Christocentric school.

The Confessional Method. This plan is simply the exposition of certain creeds and confessions in regular order. As instances of this method may be cited, Pearson (1613-1686), *Exposition of the Thirty-nine Articles;* Charles Hodge (1797-1878), *Commentary on the Westminster Confession;* Thos. O. Summers (1812-1882), in his *Systematic Theology,* edited by John J. Tigert, follows the order of the *Twenty-five Articles of Methodism.* Dr. Summers was widely known for his "conservatism, broad theological scholarship, and particularly, for careful, conscientious, and patient study of all the elements of the Arminian system of theology. His work is at once a complete system of Wesleyan Arminian divinity and an exhaustive commentary on the *Twenty-five Articles of Religion* which embody the doctrinal views of American Methodism" (*Cf.* TIGERT, *Preface,* p. 3). One of the latest representatives of this confessional method is E. J. Bicknell, who published in 1919 his *Theological Introduction to the Thirty-nine Articles,* the last impression of the book being made in 1936.

The Allegorical Method. This method was prominent in the early church, especially among the followers of Origen, but fell into decline with the rise of rationalism. The best modern representative of this method is Dannhauer (1603-1666), a professor of theology in Strassburg and the minister of the cathedral church in the same city. He describes "man as a wanderer, life as a road, the Holy Spirit as a light, the Church as a candlestick, God as the end, and heaven as the home."

The Synthetic Method. This is the method adopted by Dr. A. H. Strong in his *Systematic Theology,* and which he asserts is the most common and the most logical method of arranging the topics of theology. Dr. Gamertsfelder, who characterizes his own system of theology as "Evangelical Arminianism" follows this method also in his *Systematic Theology,* declaring that while the method has been in vogue many years it has lost none of its freshness and attractiveness. Hagenbach describes the method as one which "starts from the highest principle, God, and proceeds to man, Christ, redemption, and finally to the end of all things." The basic principle of organization is its logical order of cause and effect. This is the method of Pope in his *Compendium of Christian Theology,* Miley in his *Systematic Theology,* Hills in his *Fundamental Christian Theology,* Fairchild in his *Elements of Theology,* Ralston in his

Elements of Divinity and Wakefield in his revision of *Watson's Institutes,* known as *Christian Theology.* It is likewise the method of Charles G. Finney, Henry C. Sheldon, Enoch Pond and numerous other writers.

Miscellaneous Methods. Among these may be noted: (a) The Decretal Method which begins with the idea of the divine decrees; (b) The Patricentric Method which arranges its material around the central idea of the Divine Fatherhood, and (c) The Historical Method, followed by Ursinus (1534-1583) and later adopted by Jonathan Edwards in his *History of Redemption,* which, says Strong, was in reality a system of theology in historical form. It was "to begin and end with eternity, all great events and epochs in time being viewed *sub specie eternitatis.* The three worlds—heaven, earth and hell—were to be the scenes of this grand drama. It was to include the topics of theology as living factors, each in its own place," and all forming a complete and harmonious whole (*Cf.* STRONG, *ST*, I, p. 50). Dr. I. A. Dorner in his *System of Christianity,* makes Christian faith, the central organizing principle, while Dr. Julius Kaftan (b. 1858) in his *Dogmatics* makes the grace of God the central idea. In recent times, such works as William Adams Brown, *Christian Theology in Outline* and William Newton Clarke, *Outline of Christian Theology,* have made the conception of the Christian religion the determining factor.

There are several important results to be gained from the study of the various systems of theology. Among these may be mentioned, *first,* and most important perhaps, they give us a knowledge of what their authors regarded as central in their faith. Underlying every system is one principal truth about which all others are organized. What the dogmatic theologians of the Church in any age regard as central gives rise to the various types of Systematic Theology. Care should be exercised, however, in judging the methods of systematization in one age by those employed in another. If Anselm's *Cur Deus Home,* or Origen's *De Principiis* or St. Thomas' *Summa Theologica* do not appear to be scientific according to our standards, they doubtless were according to their standards, and these very differences prove illuminating to the earnest student of theology. *Second,* these various systems furnish us with a knowledge of the materials which the writers had at their disposal, their mental characteristics, and the methods employed to adapt their teaching to the need of the times. Dr. Dickie regards Dogmatics as a Christian religious conviction endeavoring to think itself out, and to relate itself to all other knowledge and opinion. The situation is complicated, he says, by the fact that our varying mental elements have different sources in our experience. Part of our mental content we owe to our general environment, part to our special training, and part to our individual experience. One must take into account this whole mental complex of knowledge and opinion which, whether imperfectly or altogether unsystematized, is never alike in any two minds. It is evident then that attention to the method of systematization reveals much of the author's mental characteristics, and this personal equation will be taken into account, both in the materials selected and the methods by which they are adapted, to their proposed ends. *Third,* they are important as furnishing a foundation for the study of historical theology, enabling the theologian to trace in unbroken continuity the development of truth from age to age. Since the Church in all ages is one, no age can come to its fullest expression without a knowledge of the past.

THEOLOGY A SCIENCE

Having defined theology and treated it from the standpoint of its sources and methods, we have now an objection which must be answered. It is objected that theology is not a science, in that its subject matter is not drawn from knowledge but from faith, and therefore lacks certitude. Closely related to this is the attack of Sir William Hamilton who, after defining faith as the organ by which we apprehend what is beyond our knowledge, argues that since science is knowledge, what is beyond our knowledge cannot be matter for science. He maintains, therefore, that science in its highest achievement can only build an altar to "the Unknown God." On the false assumption that faith and knowledge are antithetical, either that faith does not reach the requirements of certitude, or that it operates in a realm beyond scientific knowledge, two basic truths have been overlooked. *First,* science itself must be based upon faith, which in the scientific realm is known and treated as the assumptions of science. Physical science rests upon faith in our own existence, in an orderly world whose facts may be systematized, and in the power of the mind to logically arrange the facts presented to it. It assumes such metaphysical truths as space and time, substance and attributes, cause and effect, and also assumes the trustworthiness of the mind in its investigations. If these assumptions do not invalidate physical science, most certainly they should not be regarded as invalidating that science which deals with assumptions, admittedly without proof from the science which objects to it. "If theology is to be overthrown because it starts from some primary terms and propositions, then all other sciences are overthrown with it." Mozley defines faith as unverified reason (*Cf.* DOVE, *Logic of the Christian Faith,* p. 14).

Second, We must therefore take the position that Christian Dogmatics "is not only a science of faith but also a knowledge grounded in and drawn from faith" (MARTENSEN, *Christian Dogmatics,* p. 1). This has been the position of all leading theologians. Richard Rothe (1799-1867), who is generally regarded as belonging to the right wing of the Hegelian school, gave to theological science a clear statement of the basic elements of knowledge which has been widely used in modern theology. "Now in the devout or religious man," he says, "according to the measure in which his devoutness is living and healthy, there is immediately contained in his thought as pure thought, the notion of being determined by God. The religious man's feeling of self is at the same time a feeling of God, and he cannot come to a distinct and clear thought of self without coming to the thought of God. Thus there is provided for the devout subject a twofold point of departure for his speculative thinking, and the possibility of a twofold method of speculative inquiry. Thinking can proceed either from the consciousness of self as an *a priori* fact, or from the consciousness of God. Theological speculation is in essence nothing more than the attempt to express, in conceptual form, the immediate and certain content of the devout consciousness, the content of the feeling of the divine." Julius Kaftan, a younger contemporary of Rothe (1799-1867), takes a similar position, though admitting that the idea of faith, in Christian Theology, underwent a change in passing from the mediæval to the modern period. In the scholastic period, faith rested on authority, and was developed largely by strengthening external evidence. Now we have returned to the biblical idea of faith as a fact of human consciousness, and as a form of knowledge which strikes its roots deep into the inner practical relations sustained to its objects.

CHAPTER IV

THEOLOGY IN THE CHURCH

Having dealt with the materials and methods of theology, it is our task now to trace the development of Systematic Theology in the Church. Doctrinal discussions arise not only from original and elaborate sources, but from the simplest writings of the early church fathers. The History of Dogmatics, however, is concerned primarily with the attempts at framing an orderly and systematic representation of Christian truth as a whole, and can give attention only in a secondary manner to the discussions which have furthered or hindered the development of a Systematic Theology.

Hagenbach finds five tendencies in the development of Christian Doctrine. (I) *The Age of Apologetics,* when it was the main endeavor of the theological mind to defend Christianity against infidelity from without the Church. It extends from the Apostolic Age to the death of Origen (A.D. 70-254). (II) *The Age of Polemics or Controversies,* when it was the main endeavor of the theological mind to maintain Christianity against heresy from within the Church. It extends from the death of Origen to John of Damascus (A.D. 254-730). (III) *The Age of Systematizing Past Results* or of Scholasticism, in the widest significance of the word. It extends from John of Damascus to the Reformation (A.D. 730-1517). (IV) *The Age of Creed Controversy.* It extends from the reformation to the Leibnitz - Wolfian philosophy (A.D. 1517-1720). (V) *The Age of Philosophizing upon Christianity.* This period is characterized by criticism and speculation, the reconciliation of faith with science, and reason with revelation (A.D. 1720 to about the close of the nineteenth century).

For our purpose in reviewing the development of theology in the Church, we shall use the following outline: (I) *The Earlier Period,* from the Apostolic Age to the time of John of Damascus (A.D. 70-730). (II) *The*

Mediæval or Scholastic Period, from John of Damascus
to the Reformation (A.D. 730-1517). (III) *The Reformation Period,* covering the remaining portion of the
sixteenth century (A.D. 1517 to c. 1600). (IV) *The
Confessional Period,* covering the seventeenth and eighteenth centuries (A.D. 1600 to c. 1800). (V) *The Modern Period,* from the beginning of the nineteenth century to the present time (A.D. 1800 to the present).

THE EARLIER PERIOD

The Earlier Period may be subdivided into (I) The
Apologetic Period, from the Apostolic Age to the death
of Origen (A.D. 70-254); and (II) The Age of Polemics,
from the death of Origen to John of Damascus (A.D.
254-730). The Earlier Period is peculiarly that of the
Church Fathers, who through defenses of Christianity
against paganism from without, and controversies
against heresy from within, wrought out through patient
endurance and often at the price of martyrdom, the materials which the doctors of later periods systematized
by various methods into Christian Dogmatics.

Great Leaders of the Earlier Period. The earlier
Church Fathers are generally classified in two main
divisions: (I) the Ante-Nicene Fathers and (II) the
Post-Nicene Fathers. For our purpose, however, we
shall mention only the Apostolic Fathers and the Earlier
Apologists. The Apostolic Fathers were those of the
first and second centuries who were known to have
been personally associated with the apostles, or to have
been directly influenced by them, so that their writings breathe the same spirit as attaches to the later
epistles of the New Testament. Among these may be
named Clement of Rome (1st century) the first bishop
of Rome whose extant work known as *The Epistle of*

Among the striking and quotable sentences, McGiffert gives the
following: "It is better to keep silence and to be than to talk and not be."
"It is meet that we not only be called Christians but also be Christians."
"Where there is more toil there is much gain." "A Christian has no
authority over himself but giveth his time to God." "Christianity is a
thing of power whenever it is hated by the world." "I am God's wheat
and I am ground by the teeth of wild beasts that I may be found pure
bread."—McGiffert, *History of Chr. Thought,* I, p. 37.

Clement, is an elaborate and treatiselike writing similar
in form to the Epistle to the Hebrews. The next in
order is Ignatius of Antioch, born about the middle of
the first century. He was an immediate disciple of St.
John with whom he was contemporary for about twenty
years. There are seven letters extant, written like some
from the pen of St. Paul, while he was on his way to
Rome where he suffered martyrdom. His letters have
been characterized as "fiery, incisive, vigorous and elo-
quent beyond any other writings of the post-apostolic
period." His striking personality and the depth of his
thought characterize him as the outstanding figure of
this period. The dominant tone of his life was that of devotional love. The third in regular succession is Polycarp, Bishop of Smyrna, who wrote an Epistle to the
Philippians about A.D. 120. He was a disciple of Ignatius and is generally considered to have been personally
acquainted with St. John. He left a noble testimony
preceding his martyrdom, an account of which was sent
by the Church at Smyrna to the Church of Philomelium
some thirty years later, and is usually included with his
epistle. Papias, Bishop of Hierapolis, who likewise may
have been a disciple of St. John, wrote five books, but
of these only fragments remain of his *Exposition of the
Oracles of the Lord.* Irenæus, Bishop of Lyons (born
either between 115-125 or 130-142, the date is uncer-

In his Epistle to the Roman Church, Irenæus advises the Christians
there of his coming and begs them not to do anything to secure his release
and prevent him from martyrdom, for he regarded it as "the greatest privilege and the highest honor to die for the name of Christ." "Bear with
me," he writes. "I know what is expedient for me. Now I am beginning
to be a disciple. May nought of the things visible and things invisible
envy me, that I may attain unto Jesus Christ. Come fire and cross and
grapplings with wild beasts, wrenching of bones, hacking of limbs,
crushing of my whole body! Come cruel tortures of the devil to assail
me! Only be it mine to attain unto Jesus Christ." "The pangs of a new
birth are upon me. Bear with me, brethren. Do not hinder me from
living; do not desire my death. Bestow not upon the world one who de-
sireth to be God's, neither allure him with material things. Suffer me to
receive the pure light. When I am come thither, then I shall be a man.
Permit me to be an imitator of the passion of my God."—IRENÆUS, *Epistle
to the Romans,* pp. 5, 6.

Polycarp's noble testimony has been quoted perhaps more than any
other of the words of the Fathers. "Eighty and six years have I served
Him, my Lord and my King, and He has never done me wrong. How can
I deny Him?"

tain), was a disciple of Polycarp, and thus there is established a direct relationship from St. John to Irenæus, the last of the Apostolic Fathers.

There were also a number of anonymous writings that are of sufficient importance to demand attention. The *Didache* or Teachings of the Twelve is believed to have been published about A.D. 80-90, and if so is per-haps the oldest uninspired manuscript of the Christian Era. The *Epistle of Barnabas* is sometimes attributed to Barnabas the companion of Paul, but the weight of evidence is in favor of anonymous authorship. The *Epistle to Diognetus* claims discipleship with the apostles, but probably this is meant in the broad sense of conformity to apostolic teachings. The *Shepherd of Hermas,* commonly known as I Clement, is strictly speaking, of sub-apostolic authorship, but is generally classified with the writings of the Apostolic Fathers. Some claim authorship of this epistle for Hermes mentioned by St. Paul in Romans 16:14, but the evidence appears stronger for Hermas, the brother of Pius, Bishop of Rome c. 139-154. There is also the epistle known as II Clement which is sub-apostolic in date, but which like I Clement is classified with the writings of the Apostolic Fathers. Its author is unknown, but in all probability it is a homily written about A.D. 120-140, and therefore perhaps the earliest extant sermon preached before a Christian congregation.

During the next or Apologetic Period proper, the great names among the earlier apologists are those of Justin Martyr (died c. 165), who wrote the First and Second Apologies and the *Dialogue with Trypho;* Clement of Alexandria (c. 160-220), a voluminous writer but whose best known work is probably the *Stromateis* or Miscellanies treating of various biblical and theological subjects—other works being the *Protrepticus* written with an evangelistic purpose to make converts, and *Pædagogus,* an elementary manual intended as a handbook for the instruction of new converts; Tertullian (155-222), whose *De Testimonio Animæ* is but one of his numerous works; and Cyprian (200-258), an African bishop whose greatest contribution is found in his teachings concerning the Church.

Then there was Origen (185-254), perhaps the greatest scholar and writer of this period, whose *De Principiis* will be given further attention; Arius (d. 336), a popular and influential preacher and a scholar of no little ability, who, adopting the rationalistic positions of Lucian (d. 311 at Antioch), came into conflict with his bishop, Alexander, and thus brought about the great Arian Controversy; Athanasius (c. 296-373), the opponent of Arius, and known as the "father of orthodoxy" because of his championship of the deity of Christ; the greatest name of the period, Augustine (354-430), to whose writings both the Roman Catholic and many Protestants turn for authority; and lastly, John of Damascus (700-760), the great theologian of the Eastern Church.

Besides these there are many names of lesser importance, but of intense interest to the student of Apologetics, Aristides who addressed an apology to Emperor Antonius Pius about A.D. 150, Tatian known especially for his *Diatesseron*, Athenagoras (wrote c. 176-178) who addressed an appeal to Marcus Aurelius; a defense of Christianity written by Theophilus, Bishop of Antioch about A.D. 190; the three great Cappadocians, Gregory Nazianzen (c. 329-389), Gregory Nyssa (Bp. in 372) and Basil (c. 330-379) noted for their work in the solution of the trinitarian problem; Cyril of Alexandria (d. 444), Theodoret of Cyrus (died 457), Theodore of Mopsuesta (c. 350-428 or 429) all of whom contributed interpretations of Scripture, or devotional and apologetic tracts. Cyril's answer to Julian has been notorious in apologetic literature.

The Great Councils of the Earlier Period. No summary, however brief, can do justice to the Earlier Period without enumerating the great councils. These gave to the Church the clear and concise statements of doctrine out of which the theology of the Church was constructed. "In the lead of these controversies," says Philip Schaff, "stood church teachers of imposing talents and energetic piety; not mere bookmen, but venerable theological characters, men of a piece, as great in acting as in suffering. To them theology was a sacred business of heart and life." We give the following summary of the Ecumenical Councils. The East and West recognize seven Ecumenical Councils, but the Roman Catholic Church holds to a greater number. By "ecumenical" is meant one which, whether representative in membership or not, is accepted by the entire Church as rightly representing it in its definitions of faith. These councils with one exception were all held during the Polemic Period.

(1) The Council of Nicæa (A.D. 325) was called by the Emperor Constantine to consider, and if possible to settle, the Arian heresy. It gave the Church the first great ecumenical creed. (2) The First Council of Constantinople (A.D. 381) was called by Emperor Theodosius the Great in order to correct the errors of Apollinarianism and Macedonianism. Apollinaris (d. 392) held that Christ assumed only a human body, and that the Logos took the place of human mind or spirit. Macedonius (c. 341), Bishop of Constantinople, taught that the Holy Spirit was not a Person but a divine energy through the universe. (3) The Council of Ephesus (A.D. 431) was presided over by Cyril, Bishop of Alexandria, and was called on occasion of the Nestorian controversy which seemed to teach a Christological dualism. (4) The Council of Chalcedon (A.D. 451) was presided over by three bishops and two presbyters, who were the representatives of Leo of Rome. Six hundred and thirty bishops were present. This council condemned the Eutychian heresy which confused the two natures of Christ. It gave to the Church the creedal statement on Christology which has stood the test of the centuries. (5) The Second Council of Constantinople (A.D. 553) was called by Emperor Justinian, and presided over by the patriarch Eutychus. The council condemned the writings of Theodore of Mopsuesta, Theodoret of Cyprus and the Epistle of Ibas, Bishop of Edessa—all these being thought to favor Nestorianism. (6) The Third Council of Constantinople (A.D. 680) called by the emperor Constantine Pogonatus, was directed against Monothelit-

ism, or the teaching that the divine will supplanted the human will in Christ. (7) The Second Council of Nicæa (A.D. 787) falls across the line into the next period but is mentioned here as being one of the great councils. It had to do with the Iconoclasts and Iconduli.

The Development of Systematic Theology. While much preliminary work was done by the writers of this period, probably the first formal attempt at Systematic Theology was Origen's *De Principiis,* or "First Principles," written about A.D. 218. It is arranged in four books, the first treating of God; the second of Creation and the facts of human history; the third of man's moral and spiritual endowments; and the fourth of the Holy Scriptures as the basis of the Christian system. No adequate place is given to either Christology or Soteriology, and the doctrine of the Church is omitted entirely. Westcott points out the value of the fourth division which "he examines with reverence, an insight, a humility, a grandeur of feeling never surpassed, the question of the inspiration and interpretation of the Bible" (Cf. SMITH, *Dictionary of Chr. Biography,* iv, p. 121). In view of the four Christological heresies, the Arian, the Apollinarian, the Nestorian and the Eutychian, the writings of Athanasius are of exceptional value but cannot be said to take the form of Systematic Theology.

The second formal attempt at Systematic Theology was the *Enchiridion* of Augustine (353-430), the great dogmatic and polemic writer of the fifth century whose influence is yet strong in theological thought. As a polemical writer he opposed the Manichæans, the Donatists, the Pelagians and the Semi-Pelagians. The doctrines of Augustine when focused upon Pelagianism, show a controversial position at every point, the controversy itself being not so much between Augustine and Pelagius, as a conflict between the East and the West focused in these eminent theologians. We shall have occasion to notice these contrasts in the following sections on Theology, the Trinity, Christology, and Soteriology. The *Enchiridion* is an exposition of the Creed, and in the West became as authoritative as the creeds themselves, going far beyond them in the doctrines of sin and salvation. The work was organized on the three-fold Pauline principle of faith (*de fide*), hope (*spe*), and love (*caritate*). Of Augustine's other writings the *De Trinitate* and *De Doctrina Christiana* are regarded as important contributions to theology. His *De Civitate* or *City of God* was epoch making. The Church is regarded as the kingdom of God on earth and its government and worship as royal institutions. However, it started a trend of thought which finally resulted in the identification of God's spiritual kingdom with the visible organization of the Church, and thus gave impetus to the Roman Catholic position against which later Protestantism objected and still objects.

Another work of this period is sometimes classified as theology, the *Commonitorium* of Vincent of Lerins (d. c. 450) which supports the doctrines of the Church by reference to the Church Fathers. It is not, however, strictly dogmatic but rather a systematic exposition of Church tradition.

The third and last attempt at Systematic Theology during this period was a contribution from the East by John of Damascus (c. 700-760, date uncertain), and marks the close of the Earlier Period. The title of this work is *De Fide Orthodoxa* or the Summary of the Orthodox Faith, and by many is considered the first work worthy to be known as a Systematic Theology. It is the third section of a larger work entitled *Fons Scientia* or Fountain of Knowledge something on the order of a modern religious encyclopedia. The first two sections of *Capita Philosophica* which contain a brief treatise on the Categories of Aristotle, and a Compendium of Heresies, numbering one hundred and three, are relatively unimportant. The third section is sometimes known also as "An Accurate Exposition of the Orthodox Faith," and was a textbook at once philosophical and ecclesiastical. John of Damascus was to the East what Thomas Aquinas was to the West, and by Briggs is thought to hold even a higher position as a doctor of the universal

Church. On account of his general positions being those of the School of Constantinople, he is the normal theologian of the Greek Church. Theophanes states that he was called Chrysorrhoas, "Stream of Gold"—literally pouring forth gold—"because of that grace of the spirit which shines like gold both in his doctrine and in his life."

THE MEDIÆVAL PERIOD

The Mediæval Period covers nearly seven hundred years, and extends from the death of John of Damascus to the beginning of the Reformation (A.D. 754-1517). It is pre-eminently the period of the doctors or schoolmen, and is frequently called the Scholastic Period. Turner in his History of Philosophy, and Kurtz in his Church History subdivide this period into four main divisions. "From the tenth century, almost completely destitute of any scientific movement, the so-called *Sæculum Obscurum*, there sprang forth the first buds of scholarship without, however, any distinct impress upon them of scholasticism. In the eleventh century scholasticism began to show itself, and that in the form of dialectic, both skeptical and dogmatic. In the twelfth century mysticism assumed an independent place alongside of dialectic, carried on a war of extermination against skeptical dialectic, and finally appeared in a more peaceful aspect, contributing material to the positive dogmatic dialectic. In the thirteenth century dialectic scholasticism gained the complete ascendancy, and reached its highest glory in the form of dogmatism in league with mysticism, and never, in the persons of its greatest representatives, in opposition to it" (KURTZ, *Church Hist.*, II, p. 81).

The earlier part of this period, to the beginning of the eleventh century, while a *Sæculum Obscurum,* as to outstanding scholarship, was not so as to the events of church history. It was marked by constant strife in both church and state. In the Eastern Church there was the controversy over images, in which the Iconduli as image worshipers triumphed over the Iconoclasts or image-breakers. It was during this period also, that the great controversy arose over the insertion of the word *filioque* in the Western Creed, a controversy which finally resulted in the separation of the Eastern and Western Churches. From this one word, *filioque,* by which is meant the procession of the Holy Spirit from the Son as well as from the Father, two great systems of theology arose, widely different in both material and type. The Eastern theology was contemplative and mystical, and sought to teach by symbol rather than creed; the theology of the West was more analytical and progressive, and taught more by the logical presentation of truth as found in the creeds and confessions. The principal theologians of this period were Alcuin (735-804), a great teacher whose writings mostly concerned the doctrine of the Trinity. He was a tutor of Rabanus Maurus (776-856) known as the greatest teacher in Germany. Alcuin was himself an assistant of Charlemagne in his attempt at the revival of learning, and under his care the monastery of Tours became a great center of theological learning. Another great theologian of this period was John Scotus Erigena (c. 815-875), known as "the father of scholastic theology." In addition to his *De Divisione Naturœ,* a system of natural and speculative theology, for which he claimed a common source in the Divine Wisdom, he also wrote a treatise, *De Divina Prœdestinatione,* directed against Gottschalk and his high Augustinian position on predestination. Other and

"The pupils of Rabanus," says Briggs, "teaching in various monasteries in Northern and Western Europe, greatly enhanced theological education." Of Alcuin it was said that he distributed "the honey of the sacred writings," "the wine of ancient learning," and "the apples of grammatical subtlety."

Rabanus has this interesting paragraph: "If anyone would master the Scriptures, he must first of all diligently find out the amount of history, allegory, anagoge and trope there may be in the part under consideration, for there are four senses to the Scriptures, the historical, the allegorical, the tropological and the analogical, which we call the daughters of Wisdom. Through these Wisdom feeds her children. To those who are young and beginning to learn, she gives the milk of *history;* to those advancing in the faith the bread of *allegory;* those who are truly and constantly doing good so that they abound therein, she satisfies with the savory meat of *tropology;* while finally, those who despise earthly things and ardently desire the heavenly, she fills to the full with the wine of *anagoge.*—Cf. SCHAFF, *Hist. Chr. Ch.,* IV, p. 719.

lesser writers of this period were Strabo (809-849) who was the originator of the *Glossa Ordinaris,* or brief commentaries on the Scripture. He is known also for his *Vision of Wettin* which Sandys calls "an early precursor of Dante's *Divine Comedy.*" Servetus Lupus (805-862), a pupil of Rabanus, wrote a treatise on predestination. The works of Rabanus were more exegetical than theological and included commentaries on both the Bible and the Apocrypha. To him is attributed also the great hymn of Pentecost, *Veni Creator Spiritus* (Cf. further, BRIGGS, *Hist. Th.,* II, pp. 4-7).

The latter part of this period, beginning with the eleventh century and extending to the sixteenth, is known as the Scholastic Period, in both philosophy and theology. The rise of Mohammedanism in the East did much to bring about the transfer of theology from the churches to the schools in the West. Of this period, the first two centuries—the eleventh and the twelfth— were preparatory, and are characterized by the subordination of philosophy to theology. The schools accepted the theological doctrines as they were delivered to them by the Church, and assuming their truth sought to adjust them to human reason and deduce from them whatever corollaries were possible. Yet it is this period which marks the beginning of Systematic Theology. Following John of Damascus, who represented the theology of the East, were Anselm, Abelard, and Peter Lombard who marked the beginning of systematic treatises in the West. Anselm (1033-1109) was the first to attempt a rational theory of the atonement, and his *Cur Deus Homo,* as well as his *Monologium* and *Proslogium,* was an influential contribution to the literature of theology. Abelard (1079-1142) is known especially for his conceptualism in philosophy, a mediating position between the realism of Anselm and the nominalism of Roscelinus (1050-1100). His two principal theological works are *De unitate et Trinitate Divina,* which was condemned at Soissons under the title, *Theologia Christiana,* and *Introductio ad Theologam.* Peter Lombard (1100-1164) represented one of the earliest attempts toward a systematization of doctrine in the West.

The thirteenth century represents the period of perfection in scholasticism. Philosophy is here characterized by a friendly alliance with theology, rather than as subordinate to it. The revival of Aristotelian philosophy gave to the theologians a new principle of co-ordination and systematization. The theology of this period is therefore, the doctrines of the fathers systematized according to Aristotle. While in the former period, Systematic Theology took the form of *Sententiæ* or sentences from the Fathers, arranged in systematic order under certain rubrics, in this period it took the character of *Summa Theologiæ*, which in reality were independent systems of theology. Duns Scotus (1276-1308), was born shortly after the death of Thomas Aquinas, and though he lived only about thirty-three years, began a movement in philosophy and theology, which finally resulted in the downfall of scholasticism, and the ushering in of the period of the Reformation.

The Development of Theology in the Scholastic Period. The first great systematic work of the Scholastic Period was Peter Lombard's *Libri Sententiarum Quattuor,* or Four Books of Sentences. These were an arrangement of excerpts in systematic order from the writings of Augustine and other Church Fathers. The first book treats of God, the second, of creatures; the third, of redemption; and the fourth, of the sacraments and last things. It was adopted as a textbook by the Lateran Council (1215) and used as a text in theology for more than five hundred years. Peter Lombard, known as the *Magister Sententiarum* was a pupil of Abelard. Previous to this there were other books of sentences such as Hugo of St. Victor, *Summa Sententiarum,* and Robert Pulleyn, *Sententiarum,* but these were not as extensive as that of Peter Lombard.

The second great treatise on theology during the Scholastic Period, was the *Summa Theologica* of Thomas Aquinas, a work of great value and a source book even in modern times.

THE REFORMATION PERIOD

The preceding age was characterized by a systematizing of the results of the Polemic Period, but the Reformation becomes again a period of controversies and creed formulations, thus marking the transition from the mediæval to the modern world. The Reformation as such was the outgrowth of the Renaissance. It was in fact, a continuation of the Renaissance as it affected matters of religion, especially in Germany and England. Reuchlin and Erasmus have been called the two eyes of Germany, the one on account of his knowledge of Hebrew language and literature; the other because of his Greek learning and labors. A recent writer traces the development of thought through the four Johns—John Duns Scotus, John Tauler, John Huss and John Wesley, and then adds a fifth and a sixth—John Wessel and John Reuchlin.

The most important event of this period, and that which gave rise to the development of two radically different types of theology, was the separation of the Church into two main divisions, Roman Catholicism and Protestantism. Since that time each type has developed into a large body of divinity. While there are fundamental unities, the differences are manifest at almost every essential point in theology. The Roman Catholic positions were expressed in the Tridentine Decrees, formulated by the Council of Trent (1545-1563). They were in effect a complete system of Roman Catholic theology, and were wrought out by the indefatigable labors of the schoolmen in the universities of the Church. The positions of the Protestant Reformation were expressed in the Formula of the Concord (1580) and later in the Canons of the Synod of Dort (1618-1619). Protestantism accepted the teachings of the creeds of Nicæa, Constantinople and Chalcedon, and also in the main the Augustinian doctrines of sin and grace. It rejected the absolute authority of ecclesiastical tradition and the findings of the Church Councils. It maintained the supreme authority of the Scriptures in faith and morals, the uni-

versal priesthood of believers, and the doctrine of justification by faith alone.

The Theology of the Reformation period. The theology of the Reformation Period falls into two broad divisions—the Lutheran and the Reformed. The Lutheran
may in general be characterized as more deeply sacramentarian, while the Reformed is more intellectualistic
and doctrinal. Luther and Melanchthon are the representatives of the former, and Zwingli and Calvin of the
latter. Luther and Zwingli were primarily the reformers,
and Melanchthon and Calvin the theologians of early
Protestantism. In a discussion of the Lutheran theologians, however, it would not do to pass by Martin
Luther himself (1483-1546), whose chief work *De Servo
Arbitrio* written in 1525 has been compared to a doctrinal manifesto. But the first systematic theologian of
the Reformation period was Melanchthon (1497-1560),
who published his *Loci Communes* in 1521. This work
ran through eighty editions during the lifetime of the
author, and gave its name to countless successors. It is
characteristic of the practical spirit of the Reformation
that the *Loci* of Melanchthon grew out of his lectures on
the Epistle to the Romans and he treated the various
topics in the order in which they occurred in that epistle.
While Zwingli (1484-1531) is not generally regarded as a
theologian, he published in 1525 his *Commentarius de
Vera et Falsa Religione,* a dogmatic work which begins
with a discussion of religion, and follows with the
usual order of theology. The work stresses the sovereignty of God and absolute predestination. The epoch
making work of Reformed theology was Calvin's *Institutio Christianæ Religionis* (1509-1564). The "Institutes" appeared first in 1536 and later in 1559, and
consisted of four books divided into one hundred and four
chapters. The first three books follow the creed and the
fourth contains the doctrine of the Church. The central

Among the earlier followers of Melanchthon were Strigel (1514-
1569), *Loci Theologici;* Chemnitz (1522-1586), *Loci Theologici;* and Sel-
neccer (1530-1592), *Institutio Relig. Christ.* In connection with Calvin,
two other Swiss divines are worthy of mention, Ursinus (1534-1583) and
Olevianus (1536-1587) authors of the *Heidelberg Catechism.*

idea like that of Zwingli is the sovereignty of God, and the arrangement is essentially Trinitarian.

The Controversies of the Reformation Period. The controversial periods in Church History are usually regarded as barren and uninteresting. It is true that they are never accompanied by either the systematic development of theology or the spiritual force of evangelism, but only in this way it seems, could the materials of truth be prepared for later systematization and thence become the ground for great periods of spiritual revival. No earnest student of theology can afford to overlook the importance of these controversies, nor once he gives them his attention can he fail to admire the intellectual acuteness and moral heroism of these defenders of the faith. We can but enumerate them here as a suggestion for further study, and give them in historical order.

1. *The First Eucharistic Controversy* (1524-1529). This controversy was between Luther and Carlstadt (1481-1541) and also between Zwingli and those who upheld the Mass. Zwingli's positions were independent of Luther who could have tolerated them had he not thought them associated with the teachings of Carlstadt. As early as 1524 Luther wrote that "Carlstadt's poison is spreading in Switzerland."

2. *The Anabaptist Controversy* (1525) was concerned with the subjects and modes of baptism.

3. *The Antinomian Controversy* (1527-1566) grew out of the extreme statements of John Agricola, who insisted upon justification by faith in such a manner as to minify allegiance to the law.

4. *The Adiaphoristic Controversy* (1548) concerned certain questions of faith and morals. In its earlier form it was concerned with the question as to whether or not there was any doctrine which was purely neutral as to right or wrong. Melanchthon and Bugenhagen asserted that there were such neutral doctrines, while Placeus and Westphal held to the negative. Thomas Aquinas attempted to make a distinction between right and wrong *per se,* and right and wrong in the concrete. In the seventeenth century it broke out again; Spener

and the pietists denying any neutral positions while the opposers of the pietists affirmed that there were such.

5. *The Synergistic Controversy* (1543-1580) concerned the relation of the human and divine elements in salvation. The followers of Melanchthon affirmed that there was co-operation between the divine and the human, the Flacians denied that the sinner could be other than purely passive. The Formula of Concord rather favored the latter position. Calvinism in the main is monogeristic, while Arminianism is strictly synergistic.

6. *The Osiandric Controversy* (1549-1552) had to do with the nature of justification, Osiander (1498-1552) maintaining that it consists in the infusion of essential righteousness, or the divine nature. His position exhibits the confusion of justification with sanctification found in Roman Catholic theology, though Osiander himself was a staunch Protestant. This view of justification has never found acceptance in Protestant theology.

7. *The Second Eucharistic Controversy* (1552) was between Luther and Zwingli, and served to develop and clarify the differences between the Lutheran and Reformed Churches. Zwingli denied (a) that the body of Christ corporeally eaten does or can confirm the faith; (b) that the body of Christ corporeally or naturally eaten can or does forgive sin; (c) that the body of Christ is corporeally present in the Eucharist as soon as the words, "This is my body," are spoken over the elements. This Luther never taught: (d) that the body of Christ can be corporeally present in the elements. Luther on the other hand, asserted (a) that in the Eucharist Christ is present only to faith; (b) that whoever accepts the miracle of the incarnation has no ground for doubting the presence of Christ in and with the elements; (c) that Christ is not shut up in heaven. This Zwingli never taught: (d) that it is necessary for Christ's body and blood to be present in the Eucharist to assure the believer of the forgiveness of sins.

8. *The Majoristic Controversy* (1559) concerned the nature of good works. Major declared that good

works were essential to salvation, while Amsdorf, who led the opposition, declared them to be detrimental. The dispute was settled by the Formula of Concord which took the middle ground and laid the foundations for the generally accepted Protestant doctrine, which is, that good works are necessary as a consequence of faith, but not necessary as a condition of justification.

9. *The Arminian Controversy* (1560-1619) dealt with the doctrine of grace. The Arminians, so-called from the type of theology represented, remonstrated against five points in the Calvinistic theology. On account of this they were called Remonstrants. The Arminians were excluded from the Reformed Church, and their teachings condemned by the Synod of Dort. The Arminian theology forms the basis of the Wesleyan teaching as held by the great body of Methodism. It is also the basis of the theology of the Church of England after the time of Bishop Cranmer. The importance of this controversy demands further attention, and will be more fully discussed under the doctrines of grace.

10. *The Deistic Controversy in England* (1581-1648) was a form of the rationalistic controversy which appeared at a later period.

11. *The Pietistic Controversy* (1650). This controversy occurred a little later than the century in question but is placed here because of its connection with the earlier controversies. It was occasioned by a reaction against the dogmatic formalism of the times. The reformers had emphasized the efficacy of faith in Christ as the means of securing the forgiveness of sin, but the controversies which arose among them gradually gave a too exclusively doctrinal and polemical character to the sermons and writings of both the Lutheran and Calvinistic divines. The reaction took the form of a renewed emphasis upon feeling and good works. The direct originator of this movement was Philip Jacob Spener (1635-1705), who at meetings held in his home, repeated his sermons, expounded passages from the New Testament, and induced those present to join in conversation on religious subjects. From this they were

given the name of Pietists. The purpose of Spener was to combine the Lutheran emphasis upon Bible doctrine, with the Reformed tendency to a vigorous life.

12. *The Placean Controversy* (1633-1685). This controversy also falls outside the limits of the Reformation period. It was concerned with "mediate imputation."

Thus through struggle and debate, often with much *odium theologicum* attached, and sometimes with practices that must be viewed with disapproval, were the doctrines of the Church wrought out and preserved. Great issues were at stake, and men of intellectual acuteness and moral heroism rushed to the defense of the faith. We must believe, also, that above all was a superintending Providence which overruled the failures and shortcomings of men, and that the Holy Spirit as a Guide into all truth, Himself shaped the destinies of the Church.

THE CONFESSIONAL PERIOD

The seventeenth and eighteenth centuries (c. 1600-1800) represent the Confessional Period in theological development. During this time the doctrinal statements of the larger communions were worked out in systematic form and given to the Church as varying types of Christian Dogmatics. The theologians of this period are frequently classified as Protestant Scholastics, due to the fact that they followed in the main the same principles of systematization as were observed by the older schoolmen. Two phases of this subject demand our attention: (I) the various confessional types, and (II) the different forms which theology assumed, due to the varying influences of external circumstances. These divisions will be treated from the genetic viewpoint.

I.

The different types of theology are found within the New Testament itself, and mark the beginning of the developments found in later periods of dogmatic history. Peter represented the practical tendency; James a combination of the practical and philosophical, giving us the Wisdom Literature of the New Testament; Paul was a logician and systematizer, and gives us the Systematic Theology of the New Testament; while John was primarily a seer, announcing dogmatically what he had seen by intuition. The differentiating features of these types of theology will best be set forth by the contrasts found in chronological order in the history of the Church: (1) Eastern and Western; (2) Roman Catholic and Protestant; (3) Lutheran and Reformed; and (4) Reformed and Arminian.

The Eastern and the Western Churches. The East and the West hold in common the three Ecumenical Creeds, and also the findings of the four Ecumenical Councils—Nicæa (325); Constantinople (381); Ephesus (431); and Chalcedon (451). They separated over the controversy which began with the insertion of the word *filioque* in the creed, but perhaps the separation was due more to political and ecclesiastical reasons than to the doctrinal point of a single or double procession of the Spirit. There were two rival pontiffs, one at Constantinople in the East and one at Rome in the West. The decline of the Eastern Empire greatly aided in the development of power at Rome. After their separation they developed two distinct types of theology. That of the East was more philosophical and speculative, that of the West more progressive and practical. To the former with its fondness for metaphysical subtleties, we are indebted for the doctrines of the Trinity and the Nature of the Godhead. To the West with its more practical trend, we are indebted for the doctrines of grace and the organization of the Church.

The Confessional Standards of the Eastern Church are the three creeds mentioned above, to which were added later, the *Confessio Gennadii* (1453), and the *Confessio Orthodoxa* (1643). The doctrinal differences between the Eastern and Western Churches are these— the East (1) rejects the doctrine of the papacy; (2) modifies the seven sacraments; (3) denies the immaculate conception of the virgin; (4) circulates the Bible in the vernacular; and (5) asserts its own supremacy,

viewing the Church of Rome as the eldest born among
the schisms and heresies.

The Roman Catholic and the Protestant Churches.
As different types of theology developed in the Eastern
and Western Churches, so in the West itself, the differentiating features of Roman Catholicism and Protestantism were marked and distinct. The Roman Catholic
Church is sacramentarian, the Protestant Church is
evangelical. Evangelical Christianity holds that God
saves men directly by entering into personal and spiritual relations with them. Roman Catholicism, on the
contrary, teaches that the Church is the one divinely appointed instrument, through which spiritual blessings
are communicated by means of the sacraments. Evangelical Christianity maintains that the true Church is
composed of the whole number of those redeemed
through Christ, and that its authority is conditioned
by the immediate spiritual relation existing between its
constituent members, and the one living Lord who is its
Divine Head. While Roman Catholic theology technically admits that there is an invisible Church, practically
it identifies it with the visible organization, which it
maintains is commissioned to accomplish a certain work
in the world. It further maintains that it derives its
authority from this commission alone, apart from any
personal relation existing spiritually between Christ and
its members, or even the officials in whom the authority
is vested. Thus in the West the two branches build up an
extensive though widely divergent theology.

The Roman Catholic Standards are the three creeds,
and as especially directed against Protestantism, the
Canons and Decrees of the Council of Trent, (1545-
1563); *Professio Fidei Tridentina* (1564), which is the
creed of Pius IV; to which were added later the Vatican
decisions on the Immaculate Conception (1854), and
Papal Infallibility (1870).

Protestant Theology and Its Divergent Types. While
the divergent views of the Roman Catholic and the
Protestant Churches center largely in the conception
of the Church itself, these differences have been devel-

oped into two systems of theology which are opposed to each other at almost every point. *First,* Protestantism maintains the universality of the priesthood of believers, as over against a special order of priesthood held by Roman Catholicism; *second,* it believes that grace is communicated through the truth received in faith, as over against that which vests it solely in the sacraments; *third,* it exalts the preaching of the Word above the sacramental ministry at the altar; and *fourth,* it insists that grace is received directly from Christ through the Spirit, and that this gives membership in the Church as Christ's spiritual body, as over against the teaching that a spiritual relation with Christ must be established through the Church. The evangelical view that the Church must be approached through Christ, rather than Christ through the Church, not only marks a distinction in theology, but gives rise also to widely different types of Christian experience.

In the discussion of Protestant theology we shall consider the four following types: (1) Lutheran Dogmatics; (2) Reformed Dogmatics; (3) Arminian Dogmatics; and (4) Socinian Dogmatics.

1. *The Lutheran Dogmatic.* The Lutheran Standards are the *Augsburg Confession* with its *Apology* (1530); the *Smalcald Articles* (1537); Luther's *Smaller* and *Larger Catechisms* (1529), and the *Formulas of Concord* (1577). There have been three marked tendencies in Lutheranism, *first,* a movement toward the end of the sixteenth century and the earlier years of the seventeenth which manifested a renewed attachment to the positions of Luther as opposed to those of Melanchthon; *second,* a reaction against strict Lutheranism in favor of the earlier Ecumenical Creeds; and *third,* the mediating positions. The Lutheran theologians will be grouped under this classification.

In the movement toward a return to Luther may be mentioned Leonard Hutter (1563-1616) who is commonly known as "Luther Redivivus." His chief work, *Compendium Locorum Theologicorum,* was published in 1610, and consisted of extracts from Lutheran standards.

A second edition was published by Twesten in 1855. Here also must be classed John Gerhard (1582-1637), who was regarded as the most learned theologian of his age. His great work *Loci Communes Theologici* was published in nine volumes (1610-1622), and far excels the work of Hutter in systematic arrangement. Chemnitz (1522-1586) in his earlier years followed Melanchthon but later turned to Lutheranism. He is described as "clear and accurate, the most learned of the disciples of Melanchthon." In opposition to strict Lutheranism, George Calixtus (1586-1656) started a reactionary movement by insisting on a return to the great Ecumenical Creeds. While he followed Melanchthon rather than Luther, he was known as the "syncretistic theologian" and endeavored to find the truth in both the Reformed and the Romanist positions. His chief work was the *Epitome Theologiæ,* and represents a change from the analytical to the synthetic method of treatment. Aside from Danæus, he is the first theologian to separate between Ethics and Dogmatics. The opponent of Calixtus was Calovius (1612-1686) who in defense of Lutheranism undertakes to confute the errors which arose after the time of Gerhard. His work is entitled *Systema Locorum Theologicorum* and was published in twelve volumes. It follows the scholastic style. Akin to this, but even more dialectical in style was the *Theologia Didactico-polemica Theologiæ* of Quenstedt (1617-1688). Hollaz (1648-1713) whose work consists largely of extracts from Gerhard, Calovius and others, and shows the influence of mysticism, marks in some sense the transition from the severely scholastic theology of the seventeenth century to the pietistic type of the eighteenth century. The mediating theologians of the Jena school held a position midway between that of Calixtus and Hutter, the chief representatives being Musæus (1613-1681) and Baier (1647-1695). The latter's work, *Compendium Theologiæ Positivæ,* became an important and popular textbook for the study of the old Lutheran Dogmatic.

2. *The Reformed Dogmatic.* A movement similar to that noticed in Lutheranism is found in even a more marked manner in Reformed theology. Starting with the theology of Calvin, there was a movement in the direction of overstraining his position which led practically to "hyper-Calvinism." Against this was a reactionary movement which could not be called a return to Calvinism but to an avowed modification of it. This was represented by the Amyraldists and the Arminians, but the latter must be regarded not merely as a modification of Reformed theology but a distinct type of Dogmatics.

The Reformed theologians which immediately followed Zwingli and Calvin, were able representatives of the true Calvinistic positions. Among these may be mentioned Peter Martyr (1500-1562); Chamier (1565-1621); Wolleb (1536-1626) author of *Compendium Theologiæ Christianæ;* and Wendelin (1584-1652) whose principal works are *Compendium Christianæ Theologiæ* (1634) and *Christianæ Theologiæ Systema Majus* (1656) both of these being expositions of the strict Calvinism of that period. Theodore Beza (1519-1605) who produced no distinctly dogmatic work, began nevertheless, a powerful movement toward hyper-Calvinism which greatly influenced the theology of his time. Dr. William Twisse (1578-1646) wrote a book published posthumously at Oxford in 1653, the title of which translated is *"The Riches of God's Love unto the Vessels of Mercy Consistent with His Absolute Hatred or Reprobation of the Vessels of Wrath."* MacPherson says that this affords "perhaps the very best example of supralapsarianism developed by fearless application of logic, without necessary qualifications or reservations, to the doctrinal principles of Calvinism" (MacPherson, *Christian Dogmatics*, p. 63). Following him was Francis Turretin of Geneva (the father) (1623-1687) whose *Institutio Theologiæ Elencticæ* shows the influence of the rising federal school of theology, and Jean Alphonso Turretin (the son) (1671-1737) who sought to modify the strict Calvinism of the father, and also to promote a union of the Reformed and Lutheran Churches. Turretin, the younger, and Benedict Pictet (1655-1725), his contemporary, may both be classed as federalists and were influenced by the Cartesian philosophy.

The reactionary movement in the Reformed Church of this period was begun by Cocceius (1603-1669) who renounced the scholastic method and accepted in its stead a purely biblical method. He distributed his materials according to the covenant idea and became in this sense a federalist. His principal work was entitled *Summa Doctrinæ de Foedere et Testamentis Dei* published in two volumes. Witsius (1636-1708) attempted to reconcile the Federalists and the Orthodox party but without success. The intermediate group was represented in England by John Owen (1616-1683), Richard Baxter (1616-1685); and Thomas Ridgeley (1666-1734). The School of Saumur in France was represented by two outstanding theologians, Amyraldus (1596-1664) who made an attempt to modify the positions of the Synod of Dort; and La Place, or Placæus (1606-1655) as he is commonly known, who advanced the theory of mediate imputation of Adam's sin. The Calvinism of the School of Saumur did not meet with approval on the part of the Reformed Churches of Geneva and was condemned by the *Formula Consensus* at the Synod of Charenton (1675). The Scotch Presbyterian theologians were Thomas Boston (1676-1732); John Dick (1764-1833) and Thomas Chalmers (1780-1847). Jonathan Edwards (1703-1758) and Samuel Hopkins (1721-1803) were the chief American theologians of the period.

3. *The Arminian Dogmatic.* The Arminian or Remonstrant school arose in Holland at the opening of the seventeenth century, and came as a protest against the Calvinism of that day. James Arminius (1560-1609) was "a learned and able divine, of a meek Christian spirit." As a youth he was precocious and studied theology under Theodore Beza, a rigid Calvinist and the leading spirit in the development of hyper-Calvinism. In later life, Arminius was drawn away from the earlier positions of Reformed theology, and while a professor

at Leyden, broke into a fierce conflict with Gomarius (1563-1641). Arminius did not live long after this, but his death witnessed no cessation of the controversy. Following James Arminius, from whom this type of theology took its name, may be mentioned Simon Episcopius (1583-1643), who after the death of Arminius became the leader of the movement and carried on the controversy before the Synod of Dort. His *Institutiones Theologicæ*, published in 1643 is the clearest and most authoritative statement on earlier Arminianism. Episcopius was opposed at Dort by Gomarius, and by Maccovius (1588-1644). Voetius of Utrecht (1588-1676) was the bitterest and most violent of all the opposers of Arminianism, his *Selectæ Disputationes Theologicæ* being directed against the Arminians, the Cartesians and the Cocceians. Hugo Grotius (1583-1645) was perhaps the most outstanding theologian of the Dutch school. He is celebrated both for his "governmental theory of the atonement" and for his contribution to international law. Chief among his apologetical writings are *De Veritate Chr. Religionis,* and *Defensio Fidei Catholicæ de Satisfactione Christi,* this latter being directed against the Pelagians and Socinians but upholding the Arminian positions. Philipp van Limborch (1633-1702) not only by his life span linked the seventeenth and eighteenth centuries, but marks also the transition to rationalism. He was a professor of theology in Utrecht and a friend of John Locke, the English philosopher. His exegesis of the New Testament proved to be popular and enduring, and his *Institutes of Christian Theology* formed the most complete and best known exposition of the earlier Arminianism.

Among the Puritans in England, the most noted representative of evangelical Arminianism was John Goodwin (1593-1665). His *Redemption Redeemed* published in 1651 dealt with the questions of election, reprobation and perseverance, and his *Imputatio Fidei* or a Treatise on Justification (1642) was greatly valued by John Wesley and Richard Watson. His *Exposition of the Ninth Chapter of Romans* and *On Being Filled with the Spirit* were further contributions to the evangelical cause. John William Fletcher (1729-1785), Vicar of Madeley has been called the "Arminian of the Arminians." He was the apologist of early Methodism and his *Checks to Antinomianism* is still the best treatise on this subject. He is perhaps best known for his saintly character and his spiritual ministry. John Wesley (1703-1791) was the Father of Methodism both as to the doctrine and the polity of the Church. The development of later Arminianism commonly known as Wesleyanism occurs in the following century.

While not strictly of the Arminian type of theology, and yet thoroughly evangelical, we may mention here, George Fox (1624-1691) the founder of the Society of Friends or Quakers, and George Barclay (1648-1690) whose *Apology* represents the doctrinal standards of the society. The English Churchmen of this period were Richard Hooker (1553-1600); Gilbert Burnett (1643-1715)) and John Pearson (1613-1685) whose works on the *Creed*, the *Parables* and the *Miracles* are still standard authorities.

4. *The Socinian Dogmatic.* Frequently the Socinian theology is not regarded as a distinct type of dogmatics, but since the movement dates back to the Reformation period it is best treated here. Laelius Socinus (the uncle) (1525-1562) and Faustus Socinus (the nephew) (1539-1604) are the founders of what is known in modern times as Unitarianism. Socinianism takes its name from the former, and the latter is regarded as the founder of the sect. Their writings are collected in the *Biblotheca Fratrum Polonorum.* In the seventeenth century the doctrines were defended by Crell (1590-1631) who wrote a treatise against the Trinitarian conception of God, and Schlichting (1592-1662) who wrote a confession of faith for Polish Christians. The father of English Unitarianism was John Biddle (1615-1662) who wrote a series of tracts on *The Faith of One God,* who is only the Father; and of one Mediator between God and men, who is only the man Christ Jesus; and of one Holy Spirit, the gift of God: asserted and defended. The doc-

trinal standards are found in the Racovian Catechism. This appeared as the Rakow Catechism in the Polish language in 1605, immediately after the death of Socinus, and was completed on the basis of his writings by Statorius, Schmalz, Moscorovius, and Volkel. Latin translations appeared in 1665, 1680 and 1684.

II.

We have now to consider some of the forms which theology assumed due to the varying influences of external circumstances. We shall notice briefly (1) The Pietistic Movement; (2) The Rationalistic Movement; and (3) The Biblical Movement.

1. *The Pietistic Movement.* A strong opposition grew up in the latter part of the seventeenth and the earlier part of the eighteenth centuries against the barrenness of scholasticism, which resulted in the Pietistic Movement in Germany. Andreæ (1586-1654) and Spener (1635-1705) had waged war against a dead orthodoxy and proclaimed the need for a *theologia regenitorum* or a regeneration of theology. Spener advocated the substitution of a prayerful study of the Holy Scriptures for the official theology of his time. His special work, however, was in Eschatology, where he attempted to fill in that which he considered lacking in the Dogmatics of Luther. His views of the millennium were later worked out systematically by two of his pupils, Johann Wilhelm Peterson (1694-1727), a Lutheran mystic who was expelled from Luneburg because of his millenarian views; and Johann Konrad Dippel (1673-1734) who was known as a religious enthusiast. The work of Spener was continued by Francke (1663-1727) who was the founder of the Francke Institute at Halle. Benedict Carpzon (1679-1767) was a decided adversary of the whole Pietistic movement and under his leadership the breach widened between Scholasticism and Pietism. There developed in the minds of the people a repugnance to Scholasticism which was typically displayed in the writings of Hollaz, who has been called "the last of the orthodox theologians."

2. *The Rationalistic Movement.* Here there begins
to be felt the varying influence of the systems of philosophy upon dogmatics. There was a school of Descartes
in Holland represented by Bekker (1634-1698). His
book, *Strong Food for the Perfect,* aroused suspicions
of Socinianism and later he was deposed from the ministry. There were also schools of Wolff (1659-1754)
and Leibnitz (1646-1716) in Germany and these greatly
influenced theological study. Among the theologians of
the school of Wolff may be mentioned Stapfer (1708-
1775) whose *Theological Institutes* were widely known;
Baumgarten (1706-1757); Endemann (d. 1789); Bern-
sau (d. 1763) and Wyttenbach (d. 1779). These theologians of the earlier rationalistic period were not un-
orthodox and had as their motive the exact demonstration of dogma in such a clear manner that there could
be no true opposition offered to it. However, their very
attempts at accurate statement developed an intellectu-
alism that later gave rise to the skeptical tendencies of
rationalism. The separation between Natural Theology
and Revealed Theology became widened, and Natural
Theology was exalted at the expense of revelation. This
issued in the Deism of England and the period of the "en-
lightenment" as it is generally termed, in philosophy.
Here are the beginnings of the Rationalistic Period of the
early nineteenth century which set itself up in such
strong opposition to the truth of Christianity. After the
Reformation had freed theology in a large measure, from
the bonds of scholasticism, other philosophies soon took
its place. Semler built upon the philosophy of Wolff and
Leibnitz, and consequently represented the Scriptures as
having merely a local and temporary character. Michælis
(1716-1784) and Doederlein (1714-1789) followed Semler (1725-1791), both being aided by the philosophy of
Immanuel Kant (1724-1804). The philosophy of Herder
(1744-1803) and Jacobi (1743-1819) exemplified greater
spirituality and prepared the way for the "Father of
Modern Theology" Friedrich Daniel Ernst Schleiermacher (1768-1834).

3. *The Biblical Movement.* Against the growing tendency toward rationalism there arose a Biblical Theistic tendency which served to preserve the truth against the attacks of the rationalists. Bengel (1687-1751) with a firm faith in the inspiration and absolute authority of the Bible was perplexed at the great number of variations in the text. He set himself to study, and after twenty years published his *Apparatus Criticus,* which became the starting point for modern textual criticism of the New Testament. In his *Essay on the Right Way of Handling Divine Subjects* he states that in brief it is to "put nothing *into* the Scriptures, but to draw everything *from* them, and suffer nothing to remain hidden that is really *in them.*" Oetinger (1702-1782) followed Bengel in theology and Boehme in philosophy. He maintained that life is not only the fruit of doctrine but also its starting point and basis. Buddeus (1667-1729) was a man of genuine piety and learning, and by the conciliatory position he occupied, exerted a profound Christian influence. His *Institutiones Theologiæ Moralis* (1711) removed the casuistical elements from the Protestant treatment of Christian morals. Ernesti (1707-1781) was noted for his proficiency in Classical Languages, Rhetoric and Theology. His principal work was *Institutio Interpretis N.T.* (1761) which opened a new epoch in the history of Hermeneutics. J. H. Michaelis (1668-1738) made valuable contributions to Old Testament criticism and exegesis. He lectured at Halle and was closely associated with Francke. J. D. Michaelis (1717-1791) was recognized as an indefatigable investigator, and a prolific writer. His exegetical works on both the Old and the New Testaments are numerous, his work on the Psalms being of special importance.

THE MODERN PERIOD

Schleiermacher, the "Father of Modern Theology," may be said to have introduced into modern thought the vitality of the evangelical teaching, much as did his contemporary, John Wesley, in the field of religion. As over against the positions of the rationalists, he understood the Christian faith as something given, not merely in an external manner, but as having its seat in the consciousness. It was a consequence, therefore, not of rational thinking, but had its origin in the heart. Religion was a "feeling of dependence" and Christ and His redemption were made the center of his system of theology. As to the range of his influence Schleiermacher has been compared to Augustine and Calvin. So extensive does the history of Dogmatics become in the modern period, that it will be necessary for us to confine our thought to a mere classification of the greater theologians according to their particular schools. We shall consider the development of theology during this period under the following divisions. (1) The School of Schleiermacher; (2) The Rationalistic School; (3) The Mediating School; (4) Ritschl and His School; and (5) British and American Theology.

1. *The School of Schleiermacher.* Schleiermacher and his successors are generally regarded as belonging to the transitional school, which marks the distinction between the thought of the mediæval and that of the distinctly modern period. Here following Schleiermacher may be mentioned Alexander Schweitzer (1808-1888), who attempted to work out a system of theology based upon Christian consciousness, historical Christianity being the religion in which this ideal was realized. Schenkel (1813-1885) made conscience the distinct organ of religion. Lipsius (1830-1892) sought to develop a Christian Dogmatic purely from the standpoint of Christian consciousness, his threefold division being, (1) God-consciousness; (2) Self-consciousness; and (3) World-consciousness. Rothe (1799-1867) the pupil of Daub, occupied a position midway between rationalism and supernaturalism, and in this respect his theology is comparable to that of Schleiermacher.

2. *The Rationalistic School.* This is sometimes known as the philosophical school, due to the fact that the theology of the period was largely influenced by philosophy—especially that of Kant, Fichte, Schelling

and Hegel. Among the earlier followers of Hegel were Daub (1765-1836), Goschel (1784-1862), Hasse (1697-1783), Rosenkranz (1805-1879), Erdmann (1821-1905), and Marheineke (1780-1846). Daub was the teacher of Rothe, and shows the influence of Fichte, Schelling and Hegel in successive stages. Marheineke was a colleague of Schleiermacher and a thorough-going Hegelian. The outline of his *System of Christian Doctrine* is derived from the Hegelian triad: (1) the pure notion of God himself, embracing His nature and attributes; (2) God distinguishing Himself from Himself, the God-man, at once substance and subject. This embraces the subject of Christology and Soteriology. (3) God returning out of this distinction into eternal unity with Himself, which embraces the doctrine of the Trinity, the Administration of Grace, and the Kingdom of God. Biedermann (1819-1885) in his *Christliche Dogmatik* develops the principles of Hegelianism in a somewhat pantheistic manner. With the advent of Hegelianism in philosophy, it was asserted for a time that peace had been declared between belief and knowledge, and that theology presented the same truth in formal statement, that philosophy acknowledges in a higher conception. This self-deception, however, did not last long, and the school of Hegel split up into two parties, the first clinging to the orthodox faith, and the second making a sharp distinction between faith and knowledge as the highest wisdom. The left wing of Hegelianism was represented by Bauer (1792-1860) and the Tubingen School. Bauer applied Hegel's method of dialectical development to church history and the New Testament, and thus founded the Tubingen School which became a center of rationalism and destructive criticism. It was in Strauss (1808-1874) that the most extreme positions were reached, of whose teachings it was said, that they resembled "Christian theology as a cemetery resembles a town." Here also we should mention as having in some sense been influenced by Hegel, but more evangelical in their teaching, Otto Pfleiderer (1839-1908) and Lipsius (1830-1892). Pfleiderer's *Philosophy of*

Religion (1896) and his *Evolution and Theology* (1900) were widely influential in American thought during the latter part of the nineteenth century.

3. *The Mediating School.* This is represented by a group of outstanding theologians who sought to maintain evangelical principles and yet combine them with the best thought of modern times. As showing the marked influence of Schleiermacher there should be mentioned first of all, the incomplete *Dogmatik* of Twesten (1789-1876), who was inclined toward ecclesiastical orthodoxy, and Nitzsch (1787-1868) whose *System of Christian Faith* was a vigorous attempt to unite Dogmatics and Ethics. As other outstanding members of this school we may mention Isaac A. Dorner (1809-1884) whose great work is entitled a *System of Christian Doctrine.* His rationalistic positions appear primarily in his doctrine of the Trinity and in his Christology. Bishop H. L. Martensen (1808-1884), a Danish writer and friend of Dorner, follows in general the teachings of Lutheranism, although in the later portion of his work entitled *Christian Dogmatics* he swings more to the Reformed position. Written in an attractive style, his great contribution to theological thought exerted a wide influence in the later nineteenth and earlier twentieth centuries. This influence was due perhaps to his attractive style, and to his unusual blending of mysticism and philosophical speculation. Thomasius (1802-1875) is classed among the new Lutherans and is known especially for his treatment of the *Kenosis.* Kahnis (1814-1888) inclined toward the Sabellian idea of the Trinity. Philippi (1809-1882) bases his dogmatic on the thought of fellowship, (1) Original fellowship with God; (2) the breach of fellowship; (3) objective restoration of fellowship through Christ; (4) subjective appropriation of fellowship with God; and (5) the future completion of the restored and appropriated fellowship. Martin Kahler of Halle (1835-1912) arranges his dogmatic in three divisions: (1) the confession of the need of salvation; (2) the confession of the possession of salvation; and (3) the confession of the hope of salvation. Ebrard

presented the Reformed Dogmatic from a study of its sources in opposition to the principles of A. Schweitzer. J. P. Lange (1802-1884) in an elaborate work on dogmatics, starts with the Reformed principles and endeavors to harmonize these with later thought.

More or less independent of any particular school may be mentioned Carl Hase of Jena, who though he accepted the rationalistic position in some measure, reached his conclusions in a manner independent of other thinkers. His chief theological work is the *Evang. Dogmatik* (1826). Here also may be mentioned Cramer (1723-1788), Baumgarten-Crusius (1788-1843), and especially the *Philosophische Dogmatik* of C. H. Weisse (1801-1866) written in an attempt to harmonize the various philosophical positions. J. Müller (1801-1878) contributed to the field of theology a masterly treatise on the *Christian Doctrine of Sin* (tr. 1868). Among the apologists of this period may be mentioned C. Ullman (1796-1865) and A. Tholuck (1799-1877). Continuing the supranaturalistic position of the former period are the names of A. Hahn (1792-1863) and J. T. Beck (1804-1878) the latter endeavoring to open a new pathway in theology by using a special terminology. He was a student at Tubingen but reacted against the rationalism prevalent there. He is usually classified as a follower of Schleiermacher, but allied himself with the earlier biblical realism of Bengel. It was against his teaching that Strauss reacted so violently. A. Vinet (1797-1847), Godet (1812-1900) and Poulain (1807-1868) stand high in Switzerland and France, the latter being one of the strongest apologists against modern Naturalism.

4. *Ritschl and His School.* Albrecht Ritschl of Bonn (1822-1889) may be said more than any other of this period, to have founded a distinct school of theology. His chief work, *Justification and Reconciliation,* is the third volume of a larger work setting forth his own positions. Ritschl rejects the scholastic position, and in fact all philosophy, maintaining that philosophy and theology have no valid connection with each other. He was a firm adherent of the historical movement and therefore

insists strongly upon the recognition of the historical Christ, and the acceptance of the Scriptures as a record of revelation. His theory of knowledge is empirical, and confusion arose from an attempted union of the idealistic and realistic elements of knowledge, borrowed from Kant on the one hand and Lotze on the other. The term "value judgments" belongs peculiarly to Ritschl and his school. By these they are meant those judgments which are true and important only as they have value in producing emotional or other effects in the consciousness of the one who entertains them. This gave rise to certain phases of Higher Criticism in its destructive tendencies, such as the position that the miracles might not have been historical facts, and yet, since they produce the effect of omnipotent power, they have "value" for religion. Some of the more radical adherents of this position extended the value judgment to Christ himself, maintaining that the religious value could be dissociated from the historical background.

Among the theologians classified as Ritschlians may be mentioned Gottschick (b. 1847), Hermann of Marburg (b. 1846), Hermann Schultz (b. 1836), and perhaps Adolph Harnack (b. 1851). Julius Kaftan (b. 1848), the successor of Dorner at Berlin, modified Ritschl's position, abandoning the distinctions between scientific and religious knowledge; and Theodor Hæring (b. 1848), more than any other of the Ritschlians returns closer to the Orthodox Church.

5. *British and American Theology.* The earliest Methodist writings of a doctrinal character were John Wesley's *Sermons,* which together with his *Notes* and the *Twenty-five Articles* constitute the doctrinal standards of Methodism. John Fletcher, while in some sense the apologist of Methodism, was a member of the Established Church and Vicar of Madeley. The earliest Methodist writer to formulate a complete system of doctrine was Richard Watson (1781-1823) who published his *Theological Institutes* in 1823. This work was revised by Wakefield and with some additional material is found in Wakefield's *Christian Theology.* William Burton Pope

(1822-1903) in his *Compendium of Christian Theology,*
published in three volumes is the first British writer to
compare favorably with Richard Watson. In America,
Miner Raymond (1813-1897) published his *Systematic
Theology,* a monumental work in three volumes (1877-
1879); Thomas Neely Ralston, his *Elements of Divinity*
(1847) which was revised and enlarged by the addition
of his *Evidences, Morals and Institutions of Christianity*
(1871). In its first form it was translated into Norwegian
(1858) and in its enlarged form translated and published
in the Chinese language in 1886. Henry Clay Sheldon
published his *History of Christian Doctrine* in 1886 and
his *System of Christian Doctrine* in 1903. John J. Tigert
revised and published in 1888 the *Systematic Theology* of
Thomas O. Summers (1812-1882). John Miley's excellent work on *Systematic Theology* in two volumes appeared in 1892. Olin A. Curtis published his *Christian
Faith* in 1905, S. J. Gamertfelder, his *Systematic Theology* (Evangelical Association) in 1913; and A. M. Hills,
his *Fundamental Christian Theology* in 1931. In addition
to these a number of smaller works have been published
representative of the Arminian type of theology, among
which are Bank's *Manual of Christian Doctrine* (1897);
Binney's *Theological Compend,* (Binney and Steele)
(1875); Field, *Handbook of Christian Theology* (1887);
Ellyson, *New Theological Compend* (1905); Lowrey,
Positive Theology (1853); Weaver, *Christian Theology*
(1900).

The Lutheran and Reformed Churches in the United
States have depended largely upon German sources for
their theological teaching. Knapp, *Lectures on Christian
Theology* was translated by Leonard Woods (1831) and
widely read in America. Nitzsch, *System of Christian
Doctrine* (1849); Martensen, *Christian Dogmatics,* a
Danish work translated from the German by William
Urwick (1892); Van Oosterzee, *Christian Dogmatics*
(translated 1874), and Schmid, *Doctrinal Theology of the
Evangelical Lutheran Church* (translated 1876) repre-
sent the principal evangelical works of Lutheranism. A

more recent work, published in the United States is
Stump, *The Christian Faith* (1932)

The theologians of the Reformed Church represent
two different schools. The Older Calvinism is represented by Charles Hodge (1797-1878) *Systematic Theology;* A. A. Hodge, the son (1823-1886) *Outlines of
Theology;* Robert J. Breckinridge (1800-1871) *The
Knowledge of God Objectively Considered* (1859) and
The Knowledge of God Subjectively Considered (1860);
William G. T. Shedd (1820-1894) *Dogmatic Theology;*
Henry B. Smith (1815-1877) *Introduction to Theology*
(1883), *Systematic Theology* (1884), a representative of
the Christocentric viewpoint. These writers hold to the
views of human depravity and divine grace as advocated
by Augustine and Calvin and for this reason were known
popularly as the Old School. The New School modified
the older Calvinistic positions through a succession of
writers from Jonathan Edwards (1703-1758) to Horace
Bushnell (1802-1876). These writers follow Jonathan
Edwards in the following order: Joseph Bellamy (1719-
1790), Samuel Hopkins (1721-1803), Timothy Dwight
(1752-1817), Nathanael Emmons (1745-1840), Leonard
Woods (1774-1854), Charles G. Finney (1792-1875),
Nathaniel W. Taylor (1786-1858) and Horace Bushnell,
who held to a more or less Sabellian view of the Trinity,
and to the moral influence theory of the atonement.

Other works of Reformed writers, are Gerhart, *In-
stitutes of the Christian Religion,* William Adams Brown,
Christian Theology in Outline (1906); Pond, *Lectures
on Christian Theology* (1867); Dickie, *Organism of
Christian Truth* (1930); John MacPherson, *Christian
Dogmatics* (1898), and James Orr, *Christian View of
God and the World* (1893).

The Baptist theologians are A. H. Strong, *Systematic Theology* (1907), Alvah Hovey, *Outline of Christian Theology* (1870), William Newton Clarke, *An Outline of Christian Theology* (1917); Ezekiel Gilman Robinson, *Christian Theology* (1894); J. P. Boyce, *Abstract
of Systematic Theology* (1887).

The Anglican Theology is represented by Pearson *On the Creed,* Burnet, *The Thirty-nine Articles,* Bicknell, *Thirty-nine Articles* (a more recent work 1919, last edition 1936), Hall, *Dogmatic Theology* (a complete treatise in ten volumes), Mortimer, *Catholic Faith and Practice,* Lacey, *Elements of Christian Doctrine,* Percival, *A Digest of Theology,* Mason, *The Faith of the Gospel,* Litton, *Introduction to Dogmatic Theology,* William and Scannell, *A Manual of Catholic Theology,* and Darwell Stone, *Outline of Christian Dogma.*

CHAPTER V

THE CHRISTIAN RELIGION

Christian Theology as the science of the Christian religion, brings us at once to a consideration of its first underlying postulate, the fundamental nature of religion. The word religion is simply the Latin word *religio* brought over into the English language, and is derived from *religere* which means literally *to go over again,* or *to carefully ponder.* In the free translation of MacPherson it means "a careful reconsideration, a brooding over, a giving of the mind and all the faculties to a study of what seems to call for respectful and reverential inquiry." Lactantius held that the word is derived from *religare, to bind back* and therefore was significant of the personal relationship existing between man and his Creator. While most etymologists follow Cicero in rejecting this definition, Dr. Pope makes use of the two explanations together in describing the nature of religion. Following Lactantius, religion signifies "the eternal bond which binds man to God" and is therefore the relation of the human creature to the Supreme Creator, as acknowledged and borne witness to in all forms of theological teaching and worship; while with Cicero, the exercise of the human mind in pondering and considering divine things is signified by religion, which is, as it were, an instinctive and inwrought aspiration of human nature corrected and purified and directed to its highest issues in the true faith. Thus it is that both the objective and subjective relations of man meet in Religion, which is one of the largest and deepest terms with which we have to do (POPE, *Compend Chr. Th.,* I, p. 1).

There are two other words used in the New Testament to express the idea of religion. The first is *eusebeia* (εὐσέβεια) which is used in the sense of a reverential fear of God. At first it signified only the careful handling of anything in a general way, but finally came to mean the careful, reverential treatment of divine things (Cf. Luke 2:25, Acts 2:5; 8:2). The second word is *threskeia* ($\theta\rho\eta\sigma\kappa\epsilon\acute{\iota}\alpha$) (Cf. James 1:26, 27) and is used in a more outward sense to distinguish one form of worship from other forms (Cf. Acts 26:5, Col. 2:18, James 1:26, 27). A community, therefore, may be *threskos* ($\theta\rho\hat{\eta}\sigma\kappa o\varsigma$ James 1:26) because of its adherence to prescribed forms of worship; but it can be *eusebeia* ($\epsilon\dot{\upsilon}\sigma\acute{\epsilon}\beta\epsilon\iota a$ Cf. Acts 3:12, I Tim. 2:2) only in the sense of being made up of pious individuals. This is further evidenced by the fact that the adjective of *eusebeia*, $\epsilon\dot{\upsilon}\sigma\epsilon\beta\acute{\eta}\varsigma$ (Cf. Acts 2:5) is translated in our English version by the words "devout" and "godly" while the substantive is translated "godliness."

Definitions of Religion. In its essential idea, religion is a life in God. Stewart defines it as "fellowship with God"; Sterrett as "the reciprocal relation or communion with God and man, involving *first,* revelation; and *second,* faith"; while William Newton Clarke, followed by William Adams Brown, defines it as "the life of man in his superhuman relations." Herbert Spencer maintained that "religion is an *a priori* theory of the universe," to which Romanes added the qualifying statement, "which assumes intelligent personality as the originating cause of the universe, science as dealing with the 'how,' the phenomenal process, and religion dealing with the 'who,' the intelligent personality who works through the process." Holland makes the following distinction between natural life, which is "the life in God which has not yet arrived at this recognition that God is in all things, and is not yet as such religious. Religion is the discovery by the son of a Father who is in all His works, yet is distinct from them all." MacPherson says that "religion consists in the fact of a real relationship subsisting between God and man."

Objectively considered, religion is man's relation to the infinite and subjectively, it is the determination of human life by that relation.—HASE, *Dogmatik.*

ORIGIN AND DEVELOPMENT OF RELIGION

The question of the origin of religion has given occasion to many and widely divergent theories. Three branches of modern investigation have centered their attention upon this subject and through observation and research have made valuable contributions. These are *first,* the History of Religion, sometimes known as Comparative Religion; *second,* the Psychology of Religion; and *third,* the Philosophy of Religion.

The History of Religion. Great advances have been made in the study of religion since the publication of E. B. Tylor's famous work on *Primitive Culture* in 1871. Other works which have greatly aided this study are Menzies, *History of Religion;* M. Jastrow, *The Study of Religion;* C. P. Tiele, *Elements of the Science of Religion;* A. Lang, *Myth, Ritual and Religion;* Frazer, *The Golden Bough;* Brinton, *Religions of Primitive Peoples,* and De la Saussaye, *Handbook of Religions.* The fascination of this study in a field never before opened, led to many hasty deductions and ill-founded theories as to the origin and nature of religion. One of the distinct gains, however, was the collation of material drawn from wide fields of investigation, and its arrangement in scientific form.

The objects of worship in primitive culture were found to fall into four more or less distinct groups, (1) Nature worship; (2) Ancestor worship; (3) Fetish worship; and (4) the worship of a Supreme Being. As to which of these groups represented the most primitive form of religion was early a matter of controversy. Fetichism was for a time regarded as the earliest form of worship and the root from which all others sprang. The savage, according to this theory, took for his god some causal object of worship, and from this he was led to higher objects such as trees and mountains, sun and stars, until at last heaven became his supreme fetish. Then when he learned of spirits, he made spirit his fetish and came finally to the worship of the Supreme Being. Herbert Spencer and E. B. Tylor maintained that the worship of spirits was the earliest form of religion, but

Tylor's system of animism seemed more comprehensive. The term "animatism" has been frequently applied to Spencer's system which regarded all nature as alive or animated. Tylor, however, regarded nature as "ensouled" in man. "As the human body was held to live and act by virtue of its own inhabiting spirit-soul, so the operations of the world seem to be carried on by other spirits." It was therefore an easy step to the belief in spirits separable from the body, and moving about freely like the genii, demons and fairies which crowded the minds of antiquity. M. Reville advanced the theory that the minor nature worship was the earliest form of religion, while Max Muller and Ed. von Hartmann contended with like zeal for the primacy of the greater nature worship.

While hasty and ill-formed conclusions were soon superseded, it is now generally admitted that the most primitive form of religion known to science is a belief in *mana* as a nonpersonal, but supernatural force. It is in Melanesia that this idea finds its fullest development. Bishop Codrington says, "The Melanesian mind is entirely possessed by the belief in a supernatural power or influence, called almost universally *mana*. This is what works to effect everything which is beyond the ordinary power of men outside the common processes of nature; it is present in the atmosphere of life, attaches itself to persons and things, and is manifested by results which can only be ascribed to its operations (Cf. WRIGHT, *Philos. Religion,* p. 25). Similar conceptions are found among the pygmies of Africa where the word used is *oudah.* Among the American Indians there was a similar conception of a supernatural force, which the Algonquins called *manitou,* the Sioux *wakonda,* and the Iroquois *arenda.* Wright asserts that the *mana* idea may contain a further truth—that of a spiritual Being separate from the human minds whose support is available to men through worship. To him, therefore, *mana* may be the crude conception by which these lower strata of civilization become aware of the existence of God and the manner in which this assistance is to be obtained.

The material which enriched the study of historical religion was, according to the dominant philosophy of the time in which it was gathered, arranged on the evolutionary hypothesis. The natural religions were regarded as the basis from which, according to the process of evolution, man rose from animism and totemism to the higher religions of the spirit. These culminated in Christianity as the true ethical and spiritual religion. Hegel in his philosophy of religion classifies the lower primitive religions as the infancy of the race, the Greek religion as its childhood, the Roman religion as its early maturity, and the Christian religion as the full expression of man's religious nature. We cannot so regard it. John Caird has pointed out that one "can never get at the true idea or essence of religion merely by trying to find out something that is common to all religions; and it is not the lower religions that explain the higher, but conversely the higher religion explains all the lower religions" (CAIRD, *Fund. Ideas of Christianity*, I, p. 25). The origin of religion must be traced back to man's original constitution. Man was made for personal fellowship with God, and as originally endowed, he had personal integrity and a sufficient knowledge of God to preserve him in the state in which he was created. But with the fall and the introduction of sin, fellowship with God was broken, and man's mind became darkened through the loss of that spiritual light which forms the true principle of illumination in the things of God. We must, therefore, with Stump, regard the natural religion as "an attenuated and diluted remainder of man's original constitution and endowment." It is true that these religions possess some elements of truth, but they have lost much of what was originally revealed, and are destitute of the saving knowledge of God.

The Scriptures regard the degeneracy of religion as a direct consequence of man's sin, in which he willfully turned away from the purer knowledge and service of God. St. Paul outlines the steps in this decline in the following manner: (I) A rejection of the true God. *Because that, when they knew God, they glorified him not as God, neither were thankful; but became vain in their imaginations, and their foolish heart was darkened. Professing themselves to be wise, they became fools, and changed the glory of the uncorruptible God into an image made like to corruptible man, and to birds, and four-footed beasts, and creeping things* (Rom. 1: 21-23). Here is indicated (a) A direct refusal to worship God. The rejection is ethical. The psalmist in the expression *The fool hath said in his heart, There is no God* meant not so much a denial of the existence of God as an ethical and spiritual rejection, "No God for me." (b) Rejecting God and setting himself up in his own right, man conceived of himself in a false independence which destroyed the ground of thankfulness. (c) Man, having lost the object of his worship, did not thereby lose his craving after God, and was compelled through vain imaginations to posit objects of worship for himself. (d) These objects of worship took the character of his own corrupt heart. (e) Through a profession of worldly wisdom, systems of religion were devised which included in their scope, man, birds, four-footed beasts and creeping things. (f) Evidently St. Paul intends to indicate a gradual decline in the value of the objects of worship, through a blind impulse of a foolish and darkened heart. Man naturally would be the first object of worship, since in the rejection of God he set himself up in his own right. Dr. Dorner remarks

Indeed, when we examine the history of the ancient pagan world, we are struck by the accuracy of the description which is given of it by St. Paul in the first chapter of his *Epistle to the Romans.* He asserts that *they changed the glory of the uncorruptible God into an image made like unto corruptible man, and to birds, and four-footed beasts and creeping things.* "They paid divine worship to oxen, to crocodiles, to birds and to reptiles. They metamorphosed beasts into gods, and conversely transformed their gods into beasts, ascribing to them drunkenness, unnatural lusts, and the most loathsome vices. They worshipped drunkenness, under the name of Bacchus; and lasciviousness, under that of Venus. Momus was to them the god of calumny, and Mercury the god of thieves. Even Jupiter, the greatest of their gods, they considered to be an adulterer. At length the worship of avowedly evil beings became prevalent among them; and hence many of their rites were cruel and shockingly obscene. The floralia among the Romans, their festival in honor of Flora, the goddess of flowers, was celebrated for four days together by the most shameful actions, and with the most unbounded licentiousness."—WAKEFIELD, *Christian Theology,* pp. 33, 34.

that the oriental religions set out from the divine, and attempt to bring God down to the human, issuing often in Pantheism; but the western religions set out from the finite and attempt to lift man up to God, issuing in the deification of heroes (DORNER, *Doct. Person of Christ*, I, p. 697). The second stage would include the æsthetical and useful, hence the totemistic birds and animals; while the third would extend the deification to all life as sacred, as in some of the forms of religion found in India. (II) The second downward step is a judicial abandonment to a perverse will. Through the lusts of their hearts they desired to serve creatures and creaturely things *more than the Creator who is blessed forever. Amen.* Unregulated by truth and moved by a false impulse worship became dishonorable even to man's physical nature. *Wherefore God also gave them up to uncleanness through the lusts of their own hearts, to dishonor their own bodies between themselves: who changed the truth of God into a lie, and worshipped and served the creature more than the Creator, who is blessed forever. Amen* (Rom. 1: 24, 25). (III) The third stage downward is a judicial abandonment to evil affections. Glorifying the unclean and actuated by inordinate and unregulated affection, man degenerated into the abnormal and obscene, the results of which St. Paul presents in the shocking picture found in the next two paragraphs—Rom. 1: 26, 27. Analogous appearances of degeneration are facts which must be taken into account in any theory of religion found in organic life. (IV) The fourth and last step in the decline is a judicial abandonment to a reprobate mind. This St. Paul sums up by saying that *Even as they did not like to retain God in their knowledge, God gave them over to a repro-*

Thus, to select a few instances out of many, the rites of the goddess Cybele were no less infamous for lewdness than for cruelty; and the practice of these rites spread far and wide, and formed a part of the public worship at Rome. The *aphrodisia*, or festivals in honor of Venus, were observed with lascivious ceremonies in many parts of Greece; and Strabo tells us that there was a temple at Corinth so rich that it maintained more than a thousand prostitute women sacred to her service.— WAKEFIELD, *Chr. Th.*, pp. 33, 34.
(Cf. STORR: *Chr. Relig.* SEISS: *Apoc. Churches.* Other references on Prim. Relig.)

bate mind, to do those things which are not convenient,
being filled with all unrighteousness (Rom. 1:28, 29).
The three judicial sentences cover the entire range of
personality in its volitions, its affections and its intellect.
Desiring perverse things, they were abandoned to their
own lusts; following their own lusts they were abandoned to evil affections; and in their degeneracy, they
were given over to a reprobate mind. Or viewed from
St. Paul's summary, there was first the substitution of
a lie for the truth; then the love of that lie instead of
the truth; and lastly, the belief of that lie for the truth.
The last stage, therefore, in degeneracy, is to be filled with
all unrighteousness, which the apostle proceeds to
analyze into its constituent elements (Cf. Rom. 1:29-31).
The culmination of degeneracy, he finds in those *who*
knowing the judgment of God, that they which commit
such things are worthy of death, not only do the same,
but have pleasure in them that do them (Rom. 1:32).
According to St. Paul, then, the depth of wickedness consists in a direct and conscious violation of the will of
God, in the clear knowledge of its consequences, and conjoined with pleasure in others who are alike sinfully
minded. Thus there is built up what Martensen calls, a
"sinful society."

The arrangement of the facts in the science of religion does not concern us primarily, only in so far as they
are woven into a philosophy which is contradictory to
the plain teachings of the Scriptures. The facts themselves, however, are of great value to theology in establishing the universality of religion, and the certainty of
its being grounded in the nature and constitution of
man. For a time this was denied. Sir John Lubbock
insisted that some atheistic tribes had been found among
savage peoples, but later writers, with a much better
understanding of primitive religion, have refuted this
position. Quaterfages says, "Little by little the light has
appeared and the result has been that Australians, Kaf-
firs, Bechuanas and other savage tribes have been withdrawn from the lists of atheistic people and are recognized as religious." Tiele affirms that "No tribe or nation

has yet been met with, destitute of belief in any higher beings, and travelers who asserted their existence have been afterward refuted by the facts (TIELE, *Outlines Hist. Relig.,* p. 6). Thus the History of Religion becomes a valuable propædeutic to the study of Christian Theology, and serves to clarify and establish the view that religion belongs to the constitution and nature of man.

The Psychology of Religion. Another field of investigation has made a valuable contribution to this fundamental postulate—the Psychology of Religion. Like its companion study, the History of Religion, this new science entered with some hesitancy into its investigations, on account of the sacredness of the subject. Once, however, that it was under way, the very novelty of the field commanded the attention of scholars. Perhaps the greatest contribution that has been made to the study of religion is in establishing the fact of the variety and validity of religious experience. But in its attempts to explain the origin of religion it has made many and grotesque errors. These are not attributable to the science as such, but to the antagonistic attitude which has characterized many of its investigators. Many of the errors originate in a supposed projection of the idea of God from some inner human experience. God, therefore, on this basis has no reality. He is merely the objectification of certain inner psychological concepts. Wobbermin applies the term "illusionistic" to these theories of religion, and Knudson classifies them in three main divisions: Psychological, Sociological, and Intellectualistic.

The Psychological Theory of Illusionism, with which we are now concerned, attributes the origin of religion to a projection of psychic phenomena. This theory was held by Lucretius of Rome (B.C. 99-55), who maintained that religion had its origin in fear—especially the fear of death. Religion would not therefore exist, were it not for ignorance and timidity. But the theory that men make gods in their own likeness dates back into the dawn of Greek history. It is found in the writings of Xenophanes, the philosopher (c. 570 B.C.), whose attack was not against the existence of God, but against the anthropomorphic conception of God which men held. "If cattle could paint," he said, "horses would describe gods as horses, and oxen would describe them as oxen." For this reason "the Ethiopians represent their deities as having flat noses and black faces, while the Thracians picture theirs with red hair and blue eyes." Yet despite this attack, Xenophanes had a profound sense of the existence of God. "This Deity," he said, "is not begotten, for how can He be born of His equal; how of His unequal. If not born He cannot perish, since He is independent and by Himself."

It is in Feuerbach that this psychological type of illusionism finds its most significant expression in modern times. Here the origin of religion is attributed, not to fear, but to the quest after life and happiness. According to this theory, religion is "man's instinct for happiness which is satisfied in the imagination." The idea of God is "the realized salvation, the bliss of man." Wobbermin points out, that while Feuerbach in the beginning sought only to advance a speculative theory, he at last succumbed to the error he sought to avoid, and gave to the world a completely rationalized theory of religions—a system as completely rationalized as that of Hegel, whose philosophy he opposed. "The necessary turning point of the whole matter is this frank confession and admission that the consciousness of God is nothing but the consciousness of the species." Here one cannot fail to see the influence of Fichte's philosophy of subjectivism, which for a time was popular in philosophy as subjective theism, but which Professor Howison frankly termed "objective atheism." It must be evident to all that the philosophy of Feuerbach furnished the germ of that which later issued in Humanism. Since this theory is closely related to Positivism, it will be given further treatment as one of the Anti-Theistic Theories. But the error of Feuerbach not only issued in

Concerning his illusionistic theory of religion, Feuerbach says, "Man —this is the mystery of religion—projects his being into objectivity, and then again makes himself an object of this projected image of himself thus converted into a subject. . . . . As God is nothing else than the nature of the man purified from that which to the human individual appears, whether in feeling or thought, a limitation of evil.

Humanism, it laid the foundation for the modern development of two other theories antagonistic to the Christian faith — Freudianism, and Marxianism. The latter of these, however, must be classified as Sociological Illusionism.

Freudianism has greatly colored psychological and sociological studies in recent years. Through its theory of psychoanalysis, it has been closely related to medical science, and has sometimes been known as "medical materialism." Sigmund Freud (1856-1928) was a Viennese neuropathologist. Psychoanalysis, as he advanced it, was purely a medical method of technique. It consisted in an attempt to gain control over the subconscious life, and so of the unconscious forces in the substructure of the psychic world. Psychoanalysts have assumed that there are elementary wishes or instincts that have been repressed in the course of conscious development, but are still latent and may be uncovered. Freud and his followers, however, claim to have found these repressed instincts, almost if not exclusively, in the sphere of sexual pathology. They begin with totemism, which they attempt to explain by what they judge to have happened in the primitive horde of men. This gives rise to what is termed the Oedipus Complex in the emotional life of youth. These formulations claim to be decisive answers to the question as to what is the origin and nature of religion. Through totemism belated love and reverence were bestowed upon an animal as a substitute for the father; and this feeling for the animal as a totem and representative of the father, was in time heightened and thus arose the idea of God. It would seem that nothing could more exactly meet the description of St. Paul when he spoke of those who *professing themselves to be wise they became fools, and changed the glory of the uncorruptible God into an image made like to corruptible man, and to birds and four-footed beasts, and creeping things.* The theory has been exceptionally devastating to the minds of college youth.

The Philosophy of Religion. Having pointed out the contributions made by the History and Psychology of

Religion, we must now examine briefly the manner in which the philosophy of religion has built upon these fundamental presuppositions its various explanations of religion. These are necessary, *first,* in order to a proper understanding of the true nature of religion; and *second,* as a basis for the discrimination between a true and false emphasis of religion in the conduct of the Christian life.

The philosophy of religion has a different function from the science of religion. The former deals with the mental processes of inward development, while the latter is concerned with material processes of outward development. Comparative religion relies upon the similarities found in a community of experience, while the philosophy of religion is concerned with the eternal principle of religion which is manifested within itself. Neither of these can tell what religion is, but only the form in which it manifests itself. Nor can these afford assurance in personal religious experience. At best they can serve only as confirmatory evidences and furnish means of expression. Personal religion can be known only by the religious themselves, and carries with it the assurance of the truth of their convictions. *He that believeth on the Son of God hath the witness in himself* (I John 5:10). But religion is never belief alone. *The just shall live by faith* (Gal. 3:11). Life is equally fundamental with faith, and the adjustments of life are an essential element in religion. The broad fact, to which all religion bears witness, is a belief in a higher order, proper relation to which is essential to the right adjustments of life. Here is a sufficient basis for the philosophy of religion, but we are concerned primarily with religion itself and the possibilities contained in it for the development of a theistic and Christian conception of God. Thus we lay the foundations upon which we shall later build our theistic arguments, and gather the material which we shall use in our criticism of the antitheistic theories.

Waterhouse in his *Modern Theories of Religion* reviews nine developments in the philosophy of religion. These are (I) Religion as Feeling: Schleiermacher; (II) Personal Monism: Lotze; (III) Religious Conceptions as

Value Judgments: Ritschl; (IV) The Transcendental
Philosophy of Religion: the Neo-Hegelians; (V) Mysticism as a Religious Philosophy: Dean Inge; (VI) The
Ethical Philosophy of Religion: Martineau; (VII) The
Religious Philosophy of Activism: Eucken; (VIII) Prag-
matism as a Religious Philosophy: William James; (IX)
Personal Idealism: Rashdall. It would take us too far
afield to study these various developments, and, furthermore, it is aside from our purpose.

Schleiermacher (1768-1834) paved the way for the
modern developments in the philosophy of religion.
"Wherever a philosophy of religion is found," says
Waterhouse, "which arises from the psychology of religious experience, there is a line which runs direct,
through many junctions of converging tracts to the fervent speculation of Schleiermacher." He was the first
to analyze and evaluate religion for its own sake. Previous to his time, little was known of the true inward-
ness of religion except among the mystics; since his time,
no philosophy or theology can reckon without it. Schleiermacher was brought up among the Moravians at Halle
and was early the recipient of a profound religious experience. His entire system of theology and his philosophy as well, were dominated by his desire to give expression to the work of divine grace in his own soul. But
anchored to this intense religious experience, he allowed
himself to wander in the fields of philosophical speculation, so that he has been aptly characterized as "the
union of a pious soul with a philosophical mind." The
Moravian influence, therefore, did more than create
through Wesley, his contemporary, a revival of religion;
it created through Schleiermacher, a revival of religious
philosophy. The evangelical revival and the new epoch
in philosophy, heralded by Schleiermacher, may be justly
regarded as two sides of one and the same fact.

Like Wesley, Schleiermacher found it necessary to break with the
Moravian brethren, but the breach was caused by his intellectual independence rather than by any revolt from their spirit or from their
methods. The letters which passed between him and his father at the
time he had decided to break with the Brethren and was pleading to
be allowed to enter the wider sphere of the University, show clearly
enough the agony that he suffered.—Cf. Selbie, Schleirmacher, pp. 16, 17.

Religion is, according to Schleiermacher, a "feeling of dependence." It neither seeks like metaphysics to determine and explain the universe, nor like morals to advance and perfect the universe through the power of freedom. The feeling of dependence leads immediately to the thought of God upon which the soul must depend. Religious knowledge, therefore, is "the immediate consciousness of the universal existence of all finite things in and through the Infinite, and of all temporal things in and through the Eternal." It is to have life and to know life in immediate feeling. When this is found, religion is satisfied, when it hides itself, there is unrest and anguish, extremity and death (Cf. *Reden* p. 36). Out of this conscious knowledge of a sense of dependence and a personal relationship with the divine is built up a philosophy of religion.

Hegel (1770-1831) regarded religion as absolute knowledge. It is the relation of spirit to Absolute Spirit, and it is the Spirit only which knows and is known. Religion, therefore, becomes the standpoint for the consciousness of the True, and God is this Absolute Truth. God is conceived by Hegel, not as a Supreme Being who is back of all experience, God is rather in all experience. It may be said that the sum total of all finite experience is the Mind of God. There is according to this theory but one experience—that of the Absolute. The finite is merely an essential moment in the experience of the Infinite. Religion is not so much our knowledge of God, as God coming to a knowledge of himself through

Waterhouse maintains that Schleiermacher finds the birth chamber of religion in the mysterious moment immediately prior to the breaking forth of consciousness, an instant so momentary that it can scarcely be described as an instant—a term which implies at least a fraction of time, in which sense and object are one and indistinguishable, when there arises the first contact of the universal life with an individual and in Schleiermacher's own words "you lie directly on the bosom of the infinite world." It should be constantly borne in mind that for him, feeling stands primarily for the unity of consciousness, in which the opposition of knowledge passing through feeling to will, and will through feeling to knowledge, the common relation to feeling forming the bond of connection between them. The sphere of religion is found in this unifying element of feeling. He therefore regards sin as the conflict and salvation as the reconciliation between the God-consciousness and the world consciousness, and this is accomplished by Christ who possessed the God-consciousness in absolute measure, thereby establishing His perfection and His divinity.

finite experience. It is a function of the human spirit through which it comes to know the universe, or what is equally true, the Absolute coming to full consciousness of itself. The universe therefore is to be conceived as a single huge process in which the Absolute is constantly coming to consciousness, or in Hegel's words, "the Divine Spirit's knowledge of itself through the mediation of a finite spirit." Thus is built up on the fundamental concept of religion, a system of monism closely related to ancient gnosticism. Nor does it differ greatly from the Stoicism of the ancient Greeks. In modern philosophy, Spinoza and Hegel are closely related in their theories of a single Substance.

Ritschl (1822-1889) followed Schleiermacher and Hegel, but discounted philosophy as being detrimental to religion. His system has been characterized as "antidogmatic, antimystical and antimetaphysical." While Schleiermacher regards religion as feeling, and Hegel as knowledge, Ritschl regards it more from the volitional standpoint as power. Starting from the fundamental concept of religion, he draws a sharp distinction between the nature of things in themselves on the one hand, and what they mean for us, on the other. Science and philosophy attempt to explain the nature of things, and therefore deal with what he calls "existential judgments." This, however, is not the only way in which an object may be judged. Instead of inquiring as to its nature, we may ask, "What does it mean for us?" From this standpoint it takes on meaning as it affects the subject. This is a "value-judgment." Science and philosophy are concerned with the former, but religion is expressed in value-judgments. Thus he swings over from the idea of feeling or knowledge to that of volition, and

William Adams Brown points out that the sudden downfall of Hegelianism is one of the most striking facts in the history of philosophy. There were two tendencies, one which tended to identify religion and philosophy and developed into a critical movement. The other tended to approach the positions of traditional theology. Men like Daub and Marheinecke attempted to make Christianity the final synthesis, but the elements of conservatism were eventually overpowered by those more radical. Dr. Brown indicates that the clearest expression of this destructive tendency is found in Feuerbach's *Essence of Christianity*.

religion becomes a practical affair. "In every religion," he says, "what is sought with the help of the supernatural spiritual power reverenced by man, is a solution of the contradiction in which man finds himself, as both a part of the world of nature and a spiritual personality claiming to dominate nature. For in the former role he is a part of nature, dependent upon her, subject to her, and confined by other things; but as spirit he is moved by the impulse to maintain his independence against them. In this juncture, religion springs up as faith in superhuman spiritual powers, by whose help the power which man possesses of himself is in some way supplemented, and elevated into a unity of its own kind which is a match for the pressure of the natural world (Cf. RITSCHL, *Justification and Reconciliation*, p. 199).

Edward Caird (1835-1908) and John Caird (1820-1898) are commonly known, together with Thomas Hill Green, as Neo-Hegelians. Following the customary Hegelian procedure, Dr. Edward Caird finds in conscious life, a thesis, the self; an antithesis, a not-self or the objective world; and a synthesis which is God. He differs from Hegel, however, in that he does not make this triad in consciousness, but is more closely related to Lotze, who identifies God with the principle of unity. He sets out from the basic principle of religion to demonstrate the necessity of God, and he does this by interpreting religion as a rational consciousness. The principle, then, out of which the consciousness of God arises, is as much a primary element of knowledge as our consciousness of the self or of the objective world. The idea of God is accordingly described as "the ultimate presupposition of our consciousness."

Martineau (1805-1900) develops an ethical philosophy of religion. Here one would suppose the Kantian idea of religion as morality would be given a modern turn, but Martineau gives more attention to the argument from causality than he does from conscience, though the latter is not neglected. His idea of causality is that of Will, and that Will regarded as free. He admits of no second causes other than that of created minds.

Religion resolves itself, therefore, into "a conscious relation on our part, to a higher than we; and on the part of a rational universe as large, to a higher than all" (MARTINEAU, *Study of Religion*, II, p. 1). It consists of an inward source, personally revealed, though Martineau regards this as intuition rather than as feeling. "Just as in perception we are immediately introduced to another than ourselves that gives us what we feel, so in the acts of consciousness we are immediately introduced to a Higher than ourselves which gives us what we feel." "I care not," he says, "whether this be called an immediate vision of God in the experience of conscience, or whether it is to be taken as an inference drawn from the data they supply. It is the truth contained in them" (MARTINEAU, *Study of Religion*, pp. 27, 28).

FALSE CONCEPTIONS OF RELIGION

The philosophies which have been advanced in support of religion have, in most instances, served an admirable purpose. But philosophy has a tendency to usurp the place of religion and as such its influence is always baneful. The false conceptions of religion to which we call attention are such by virtue of an improper synthesis of the factors of personality. True religion must call out the whole personality and in its forms of expression represent a balanced emphasis upon the primary element of feeling, intellect and will.

Religion is not mere feeling. We tread on delicate ground here, for the term feeling is used in widely different senses. As Schleiermacher most commonly uses it, feeling is the unity of consciousness in which knowledge and volition meet. It is not, therefore, what is com-

In order to complete his construction, Martineau produces three reasons for the identification of the Will he has discovered behind phenomena, with the Law-giver revealed by conscience: (1) We unite in our persons subjection to both moral and physical law, inseparably intertwined. (2) Our springs of action are aroused by the external world; the data of conscience are found in life and humanity, and its problems set by the condition these impose. (3) The discipline required by moral law is enforced by physical law. . . . . These two aspects, however, the physical and the moral, are separate only in human apprehension, not in the divine existence.—MARTINEAU, *Study of Religion*, pp. 26ff.

monly termed emotion, but the deep underlying source out of which both intuition and emotion arise. Religion is neither doctrine nor ceremony, but experience. It is deeper down than either thought or conscience. It is to know life in immediate feeling. Those who agree with Schleiermacher interpret his idea of feeling in the scriptural sense of the *heart* or the *spirit*. To this there can be no exception, but it is not always clear that Schleiermacher uses the term feeling wholly in this sense. Apparently he sometimes means merely organic sensation. He argues that since "religion is feeling," then "feeling is religion." Consequently he maintains that there is in the breast of every man, that which needs only recognition to be religion. Such a confusion of the spiritual affections of the heart with mere organic sensation destroys the very place which religion should occupy, and reduces it from the supernatural to a mere naturalistic plane. This position finds a modern exponent in Horace Bushnell, who conceived of grace as communicated through the natural relations of life, and therefore stated as a thesis, that the child should grow up so as to never know himself other than as a Christian. This theory forms the basis of much of the present day teaching on religious education. Religion is not a matter of unregulated emotion, nor is it "morality tinged with emotion." The religion of the heart must develop into a living consciousness through rational thinking, and must test its validity through action—the processes of which are induced and perfected by the conscience. In the Pauline statement, it is *Love out of a pure heart, and a good conscience and a faith unfeigned* (I Tim. 1: 5) that is, the stream of perfect love, flowing out of a pure heart, regulated by a good conscience, and kept full and fresh and flowing by an unfeigned faith.

Religion is not mere knowledge. Hegelianism has been a determining factor in the rationalization of religion. But it has also emptied it of its emotional content and left it barren and unfruitful. Hegel did not entirely ignore feeling. Like Schleiermacher, he made it the primal element in consciousness, but he makes it too elemental to be of any worth. Feeling as such, he says, is full of contradictions, the most debased as well as the highest and noblest. The value of religion lies in its rational content. Emotion in religion therefore came under the ban and the feelings were repressed until their sources were dried up.

The Hegelian triad furnished an unworthy concept of sin. All progress is by means of a thesis, an antithesis and a synthesis. Evil is such on any plane merely through contrast with its corresponding thesis. It may, however, be conjoined with this thesis in a higher synthesis, thus removing the distinctions and forming a new and higher thesis. Sin, therefore, is merely a relative matter. It is only partial good. It is regarded as evil, solely because we fail to see it in its higher meanings. It therefore becomes impossible to hold to the exceeding sinfulness of sin as the Scriptures teach us, and thus the whole redemptive idea is weakened. It is for this reason that Dr. Olin A. Curtis abhors any touch of the psychological climate of naturalism. The emphasis upon development has weakened also the belief in the crises of religion, at least in its practical outworkings. The deterministic position of Hegelianism has given rise to a new interpretation of freedom which regards man as self-determined in the sense that his actions are the expression or realization of himself. This puts the ultimate source of moral accountability in character, which is regarded, not as the result of free and responsible choices, but proceeds from man's will as the expression of his whole self. Outward authority is therefore minified and man's will becomes his rule of life.

Religion is not simply action. We have pointed out some of the dangers of a disproportionate emphasis upon feeling and knowledge as factors in religion, and it remains to be shown that volition can no more lay claim to the prime place than those just considered. Attempts to identify religion with morality usually date back to the philosophy of Kant with its categorical imperative. While the two coincide, and there can be no true religion without morality, nor no true morality without religion, the two must be clearly distinguished in thought. Morality presupposes a capacity which has been developed by practice, while religion is a power bestowed from above. Morality knows no sin as such, only failure or deficiency. Sin and repentance are distinctively religious terms. The moral life calls for no worship and is essentially action; religion, while manifesting itself in activity toward men, manifests itself also in worship toward God. Morality is primarily obedience to law; religion is submission to a Person. Christianity forever sweeps away all hope of justification through law, for by the law is the knowledge of sin; but as a redemptive religion declares that men may be *justified freely by his grace through the redemption that is in Christ Jesus* (Rom. 3:24). Neither ethical philosophies, metaphysical cults, formal worship nor any other form of religion relying upon self-righteous works can bring man to a sense of deliverance from sin. "You are doubtless acquainted with the histories of human follies," cried Schleiermacher, "and have reviewed the various structures of religious doctrine, from the senseless fables of wanton peoples to the most refined deism, from the rude superstition of human sacrifice to the ill-put-together fragments of metaphysics and ethics, now called purified Christianity, and you have found them all without rhyme or reason. I am far from wishing to contradict you."

THE NATURE OF RELIGION

Having examined the results of both the science of religion and the philosophical developments based upon the history and psychology of religion, we are now able to determine more fully the true nature of religion regarded in its most general sense. Four fundamental characteristics appear, and these may be found, whether in the lowest and most primitive forms of religion, or in the supreme and final Christian religion. No form or degree of religion is without them. *First*, there is the thought of a supernatural power—God—in the religion of revelation, or gods in the naturalistic religions.

Second, there is a sense of need which seeks satisfaction from this supernatural power. *Third,* there is the idea of reverence, and the feeling that it is incumbent to do homage in worship, and to render willing obedience to the supernatural. *Fourth,* there is some sort of assurance of the manifestation of God. It is evident that the first three are dependent upon the interchange of relations between God and man; while the fourth or Revelation is recognized as a special favor from God.

A careful consideration of these characteristics reveal the fact of their necessity in religion. The Supernatural, for instance, may be regarded as the gods in polytheism, or even lower powers in animism, totemism, and Shamanism. In Christianity, there is a clear idea of the personal God as Father. The sense of need likewise may reach to the lowest forms of physical necessity in which divine aid is sought through superstitious practices and for lower ends. The third likewise varies, giving rise to heathen sacrifices on the one hand, and on the other to the loftiest moments of prayer and adoration in Christian worship. The fourth approaches the distinctness of the Christian religion, for only in the Old and New Testaments, given to Judaism and to Christianity as parts of one revelation, do we find a true manifestation of God, and this is in turn dependent upon Christ as the Eternal Word made flesh, thereby bringing to man the glorious and express image of the Father.

From the time of Barnabas the early apologist, to that of Kant in modern times, it was the custom of the Church to draw a sharp line of demarcation between the Christian religion and ethnic religions, declaring that the former was true and the others totally false. The fact that these other religions contained much of truth was wholly overlooked. With the development of the modern science of religion there has come a changed attitude, and with it the recognition of the true Pauline view so long submerged—that the Gentile religions were "wild olive branches" as over against the cultured branches of Judaism. But neither has St. Paul any place for the modern syncretistic position that Christianity is but one among many other religions, which are equally beneficial expressions of the profound religious nature of man. While admitting the truth in any and all ethnic religions, he makes a sharp distinction between these and Christianity on a twofold basis, *first* the difference in ethical quality; and *second,* the difference in the character of the Founder. The first is found in his condemnation of the heathen religions, a fact attested by all who are familiar with the low moral tone, not only of primitive religion, but also of the so-called universal religions. The latter will form the basis of our next proposition.

From the historical viewpoint, we base our argument for the supremacy of the Christian religion over the ethnic religions on the fact of its all inclusiveness. Christianity is distinctive and therefore exclusive, because it is absolutely inclusive. "It is not an amalgamation of other religions," says Matheson, "but it has in it all that is best and truest in other religions. It is the white light that contains all the colored rays. God may have made disclosures of truth outside of Judaism, and did so in Balaam and Melchizedek. But while other religions have a relative excellence, Christianity is the absolute religion that contains all excellencies." By this method, therefore, we take firmer ground for the distinctness and finality of the Christian religion, than is possible by regarding it either as one religion among many, or one over against many, and we preserve what is true in both positions.

Christianity is the distinctive and final religion. Having examined the false religions, it is evident that there is and can be but one religion in the sense of embracing all truth within itself. "Man is a religious being, indeed, as having the capacity for the divine life. He is actually religious, however, only when he enters into this living relation to God. False religions are the caricatures which men give to sin, or the imaginations which men, groping after light, form of this life of the soul in God" (Cf. STRONG, *Systematic Theology,* I, p. 23). We sum up our arguments for Christianity as the distinctive and final religion in the following propositions:

1. *Christianity Is a Historic Religion.* Christianity is something more than a philosophy of religion or a cult of worship. It is not a theory of the intellect but a redemptive power worked out on the plane of human history in the person of Jesus Christ, who, tested in all points as are other men, was yet triumphant over sin and death. It must therefore occupy a place in the history of religion, and be classified with the so-called universal religions which take their character from the personality of their founders. The difference between Christianity and the ethnic religions lies in the character of the founders—the infinite stretch between the human and the divine.

2. *The Founder of Christianity Is Jesus Christ, the Divine Son of God.* Christianity takes both its distinctive character and its exclusiveness from the personality of its Founder. The argument of the author to the Hebrews is essentially this: *God, who at sundry times and in divers manners spake in time past unto the fathers by the prophets, hath in these last days spoken unto us by his Son, whom he hath appointed heir of all things, by whom also he made the worlds* (Heb. 1: 1, 2). Here the argument is, that in the olden time the revelation of God was partial and imperfect in that it was mediated through human means; now it can be perfect because mediated through divine means. This is the essential difference between Judaism and Christianity. The prophets furnishing only a human mediation, the revelation must therefore be external; being external it must necessarily be ceremonial; and being ceremonial must be preparatory. Christianity mediated through the divine Son is internal rather than external; is spiritual rather than ceremonial, and perfect instead of preparatory. Thus Judaism with its prophetic offices could be only preparatory to the fuller revelation of Christianity. This is brought out clearly by St. Paul, who, being asked what advantage the Jews have over the Gentiles, says, *Much every way; chiefly because unto them were the oracles of God*—that is, they were the intermediaries between God and the religions of the world. They were

thus not an end but a means—elected for a purpose. Their condemnation lay in this, that they ceased to regard themselves as a people with a ministry, and made themselves an end in the revelation of God, and consequently despised others. But the Apostle John, in the Fourth Gospel, links the work of Christ directly to that of the Father apart from all earthly relationships. Choosing for his words, not the Jewish but the Greek concepts and terminology, he declares that *In the beginning was the Word, and the Word was with God.*

Paul's argument has been condensed into what amounts to a creedal statement — *Our Lord Jesus Christ*—the *Lord* (or *kurios*) signifying his divinity as the highest term applied to deity; *Jesus* the human and historical relationship, and *Christ,* or the anointed one, as the office or mission of Christ.

3. *Christianity Is a Redemptive Religion.* Throughout the entire New Testament, Christ is regarded in his redemptive aspects. Perhaps the most familiar text illustrative of the purpose of God in the incarnation is that of John 3: 16, *God so loved the world, that he gave his only begotten Son, that whosoever believeth in him should not perish but have everlasting life.* Paul makes the soteriological aspect of Christ's coming the thesis of perhaps his most outstanding and systematic treatise on theology—the Epistle to the Romans. This thesis is, *I am not ashamed of the gospel of Christ, for it is the power of God unto salvation to every one that believeth. For therein is the righteousness of God revealed from faith to faith: as it is written, the just shall live by faith.* St. Peter likewise expresses the same profound truth. *Blessed be the God and Father of our Lord Jesus Christ, which according to his abundant mercy hath begotten us again unto a lively hope by the resurrection of Jesus Christ from the dead, to an inheritance incorruptible, and undefiled, and that fadeth not away, reserved in heaven for you, who are kept by the power of God through faith unto salvation ready to be revealed in the last time* (I Peter 1: 3-5). To Paul and Peter and John, Christianity was not simply a doctrine but a power. To

the Jews it might appear a stumblingblock, and to the Greeks foolishness, but to the saved, Christ was the power of God and the wisdom of God. Christ they regarded not solely as a prophet, or a teacher, or a great man, but as a redeemer. Much that passes for the gospel therefore is no more than a system of ethics, or a profound philosophy of life. Anything which stops short of the power of God in salvation, stops short of the place where the message of Christ becomes a gospel.

CHAPTER VI

THE CHRISTIAN REVELATION

Christian Theology is based upon the revelation of God in Christ, the record of which, in both its preliminary and its perfect stages, is given in the Scriptures of the Old and New Testaments. Referring the reader to our basic assumptions concerning the relation of the written word to that of the Personal and Eternal Word, as found in our discussion of the Scriptures, we may here in an introductory way speak of revelation and the Christian faith as the objective and subjective forms of God's disclosure of Himself to man. But Revelation refers them to God as the Revealer, while the Christian faith regards them as received by men. It is well to keep this before us in our discussions, for thus we preserve intact, both the formal and the material principles of revelation. What God is pleased to make known, man's acceptance makes his faith. Both the revelation and the Christian faith are coincident with the Scriptures. We do not say identical, for Christian Theology must ever make Christ, the Living and Eternal Word, the supreme revelation of God. But the Holy Scriptures as the true and inerrant record of the Personal Word, and the medium of continued utterance through the Holy Spirit, must in a true and deep sense become the formal aspect of the one true and perfect revelation. Regarding the Scriptures, therefore, as the formal Rule of Faith, our subject divides itself naturally into three main divisions: (I) The Nature of the Christian Revelation; or REVELATION; (II) The Origin of the Christian Revelation, or INSPIRATION OF THE SCRIPTURES; and (III) The Evidences of the Christian Faith, or THE CANON OF HOLY SCRIPTURE.

By revelation, in the broader sense of the term, is meant every manifestation of God to the consciousness of man, whether through nature and the course of

human history, or through the higher disclosures of the
Incarnate Word and the Holy Scriptures. It thus becomes at once, "the most elementary and the most comprehensive word of our theological system." It is customary to divide the subject broadly into (I) General
Revelation; and (II) Special Revelation. Other terms
used to express this twofold division are Natural and
Supernatural, or External and Internal Revelation. Mac-
Pherson suggests the use of the terms Mediate and Immediate—the former being that made indirectly through
the various mediating agencies and instrumentalities,
the latter, the revelation made immediately to the spiritual nature of man. While these divisions are more or
less conventional, they are distinctions admitted by the
Scriptures themselves (Psalm 19, Romans 1:20, 2:15,
Acts 14:17, 17:22-31); and the later and higher revelations of divine truth instead of abrogating them, seem to
set them out in clearer light.

GENERAL REVELATION

By General Revelation as the term is used in theology, we mean that disclosure of Himself which God
makes to all men—in nature, in the constitution of the
mind, and in the progress of human history. There is a
tendency frequently found among certain classes of theologians, to regard revelation as the divine aspect, of
that which from the human plane may be viewed as the
ordinary learning process. Thus Lipsius states that all
revelation, both as to its form and its contents, is at once
supernatural and natural; supernatural because it is
the effect of the Divine Spirit in man, natural because
it operates both psychologically and historically through
consciousness regarded as embraced within the spiritual
nature of man. MacPherson calls attention to this fallacy, and warns us that it resolves itself into practically
a deistical theory of God and the universe. More modern views of inspiration, as being merely differences in
degree rather than in kind, have likewise proved detrimental to a right conception of the Holy Scriptures.

From the scriptural standpoint, however, the two terms ἀποκάλυψις or an "unveiling," and φανέρωσις or a "showing forth" or "making known" are applied to the mysteries of religion solely, and not to the mere discoveries made slowly and gradually through the intellectual processes of learning.

We have now to set forth in an enlarged manner, the results of the investigations learned in the science and philosophy of religion. These furnish undisputed evidence of the universality of religion, and of its ground in the nature and constitution of man. The philosophy of religion has shown that this natural religiousness of man is itself a revelation, and in its unfoldings, directly and of necessity leads to the revelation of the objective existence of God. Religion takes its moral character from the fact of conscience, by which man knows the fundamental distinction between right and wrong, and this leads immediately to the nature of the Supreme Being as holy. We approach the subject from a different angle, but we reach the same results when we use the term Revelation instead of Religion. Revelation in its general sense is made to man, (I) through nature, (II) through the constitution of man himself; and (III) through the progress of human history.

Revelation through Nature. Here we mean the disclosure of God through the physical universe considered apart from man. This we have already pointed out in our discussion of nature as a source of theology. The argument need not be repeated. Nature is filled with the Divine Spirit and reveals God as the atmosphere is filled with sunlight and reveals the sun. But the language of nature falls upon darkened intellects and dulled sensibilities and must be read in the dim light of a vitiated

In this more general application other words are used besides ἀποκάλυψις or revelation: such as φωτίζειν or the light of the Son in human reason which lighteth every man that cometh into the world; φανερουν, or the declaration of the divine glory in the universe, and of the testimony of the Supreme to all men which may be manifest (Rom. 1:19) and to the providential guidance of the Gentiles before whom He left not himself without a witness οὐκ ἀμάρτυρον (Acts 14:17). All of these lower and more restricted or improper revelations and methods of revelation are taken up into Revelation proper.—POPE, *Compend Chr. Th.*, I, pp. 36, 37.

spiritual nature. However, as Ewald points out, "the more God is otherwise known, the more this whole infinite, visible creation declares His invisible glory, and reveals His hidden nature and will," and to this the testimony of every spiritually renewed soul bears joyful witness.

It may be well to call attention to the fact also, that otherwise extraordinary experiences become through frequent repetition common and ordinary, and thereby lose the aspect of the miraculous. The most illuminating presentation of this fact which we have found is by Dr. Samuel Harris of Yale in his *Self-revelation of God*—an older work but a rich apologetic for Christian Theology. "Persons sometimes imagine," he says, "that if God had revealed Himself continually and to all men by working miracles before them, it would have been impossible to doubt His existence. But miracles are presented to the senses, and therefore, like the familiar works of nature are a veil which hides God while revealing Him; the mind must pass through them; just as it passes through the sensible phenomena of nature, to the God unseen and spiritual, behind the veil. And if miracles were as common as summer showers and rainbows, they would attract no more attention than they. It is sometimes thought that if God should habitually reveal Himself in theophanies such as the Bible records, doubt would be no longer possible. But even in the theophanies the prophets did not see God; they saw only signs and symbols through which their spiritual eyes saw what can be only spiritually discerned. Ezekiel saw a cloud coming out of the north with whirlwind and with infolding fire and flashing lightning; and from its amber brightness a crystal firmament evolved borne on four cherubim, with wheels of beryl so high that they were dreadful, and all moving with flashing light and, to the very wheels, instinct with the spirit of life. On the firmament was a sapphire throne, and on the throne the appearance of a man. But if that vision should rise on our view every morning from the north, wherein would that miniature firmament reveal God any more than the sun which rises every morning in the east, or the firmament with its thousands of stars which wheels majestically above us every night? What theophany presented to the senses can open to view such energies, such swiftness of motion, such greatness and such fineness of being, such grand and harmonious systems, such powers instinct with the spirit of life, such manifestations of reason, such manifestations of God, as science is disclosing in the physical universe itself. We discover also a certain limitation in the nature of things to the revelation of God through words. Some may think it would be a great help to faith if "GOD IS LOVE" were written across the sky in letters of stars. We might ask in what language it should be written, and might suggest that such an arrangement would imply that the earth is the center of the universe, and that all other worlds exist for it. But were the words written thus, it would still be only an orderly arrangement of the stars through which the mind must look to read its significance; and such orderly arrangements we see everywhere in nature. How immeasurably more significant the revelation of His love which God has made in the life and self-sacrificing love of Jesus the Christ. . . . . So the words of the prophets and apostles fall without significance on the ear, until God by His divine action has disclosed their meaning. The hearer must first know God by his own experience of God's grace, or by his knowledge of God's action in nature, or in human history, or above all in Christ, in order to understand the prophet's communication" (HARRIS, *Self-revelation of God,* pp. 70, 71). Here we anticipate our argument for the necessity of a supplementary revelation.

The Revelation of God in the Nature and Constitution of Man. The next stage in natural revelation is to be found in the nature and constitution of man himself. Man knows himself to be a spiritual, personal being, and in the unity of this personality, he finds three moments or aspects of his being, that of intellect, feeling and will. Man knows himself also to have a conscience, from which arises a sense of duty to an over Master or Lord. Nor can the root word be entirely overlooked. Conscience is the knowing along with someone. We may say, therefore, that consciousness is the self, apprehending the world and thereby distinguishing itself from the world; and we may say that conscience is the self apprehending God and thereby distinguishing itself from God. It knows further that as a person it is made for fellowship with the Supreme Person. In thinking of creation, the self posits a Creator; and in the idea of preservation, it posits a Ruler. But we are not through with this matter of conscience. Dr. Phineas F. Bresee in his chapel addresses frequently referred to Carlyle's definition which he would ask the students to repeat with him, commenting on the importance of each word. Conscience is "that Somewhat or Someone within us which pronounces as to the rightness or wrongness of the choice of motives." Were the word "Somewhat" omitted, he asserted, we should have Isaiah's definition of conscience. What is this which is a very part of our being, which when we have done our best to identify it with our own inner impulses, and know that however intimately it is related to our selfhood, it is not of our earth-born nature, nor is it an individual possession, but is in its essence, timeless and eternal? Nor is this inner reality impersonal, a mere abstraction or quality, but "a vital, concrete personal Presence." This is what Dr. Bresee sought to impress upon those who were so fortunate as to sit under his ministry. We are driven to the conclusion, that as consciousness is that quality of the self which knows itself in relation to external things, and cannot exist apart from its object in the temporal order; so also conscience cannot exist without a Personal Object in the timeless and eternal order.

Referring again to the elements of personality, we may say that God is known to man through his reason, both immediately in his consciousness and mediately through the universe. It is a necessary intuition of the mind. "By a necessary intuition," says Dr. Miley, "we mean one that springs immediately from the constitution of the mind, and that, under proper conditions, must so spring" (MILEY, *Syst. Th.*, I, p. 68). These revelations are not merely products of thought. "As everywhere diffused daylight comes from the reflection of the light of the sun from the atmosphere and innumerable objects, the mind is illuminated with intelligence by thought reflected from innumerable points of reality around it." Goethe says, "All thinking in the world does not bring us to thought. We must be right by nature, so that good thoughts may come before us like free children of God, and cry, 'Here we are!'" These thoughts are reflected from the objects of the physical and moral universe, and reveal the spiritual and divine that is in them. "So in the spiritual life," continues Dr. Harris, "the knowledge of God is not originated by thinking, but presupposes revelation. And there is a spiritual insight which sees into the significance of the reality revealed. In the revelation of God in Christian consciousness, the humblest mind has a vision of God and of the universe in relation to Him, which ungodly genius with all its powers cannot see" (Cf. HARRIS, *Self-revelation of God,* p. 87).

We must not allow a mechanistic psychology, or an agnostic philosophy to tie us down to the earth, nor must we lose the sense of reality through a false idealism. "Rationalism dug so deep for a foundation for faith," says Dr. Buckham, "that it was buried under the soil upon which it should have built. Absolute Idealism spurned the earth and has always remained in the air." Man is at once a creature in nature, and a personal being transcending nature. The Scriptures tell us that he is the highest of the created earthly creatures from the physical standpoint, and also that God breathed into his nostrils the breath of life and man became a living soul. In this he is the recipient of an imparted life and thus a son of God. Dr. Harris uses the terms "natural" and "supernatural" in this connection, but he does so by limiting the term "supernatural" to its strictly literal meaning as being "above nature," not as divine. The contrast between the human and the divine he thinks

is better expressed by the terms "finite" and "infinite."
"Man, therefore, as a personal and spiritual being is
supernatural. He knows in himself reason and free will
and rational motives, the essential attributes of a supernatural or spiritual being. As a spirit, he is like God
who is a Spirit; he participates in reason the same as
God, the eternal Reason; he recognizes as imperative
in his own reason the same law of love which God
commands, he can love like God. Thus he has something in common with God, while as to his physical
organization he is in nature as really as the trees, is
sensitive to its action on him, and so knows it in his conscious experience. In his spirit he is supernatural, is
sensitive to the action of the supernatural on him, and
knows it in his conscious experience. Thus he knows
two systems in the universe, the natural and the spiritual or supernatural. . . . . His consciousness is the center
upon which the powers of nature converge and reveal
themselves; it is likewise the center on which the powers
of the spiritual system converge, and in which they
reveal themselves. Thus he has knowledge of the system of nature and of the rational and moral system, and
of their unity in the universe, which is the manifestation
of God. The unity of the two appears in the subordination of nature to spirit and its harmony with it as the
sphere in which it acts and through which it is revealed.
If the physical organization of man is but the form and
medium through which the human spirit reveals itself,
if all nature is but the form and medium in and through
which God and the spiritual system are revealed, the
antagonism between nature and the supernatural dis-
appears, but the distinction between them remains; and
man by virtue of his spiritual and supernatural powers
is participant in the light of the Divine Reason, and is
capable of knowing God and communing with Him, of
knowing the supernatural and participating in it. Thus
man is at once a supernatural being in a supernatural or
spiritual environment, and a participant of nature in a
physical environment. If we once grasp this reality it

will be impossible to doubt that his spiritual environment may reveal itself in his consciousness through his spiritual sensibilities or susceptibilities, as his physical environment reveals itself through his senses. The spirit will no longer be conceived as ghostly or ghastly, but as essentially and distinctively human" (HARRIS, *Self-revelation of God,* pp. 85, 86).

The Revelation of God in History. The progress of human history reveals the purpose of God in a higher manner than is possible in the constitution of a single individual. This fact, which forms the basis of the teleological argument concerning the existence of God, must likewise be unfolded in our discussion of the subject of Divine Providence. It is sufficient here, however, to deal only with those aspects which will not be included in the later discussions. History is not a disconnected series of events. History belongs to human volition. It is a record of what men have done. But there is an inner directing Presence in history and an Authoritative Will above it which directs all to an expressed goal, a fullness of time. This goal is the coming of the Word made flesh, the Incarnate Son of God standing out on the plane of human history as God manifest in the flesh. In the light of this historical fact, we are able to look back through the pages of history and recognize purpose in its events; and we are able to read the words of the prophets and see their predictions fulfilled. But as the central point of all history, He has had His impress upon it. "The striking and significant fact concerning this fresh illumination of the Jesus of history is that He proves so real and so magnetic to the world of today. Many centuries separate Him from us; mighty changes have swept across the intervening generations; civilization has moved on through diverse periods and vast developments, but the Man of Nazareth is the same yesterday, today and forever in His hold upon men. Above

MacPherson emphasizes the fact that although revelation is a spiritual communication to man, it is not concerned with natural knowledge, and therefore does not take into consideration the niceties of a metaphysical or psychological kind, but only with the facts that bear upon the relation of man to God (Cf. MACPHERSON, *Chr. Dogm.,* p. 20).

the now curious and outgrown ideas of His time, the meager life, the archaic customs, He rises supremely real, supremely commanding and supremely winsome" (BUCKHAM, *Christ and the Eternal Order,* p. 65). History in its clearer light of the revealed Christ, sheds its searching rays back along the path and we see that *He was in the world, and the world was made by him, and the world knew him not.* As in the metaphysical realm, He was the Light that lighteth every man coming into the world, and yet a Light which shined in the darkness, and the darkness apprehended it not; so in the course of human history he was forever coming to His own, yet His own received Him not. This "somewhat" proves to be in clearer light a "some one," who as the pre-existent and eternal Word, in whose image man was made, by whose power the worlds were formed, and by whose presence the course of history has developed in spite of the darkness and antagonism of sin; so this One must continue until, according to the Scriptures, all things are gathered together in one, both in heaven and in earth, even in Him (Eph. 1:10).

Watson tell us that Revelation gives information on those subjects which most immediately concern the Divine Government. It must, therefore, (1) contain explicit information on those important subjects on which mankind had most greatly and most fatally erred. (2) That it should accord with the principles of former revelations, given to men in the same state of guilt and moral incapacity as we find them in the present day. (3) That it should have a satisfactory external authentication. (4) That it should contain provisions for its effectual promulgation among all classes of men. The Christian Revelation therefore must give us a knowledge of God's will, the knowledge of the Mediator between God and man, Divine Providence, the chief good of man, his immortality and accountability and the future state (WATSON, *Institutes,* I, pp. 62, 63).

The writers of the mediæval period made this distinction: Natural religion gives truths which can be learned by the unaided reason; Revelation is concerned with truths which are beyond the power of natural reason. Natural Theology, however, has generally gone too far, (1) in claiming for its arguments a stronger and more coercive proof than rightfully attaches to it; and (2) the assumption that Revelation lies wholly without the realm of reason. Thomas Aquinas maintained that revelation operates through an inward light, which exalts the mind to the perception of those things which it cannot of itself attain. Just as intelligence, therefore, is assured of what it knows by the light of reason, so in the realm of revelation it has an assurance by means of this inward supernatural light.

SPECIAL REVELATION

By Special Revelation we refer to the redemptive purpose of God manifested in Christ Jesus, as over against the more general revelation of His power as manifested in His creative works. Some have objected to the idea of a special revelation as being derogatory to the wisdom of God in that it appears to represent Him as mending or supplementing the former disclosures of Himself. The objection is not valid. God created the earth as a theater for the activities of men as personal beings, who indeed as to their bodies are an integral part of nature, but who in their spiritual beings transcend nature and form a spiritual fellowship. General revelation is basic and fundamental, but from the very nature of things, implies a revelation on a higher and personal plane. Thus by the union of these two forms of revelation, man comes to know God not as mere law, or as force working through law, but as a Supreme Personality, who is not only capable of entering into fellowship with men, but who has created men specifically for communion with Himself. Again, since man has been created for personal fellowship with God, it is rational to suppose that He would make disclosures of Himself through human personality beyond those possible through restricted and impersonal nature. Finally, the fact that sin entered the world as an event later than the creative fiat, necessitates a special revelation if God's attitude toward sin is to be understood, and His purpose of redemption effectually made known to men. As a corollary to this last position, a special revelation is necessary, because divine tuition must contend against the abnormal consequences of sin as discovered in the apathy, perversity and spiritual darkness which characterize the minds of men. "A single glance," says Sheldon, "at the tragedy of human sin and folly, ought to dissipate the fiction that nature affords an adequate revelation for man in his actual condition. It may indeed be sufficient to involve a measure of responsibility, but it is not sufficient to supply the highest motive power or the most efficient guidance" (SHELDON, *System of Chr. Doct.*, p. 75).

Strictly speaking we have here three grades of revelation—that made through impersonal nature, that made through man as a personal being in a peculiar sense transcending nature; and lastly that made through Jesus Christ as the Incarnate Word of God. It is evident, therefore, that the spiritual nature of man becomes the theater for the special revelation of God. Regarded from the lower standpoint, man represents the culmination of the revelation of God through Nature. Viewed from above, human nature becomes the organ of the Divine Revelation through Christ. In man, the human spirit rests in nature; in Christ the divine rests in the human. From the days of the early Church, there has been a speculative interest in the question as to whether or not Christ would have become incarnate in order to perfect the revelation of God through man, or whether He came solely in His redemptive purpose and power. However we view the question two comings are involved—one in humiliation, due to sin; the other a second coming in glory without sin unto salvation. Whether this second coming would have become a first, had sin not entered the world, can be only a matter of private conjecture. We are on safe ground, however, when we consider the revelation of God in Christ in its profoundest depths as an unfolding of the redemptive purpose of God.

In thus limiting the idea of a special revelation to the unfolding of the eternal counsel of God as it concerns the redemption of men through Christ, we bring before us three salient points. *First*, the redemptive purpose of God as revealed in Christ; *second*, the perfected Scriptures as the final testimony of Jesus to sinful men; and *third*, the coincidence of these with the Christian Faith.

Christ's Redemptive Mission. Only in a preliminary manner, and as it is directly concerned with the revealing work of Christ, do we call attention to the nature of His mission. "Revelation proper," says Pope, "is consecrated to the mystery hid with Christ in God, the one secret which it unfolds." To this the prophets bear witness, and it is common burden of both our Lord and His apostles. Christ himself is the sum of all revelation, *the brightness of his glory, and the express image of his person, and upholding all things by the word of his power* (Heb. 1:3). The incarnation is referred to as *the mystery of godliness* (I Tim. 3:16); and Christ is himself called the *Mystery of God* (Col. 2:2) *in whom are hid all the treasures of wisdom and knowledge* (Col. 2:3). St. Paul tells us that the knowledge of the glory of God is seen *in the face of Jesus Christ* (II Cor. 4:6). John sounds a deep and authoritative note in the prologue to the Fourth Gospel especially in such verses as *In the beginning was the Word and the Word was with God and the Word was God* (John 1:1); and again, *No man hath seen God at any time; the only begotten Son which is in the bosom of the Father, he hath declared him* (1:18). And in another place, *He that hath seen me hath seen the Father* (John 14:9). Matthew likewise tells us that *no man knoweth the Son, but the Father; neither knoweth any man the Father, save the Son, and he to whomsoever the Son will reveal him* (Matt. 11:27). In Christ, all the prophets with their lamps, all the priests with their altars and sacrifices, and all the kings with their thrones and scepters, are lost in Him who is our Prophet, Priest and King.

The Scriptures Contain and Are the Word of God. Christ was Himself the full and perfect revelation of the Father—the effulgence of His glory and the express or exact image of His Person. His testimony is the spirit of prophecy—the last word of all objective revelation. It is because this testimony is perfected in the Scriptures, that they become the Word of God objectified. Dorner maintains that neither faith nor the Scriptures but only God in Christ, and in the Holy Spirit, is the principle of the existence of Christianity (*principium essendi*), while faith is primarily the principle of the knowledge of Christianity (*principium cognoscendi*); and that for dogmatic theology, faith with its contents appropriated from the Scriptures, constitutes the immediate material. On the contrary, we must hold with MacPherson, that it is not faith with the Scriptures as its content, but the Scriptures, as the record of divine revelation, which claim acceptance from man. When received by faith in God who therein reveals Himself, the Scriptures become the principle of knowledge, and the Rule of Faith. Francke's position against which Dorner argues, is much more in harmony with the Protestant doctrine of the Holy Scriptures, which makes the Scriptures the *principium cognoscendi objectivum*, and then places the believing subject alongside, co-ordinated with the Scriptures as the *principium cognoscendi subjectivum*. God himself, then as the *principium essendi*, binds these two together into ultimate unity. "Christianity thus owes its existence to Christ, the revealer of God, but the knowledge of Christianity is immediately set forth in the Scriptures, which must be received and understood by the heart and mind of the believer" (Cf. MacPherson, *Chr. Dogm.*, p. 27).

The Scriptures and the Christian Faith. The Revelation of God given to man in the Holy Scriptures, becomes the Christian faith when received by him. We must therefore regard the body of truth as addressed primarily to the principle of faith, and secondarily as presenting its credentials to reason in order to win the assent of those who are not yet of the household of faith. Concerning the first, we must now discuss more at length (I) The Christian Book and (II) The Christian Faith. Concerning the second we must give attention to (III) The Credentials of Revelation with its subtopics.

THE CHRISTIAN BOOK

The first subject in any discussion of the Christian revelation must of necessity be the Christian Book since here alone are to be found its documentary records. This leads us immediately to a consideration of the nature and function of the Scriptures as the oracles of God. Christ the Personal Word was Himself the full and final revelation of the Father. He alone is the true Revealer. Not merely His words and acts, but He himself as manifested in His words and acts. In this sense it may be truly said that "the Oracle and the oracles are one." To rightly understand, then, the nature and function of the Bible, it must be viewed as occupying an intermediate position between the primary revelation of God in nature, and the perfect revelation of God in Christ—the Personal Word. If we place at the very center of Revelation the idea of the Eternal Word, and draw about it a series of concentric circles, the first and nearest would represent the Word incarnate or the revelation of God in Christ the Personal Word. The second circle farther removed would represent the Bible as the written Word. It is in this sense that the Bible is at once the Word of God and the record of that Word. The Gospels were given to us by the evangelists who, under the inspiration of the Spirit, recorded the words and deeds of the Christ in the flesh. The Acts, the Epistles and the Apocalypse were given by the direct energizing of the Spirit, in fulfillment of Christ's purpose to give the Church the Scriptures of the New Testament as supplementary to, and a completion of, the Old Testament. It is evident, then, that the Bible bears the same relation to the Living and Personal Word, that our words spoken and recorded bear to our own persons. The third and outer circle would represent the revelation of God in nature and the created universe. In order, therefore, to correctly understand the Bible as the written Word, we must estimate it in its relation to nature on the one hand, and the Personal Word on the other.

The Relation of the Bible to Nature. The revelation of God in the Holy Scriptures is not meant to supersede His revelation in nature but to supplement it. It is important that we keep before us, constantly, the fact that the mind rises to spiritual conceptions through the use of material things. *That was not first which is spiritual, but that which is natural: and afterward that which is spiritual* (I Cor. 15:46). What did we know of spiritual things when we were children? And how could we

ever have learned them, had it not been for the analogy
of earthly things? Is not this the meaning of Jesus of
whom it is recorded that *without a parable spake he
not unto them?* (Matt. 13:34). When Jesus would
lead His disciples into the deeper truths of the Spirit, He
pointed to the lilies by the roadside, the grass of the
field, the sparrows. From these observations He leads
not directly to spiritual truth, but first to the realm of
historical fact and then to spiritual values. *Consider
the lilies of the field*—this is His primary observation,
the basis of all scientific investigation. *Solomon in all
his glory was not arrayed like one of these*—this is the
realm of secondary or historical knowledge. *How much
more shall your heavenly Father clothe you*—this is
the spiritual value which forms the ultimate goal of His
instruction—a knowledge of the Father and personal
trust in Him. There is a deep and profound philosophy
here. The Earth and the Bible are God's two texts, each
having its place, time and function in progressive revelation. Nature is the primary source of knowledge, the
Bible is the supplementary source. Nature proposes
mysterious questions, and the Bible in so far as it is
understood solves them. The Bible furnishes us with
ideals, Nature gives us the tools with which to work
them out. The one tells us of His eternal power and
Godhead, the other of His mercy and love. Without the
Bible the universe would be a riddle; without Nature,
the Bible would be meaningless. When Nicodemus desired the knowledge of spiritual things, Jesus said unto
him, *If I have told you earthly things, and ye believe not,
how shall ye believe, if I tell you of heavenly things?*
(John 3:12).

*The Relation of the Written Word to the Personal
Word.* The Bible on the other hand, must be considered
in relation to Christ the Living Word. Not from themselves do the inspired books give forth light. The
original source of the Christian knowledge of God must
ever be, the Lord Jesus Christ. To Him as the ever-
living Light the written word is subordinate. The Personal Word manifests Himself in and through the writ-

ten Word. The books which were written concerning
Him by evangelists and apostles bear a relation to His
Divine-human life resembling His own spoken words to
His Person; and these books through the succeeding ages
derive their light and their truth uninterruptedly from
Him who is the Light and the Truth. Mystically connected with the Christ of God, the Scriptures continue
to be the objective medium through which by the Spirit,
the original Light shines into the hearts of true believers.
When, however, the living synthesis of the written Word
and the Personal Word is lost, the Church thereby sun-
ders the Bible from the spiritual communion in which
it perpetually stands, and comes to view it as an independent book, apart from the living Presence of its
Author. Divorced from its true meaning and mystical
ground, the Bible holds a false position for both theologian and teacher.

False Conceptions of the Bible. It is evident that anything, however good, which sets itself up in a false independency and thus obscures or obstructs the revelation of the Living Word, becomes in so far a usurper or
pretender to the throne. The history of Christendom
reveals three such perversions of divine things. Three
worthy monarchs have had scepters thrust into their
hands and were thereby forced into a false and unworthy
position before both God and man. The first of these was
the Church. Founded by her Lord as a holy fellowship
of Christ with His people, the Church was composed of
redeemed saints in loving obedience to their Lord. As
such, the Church was spiritual and triumphant. Nothing
could withstand the power and the glory which were
hers in communion with her Lord. But through false
teachers and a mistaken concept of the Church itself,
she soon set herself up in the place of her Lord. She became an end in herself, instead of a medium through
which the believer could approach to God, and thus a
usurper of Christ's throne. It was against the tyranny
of a false position concerning the Church that Protest-
tantism revolted. Those who protested did not thereby
cease to be Christians, but they did assert that they were

free in Christ, and refused to be entangled again with the yoke of bondage. They insisted that one is their Master, even Christ, and that all they are brethren (Matt. 23: 8-10).

The next worthy monarch to be forced into the position of a usurper was the Bible. Before the second generation of Reformers had passed away, a movement was set up to place the Bible in the position formerly held by the Church. The Reformers themselves strove earnestly to maintain the balance between the formal and the material principles of salvation, the Word and Faith, but gradually the formal principle superseded the material, and men began unconsciously to substitute the written Word for Christ the Living Word. They divorced the written Word from the Personal Word and thus forced it into a false position. No longer was it the fresh utterance of Christ, the outflow of the Spirit's presence, but merely a recorded utterance which bound men by legal rather than spiritual bonds. Men's knowledge became formal rather than spiritual. The views of God attained were merely those of a book, not those of the Living Christ which the book was intended to reveal. As a consequence Christ became to them merely a historical figure, not a living Reality; and men sought more for a knowledge of God's will than for God himself. They gave more attention to creeds than to Christ. They rested in the letter, which according to Scripture itself kills, and never rose to a concept of Him whose words are spirit and life. The Bible thus divorced from its mystical connection with the Personal Word, became in some sense a usurper, a pretender to the throne.

Lastly, Reason itself was forced into a false authority. Severed from its Living Source, the Bible was debased to the position of a mere book among books. It was thus subjected to the test of human reason, and as a consequence there arose the critical or critico-historical movement of the last century known as "destructive criticism." Over against this as a protest arose a reactionary party, which originating in a worthy desire to maintain belief in the plenary inspiration of the Bible, and its genuineness, authenticity and authority as the Rule of Faith, resorted to a mere legalistic defense of the Scriptures. It depended upon logic rather than life. Spiritual men and women—those filled with the Holy Spirit, are not unduly concerned with either higher or lower criticism. They do not rest merely in the letter which must be defended by argument. They have a broader and more substantial basis for their faith. It rests in their risen Lord, the glorified Christ. They know that the Bible is true, not primarily through the efforts of the apologists, but because they are acquainted with its Author. The Spirit which inspired the Word dwells within them and witnesses to its truth. In them the formal and material principles of the Reformation are conjoined. The Holy Spirit is the great conservator of orthodoxy. To the Jew, Christ was a stumblingblock, and to the Greeks foolishness; *but unto them which are called, both Jews and Greeks, Christ the power of God, and the wisdom of God* (I Cor. 1:24).

THE CHRISTIAN FAITH

The next subject in our discussion of revelation is the *Christian Faith*, which may be defined as the acceptance by man of the revelation of God given in Christ and recorded in the Holy Scriptures. It becomes, therefore, the body of external revelation as surely accepted and believed by all Christians, because they are assured of its evidences, and have made it the ground of their personal trust. It is something more than merely external revelation, it is that revealed truth incorporated in personal life, it is the truth made vital and living by being embodied in human personality. The body of Christian truth is addressed primarily to faith, and only secondarily to reason. As appealing to that universal principle of human nature, the faculty of believing, this body of truth is the Christian Faith. As related to reason, it presents its credentials in order to acceptance on the part of those who seek the truth.

The Body of Truth as Addressed to Faith. The principle of faith belongs to human nature as certainly as does reason. Faith is the highest exercise of man as a personal being, and calls into action the full range of his powers—the understanding of the mind, the love of the heart and the volitional powers of the will. It is that power of personality, deep-seated in its spiritual constitution, by which it is able to accept truth presented to it on sufficient evidences, whether that evidence be consciousness, intuition or testimony. The revelation of God is personal. The Spirit demonstrates the truth to the intellect, the feelings and the will. Furthermore, the divine revelation is always made ultimately to the understanding. It is not always immediately so, for it is frequently mediated through the feelings, or the will. As such, however, the revelation may not be said to be fully personal. If the feelings be overemphasized in our knowledge of God, we have mysticism, which in so far as it insists upon immediate communion with God in the conscious experiences of men, is true and strong. Its chief error lies in the fact that it attempts to limit re-

We are justified, therefore, in holding that the Scriptures of revelation and Christianity, as the Christian Faith, cover the same ground and strictly coincide. . . . . We have to do only with the general fact that in all sound theology the Bible and Christ are inseparably connected. Not that they are in the nature of things identical: we can suppose the possibility of an Incarnate Revealer present in the world without the mediation of the written Word. Indeed we are bound to assume, as has already been seen, that there is a wider revelation of the Word in the world than the Scriptures cover. Moreover we may assert that His revelation of Himself is still, and even in connection with the Scriptures, more or less independent of the Word. But as the basis for the science of theology the Bible is Christianity. It has pleased God from the beginning to conduct the development of the great mystery by documents containing the attested facts, the authenticated doctrines, and the sealed predictions of enlargement of the Volume of the Book. That Book is the foundation of Christianity; the Lord of the Bible and the Bible are indissolubly the Rock on which it is based. We have no other Christian religion than that which is one with its document and records; we have no documents and records which do not directly pay their tribute to the Christian Religion; and there is no revelation in any department of truth of which the same may be said. All revelation is identical with Christianity and summed up in it. Hence, generally speaking, and as yet regarding the Scriptures only as a whole, we may say that the character of Christianity is the character of the Bible; the claims and credentials of the one are the claims and credentials of the other. This observation will lead us by an easy transition to the counterpart of Revelation: the Christian Faith.—POPE, *Compendium of Christian Theology,* p. 41.

ligious experience to the range of the emotions, instead of recognizing it as rooted in the spiritual constitution of man. It thus excludes the light of reason, and degrades the Word of God by claiming for itself an inspiration equal to the theopneustic utterances of Holy Scripture. It is a direct inlet to the most baneful error, that the body of truth accepted as the Christian Faith was not given from above as a complete whole, but left by the spirit of inspiration to be finished by endless supplements and communications made to individuals. On the other hand, if reason be unduly emphasized, or unchecked by religious experience and historical revelation, it issues in rationalism and falls short of the true knowledge of God. To those who receive the truth, however, revelation becomes an organic whole. To them it is both objectively and subjectively the Christian Faith—objectively as a body of revealed truth, subjectively as having become their own in faith and assurance. It is more than a philosophy of life, the glory of their powers of reason; and it is more than a tradition received by inheritance however rich that might be—it is the richer inheritance of the Holy Spirit who has quickened their belief into the assurance of personal knowledge and experience. As reason did not give them this body of truth, it cannot

Dr. Daniel Steele describes a fanatic as one who "abjures and pours contempt upon that scintillation of the eternal Logos, human reason. This lighted torch placed in man's hand for his guidance in certain matters, he extinguishes in order ostensibly to exalt the candle of the Lord, the Holy Ghost, but really to lift up the lamp of his own flickering fancy. Reason is a gift of God, worthy of our respect. We are to accept it as our surest guide in its appropriate sphere. Beyond this sphere we should seek the light of revelation and the guidance of the Spirit. The fanatic depreciates one perfect gift from the Father of Lights, that he may magnify another. Both of these lights, reason and the Holy Ghost, are necessary to our perfect guidance. To reject one is to assume greater wisdom than God's. Such presumptuous folly He will glaringly expose. He who spurns the Spirit will be left to darkness outside the narrow sphere of reason; and he who scorns reason will be left to follow the hallucinations of his heated imagination, instead of the dictates of common sense."

" 'Tis reason our great Master holds so dear;
'Tis reason's injured rights His wrath resents;
'Tis reason's voice obeyed His glorious crown;
To give lost reason life, He poured His own;
Believe, and show the reason of a man;
Believe, and taste the pleasure of a God.
Through reason's wounds alone thy faith can die."

take it away. They received it by faith, and hence live and move in that realm which is *the substance of things hoped for, the evidence of things not seen* (Heb. 11:1).

Faith as Allied with Reason. The Christian Faith is addressed to the principle of believing in man, and also to reason as subordinate to that faith. God is revealed to man through reason, both immediately in consciousness and mediately through the physical and moral systems of the universe. Basing his argument upon the threefold nature of personality as involving the affections, the will and the reason, Harris points out that there are three elements in our knowledge of God—the experiential, the historical, and the rational; and that only in the synthesis of these three is the largest knowledge of God possible. Each of these must test, correct and restrain the others, and at the same time clarify, verify and supplement them. To attain this synthesis is the great problem of religious thinking, a synthesis which can be attained only through the medium of historical revelation. Religious experience and theological thought must center in the living Christ. In Him is life;

There are therefore three elements in the knowledge of God, which may be called the experiential, the historical, and the rational or ideal. Theological knowledge is the comprehension of these three elements in a unity or synthesis of thought. The historical is the medium for the synthesis of the experiential and the rational. . . . . The necessity of this synthesis is evident from the fact that thought, which recognizes only one or two of these three elements, issues in disastrous error. When the experiential belief withdraws into itself, the result is mysticism. When the rational or ideal isolates itself, the first result is dogmatism; the later result is rationalism. In each case the Bible, as the record of God's revelation of Himself recedes toward the background, and ultimately is disregarded. When the historical isolates itself, the result is unspiritual and arid criticism of the Bible, and anthropological and archæological investigation.—HARRIS, *Self-Revelation of God*, p. 122.

Christianity does not come to men primarily as a system of doctrine demanding the assent of the intellect, but rather as a practical remedy for sin asking the consent of the will to its application. The gospel offers pardon for sin on the ground of Christ's atoning work, restoration to fellowship and sonship with God, and the grace of the Holy Spirit as the power by which sin may be overcome and holiness attained. The means or instrument by which this is appropriated is faith in Christ—a faith which consists primarily in trust, an act of the will, a giving of oneself in entire submission into the hands of the Saviour. Now this offer can be tested in only one way, that is, by personal trial. It belongs to the realm of inward and personal experience, and those who have fully and fairly tried it have never found it to fail.—STEARNS, *Present Day Theology*, pp. 37, 38.

in Him also are hid all the treasures of wisdom and knowledge. The Bible as the objective body of Christian truth must be held in solution in theological thought, and through the Spirit must be made vital in Christian experience. The gracious work of the Holy Spirit which awakens faith in the believer exerts an influence upon the whole range of his being. It not only purifies the affections so that they center in their living Lord, but it humbles reason to receive those mysteries which it cannot understand. Nor is this in any sense derogatory to reason. Faith honors reason, when thus restored to soundness, and gives to it perfect authority in that field over which reason should preside. Reason approves the evidences upon which faith rests, and therefore in the whole economy of redemption, the Scriptures of revelation and the voice of sound reason blend into one perfect and harmonious whole. This leads us immediately to the credentials of revelation, presented to the reason as evidences.

THE CREDENTIALS OF REVELATION

Having discussed the objective character of revelation, and having treated it from the subjective standpoint as the Christian faith presented for man's acceptance, it remains now to consider the subject as presenting its evidences to reason. For this we have scriptural authority. The believer is exhorted to be ready, or prepared, to give a reason or an apology ($\pi\rho\grave{o}s$ $\mathring{a}\pi o\lambda o\gamma\acute{\iota}a\nu$) for the hope that is within him (I Peter 3:15). So also Luke, known as the Evangelist of the Evidences, ad-

The Christian Faith presents to the faculty by which the infinite and eternal are perceived a system of truth which human reason cannot fathom or understand, against which it naturally rebels. But the same Spirit who opens the eye of faith gives reason its perfect soundness, so that it consents to accept what it cannot itself verify. Here, of course, we regard Revelation as one organic whole, which has for its unifying principle one overwhelming truth, the union of God and man in Christ. Around this center revolve other equally incomprehensible doctrines; and beyond these in a wider orbit many which are not in the same sense beyond the human faculties. And speaking of the one vast Revelation we may say that it is committed to faith and submissively wondered at by reason. Faith is elevated to receive it and reason humbled to submit to it.—POPE, Compendium of Christian Theology, I, pp. 45, 46.

dresses his Gospel to Theophilus that he might "know the certainty of those things" wherein he had been instructed (Luke 1:4). Here the word ἐπιγνῷς denotes accurate and systematic knowledge. While the Christian believer has the stronger evidence of the *testimonii Spiritus sancti,* he must not overlook the value of the credentials as a means of bringing the unbeliever to listen to the voice of revelation. And yet these external evidences apart from the internal demonstration of truth by the Holy Spirit, cannot have the same strength as the combined credentials and therefore too much cannot be expected of this form of evidence.

We present the Credentials of Revelation under the following heads: (1) Miracles; (2) Prophecy; (3) The Unique Personality of Christ; and (4) The Witness of the Holy Spirit.

We cannot give attention to the so-called "presumptive evidences" other than to point out that the rudimentary nature of religion as grounded in a feeling of dependence, necessitates such a revelation of God as shall satisfy the natural cravings of his heart. This was the plea of Augustine—"Thou hast created us for Thyself, and our hearts are restless till they rest in Thee." The Christian revelation evidences its value in that it appeals directly to a preparation in the human spirit. Throughout the whole of Scripture, the Voice of the Creator speaks directly to the inner needs of His creatures. The positive strength of the Scriptures, therefore, lie in this, that there is no possible question growing out of created human nature, to which response is not given by the Creator. Again, man requires immediate communion with God in order to preserve him from moral degradation. We have shown that the ethnic religions are the outgrowth of a failure to retain the knowledge of God. It may be presumed, therefore, that God who created man a social being, would provide such instruction as to order social institutions in righteousness. Consequently, not only did John, the Forerunner of Jesus, begin his preparatory ministry with the cry, *Repent, for the kingdom of heaven is at hand* (Matt. 3:2); but

Jesus also came *preaching the gospel of the kingdom of God* (Mark 1:14). Thus there is given a corrective to the false structures of religious and social life by the revelation of Jesus Christ who becomes the center of a new redemptive order. Thus, also, is fulfilled the ancient prophecy, *he correcteth the Gentiles*—their chastisement performing the functions of the law in Israel—that of a schoolmaster to bring them to Christ (Cf. Psalm 94:10; Gal. 3:24). Lastly, since the former revelations were imperfect, we may presume that God, who reveals Himself through His created works and in the progress of human history, would perfect this revelation by an authoritative and satisfying disclosure of Himself in His spiritual perfections. Christianity answers as a credential of revelation, in that it is the explanation of all the preparatory disclosures, and the consummation of them all. God has not left Himself without a witness in every age, a chosen company to whom He has made known His will, and these preliminary revelations of truth have at once satisfied human hearts and kindled within them deeper desires and higher aspirations. Christianity comes, then, as the final answer to this continuous expectation. It comes "as the perfecting of its earlier self, the final and sufficient response to the expectation it had kept up from the beginning. This is its supreme preparatory credential. It is the last of many words, and leaves nothing to be desired in the present estate of mankind" (POPE, *Compend. Chr. Th.*, I, p. 59).

This is in fact, the crowning presumptive argument in its favor, that it is the end and completion of a revelation that has been going on from the beginning. It is not a religion that literally began in Judea with the advent of Jesus. It does not profess to be the first supernatural communication to mankind, it is not the opening of the heavens for the first time. It finishes a testimony that began with the fall of man; in the best sense, therefore, it is as old as Creation. . . . . This is in fact its glory. It is the last accent of a Voice which spoke first at the gate of Paradise. That Voice was the primitive revelation from the perversions of which all the innumerable forms of mythology arose. But that Voice awakened the desire of the human race to which all revelation has been a response, and has constantly deepened that desire whilst it responded to it, but only in a peculiar line and within a limited area. On either side of that line, and beyond that area, men groped after the lost Creator and the forfeited Paradise in their own way, being dealt with in both justice and mercy. The mercy of the Supreme has in every age guided the instincts of all the sincere. (Cf. Acts 10:34, 35; Rom. 1:21) POPE, *Compendium of Christian Theology*, I, p. 58.

The Evidence of Miracles. Before turning our attention directly to a consideration of miracles, we need to remind ourselves that Revelation is throughout wholly supernatural. God is immanent in the world, but not in the same sense that He is the Personal Presence in the economy of revealed Truth. Nature, as governed by certain fixed physical and metaphysical laws, must be touched if not permeated by the supernatural. But God is transcendent as well as immanent, and the invisible world and all spiritual interventions must necessarily be supernatural, if they are to bear witness to the transcendent purpose of God. "Hence it follows that the introduction of man into this system of things was a supernatural intervention; and all revelations of the unseen in the constitution of his nature are supernatural; and all evidences of the presence and glory of God in the universe as seen by man are supernatural" (POPE, *CCT*, I, p. 62). God, as a free Personality, is not merely back of nature as its metaphysical ground, but over it, and free to work within it or upon it according to His pleasure. *It is manifest,* says St. Paul, *that he is excepted which did put all things under him.* In a preliminary way we may say, then, that an intervention of Divine Power in the established course of nature, beyond that of creaturely measure, is regarded as a Miracle; while the same intervention in the realm of knowledge is termed Prophecy.

The intervention of God as a free Personal Being, is not a violation of law nor a suspension of it, but the introduction of a sufficient cause for any effect He would produce. Sheldon points out that the free working of men introduces effects into nature without destroying the integrity of the system, and the higher range of mir-

These three credentials of Miracle, Prophecy and Inspiration ought to be united; they mutually give and receive strength and are strongest when combined. The miracle, of course, is most demonstrative to the extant generations of beholders, the prophecy only to the generations which come afterward. . . . . Inspiration embraces the two in one; it records the fact of the miracle, and as inspiration makes it present to every age; while as inspiration, its record of a prophecy makes the fulfillment as if it were already come or were already past to those who hear it.—POPE, *Compendium of Christian Theology,* I, p. 98.

acles has the same effect, so that the greatest miracle is as harmless as the least physical expression of man's free agency. As an illustration of the harmonious blending of the natural and supernatural, he calls attention to a man who may by his free choice cast a branch into a stream, which is immediately borne on in accordance with the laws of nature, though those laws might never have brought it into the stream. So also the physical effect of a miraculous work enters immediately into the stream of natural causes and is borne on by its ceaseless flow. Miracles, then, do not undermine nature, any more than the stream generates the effect or is turned aside by it (Cf. SHELDON, *System of Christian Doctrine,* p. 106ff).

Miracles are expressed in the Scriptures by a variety of terms. In his sermon on the Day of Pentecost Peter describes the Lord Jesus as *a man approved of God among you by miracles and wonders and signs, which God did by him in the midst of you* (Acts 2:22). Here are three words used to describe what we commonly term miracles, and the Apostle John uses a fourth, that of "works." The first is *dunamis* (δυνάμεις), which signifies "powers" and looks more especially to the agency by which they were produced—which God did by Him. This power dwells in the Divine Messenger (Acts 6:8, 10:38, Rom. 15:19), and is that by which he is equipped of God for his mission. The word came later to mean "powers" in the plural, as separate exertions of power, and is translated "wonderful works" (Cf. Matt. 7:22). The second term is *terata* (τέρατα), which denotes wonders, and has regard primarily to the effect produced on the spectator. The astonishment with which the beholders were seized is frequently described by the evangelists in graphic terms. Origen points out that the term "wonders" is never applied to the miracles except in connection with some other name. They are constantly described as "signs and wonders" (Cf. Acts 14:3, Rom. 15:19, Matt. 24:24, Heb. 2:4). The third term *semeia* (σημεῖα) is that of signs. It has particular reference to their significance as the seals which God uses to authenticate the persons by whom they are wrought. These three terms, "wonders," "signs," and "powers" occur three times in connection with one another (Acts 2: 22, II Cor. 13: 12 and II Thess. 2: 9) and are to be regarded as different aspects of the same work rather than different classes of works. This is illustrated in the healing of the paralytic (Mark 2: 1, 2) which was a *wonder* for "they were all amazed"; it was a *power,* for at Christ's word the man took up his bed and went out before them all; it was a *sign,* for it was a token that One greater than man was among them, and was wrought that they might know *that the Son of man hath power on earth to forgive sins* (Cf. also I Kings 13: 3, II Kings 1: 10). The fourth term *erga* (ἔργα), signifying works, occurs only in the Gospel of John. It occurs frequently in the words of Jesus himself as when He says, *though ye believe not me, believe the works";* or again, *if I had not done among them works which none other man did, they had not had sin* (John 10: 38, 15: 24). Taken in connection with the deity of Christ, the term suggests that what men regarded as wonders requiring the exercise of mighty power, were in the estimation of the Lord himself simply works. They required no more exertion at His hands than that which was common or ordinary with Him as Divine. In this connection Trench says, "He must, out of the necessity of His higher being, bring forth these works, greater than man's. They are the periphery of that circle whereof He is the center. The great miracle is the Incarnation; all else, so to speak (Isaiah 9: 6), are works of wonder; the only wonder would be if He did them not. The sun in the heavens is a wonder; but it is not a wonder that, being what it is, it rays forth effluences of light and heat. These miracles are the fruit after its kind which

The Hebrew historian or prophet regarded miracles as only the emergence into sensible experience of that divine force which was all along, though invisibly, controlling the course of nature.—SOUTHAMPTON, *Place of Miracles,* p. 18.

If we look at a conflagration through smoked glass, we see buildings collapsing, but we see no fire. So science sees results, but not the power which produces them; sees cause and effect, but does not see God.—GEORGE ADAM SMITH, Isaiah 33: 14.

the divine tree brings forth; and may, therefore, with deep truth, be styled the "works" of Christ with no further addition or explanation" (TRENCH, *The Miracles*, p. 6). Donne calls attention to the fact, also, that there is in every miracle a silent chiding of the world, and a tacit reprehension of them who require or need miracles. Did they serve no other purpose than to testify of the liberty of God, whose will, however habitually declared in nature, is yet above nature; were it only to break a link in the chain of cause and effect which otherwise we should substitute for God, and be brought thereby under

The miracles, then, not being against nature, however they may be beside and beyond it, are in no respects slights cast upon its everyday workings; but rather when contemplated aright, are an honoring of these in the witness which they render to the source from which these all originally proceed, for Christ healing a sick man with His word, is in fact claiming in this to be the Lord and Author of all the healing powers which have exerted their beneficent influence on the bodies of men, and saying, "I will prove this fact, which you are ever losing sight of, that in me, the fontal power, which goes forth in a thousand gradual cures resides and is manifested on this occasion by only speaking a word and bringing back a man to perfect health"; not thus cutting off those other and more gradual healings from His person, but truly linking them to it. So when He multiplied the bread, when He changed the water into wine, what does He but say, "It is I and no other, who by the sunshine and the shower, by the seedtime and the harvest, give food for the use of man; and you shall learn this, which you are evermore unthankfully forgetting, by witnessing for once or twice, or if not actually witnessing, yet having it rehearsed in your ears forever, how the essence of things are mine, how the bread grows in my hands, how the water, not drawn up into the vine, nor slowly transmuted into the juices of the grape, but simply at my bidding changes into wine. The children of this world sacrifice to their net, and burn incense to their drag, but it is I who, giving you in a moment the draught of fishes which you yourselves had long labored for in vain, will remind you who guides them through the ocean paths, and suffer you either to toil long and to take nothing, or to crown your labors with a rich and unexpected harvest of the season." Even the single miracle which wears an aspect of severity, that of the withered fig tree, speaks the same language, for in that the same gracious Lord is declaring, "The scourges are mine, wherewith I punish your sins, and summon you to repentance, continually miss their purpose altogether, or need to be repeated again and again; and this mainly because you see in them only the evil accidents of a blind nature; but I will show you that it is I and no other who smites the earth with a curse, who both can and do send these strokes for the punishing of the sins of men." And we can perceive how all this should have been necessary. For if in one sense the orderly workings of nature reveal the glory of God (Psalm 19:1-6), in another they hide that glory from our eyes; if they ought to make us continually remember Him, yet there is danger that they may lead us to forget Him until this world around us shall prove not a translucent medium through which we behold Him, but a thick, impenetrable curtain, concealing Him wholly from our sight." —TRENCH, *The Miracles*, pp. 15, 16.

the iron chain of inexorable necessity, miracles would serve a great purpose in the religious life of mankind.

Miracles are commonly defined as manifestations of the supernatural which have their theater in the sphere of sense-perceptions. Fisher defines a miracle as an event which occurs in connection with religious teaching, and which the forces of nature, including the natural powers of man, cannot of themselves produce, and which must therefore be referred to a supernatural agency. Dorner's definition is similar: "Miracles," he says, "are sensuously cognizable events not comprehensible on the ground of causality of nature and the given system of nature as such, but essentially on the ground of God's free action alone" (DORNER, *System of Chr. Doct.*, Sect. 55).

We come now to a consideration of the nature of miracles as credentials, and to an examination as to wherein their value as evidences lies. We may say, in a general way, that revelation appeals to the whole body of evidence that God has interposed in human affairs; and that this evidence is so transcendent and extraordinary as to warrant a belief in the miraculous. Christian Faith, therefore, rests a strong claim on the fact that to the whole scope of Christianity, in both its preparatory stage and its perfect fulfillment, there attaches a series of miracles and signs and wonders which no candid person should deny. But in a more specific sense, their value

A created universe which was in itself so perfectly organized that the entrance of the direct agency of God could not be admitted . . . . would be a barrier for God, and consequently, as a creature, most imperfect.—RICHARD ROTHE.

Lotze, that great philosopher, whose influence is more potent now than at any other time in present thought, does not regard the universe as a plenum to which nothing can be added in the way of force. He looks upon the universe rather as a plastic organism to which new impulses can be imparted from him of whose thought and will it is an expression. These impulses, once imparted, abide in the organism and are therefore subject to its law. Though these impulses come from within, they come not from the finite mechanism, but from the immanent God. "He makes the possibility of the miracle depend upon the close and intimate action and reaction between the world and the personal Absolute, in consequence of which the movements of the natural world are carried on only *through* the Absolute, with the possibility of a variation in the general course of things, according to the existing facts and the purpose of the Divine Governor" (Cf. STRONG, *Systematic Theology*, I, p. 123).

lies in the fact that they are an authentication of the
messengers of God to their contemporaries. This seems
to be generally expected by men and was given expression by Nicodemus in the words, *Rabbi, we know that
thou art a teacher come from God; for no man could do
these miracles that thou doest, except God be with him*
(John 3:2). Here, however, the sign precedes the
teaching, while for later generations, the message is the
more prominent and the attestation secondary. We must
therefore include original miracles with other branches
of evidence, and examine more particularly wherein
their evidential values lie, this being commonly known
as the criteria or test of miracles.

Since miracles are signs intended to convey truth as
well as to attest it, we may say *first,* that they must be an
integral part of revelation itself. Their evidential value,
important as it is, must never be regarded as secondary,
and the divine impulse and the needs of men primary.
In this sense there is not a miracle in Scripture that does
not demonstrate either the power or the wisdom of God,
His mercy or His justice. They are never regarded as
mere portents, but always faithful to the character of
God. *Second,* the missions which miracles authenticate must be worthy of God. Here again the miracles of
the Bible meet every demand of a true credential. The
earlier miracles were not only authentications of the
messengers of God, but also of the dread name of Jehovah. The miracles of Moses and his economy attested at
every critical hour that God reigned. This is equally
true in the New Testament as in the older economy. The
supreme miracle, however, is that of the Divine Person,
which because of its importance must be considered as
a separate credential. *Third,* as credentials, miracles
must allow the application of proper criteria in the case
of those who witnessed them, and must be supported by
such evidence as their posterity may demand. Our Lord
recognized this when He said, *I spake openly to the
world; I ever taught in the synagogue, and in the temple,
whither the Jews always resort; and in secret have I
said nothing* (John 18:20). What was true of His words

was equally true of His miracles. As to the historical evidences for posterity, there are no events which have been better substantiated, or more circumstantially attested than the whole range of central miracles. Of these the resurrection was crucial, the establishment of which assured all the rest. This was guaranteed by many infallible proofs, and believed by a large body of mentally sound and conscientious persons, many of whom sealed their faith with their blood. Again, the miracles are witnessed by their connection with public monuments. As the Passover was an abiding testimony to the deliverance of Israel from Egypt, so the Lord's day is an undeniable testimony to the resurrection of Christ. So also the Church as an institution is a perpetual memorial of Christ's life, death and resurrection, and has been so regarded from the earliest time to the present. *Fourth,* there is a credential or postulate which belongs to faith more specifically than to reason—that which regards the miracles as the economy of a supernatural order. This we have discussed in the opening paragraphs of this chapter. Two questions arise, *first,* the undeniable occurrence of what the Scripture terms "lying miracles" and which admit that these things are permitted for reasons too incomprehensible for us to understand. They are readily identified as being out of harmony with the character of God and are a stumbling block to those only whose faith does not recognize this clear distinction. We are commanded to try the spirits and John gives us the distinguishing test. *Hereby know ye the Spirit of God; Every spirit that confesseth that Jesus Christ is come in the flesh is of God; and every spirit that confesseth not that Jesus Christ is come in the flesh is not of God; and this is that spirit of antichrist, whereof ye have heard that it should come; and even now already is it in the world* (I John 4: 2, 3). Here the test is ethical and spiritual. That which admits the incarnation as a divine revelation of God to man, and is in conformity with the spirit and purpose of Jesus Christ in His life among men, is of God. That which is out of harmony with character and works of Christ is not of God. This test is infallible. *Second,* there is the question of the continuation of miracles in the Church. To a faith, however, that views miracles as belonging to a supernatural economy, and God as an Infinite Personality over against a mere philosophical Absolute, or a metaphysical ground of Reality, there is no occasion for doubting that God, according to His good pleasure, may endow His servants with the gift of prophecy or of miracle.

Prophecy as a Credential of Revelation. Prophecy, like miracle, is vitally connected with revelation. Unlike it, however, prophecy is cumulative in its evidential value, each fulfilled prediction becoming the basis for further prediction. As a credential, therefore, it is of the highest order. Prophecy may be defined as a declaration, a description, a representation, or a prediction of that which is beyond the power of human wisdom to discover. The primary meaning of the word is "forth-telling" by which is meant the declaration of the will of God without special reference to the time order. It is also used in the narrower sense of prediction or "fore-telling," this latter being the meaning most commonly attached to it in ordinary speech. There are two Hebrew words applied to the prophets also. The earliest is that of *seer,* which carries with it the implication that the prophets received their messages through visions from the Lord. The second term is *announcer,* and directs the thought more to the message itself. This message, however, was not merely the expounding of the law already given, as was done by the priests, but a fresh utterance from the Lord, a supernatural and authoritative disclosure of divine truth. There is a reference to this distinction in I Samuel 3:1 where it is stated that *the word of the Lord was precious in those days; there was*

No divine act can contradict divine righteousness. By the verdict of the Bible, no impure wonder-worker has any claim to credence. All marvels, in proportion as they are not plainly linked with the holy ends, are properly subject to doubt, while those which are discovered to be antagonistic to moral interests are but lying wonders, products of human or diabolical fraud. In general, it may be affirmed that an increased demand is placed upon testimony in the measure that any supposed case of miracles fails to meet either of the two other tests.—SHELDON, *System of Christian Doctrine,* p. 107ff.

no open vision. Whether, therefore, a vision was presented to the interior eye of faith, or whether the truth was lodged in the understanding, the prophet in his utterance performed what in another domain would be called miracle, and what in the realm of prophecy is frequently termed a "miracle of knowledge."

Prophecy as prediction is the divine impartation of future knowledge. It is plain from the whole tenor of the Scriptures, that prophecy in this sense of foreannouncement was intended to be a permanent credential in the Church. God in speaking through Isaiah the prophet sanctions this form of credential. *Remember the former things of old;* he says, *for I am God, and there is none else; I am God and there is none like me. Declaring the end from the beginning* or, *futurity from the former time and from ancient times to the things that are not yet done* (Isa. 46: 9, 10). Our Lord gives the same sanction for the New Testament. *And now I have told you before it come to pass, that when it is come to pass ye might believe* (John 14: 29). But prediction itself follows certain well-defined principles. Dr. Pope in his excellent discussion of this subject calls attention to four of these laws of prophetic prediction. (1) *Christ is its Supreme Subject.* It is to Him that all the prophets give witness (Acts 10: 43). "Nothing is more certain in the annals of mankind," he says, "than that a series of predictions runs through the ancient literature of the Jews which has had a most exact fulfillment in the advent and work of Jesus. This is the supreme credential of prophecy in revelation." (2) *The Law of Progression.* According to this principle, each age is under the sway of some governing prophecy, the accomplishment of which introduces a new order of prophetic expectation. Thus the first period of prophecy was from the protevangelium, which was the first prophecy with promise, to that of the exilic prophets, the theme being the gospel which binds time and eternity into one and commands the whole scope of redemption. The second prophetic period was from the exile to "the last days" or the "fulness of time," when all the prophecies were gathered up and fulfilled in Christ. Three things characterize the prophecy of this period, "the voice of the Son" (Heb. 1:2), the Atoning Blood (I Peter 1:11, 20), and the Effusion of the Spirit" (Acts 2:17). With Christ the supreme fulfillment, a new age of prophecy begins, and to His second coming we now bear the same relation, as did the ancient Jews in their expectation of the Messiah. (3) *The Law of Reserve,* by which He has so ordered that in every prediction, and every cycle of predictions, sufficient truth is given to encourage hope and anticipation, and enough concealed to shut up the prediction to faith. "Every generation could rejoice in the fulfillment of the prophecies that had gone before concerning itself; but as to its own future it was under the sway of an indefinite hope. There is no exception to this law throughout the economy of prophecy" (Cf. POPE, *CCT,* I, p. 83). (4) *Prophecy has been constituted a sign to each succeeding generation.* The books of the prophets furnish an inexhaustible fund of information and instruction apart from the predictive elements, and this makes it clear that prophecy was intended to be an abiding credential throughout the whole course of time.

The Unique Personality of Christ. The supreme credential of Christianity is Christ. He is the Great Fulfillment of all prophecy. In Him are hid all the treasures of wisdom and knowledge (Col. 2:3). To Him also is given all power in heaven and in earth (Matt. 28:18). In Him Revelation becomes essentially an organism of redemption. In His sacred presence, the sphere of miracle is immediately enlarged. His advent was a miracle, and His words and works, His life, death, resurrection and ascension were but a continuation of this one great miracle. In Him there is an immediate act of divine omnipotence and an immediate display of divine omniscience, both of which find their expression in the redemptive economy. Here it may be clearly seen that miracle is essential to redemption, and without it there can be no genuine Christian revelation.

We may be permitted now to lift our discussion of miracles to a higher plane, and to consider them from a

scriptural rather than a philosophical viewpoint. Since
the evangelists could not record all the miracles of our
Lord (John 20:30) a careful analysis shows that the
recorded miracles were selected according to a twofold
plan, *first,* their theandrical considerations as Pearson
uses the term; and *second,* for their evidential value.
By the first is meant a consideration of miracles as the
outflow of Christ's nature or as an influence radiating
from His Person. The great miracle is the hypostatic
union before which the miracles of nature pale into comparative insignificance. Hence the Evangelists regard the
miracles of Christ as having their source in this hypostatic union. This is perhaps expressed most simply in
the healing of the woman who touched the hem of
Christ's garment and virtue went out from Him (Mark
5:30); and again when *the whole multitude sought to
touch him; for there went virtue out of him, and healed
them all* (Luke 6:19). The aim of the miracles was to
manifest the glory of God, this being expressly stated
in the first miracle of Cana in Galilee (John 2:11). The
transfiguration revealed the majesty of Christ (Matt.
17:1-8, II Peter 1:16-18; the raising of Lazarus was for
the inspiration of faith in His power (John 11:15);
while the high priestly prayer of Jesus (John 17) has
as its supreme purpose the glory of the Father (Cf.
John 17:1, 4, 5, 6, 26). The miracles of Christ were a
revelation also of His mercy, not merely as transitory
and dissociated acts of sympathy, but the deep and abiding principle which characterizes the whole work of redemption. Both Irenæus and Athanasius taught that the
works of Christ were manifestations of the Divine Word,
who in the beginning made all things, and who in the
incarnation displayed His power over nature and man.
These works include both a manifestation of the new
life imparted to man, and a revelation of the character
and purposes of God (Cf. John 1:14). We must therefore regard the redemptive purpose of the miracles in
the same light as the doctrine and life of the Eternal Son
of God.

In the second place, as indicated above, the miracles were selected for their evidential value. This follows naturally from the previous discussion. Referring again to the miracle of Cana, it is recorded that because of this *the disciples believed in him.* Jesus himself constantly referred to His works as evidences of His deity and His mission, declaring that they had greater value than the testimony of John the Baptist (John 20: 31). While a few miracles have been selected and the details given more or less minutely, it must be borne in mind that for the people living in the time of Christ, the multitude of unrecorded miracles had great bearing on His mission.

Prophecy also takes on a new aspect when considered in direct relation to the unique personality of Christ. What earthly biography was ever preceded by such a preface as that furnished our Lord in the Messianic prophecies. For a thousand years, a picture was gradually unfolded of One who should be Son of man and Son of God; and who should within His unique personality manifest the full range of both divine and human attributes in glorious harmony. The rough outline given at the very gates of Eden was filled in by more than a

Are the miracles, then, to occupy no place at all in the array of proofs for the certainty of the things which we have believed? On the contrary, a most important place. We should greatly miss them if they did not appear in sacred history, for they belong to the very idea of a Redeemer, which would remain most incomplete without them. We could not without having that idea infinitely weakened and impoverished, conceive of Him as not doing such works; and those to whom we presented Him might very well answer, "Strange that one should come to deliver men from the bondage of nature which was crushing them, and yet Himself have been subject to its heaviest laws—Himself wonderful, and yet His appearance accompanied by no analogous wonders in nature —claiming to be the Life, and yet Himself helpless in the encounter with death; however much He promised in word, never realizing his promises indeed; giving nothing in hand, no firstfruits of power, no pledges of greater things to come." And who would not feel that they had reason in this . . . . that He must show Himself, if He is to meet the wants of men, mighty not only in word but in work? When we object to the use often made of these works, it is only because they have been forcibly severed from the whole complex of Christ's life and doctrine; and presented to the contemplation of men apart from these; it is because when on His head are "many crowns," one only has been singled out in proof that He is King of kings and Lord of lords. The miracles have been spoken of as though they borrowed nothing from the truths which they confirmed (but those truths, everything) when indeed both are held together in a blessed unity, in the Person of Him who spake the words and did the works.—TRENCH, *The Miracles*, pp. 73, 74.

hundred predictions uttered by men of all types and under varying circumstances of time and place. The psalmist describes Him as the Lord's Son to whom the heathen will be given as an inheritance, and the uttermost parts of the earth for His possession (Psalm 2: 7, 8). He will be a priest forever, after the order of Melchizedek (Psalm 110: 4). He shall judge the people with righteousness and the poor with judgment, and shall have dominion from sea to sea, and His name shall endure forever (Psalm 72: 2, 8, 17). In glowing terms Isaiah declares that *there shall come forth a rod out of the stem of Jesse, and a Branch shall grow out of his roots: and the spirit of the Lord shall rest upon him, the spirit of wisdom and understanding, the spirit of counsel and might, the spirit of knowledge and of the fear of the Lord; and shall make him of quick understanding in the fear of the Lord* (Isaiah 11: 1-3). He should have as His mission, *to open the blind eyes, to bring out the prisoners from the prison, and them that sit in darkness out of the prison house* (Isaiah 42: 7), words which Jesus applied to Himself in the synagogue at Nazareth (Luke 4: 18-21). Jeremiah shared the same hope with the rest of the prophets and exclaimed, *Behold, the days come, saith the Lord, that I will raise unto David a righteous Branch, and a King shall reign and prosper, and shall execute judgment and justice in the earth. In his days Judah shall be saved, and Israel shall dwell safely: and this is his name whereby he shall be called, THE LORD OUR RIGHTEOUSNESS* (Jer. 23: 5, 6). Micah and Zechariah give utterance to the prophecies which were used during the lifetime of Jesus on earth as evidences of prophetic prediction. *But thou, Bethlehem Ephratah, though thou be little among the thousands of Judah, yet out of thee shall he come forth unto me that is to be ruler in Israel; whose goings forth have been from of old, from everlasting* (Micah 5: 2). *Rejoice greatly, O daughter of Zion; shout, O daughter of Jerusalem: behold, thy King cometh unto thee: he is just, and having salvation; lowly, and riding upon an ass, and upon a colt the foal of an ass* (Zech. 9: 9). It is Daniel, however, who gives us the picture of the majesty of Christ, and who prophesies of the kingdom beginning in Him and stretching on into the future when all things shall be put into subjection to Him and God be all in all. *I saw in the night visions, and, behold, one like the Son of man came with the clouds of heaven, and came to the Ancient of days, and they brought him near before him. And there was given him dominion, and glory, and a kingdom, that all people, nations and languages, should serve him: his dominion is an everlasting dominion, which shall not pass away, and his kingdom that which shall not be destroyed* (Daniel 7: 13, 14).

The wealth of Christ's person, however, transcends the predictions of prophecy. His historical manifestation exceeds in glory anything that the heart of men might conceive, or that perhaps the prophets themselves could fully comprehend, even when speaking under the inspiration of the Spirit. One can but sympathize with Herman Shultz, who in commenting upon Isaiah 53 says, "The figure from which he starts is the actual historical figure of which he has so often spoken. But he is raised above himself. The figure which he beholds is embodied in an ideal figure in which he sees salvation accomplished, and all the riddles of the present solved. If it is true anywhere in the history of poetry and prophecy, it is true here, that the writer, being full of the Spirit, has said more than he himself meant to say, and more than he himself understood" (SCHULTZ, *Old Testament Theology*, II, pp. 431-433). That God should Himself create a living creature in His own image, a reflection of Himself is glorious; but that God himself in the Person of His Son should appear in the flesh, and take upon Him the likeness of men, transcends in glory all other manifestations human or divine. When we consider that the Incarnation was in itself redemptive as representing a new order of creation; and that it was provisional in its relation to the crucifixion, resurrection and ascension; and further, that to this glorious being was given the power of so transforming a sinful creature as to bring him into possession of the divine holiness, and so exalt a debased and groveling worm of the dust that he shall sit with Him on the throne of His majesty; then, this is not only indescribable but inconceivable. Yet here the glory of God and the glory of man are conjoined. In Him we find not only our calling's glorious hope, but in Him likewise are made the praise of His glory.

The Witness of the Holy Spirit. The last and highest evidence of revelation is found in the presence of the Holy Spirit in the Church, and His witness to sonship in the hearts of individuals. It must be constantly kept in mind that the Holy Spirit was not given to supersede Christ, but to enlarge and make more effective the work begun in the Incarnation. The spiritual Christ, or the Christ of the Holy Ghost, is not less personal than the historical Christ, nor is He less potent, but rather more potent than when tabernacling in the flesh. This our Lord himself conceded when He said to His disciples, *I have a baptism to be baptized with; and how am I straitened till it be accomplished!* (Luke 12: 50). In His farewell address, therefore, our Lord promises the Comforter to His disciples saying, *It is expedient for you that I go away; for if I go not away, the Comforter will not come to you; but if I depart, I will send him unto you* (John 16: 7). This Comforter is the Spirit of truth, which proceeds from the Father and testifies of Christ (John 15: 26); *He will reprove the world of sin, and of righteousness, and of judgment* (John 16: 8) and shall glorify Christ, speaking not of Himself, but receiving from Christ the things to be revealed to the disciples (John 16: 14).

The early Church recognized this testimony as its strongest evidence. Peter in his sermon at Pentecost declares, *This Jesus hath God raised up, whereof we are all witnesses,* and follows this with his testimony concerning the Holy Ghost as the promise of the exalted Christ. This is stated with even greater clearness in his address to the council, where he declares that *We are his witnesses of these things; and so is also the Holy Ghost, whom God hath given to them that obey him* (Acts 2: 32, 33, 5: 32). The Apostle Paul builds a strong argument upon the witness of the Holy Ghost, maintaining that the presence of unbelief as regards the Christian revelation is directly due to the rejection of the Spirit. He reminds the Corinthians that *No man can say that Jesus is the Lord, but by the Holy Ghost* (I Cor. 12: 3). He declares further, that his preaching was not with enticing words of man's wisdom *but in demonstration of the Spirit and of power; that their faith should not stand in the wisdom of men, but in the power of God* (I Cor. 2: 3, 4). Here St. Paul bears witness to a principle which is found throughout the Scriptures, that the Christian revelation is a gift of God, bestowed in connection with the prudent and prayerful use of our human faculties. John in his first epistle cites the double witness of the human and the divine. He opens his epistle by referring to that *which we have heard, which we have seen with our eyes, which we have looked upon, and our hands have handled of the Word of life* (I John 1: 1); but adds to this *if we receive the witness of men, the witness of God is greater* (I John 5: 9). As to the nature of this witness he says, *it is the Spirit that beareth witness, because the Spirit is truth* (I John 5: 6). But close attention to the apostle's thought shows that not only the individual believer *hath the witness in himself* (I John 5: 10); but that the Holy Spirit witnesses to the entire objective economy of salvation, both the water and the blood. The water evidently refers to Christ's baptism, by which He entered upon a new order of ministry and opened a new order of life to the believer; and the blood refers to the atonement by which full propitiation was made for the sins of the past. The author of the Epistle to the Hebrews likewise bears witness to the objective work of Christ. *But this man*, he says, *after he had offered one sacrifice for sins forever, sat down on the right hand of God; from henceforth expecting till his enemies be made his footstool. For by one offering he hath perfected forever them that are sanctified. Whereof the Holy Ghost also is a witness to us* (Heb. 10: 12-15). Here the Holy Spirit is regarded not in the specific sense as witnessing to the salvation of the individual believer, though this is included, but in the more general sense of attesting the truth of the atoning and intercessory work of Jesus Christ. The weight of this evidence as the writer regards it, and as the Church has ever received and borne witness to it, is best shown in the exhortation with which we close this discussion of the credentials of revelation. *See that ye refuse not him that speaketh. For if they escaped not who refused him that spake on earth, much more shall not we escape, if we turn away from him that speaketh from heaven: whose voice then shook the earth: but now he hath promised, saying, Yet once more I shake not the earth only, but also heaven* (Heb. 12: 25, 26).

Works on prophecy are numerous. Ralston treats the subject under three main heads, (I) Prophecies in relation to the Jews; (II) Prophecies in relation to Nineveh, Babylon and Tyre; and (III) Messianic Prophecies. Watson states that there are more than one hundred references to the Messiah in the various prophecies, and discusses several of these at great length. Riehm in his work on *Messianic Prophecy* cites such references as I Kings 22:17-36 where it was predicted that Ahab and Josiah would be defeated by the Syrians; Isaiah 7:18-25; 8:5-7 that Rezin and Pekah would not succeed in taking Jerusalem; also Isaiah 7:18-25 where Assyria would afflict Judah; and the destruction of Sennacherib's army 14:24-27. Jeremiah predicted the overthrow of the Jewish kingdom (Jer. 5:15-18) and also the return after seventy years (Jer. 25:12).—A. KEITH, "Evidences from Prophecy" is one of the older but authoritative books on this subject. Another of the older and standard works is Horne's "Introduction to the Scriptures" which has in the Appendix a large collection of the prophecies and their fulfillment.

CHAPTER VII

THE INSPIRATION OF THE SCRIPTURES

Religion and Revelation as we have seen, indicate the particular sphere in which the material of theology is to be sought. They must, therefore, in their application to religious faith in general, be regarded as more inclusive than Christian Theology. But these must be regarded in the broader sense of religious faith in general, rather than that of Christian Theology. The latter, as the science of Christianity, is based upon the documentary records of God's revelation of Himself in Christ Jesus. The Holy Scriptures are thus recognized by all schools as the *fons primarius* or true source of Christian Theology. They are the documents of the Christian religion, the depository of the Christian revelation. It is evident, therefore, that we should direct our inquiry to the nature and authority of the Holy Scriptures, which contain both the records of historical development and the finished result of divine revelation. This authority lies in the fact that they are an inspired revelation of God to man. They are divine in their origin—the product of the Holy Spirit's inspiration. In a theological sense, then, inspiration signifies the operation of the Holy Spirit upon the writers of the books of the Bible in such a manner that their productions become the expression of God's will. It is by this means that the Scriptures become the Word of God.

Definitions of Inspiration. Having pointed out the general nature of inspiration, it remains for us to define it more specifically, and to point out the varying uses of the term. The term "inspiration" is derived from the Greek word *theopneustos*, which signifies literally, "the breathing of God," or "the breathing into," and is therefore "that extraordinary agency of the Holy Spirit upon the mind in consequence of which the person who partakes of it is enabled to embrace and communicate the truth of God without error, infirmity, or defeat" (DR.

HANNAH). And this must be understood to apply to the
subjects of communication whether immediately revealed to them, or with which they were before acquainted. "By inspiration," says Farrar, "we mean that
influence of the Holy Spirit which, when inbreathed into
the mind of man, guides and elevates and enkindles all
his powers to their highest and noblest exercises." Pope
defines it as "the inbreathing of God and the result of
it." Strong shifts the emphasis of inspiration from a
mode of the divine agency to the body of truth which is
a product of this agency; and further, he holds that inspiration applies only to the whole body of Scripture
when taken together, each part being viewed in connection with what precedes and what follows. His definition
is as follows: "Inspiration is that influence of the Spirit
of God upon the minds of the Scripture writers which
made their writings the record of a progressive divine
revelation, sufficient when taken together and interpreted by the same Spirit who inspired them, to lead
every honest inquirer to Christ and salvation." In an
earlier but scholarly work entitled, *The Inspiration of
Scripture*, William Lee takes essentially the same position, maintaining that "the various parts of Holy Scripture, in order to be rightly understood, or justly valued,
must be regarded as the different members of one vitally
organized structure; each performing its appropriate
function, and each conveying its own portion of truth.
.... Had there been but one Gospel, the Church's teaching might have been, in like manner, one-sided. From
the Gospel of St. Matthew the higher nature of Christ
could not have been so clearly proved to the Ebionites,
as from that of St. John; while the former was better

"By inspiration we understand that actuating energy of the Holy
Spirit, guided by which the human agents chosen by God have officially
proclaimed His will by word of mouth, or have committed to writing
the several portions of the Bible.—FIELD, *Handbook of Christian Theology*, p. 53.

"On this subject the common doctrine of the Church is, and ever has
been, that inspiration was an influence of the Holy Spirit on the minds
of certain select men, which rendered them the organs of God for the
infallible communication of His mind and will. They were in such a sense
the organs of God, that what they said, God said."—HODGE, *Systematic
Theology*, p. 154.

calculated to oppose the dreams of the Gnostics. But the four Gospels, having been combined in the Canon, the Church has thus been defended on all sides. Hence the Gospels were well termed by an early father (Irenæus) the four pillars of the Church, each supporting its own portion of the structure, and guarding it from subsiding into any of those forms of false doctrine to which partial views of the truth had given rise" (pp. 31, 32). While the views of the Church concerning the theories have varied widely, there is no subject on which there has been a closer agreement as to the fact of inspiration itself. This we may summarize in this general definition, Inspiration is the actuating energy of the Holy Spirit by which holy men chosen of God have officially proclaimed His will as revealed to us in the sacred Scriptures.

Inspiration and Revelation. By *Revelation* we understand a direct communication from God to man of such knowledge as is beyond the power of his reason to attain, or for whatever cause was not known to the person who received it. By *Inspiration* we mean the actuating energy of the Holy Spirit through which holy men were qualified to receive religious truth, and to communicate it to others without error. The disclosure of the mind of God

"But whence the title Holy Scriptures?" inquires William Lee. "Traced to its true source, this notion depends upon the fact, that the ideas of the Eternal Word, and of the Divine Spirit, are here to a certain degree correlative. The Word as divine and eternally *creative*, has the Spirit as the divine and eternally *animating* principle, in and with Himself. By the agency of the Divine Spirit the meaning and will of the Eternal Word are introduced into the real being of things. All divine activity in the world is organic. So also the arrangements of God's Revelation form a system which comprehends all things; which aids in bringing light into darkness; whose center is Christ, to whom every revelation in earlier times must be referred, and from every revelation, of a later period, has proceeded, by virtue of that Holy Spirit imparted through Him to the world. This agency of the Holy Spirit, by the very force of the term, forms the essence of the idea of inspiration; and the two conceptions thus pointed out, of the Eternal Word as the Divine Person who reveals, and of the Holy Spirit as the Divine Person who inspires, are the pillars upon which must rest any theory respecting the Bible and its origin which can deserve serious notice.—WILLIAM LEE, *The Inspiration of the Scripture,* pp. 25, 26.

In God as Logos, Word and Act are ever united: He spake, and it was done, He commanded, and it stood fast (Psalm 33:9).

The transition to a written document, composed according to God's will, can detract in no respect from the power and efficacy of His Word. On this assumption rests the whole notion of Inspiration.—RUDELBACH (Cf. LEE, *Inspiration,* p. 25).

to man is Revelation when viewed from the standpoint of the truth unveiled; it is Inspiration when viewed in relation to the methods of its impartation and transmission. These distinctions find their deepest meaning in the differences of office as it pertains to the Son or to the Spirit. The Son is the Revealer, the Holy Spirit is the Inspirer. The Son is the living and eternal Word of God in whom dwelt the fullness of grace and truth (John 1: 14), and *in whom are hid all the treasures of wisdom and knowledge* (Col. 2: 3). Jesus as the Divine Word was both Revealer and Revelation. As Revealer, our Lord declared that no man knoweth the Father, *save the Son, and he to whomsoever the Son will reveal him* (Matt. 11: 27 cf. Luke 10: 22). As Revelation He is God *manifest in the flesh* (I Tim. 2: 16). The Holy Spirit is the inspirer, whose office work is to make known to men the truth as it is in Christ Jesus. Jesus is the Truth, the Holy Spirit is the Spirit of truth. Hence it is said, *He shall glorify me: for he shall receive of mine, and shall shew it unto you* (John 16: 14). There are some expressions in Scripture which exhibit both revelation and inspiration, as in Hebrews 1: 1, 2. *God who at sundry times and in divers manners spake in times past to the fathers by the prophets; hath in these last days spoken unto us by his Son.* Here there is a reference to revelation as the body of truth received by the prophets, and also to inspiration as the method by which they received and administered this truth. The "sundry times" can only refer to the progressive nature of revelation and indicates the successive stages in which God revealed the truth to the ancient prophets. The "divers manners" refers more especially to the fact of inspiration which includes visions, dreams, ecstasy or other forms of manifestation found in the Old Testament. Here then revelation and inspiration are conjoined, and what was implicit in the Old Testament comes to its perfection in the New Testament, and this as it concerns both content and method.

The Possibilities of Inspiration. Unquestionably the Father of spirits may act upon the minds of His creatures, and this action may be extended to any degree necessary for the fulfillment of the purposes of God. This truth has given rise to what is known as degrees in revelation, but which more strictly should be regarded as factors in all revelation. The first is "superintendence," by which is meant a belief that God so guides those chosen as the organs of revelation, that their writings are kept free from error. Following this is the factor of "elevation," in which the minds of the chosen organs are granted an enlargement of understanding, and an elevation of conception beyond the natural measure of man. The highest and most important is the factor of "suggestion," by which is meant a direct and immediate suggestion from God to man by the Spirit, as to the thoughts which he shall use, or even the very words which he shall employ, in order to make them agencies in conveying His will to others. These factors in varying degrees must enter into any clear thought of inspiration, but to regard them as different degrees of inspiration, as if the several portions of the Scripture were in different degrees the Word of God is necessarily to weaken the authority of the Bible as a whole. The error springs from a failure to distinguish between revelation as the varying quantity, and inspiration as the constant; the one furnishing the material by "suggestion" when not otherwise attainable, the other guiding the writer at every point, thus securing at once the infallible truth of his material, and its proper selection and distribution. For this reason we conclude that the Scriptures were given by plenary inspiration, embracing throughout the elements of superintendence, elevation and suggestion, in that manner and to that degree that the Bible becomes the infallible Word of God, the authoritative rule of faith and practice in the Church.

Nor can our inability to explain this extraordinary

Abstract the idea of the inspiring Spirit guiding the pen of the sacred writer in every sentence, word and letter, from the holy Gospels, and the heavenly unction—the divine power of the Book is gone. It is no longer the record of heaven we trace—no longer the voice of God which we hear. The Shekinah has left the mercy seat; the divine sacrifice ceases to smoke upon the altar, and the glory has departed from the Christian temple.—RALSTON, *Elements of Divinity*, p. 600.

action of God upon the human mind be an objection to the doctrine of inspiration. Psychology cannot satisfactorily explain the interaction between the mind and body in human personality, nor the manner in which ideas are impressed upon the mind. But it would be impertinent to deny the existence of such interaction. If men can communicate their thoughts by means of language and thus make themselves understood by others, most certainly the Author of our being can reveal Himself to men. It is unreasonable to suppose that God as the "Father of spirits" does not have it in His power to communicate truth to the minds of men, or to instruct them in those things which concern their eternal wellbeing.

The Necessity of Inspiration. That inspiration is necessary, grows out of the nature of the subjects which the Scriptures unfold. *First,* there are truths which could not otherwise be known except by special inspiration. There are historical truths, past facts, which if God had not revealed them in a supernatural manner could never have been known, such as the creation of the world and the history of antediluvian times. Granting that there were written sources and oral traditions which had been handed down from former times, even then the inspiration of superintendence would have been necessary in order to a true and inerrant account. *Second,* the authoritative language of the Scriptures argues the necessity of inspiration. The writers do not present to us their own thoughts but preface their communications with a *Thus saith the Lord.* On this ground alone they demand assent. It follows, then, that either the sacred writers spoke as they were moved by the Holy Spirit,

It is reasonable that the sentiments and doctrines developed in the Holy Scriptures should be suggested to the mind of the writers by the Supreme Being himself. They are every way worthy of His character, and promotive of the highest interests of man; and the more important the communication is, the more it is calculated to preserve men from error, to stimulate them to holiness, and to guide them to happiness, the more reasonable it is to expect that God should make the communication free from every admixture of error. Indeed, the notion of inspiration enters essentially into our ideas of a revelation from God, so that to deny it is the same as to affirm that there is no revelation.— WAKEFIELD, *Christian Theology,* p. 72.

or they must be acknowledged as impostors, a conclusion invalidated by the quality and enduring character of their works. Again, if the Scriptures were not divinely inspired, they could not claim as they do, to be the infallible standard of religious truth. Only as we are convinced that the writers were aided by a supernatural and divine influence, and this in such a manner as to be infallibly preserved from all error, can the sacred Scriptures become a divine rule of faith and practice.

THEORIES OF INSPIRATION

Various theories have been advanced, in an attempt to harmonize and explain the relation of the divine and human elements, in the inspiration of the Scriptures. Christianity, however, is based upon the fact of inspiration, and is not dependent upon any particular theory as to the origin of its sacred writings. The rationalistic explanations emphasize unduly the human element, while the supranaturalistic theories minify it, maintaining that the sacred writers were so possessed by the Holy Spirit as to become passive instruments rather than active agents. The dynamical theory is advanced in an attempt to mediate between the two extremes, and is the theory most generally accepted in the Church. The so-called erroneous theories it will be noted, are such, not because they are essentially wrong, but because by unduly emphasizing one particular element, they thereby become inadequate as explanations of the wide range of Scripture phenomena. We shall classify these theories as follows: (1) The Mechanical or Dictation Theory which emphasizes the supranaturalistic element; (2) the Intuition and Illumination Theories which stress the human element; and (3) the Dynamical or Mediating Theory.

The Mechanical or Dictation Theory. This theory emphasizes the supranaturalistic element to such an extent that the personality of the writer is set aside, and he becomes under the direction of the Holy Spirit a mere amanuensis or penman. As a representative of this extreme position, Hooker says, "They neither spake nor wrote any word of their own, but uttered syllable by syllable as the Spirit put it into their mouths." In order to account for the peculiarities of individual expression on this theory Quenstedt says, "The Holy Ghost inspired his amanuenses with those expressions which they would have employed, had they been left to themselves." An extravagant doctrine of mechanical inspiration grew up among the Jews after the exile and prevailed in the time of Christ. Some of the Talmudists held that Moses wrote all the Pentateuch including the description of his own death which he did with tears. By most Talmudists the last eight verses are attributed to Joshua. Christ's freedom in the use of the Scriptures shows how far He rose above the bondage of the letter. If He said, "It is written," He also said, "But I say unto you." Against the weakness of this theory may be urged the following objections. *First,* it denies the inspiration of persons and holds only to the inspiration of the writings; whereas the Scriptures teach that *holy men of God spake as they were moved by the Holy Ghost* (II Peter 1: 21). It is for this reason that Dr. I. A. Dorner in his *System of Christian Doctrine* (I, p. 624) speaks of this as a "docetic theory," in that the writers were only so in appearance, all second causes being done away in the pure passivity of the instruments. *Second,* the Mechanical Theory does not comport with all the facts.

According to Philo, "A prophet gives forth nothing at all of his own, but acts as interpreter at the prompting of another in all his utterances, and as long as he is under the inspiration he is in ignorance, his reason departing from its place and yielding up the citadel of the soul, when the divine Spirit enters into it and dwells in it and strikes at the mechanism of the voice, sounding through it to the clear declaration of that which he prophesieth." "Josephus holds that even the historical narratives were obtained by direct inspiration from God," so that as the Rabbis said, "Moses did not write one word out of his own knowledge."

Dr. Charles Hodge, who holds that the inspiration of the Scriptures extends to the words, says that "this is included in the infallibility which our Lord ascribes to the Scriptures. A mere human report or record of a divine revelation must of necessity be not only fallible, but more or less erroneous. The thoughts are in the words. The two are inseparable. If the words priest, sacrifice, ransom, expiation, propitiation by blood, and the like, have no divine authority, then the doctrine which they embody had no such divine authority." It is evident, however, that in so far as Dr. Hodge's statement is true, it belongs rather to the dynamical than to the mechanical theory of inspiration.

It is evident from the Scriptures themselves that the writers were actuated in different ways—though by the inspiration of one Spirit. Some of the disclosures of truth were in audible words. *And when Moses was gone into the tabernacle of the congregation to speak with him, then he heard the voice of one speaking unto him from off the mercy seat that was upon the ark of testimony, from between the two cherubims: and he spake unto him* (Num. 7:89). Again in Acts 9:5 Paul exclaims, *Who art thou, Lord? and the Lord said, I am Jesus whom thou persecutest.* These Scriptures can mean nothing else than a revelation in audible words. (Compare also Exod. 2:4, 20:22, Heb. 12:19, Dan. 4:31, Matt. 3:17, 17:5, Rev. 19:9 also 1:10, 11.) But the writers in a number of instances referred to sources, or they used their own knowledge of history, or recorded their own experiences. Such is the case in Luke's Gospel and also in the Acts of the Apostles. *Third,* and perhaps the strongest argument against this theory is the fact that it is out of harmony with the known manner in which God works in the human soul. The higher and more exalted the divine communications, the greater the illumination of the human soul and the more fully does man come into possession of his own natural and spiritual faculties. The Mechanical Theory may apply in a few instances, but it is too narrow and insufficient to establish a general theory of inspiration.

The Intuition Theory. According to this theory, inspiration is only the natural insight of men lifted to a higher plane of development. It is rationalistic in the extreme, and virtually denies the supernatural element in the Scriptures. Its weakness lies in this, that man's insight into truth is vitiated by a darkened intellect and wrong affections. *The natural man receiveth not the things of the Spirit of God: for they are foolishness unto him; neither can he know them, because they are spiritually discerned* (I Cor. 2:14). He cannot therefore of himself penetrate the divine mysteries, and needs a direct communication of truth through the Spirit. "The Intuition Theory," says Sheldon, "disparages the notion

of the direct operation of the Holy Spirit, and implies
that the educated faculties of the scriptural writers, by
their own virtue grasped all the truth which they conveyed."

The Illumination Theory. This theory differs from
the preceding in that it holds to an elevation of the religious perceptions instead of the natural faculties. It
has been likened to the spiritual illumination which
every believer receives from the Holy Spirit in Christian experience. The inspiration of the writers of sacred
Scripture, according to this theory differs only in the degree not in kind,. from that which belongs to all believers. While illumination through intensification of experience may prepare the mind for the reception of truth,
it is not in itself a communication of that truth. It will
be seen that the element of "elevation" mentioned previously is here expanded beyond its rightful place, and
thus becomes the basis of an erroneous theory of inspiration.

The Dynamical Theory. This is a mediating theory
and is advanced in an effort to explain and preserve in
proper harmony, both the divine and human factors in
the inspiration of the Scriptures. It maintains that the
sacred writers were given extraordinary aid without any
interference with their personal characteristics or activities. It preserves the scriptural truth that God speaks
through human agencies, but insists that the agent is
not reduced to a mere passive instrument. Against this
theory little objection can be urged. It has been held by
such standard theologians as Pope, Miley, Strong, Wat-

Among those who have held to the Illumination Theory may be mentioned the following: E. G. Robinson, "The office of the Spirit in inspiration is not different from that which he performed for the Christians at the time when the Gospels were written"; Ladd, "Inspiration,
as the subjective condition of biblical revelation and the predicate of
the Word of God, is specifically the same illumining. quickening, ele-
vating and purifying work of the Holy Spirit as that which goes on in
the persons of the entire believing community."

A. A. Hodge rejects the Illumination Theory. "Spiritual illumination," he says, "is an essential element in the sanctifying work of the
Holy Spirit common to all true Christians. It never leads to the knowledge of new truth, but only to the personal discernment of the spiritual
beauty and power of truth already revealed in the Scriptures."—HODGE,
Outlines of Theology, p. 68.

son, Wakefield, Summers, Ralston and Hills, and with some modification by Curtis, Sheldon, Martensen and Dorner. In opposition to the Intuition Theory, it maintains there is a supernatural element in inspiration, as over against mere intuitive natural reason. In harmony with the Illumination Theory, it maintains that there was an "elevation" on the part of the sacred writers which prepared their minds and hearts for the reception of the message, but insists that the theory is inadequate, in that to the prepared agencies there must be in addition a divine communication of truth.

SCRIPTURAL PROOFS OF DIVINE INSPIRATION

The Scriptures claim to be divinely inspired. Since the term inspiration denotes the specific agency of the Holy Spirit as Author of the sacred Scriptures, it is required of us to give first place to the testimony of the Bible itself. Pope points out that it is not arguing in a circle to receive the witness of the Bible concerning itself, if we remember that in things divine credentials are always first, and must be sustained by their own evidences. These credentials will be considered in the following order, *First,* the Witness of the Old Testament; *Second,* the Declaration of our Lord; and *Third,* the Testimony of the Apostles.

The Witness of the Old Testament. Communications of divine truth were given at sundry times and in divers manners, to the writers of the Old Testament. The patriarchs received revelations from God, and some of these were written down, but it is evident that these records were not by themselves officially declared as Scripture. Moses seems to have been given a special prerogative as the founder of Israel as a nation, for it is recorded of him that *there arose not a prophet since in Israel like unto Moses, whom the Lord knew face to face* (Deut. 34:10). To him was granted the privilege of creating the first body of literature known as sacred Scripture. Knowing that he was inspired of the Spirit, Moses frequently reminded those whom he addressed, that his messages were given by divine authority and no phrase is of more frequent recurrence than the well-known words, *The Lord spake unto Moses.* David laid claim also to divine inspiration, saying, *The Spirit of the Lord spake by me, and his word was in my tongue* (II Sam. 23:2). The later prophets delivered their predictions, not only in the name of the Lord, but as messages immediately inspired by the Spirit. Isaiah frequently introduced his prophetic messages with the words, *Thus saith the Lord;* while Jeremiah, Ezekiel and a number of the minor prophets used such expressions as *The word of the Lord came unto me, The Lord said unto me,* or *Thus saith the Lord.* Moses seems to have anticipated in his prophecy the coming of a new age, in which the Holy Spirit should be communicated in His prophetic offices to all the people of God. *Would God that all the Lord's people were prophets, and that the Lord would put his spirit upon them!* (Num. 11:29). This is doubtless a prophetic reference to Pentecost, and must be understood in a different sense from that by which original revelations were given to men. Christ is the true and highest revelation of God, and the coming of the Spirit is the realization and interpretation of the truth as it is in Him.

The Declaration of Our Lord. Christ declared the Old Testament to be of divine authority, and His testimony must be the final word as to the nature and results of inspiration. His witness is perfect in meeting the demands of Christian faith. He regarded the Old Testament as a completed canon, and expressly declared that the least ordinance or commandment must have its perfect fulfillment. This is the meaning of the words *one jot or tittle* (Matt. 5:18). To this we may add that the nature of our Lord's testimony is such, that while sanctioning the whole body of sacred writers, he speaks as one above them. He never claims for Himself the limited inspiration of the prophets for *it pleased the Father that in him should all fulness dwell* (Col. 1:19) and again, *For in him dwelleth all the fulness of the Godhead bodily* (Col. 2:9). In this connection, also, we have the testimony of John the Baptist to the supreme authority of Christ. *He that cometh from above is above all; he that is of the earth is earthly, and speaketh of the earth: he that cometh from heaven is above all. . . . . For he whom God hath sent speaketh the words of God: for God giveth not the Spirit by measure unto him* (John 3: 31, 34). Here the fullness of revelation and the highest form of inspiration are conjoined in the words of Christ.

To the Jews who opposed Him, He said, *Why do ye also transgress the commandment of God by your tradition?* (Matt. 15: 3, 6). Here the Old Testament is expressly stated to be the Word of God. To the tempter in the wilderness, Christ replied, *It is written,* a formula which among the Jews signified that the quotation was from one of the sacred books and therefore divinely inspired. Jesus quotes from four out of the five books of Moses, from the Psalms, from Isaiah, Zechariah and Malachi. He recognized the threefold division of the Scriptures which was common among the Jews—the law, the prophets and the psalms (Luke 24: 44, 45), and declared that these testified of Himself. This is brought out again in a controversy with the Jews, in which He says, *Search the scriptures; for in them ye think ye have eternal life: and they are they which testify of me* (John 5: 39). He further asserted that the Scriptures were the Word of God, and that the Scriptures cannot be broken (John 10: 35). In His postresurrection exposition to the two disciples on the way to Emmaus, it is said that *beginning at Moses and all the prophets, he expounded unto them in all the scriptures the things concerning himself* (Luke 24: 27). Here He recognized the whole content of Scripture in its unity and declares specifically that it refers to His own Person and work.

The Testimony of the Apostles. It remains for us to consider now, the testimony of the apostles concerning the inspiration of both the Old and the New Testaments. First, consideration must be given to the testimony of the Apostle Peter, who immediately before Pentecost stood up among the apostles and other disciples and said, *Men and brethren, this scripture must needs have been fulfilled, which the Holy Ghost by the mouth of David spake before concerning Judas, which was guide to them that took Jesus* (Acts 1:16). This statement has been regarded by some as a general definition of inspiration—*the Holy Ghost spake, the mouth of David* was the instrument, and the result was *Scripture*. (Cf. POPE, *Compend. Chr. Theology*, I, p. 164). St. Paul quotes the Old Testament constantly in his writings, using a wide variety of terms, such as *the scriptures of the prophets* (Rom. 16:26), *the holy scriptures* (II Tim. 3:14), and other similar expressions. He asserts the unity of the scripture in the text, *All scripture is given by inspiration of God,* and declares its purpose as *profitable for doctrine, for reproof, for correction, for instruction in righteousness: that the man of God may be perfect, thoroughly furnished unto all good works* (II Tim. 3:16, 17). The nature of the Epistle to the Hebrews is such that the whole composition depends upon the Old Testament as Holy Scripture. This it regards as the oracles of God, spoken by the Holy Spirit and preserved to the Christian Church in a book quoted as authoritative and infallible. Another peculiarity of this epistle lies in the fact that the same expression is used to indicate both the testimony of the Spirit and the personality of the writer. In quoting Jer. 31:31 the writer of the epistle says, *The Holy Ghost also is a witness to us; for after that he had said before, This is the covenant that I will make with them after those days, saith the Lord, I will put my laws into their hearts, and in their minds will I write them* (Heb. 10:16, 17). A further contribution of this epistle is to be found in the fact that it regards the Old Testament as a rudimentary phase of divine revelation, and the Christian or New Testament as the completion of that previously begun. Hence we read the injunction of the writer that *ye have need that one teach you again which be the first principles of the oracles of God,* that is, the Old Testament (Heb. 5:12).

We must consider also the testimony of the apostles as to the inspiration of the New Testament Scriptures. As a body of men, they are united in their belief that their messages are from God their Saviour and by His Holy Spirit. Everywhere the fact of inspiration is implied. But there are direct assertions also which form indisputable evidence of inspiration. Referring to St. Peter we have the exhortation to be *mindful of the words which were spoken before by the holy prophets, and of the commandment of us the apostles of the Lord and Saviour* (II Peter 3: 2). Here the revelation made to the Old Testament prophets, and that made to the New Testament apostles, are placed side by side as being of equal authority. This thought is further developed later on in the chapter, where he speaks of some things hard to be understood in the writings of St. Paul, *which they that are unlearned and unstable wrest, as they do also the other Scriptures, unto their own destruction* (II Peter 3: 16). Here is a direct and definite testimony to the inspiration of the writings of St. Paul, which are classed with *"other scriptures"* as of equal authority. St. Paul himself, ascribes his revelations to Christ, and his inspiration to the Holy Spirit. Of the first he testifies that God called him by His grace, *to reveal his Son* in him, that he might preach Him among the heathen (Gal. 1: 16); and again that it was *by revelation* that the mystery was made known unto him (Eph. 3: 3); while of the second he testifies, *Now we have received, not the spirit of the world, but the spirit which is of God; that we might know the things that are freely given to us of God. Which things also we speak, not in the words which man's wisdom teacheth, but which the Holy Ghost teacheth: comparing spiritual things with spiritual* (I Cor. 2: 12, 13). Nor can we omit the testimony of St. John, who in his First Epistle speaks of *an unction from the Holy One* (I John 2: 20), a privilege which in some measure belongs to all true believers, but in its highest degree, as before pointed out, belongs only to the company of apostles and prophets as the writers of the Christian Scriptures. However, in the Apocalypse, it is expressly stated that he was *in the Spirit* (Rev. 1: 10), which in connection with a verse in the last chapter indicates that the writer was thinking of the expression in the sense in which it was used of the Old Testament prophets who spoke by inspiration. Consequently we read, *These sayings are faithful and true: and the Lord God of the holy prophets sent his angel to shew unto his servants the things which must shortly be done* (Rev. 22:6). As to the two historical evangelists, St. Mark and St. Luke, these did not share directly and immediately in the promise to the apostolate, but only indirectly and mediately through St. Peter and St. Paul. Further consideration will be given to these writers in the study of the Canon.

VALUE OF THE SUBJECT FOR THEOLOGY

No subject has been of greater importance in the study of theology, than that which has been under consideration—the Inspiration of the Scriptures. Referring again to the verse, *the Holy Ghost spake through the mouth of David* (Acts 1:16) we may consider the theological value of the subject from three aspects: *first,* the Holy Spirit as the Source of Inspiration; *second,* holy men as the organs of inspiration; and *third,* the Holy Scriptures as a divinely inspired body of truth.

The Holy Spirit as the Source of Inspiration. As paternity is the property of the Father and filiation the property of the Son, so procession belongs to the Spirit. As the Son is the revealer of the Father and therefore the eternal Word, so the Inspiring Spirit proceeding from the Father and the Son, is the sole basis of communication between God and man. It is seen, therefore, that the Holy Spirit is the Spirit of truth, and as such, presides over the impartation of all truth. As it relates to the revealing work of the Son, He alone is the Author of Inspiration. We may say, then, "that while the Scripture is God-inspired, only the Spirit is the inspiring God."

The Organs of Inspiration. In stressing the fact that the Bible is the Word of God, and hence inspired by the Spirit which gives it divine authority, we must not overlook the fact, also, that the Bible has in it a human element. Not only did the Holy Spirit speak through David, David also spoke. *Holy men,* we are told, *spake as they were moved by the Holy Ghost,* a better rendering being, "Holy men spake from God, being moved by the Holy Ghost." The two Scriptures are not opposed to each other, but together express the full-orbed range of inspiration. As Jesus the Word of God was at once divine and human, so the written Word of God must be viewed in the same light. To overlook the two natures in Christ is to turn to unitarianism on the one hand or docetism on the other. To overlook the two elements in the written Word, is to undervalue either its divine authority or its human appeal. As Jesus was crucified through weakness, yet lived by the power of God, so the Bible has been ceaselessly and bitterly attacked by its enemies, yet ever lives as an enduring monument of divine truth. As it was necessary for Jesus to become a partaker of our infirmities in order to appeal to the hearts of men, so also the Bible is extremely human in its character, searching the hearts of men, *quick and powerful, and sharper than any twoedged sword, piercing even to the dividing asunder of soul and spirit, and of the joints and marrow, and is a discerner of the thoughts and intents of the heart* (Heb. 4:12).

The organs of inspiration had both character and preparation. They were holy men. They were sanctified through the truth and thus prepared for their office and work. As moral and spiritual truth can be understood only by moral and spiritual men, the organs of inspiration must of necessity have been holy in heart and life. Their faculties were prepared by the immediate influence of the inspiring Spirit, and He used them for the accomplishment of the end in view, the formation of the sacred Scriptures. They were not merely passive instruments, but active agents in the full range of their powers. Their natural characteristics and endowments were not submerged but elevated and strengthened.

The Holy Scriptures as a Divinely Inspired Body of Truth. It follows that if God spake through holy men, their utterances must constitute a body of divine truth. It is to this body of truth that we apply the term Holy Scripture. As such we must regard the Bible as given to us by plenary inspiration. By this term we do not refer to any one of the particular theories of inspiration already cited, but to the character of the whole body of truth. By plenary inspiration, we mean that the whole and every part is divinely inspired. This does not necessarily presuppose the mechanical theory of inspiration, as some contend, or any particular method, only that the results of that inspiration give us the Holy Scriptures as the final and authoritative rule of faith in the Church.

In this connection the question sometimes arises as to what assurance we have that Christ intended to preserve and continue His teachings in a new volume of sacred Scripture. All that we need is given to us in one comprehensive promise made to His disciples. *I have yet many things to say unto you, but ye cannot bear them now. Howbeit when he, the Spirit of truth, is come, he will guide you into all truth: for he shall not speak of himself; but whatsoever he shall hear, that shall he speak: and he will shew you things to come. He shall glorify me: for he shall receive of mine, and shall shew it unto you* (John 16:12-14). Our Lord sanctioned the Old Testament Scriptures as the preparatory records of His own gospel and kingdom. It was necessary, therefore, that these be brought to their perfection by the New Testament Scriptures, which should fill out their meaning, and set upon the entire body of Scripture the seal of His perfect revelation.

Christ made full provision for the preservation of His perfected doctrine. All that we need to assure our hearts was given in one large promise, which declared that His sayings should be revived in their unbroken unity in His disciples' memory. He shall teach you all things, and bring all things to your remembrance whatsoever I have said unto you; that which He could not yet speak concerning His Person, His Spirit should reveal, He will guide you into all truth; and that the same Spirit should show them things to come. The Spirit was no other than Himself by His Agent reuttering His own words, revealing His own Person and work, and filling up His prophecy of the future. Hence, lastly, our Lord's sanction makes the complete Scriptures the finished revelation, never to be superseded. Nothing can be more plain that the entire fullness of what the Revealer had to say to the world was to be communicated to the apostles by the Holy Ghost; and that, not as a further disclosure on the part of the Spirit, but as the consolidation of the Saviour's teaching into its perfect unity, and its expansion into its perfect meaning. No future streams of revelation were to rise higher than the fountainhead of truth opened in Himself. Hence we may repeat concerning the Book what has been said concerning our Lord's teaching; the Bible means all revelation, and all revelation means the Bible.—POPE, *Compend. Chr. Th.*, I, pp. 40, 41.

CHAPTER VIII

THE CANON

We have considered the subject of Revelation, objectively as an apocalypse or divine unveiling of the truth, and subjectively as the faith received by man; and we have further considered the divine-human manner in which this revelation was committed to writing through the inspiration of the Spirit; it remains for us to complete this study by considering more in detail the specific character of the Bible as containing the divinely authorized documents of the Christian faith. This leads us directly to a study of the Canon of Holy Scripture, which we must regard not only as the Christian rule of faith and practice, but also as the ultimate critical standard of religious thought.

By the canonicity of a book is meant its right to a place in the collection of sacred writings. The word canon (*κανών*) means literally, a straight rod, or a measuring reed. It is used in both an active and a passive sense—active as a test or standard of measurement, passive as applied to that which has been measured. In this dual sense, the word *canon* is applied to Holy Scripture. In the objective sense, the canonical books are those which have measured up to the standard tests. In a subjective sense, these measured or canonical books become the Rule of Faith in the Church. This seems to be the meaning of Gal. 6: 16 where the Apostle Paul pronounces a benediction upon *as many as walk according to this rule*. Semler and others held that the word *canon* originally meant simply a *list* and was employed by early ecclesiastical writers to designate a catalogue of things that belonged to the Church. In this sense it was applied to a collection of hymns to be sung on festival occasions, and in some instances to the list of the names of church members. It was particularly applied to the publicly approved catalogue of all the books that

might be read in the Church for edification and instruction. In this sense it is thought to discriminate between
the canonical books which might be read authoritatively
in the Church, and the apocryphal which might be read
for instruction but not as a standard or rule of faith.
Bicknell agrees with this, pointing out that the word
canonical (κανονίζειν) was sometimes applied to a single
book, but indicates that it soon came to be used in the
more general sense as a standard to which an appeal
could be made (Cf. BICKNELL, *Thirty-Nine Articles,*
p. 176).

The word *canon* is first found in the writings of
Amphilochius (380), though Athanasius uses the word
canonical in his *Festal Epistle* (367). Since the time of
Jerome, the term *canon* has been used in both the objective and subjective senses, the one dependent upon
the other. The word *Biblia* has been in use since the
fifth century and signifies a collection of books *par excellence.* It was probably first used by Chrysostom.

Before taking up a more detailed study of the development of the canon, the following observations are
necessary.

1. The canonicity of a book was not settled by the
authority of the primitive Church, but by its testimony.
This is an important distinction. As the church does
not rest its belief in miracles on the authority of the
early Christians, but on their witness and attestation,
so in the matter of the Gospels and Epistles, it was not
their decision as to the inspiration of the contents that
renders them authoritative now, but their tesimony as
to their apostolic authorship. "The authority of the first
Christians," says Dr. Shedd, "is no higher than that of
any other Christians, but their testimony is" (SHEDD,
Dogm. Th., I, p. 142).

   Dr. Shedd refers to a statement by Coleridge to this effect, that "we
receive the books ascribed to John and Paul as their books, on the
judgment of men for whom no miraculous discernment is pretended.
Shall we give these less credence than to John and Paul themselves? The
modern Church does not receive John's Gospel and Paul's Epistles as
canonical, on the 'judgment' or decision of the primitive Church respecting their contents, but on their testimony respecting their authorship."—
SHEDD, *Dogm. Th.,* p. 142.

2. The tests which the early Christians applied to the books circulated among the churches were simple, being limited generally to apostolic origin or authorization. It was held as an unquestioned fact that the Lord committed to the apostles alone the authority to direct the Church, and therefore all that was demanded was a certain knowledge of apostolic authority. For this reason the Gospels of St. Mark and St. Luke were never questioned, for they were understood to have been written by the authority of St. Peter and St. Paul. When authorship was uncertain, the so-called *Regula Fidei*, or "rule of faith" as indicated above was brought to bear, and in addition to this the testimony of those churches that held these documents. But this harmony with the rule of faith, and this testimony of the individual churches, were always regarded as subordinate though sufficient tests.

3. The human element in the formation of the canon needs to be given proper consideration also. In this respect there is a parallel between the Holy Scriptures and Him of whom they testify. This parallel we have already indicated, but must now give it further emphasis. As there is in the Person of our Lord a divine and a human side, united in the one life of the God-man; so in the sacred Scriptures there is divine revelation, law and promise on the one side, and human apprehension and representation on the other. As in the doctrines concerning the Person of Christ there was Docetism on the one hand which minified the humanity of Christ in order to exalt His deity, so there was on the other hand, Socinianism which magnified His humanity at the expense of His divinity. The Scriptures have likewise had their Docetists and their Socinians, an exaltation which amounted almost to bibliolatry on the one hand and a rationalism on the other, which had as its avowed purpose and attempt to reduce the Bible wholly to a human plane. Van Oosterzee says that at every step the impartial reader must exclaim, "How divine!" and again "How human!" As a failure to grasp and hold the great truth that the Personal Word incarnate was both divine and human led to heretical opinions, so any undue emphasis

upon either phase of the Scriptures to the detriment of the other will prove disastrous, to both correct doctrine and genuine experience.

THE OLD TESTAMENT CANON

The Old Testament Scriptures were arranged in three main divisions, (I) The Law *(Torah);* (II) The Prophets *(Nabiim)*; and (III) The Writings *(Kethubim)*, the latter being generally known as the *Hagiographa*. The first division included the Pentateuch; the second was divided into the Former or Earlier Prophets which included the historical books of Joshua, Judges, Samuel and Kings; and the Latter Prophets, Isaiah, Jeremiah, Ezekiel and the Twelve; the third division included the Psalms, Proverbs and Job, Daniel, Ezra, Nehemiah, the Chronicles, and the five "rolls" or *Megilloth*—Songs of Solomon, Ruth, Lamentations, Ecclesiastes and Esther. Since the Psalms formed the first book in the third division, the Scriptures are sometimes referred to as the *Law,* the *Prophets* and the *Psalms* (Matt. 11:13, Luke 16:16, Acts 26:22, Rom. 10:5).

The beginnings of the Old Testament canon are shrouded in mystery. We are told that Moses before his death wrote a book of the law, which he commanded the Levites to put in the side of the ark, *that it may be there for a witness against thee* (Deut. 31:26). In this book of the law it is enjoined upon every future king that *it shall be, when he sitteth upon the throne of his kingdom, that he shall write him a copy of this law in a book out of that which is before the priests the Levites: and it shall be with him, and he shall read therein all the days of his life* (Deut. 17:18, 19). Later it is recorded that Joshua made a covenant with the people *and wrote these words in the book of the law of God* (Joshua 24:26). This appears to have been an addition to that which was in the keeping of the Levites. Still later Samuel, previous to the establishing of the people under the kingship of Saul, *told the people the manner of the kingdom, and wrote it in a book, and laid it up before the Lord* (I Sam.

10:25). Under the reforms of Jehoshaphat (c. 914 B.C.) there was a purification of worship which took away the elements of Baalim and exalted the worship of Jehovah. At this time under the direction of the king, the princes together with certain Levites and priests taught in Judah *and had the book of the law . . . . with them, and went about throughout all the cities of Judah, and taught the people* (II Chron. 17:9).

But the outstanding date in the formation of the Old Testament canon, is 621 B.C., when Hilkiah the high priest discovered the book of the law in the temple, during the earlier part of the reign of Josiah. *And Hilkiah the high priest said unto Shaphan the scribe, I have found the book of the law in the house of the Lord. . . . . And Shaphan the scribe shewed the king, saying, Hilkiah the priest hath delivered me a book. And Shaphan read it before the king* (II Kings 22:8, 10). Immediately following this Josiah the king called a great convocation composed of the elders of Judah and Jerusalem, the priests, the prophets and all the people, both small and great, *and he read in their ears all the words of the book of the covenant which was found in the house of the Lord. And the king stood by a pillar and made a covenant before the Lord . . . . that were written in this book. And all the people stood to the covenant* (II Kings 23:1-3). This is considered a landmark in the history of the canon. While there are references to the law of God as early as Amos (B.C. 759-745) and Hosea (B.C. 743-737), they do not give us the extent of the books which were then included in the canon. (Cf. Amos 2:4 and Hosea 8:12). In commenting on this convocation of Josiah, Sanday says that we have here a solemn religious act, by which the king and the people alike accepted the book read before them as expressing the divine will, and took its precepts as binding upon themselves. This is the essential meaning that, as applied to a book, is contained in the epithet "canonical" which means "authoritative," and authoritative because in its ultimate origin it is divine (Cf. SANDAY, *Bible E. R. E.,* ii 565).

The next important date concerning the first division
of the Old Testament canon is the promulgation of the
Law in the time of Ezra and Nehemiah (c. 500-450 B.C.).
The Law of Moses, *which the Lord had commanded to
Israel* (Neh. 8: 1ff) was read before the people, and a
covenant was made which was sealed by the princes,
Levites and priests (Neh. 9: 38, 10: 1ff). From a study
of Nehemiah chapters 8-10 it seems evident that the
Book of Joshua was included with the Pentateuch, or
the Hexateuch substantially as we now have it. There is
in this connection also, the testimony of the Samaritan
Pentateuch which likewise dates from the time of Ezra
and Nehemiah (500-450 B.C.). It is significant, however, that the Samaritans accepted as canonical, only
the Pentateuch, which seems to indicate that at this early
date when the Jews and Samaritans formed their separate communities, the canon contained only the Pentateuch. We may allow that the first division of the
Hebrew Scriptures—that of the Torah or Law, was fully
accepted as canonical by 440 B.C.

The story of the Samaritans is told in II Kings 17: 6,
24, 26, 27, 28, 33. The king of Assyria brought these people to Palestine to take the place of the Jewish captives
which had been carried away to his own land. Later, ow-
ing to their belief that the God of Israel was against
them, a captive Jewish priest was sent to teach them,
but the people combined Jehovah worship with that of
their own gods. When Nehemiah restored Jerusalem,
hostility arose between them and the Jews. Green says,
"that after being repulsed by the Jews, the Samaritans,
to substantiate their claim of being sprung from ancient
Israel, eagerly adopted the Pentateuch which was
brought to them by a renegade priest." But this fact
witnesses to our Pentateuch as existing in its present
form as far back as the time of Ezra and Nehemiah.

The second or Prophetico-Historical section of the
Old Testament canon, commonly known as the "Prophets," was likewise gradual in its development. Bicknell
thinks that the reason Ezra and Nehemiah, as well as
Chronicles were not included in this second division was

due to the possibility that when these books were composed, the canon was at least well on its way to being closed. Also that the free manner in which the Chronicler treats the text of Samuel and Kings, together with the strange variations in the Septuagint translation of Samuel, seems to indicate that these books were not fully recognized as canonical by the year 300 B.C. The earliest reference to the "Prophets" as a definite collection of writings is found about 200 B.C. There is a reference in Ecclesiasticus (c. 180 B.C.) to the "twelve prophets" as being parallel to Jeremiah and Ezekiel (Ecclus. 49: 10), and a reference in Daniel which quotes Jeremiah as authoritative (Dan. 9: 2). We may regard this portion of the canon, therefore, as being closed about 200 B.C.

The third division or Hagiographa is even more obscure. As the name indicates, this division contained writings of a diverse character. The earliest reference made to it is in the prologue to Ecclesiasticus (130 B.C.), where the expression "The Law, the Prophets and the other writings" is used. In I Maccabees (7: 17) Psalm 79 is referred to as Scripture. We may regard this section of the canon as being closed about 100 B.C. Wakefield thinks that the canon of Old Testament Scripture originated somewhat in the following manner. When the Jews returned from Babylon and re-established divine worship, they collected the inspired books which they

"There is no sufficient reason," says Pond, "for supposing that any of the canonical books of Scripture have been lost. We can hardly reconcile it with our ideas of the wisdom and the goodness of God, that He should suffer such an event to take place; nor is it likely that He has. Mention is indeed made in the Old Testament of certain books which are no longer extant; such as "the book of Jasher" (Josh. 10:13) and "The book of the Wars of the Lord" (Numbers 21:14). But there is no evidence that either of these was ever included in the Jewish canon, or was entitled to be there. And the same remark may be made respecting "The book of the Chronicles of the kings of Israel," so often referred to in the first Book of the Kings. This was not the Book of Chronicles which we have in our Bibles, but the authorized records of the kingdom of Israel, made and kept by the kings' scribes. It was the register of what we would call the Secretary of State. The three thousand proverbs of Solomon, and his songs which were one thousand and five, together with his works on botany and natural history, would no doubt, be very entertaining, if we had authentic copies of them; but there is no evidence that these works ever claimed inspiration, or were ever admitted into the sacred canon of the Jews.—POND, *Lectures on Christian Theology*, p. 53.

still possessed, and in this manner began a sacred library
as before they had done with the Law. To this collection
they afterward added the writings of Zechariah, Malachi,
and other distinguished prophets and priests, who wrote
during the captivity or shortly after; and also the Books
of the Kings, Chronicles, and other historical writings,
which had been compiled from the ancient records of the
nation. The collection thus made was ever afterward
considered complete, and the books composing it were
called the Holy Scriptures; or the Law and the Prophets.
Sometimes also they used the threefold division as we
have previously pointed out, referring to the Scriptures,
as "the Law, the Prophets and the Psalms."

Jewish authorities recognized the canon of the Old
Testament as we now have it, as being in existence at
the time of Christ. Josephus says, "We have only twenty-two books which are to be trusted as having divine
authority, of which five are the books of Moses. From
his death to the reign of Artaxerxes, king of Persia, the
prophets, who were the successors of Moses, have written thirteen books. The remaining four contain hymns
to God, and documents of life for human edification"
(*Against Apion* 1:8). Our present Bible makes twenty-
four by separating Ruth from Judges, and Lamentations from Jeremiah. Philo of Alexandria never quotes
from an apocryphal book, although he does quote from
nearly all the books of the Hebrew canon. We may regard the action taken by the Council of Jamnia 90 A.D.
as the final stage in the fixing of the Jewish canon. After
the fall of Jerusalem, Jamnia became the center for
Palestinian Judaism, and the action taken there included in the canon all the books in the English Old Testament and no others (Cf. BICKNELL, *Thirty-Nine Articles,* p. 178).

The highest witness to the canon of the Old Testament as divinely inspired, is for the church, to be found
in the fact that it was ratified by our Lord and His
apostles. The importance of such supreme testimony
cannot be overestimated, in establishing the Old Testament Scriptures as the sufficient and infallible Oracles

of God, for the preparatory dispensation. It is just this, in fact, that seals the Jewish canon as Christian Scriptures to be united with those which should afterward be given by the same Spirit, thus completing the objective canon of all the sacred Scriptures of the two dispensations. Of this evidence Dr. Pope writes that their divine origin is guaranteed to the Church by the fact "that the Saviour has given His authenticating testimony to the whole body of them in their integrity. That sanction, first, makes the Old Testament the revelation of Christ. As it testified of Him so He testifies of it. He took it into His hands, and blessed it, and hallowed it forever as His own. As revelation is Christ, and Christ is the subject of the Old Testament, the Old Testament is of necessity the revelation of God. Knowing better than any human critic can know all its internal obscurities, He sealed it nevertheless for the reverence of His people. The canon of the ancient oracles, precisely as we hold them now, no more no less, he sanctified and gave to the Church as the early preparatory records of His own Gospel and kingdom. That sanction, second, assures us that the New Testament is His own authoritative completion of the Scriptures of revelation" (POPE, *Compend Chr. Th.*, pp. 39, 40).

THE NEW TESTAMENT CANON

The formation of the canon of the New Testament Scriptures was likewise a gradual process, extending over a considerable period of time. It runs through the entire ante-Nicene period, and may be said to have been closed at the end of the fourth century—every vestige of doubt concerning any of the books having disappeared by that time. The earliest stage in the formation of the New Testament canon, is to be found in the collections of writings made by the local churches, and in some instances by churches within a given area. That there was an early collection of the Pauline Epistles is indicated in II Peter 3: 16 where it is stated that *in all his epistles, there are some things hard to be understood.*

In Col. 4:16 the author requests that *when this epistle is read among you, cause that it be read also in the church of the Laodiceans; and that ye likewise read the epistle from Laodicea.* There is evidence also that the epistle to the Ephesians was at first a circular letter, for in the two oldest MSS the words "at Ephesus" (1:1) are omitted. On this basis these words were added because the epistle was finally lodged at Ephesus. Some have thought, also, that the Epistle to the Romans was used as a circular letter without the addition of the last chapters. It may be readily understood how each church would preserve its own epistles and thereby, almost unconsciously, began the growth of the New Testament canon.

The Earliest Canons. The earliest mention of a definite canon is that of Marcion (140 A.D.). He collected St. Paul's Epistles, rejecting the Pastoral Epistles, and adding a mutilated version of St. Luke's Gospel. Regarded as a heretic by the Church, he recorded only those epistles which seemed to accord with his heretical opinions, and made changes in the Gospel of Luke to substantiate his positions. The other three Gospels were rejected. The Muratorian Canon was formed about 200 A.D., a fragment which contained a list of the books regarded as authoritative in Rome. This includes the four Gospels, Acts, all the Epistles of St. Paul, the Apocalypse, two Epistles of St. John, St. Jude, and the first Epistle of St. Peter. Hebrews, St. James, and one, probably the third Epistle of St. John, are omitted. The second

The only books of the New Testament which have been accounted lost, are an Epistle of Paul to the Corinthians, supposed to precede what we are accustomed to regard as his first epistle; and his Epistle to the Laodiceans (Col. 4:16). But the epistle of which Paul speaks in I Cor. 5:9 was undoubtedly the very epistle which he was then writing. The passage is badly translated in our version; not "I wrote unto you in *an* epistle," but "I have written unto you in *the* epistle"; that is, in *this* epistle—the very writing which I now send. . . . . The Epistle to the Laodiceans has been justly regarded as no other than the Epistle to the Ephesians. As Ephesus was the chief city of proconsular Asia, this epistle may have been designed for all the churches in the province; among which was the church of the Laodiceans. There was an Epistle of Paul to the Laodiceans extant in the fifth century; but it was manifestly a forgery, and never had a place in the sacred canon.—POND, *Lectures on Christian Theology*, p. 53.

Epistle of St. Peter is regarded as doubtful. Hermas is to be read privately but not in the Church. Dr. Shedd thinks that the reference made here is to a conception that was gradually forming in the minds of Christians, that of a New Testament as a companion to the Old Testament, and therefore the books of the New Testament are cited as Scripture.

The Early Catalogues of Scripture. At a very early period, catalogues or lists of the books of the New Testament were drawn up by different persons. The earliest of these was that of Origen (210 A.D.), who for some reason omits the Epistles of James and Jude, while acknowledging them in other parts of his writings. The next is that of Eusebius (315) A.D., who makes a distinction between the *homologoumena* and the *antilogoumena* which we shall treat in our next section. The catalogue of Athanasius is of the same date as that of Eusebius, and exactly corresponds with our present canon. Bicknell places this catalogue at even an earlier date than that of Eusebius (307 A.D.), and states that the canon of Epiphanius in his work on Heresies is also identical with our own. The catalogue of Cyril of Jerusalem (340 A.D.) and that of the Council of Laodicea (364 A.D.) contain all the New Testament books except the Apocalypse, which is rejected also by Gregory Nazianzen (375 A.D.) and Amphilochius of Iconium. Philostrius, Bishop of Brescia (380 A.D.) leaves out both the Apocalypse and the Epistle to the Hebrews; but Jerome (382 A.D.), Ruffinus (390 A.D.) and Augustine (394 A.D.) contain the full lists of the New Testament books as acknowledged. It may be mentioned in this connection also, that the Vatican and Sinaitic MSS belong to the middle of the fourth century (c. 325-350 A.D.). The former contains all the books except Philemon, Titus, I-II Timothy, Hebrews and the Apocalypse. The latter contains all the Gospels, all the Epistles and the Apocalypse.

The Homologoumena and the Antilogoumena. The catalogue of Eusebius as previously mentioned, gives a list of all the books as accepted by his contemporaries, but arranges them in two classes as the acknowledged books, *homologoumena* (ὁμολογούμενα), and the disputed books, *antilogoumena* (ἀντιλογόμενα); to which he adds a third class also, the spurious or rejected books, *notha* (νόθα). In the first class, he places the following: the four Gospels, Acts, the Epistles of St. Paul, I Peter and I John, and with some hesitation mentions the Apocalypse. In the second class are the following: St. James, St. Jude, II and III John and II Peter. Here he again mentions the Apocalypse. Hebrews is not mentioned, but it is probably classed with the Epistles of St. Paul. He admits, however, that the authorship is disputed by the Roman Church. In the last class he mentions the Acts of Paul, Hermas, the Apocalypse of Peter, the Epistle of Barnabas, and the *Didache* or so-called "Teachings of the Apostles." It seems, also, that the Apocalypse is included, though this is doubtful. It will be seen from this that the Apocalypse was not as yet fully classified. It should be observed that the seven books classified as *antilogoumena* were not rejected books, but subjected merely to suspended judgment, some because the authorship was not certain, as in the case of the Epistle to the Hebrews, some were written to the Christians at large and were not under the protection of any particular church, while others were addressed to individual men, and on that account were not readily accepted. In later times the *antilogoumena* were sometimes classified as *Deutero-Canonical*. In the third class mentioned above, the rejected books were not regarded as spurious in the sense of not being truthful, but only as not having sufficient warrant for canonicity. A few of these small treatises were received in the earlier church with great veneration, as written by men who had been companions to the Apostles. Among these were the epistles of Clement of Rome, Barnabas and Hermas. They were included in the earliest Codices, where they still may be found, but only as supplements.

Conciliar Action. The first conciliar action concerning the establishment of the canon, was taken by the Synod of Carthage, which formally ratified the canon as it now stands. This date according to Bicknell is either 397 A.D. or 419 A.D. This decision was confirmed by the Trullan Council in 692 A.D. As previously stated, the action of these councils did not authorize the present canon of Scripture, but only confirmed what had already been accepted by general usage. "So we may sum up the history of the Canon," says Bicknell, "as the gradual work of the collective consciousness of the Church, guided by the Holy Spirit. It was a task of not only collecting but sifting and rejecting. . . . . It was a work in which all members of the body played their part. The devotional taste of the multitude was guided and corrected by the learning and spiritual enlighten-

The final ratification was brought about by the pressure of persecution directed against the sacred writings; but there ought to be no doubt that this was under the special supervision of the Holy Ghost. The parallel (with the formation of the Old Testament canon) is so far complete. But there were some peculiarities in the case of the new collection. The gospel was diffused over the world, and every church was the guardian of its own holy books, while every province of early Christendom had its own special selection of Scriptures; there were also numberless heresies, multiplying their spurious productions. These two circumstances tended to make the concurrence of the Christian Church in the final acceptance of the New Testament writings a more remarkable fact than the unanimity of the Jewish Church in regard to the Old Testament."—POPE, Compend. Chr. Th., I, p. 199.

The four Gospels were from the first distinguished from the apocryphal. Justin Martyr (163 A.D.) speaks of "memoirs" of Christ as the work of the evangelists. Irenæus (202 A.D.) cites passages from all four of the canonical Gospels. Clement and Tertullian (220 A.D.) do the same. Tatian (172 A.D.), and Ammonius (200 A.D.), arranged harmonies of the four Gospels. Theodoret (457 A.D.) found two hundred copies of Tatian's harmony in the Syrian churches, which he took away from them, because of some heresy it contained. Neander supposes that Tatian mixed some things with the canonical Gospels from the apocryphal. Origen (250 A.D.), writes a commentary on Matthew and John. These facts prove the general acceptance of the four Gospels as canonical, prior to 250 A.D. Yet there was no action of the church in a general council to this effect.—Cf. SHEDD, Dogm. Th., p. 146.

As an evidence of the genuineness of the New Testament writings, we may cite quotations from Clement as early as the first century. Also from Ignatius, Polycarp, Justin Martyr, Irenæus, Athenagoras and Theophilus of Antioch. Eusebius collected this testimony, especially that of the ecclesiastical writers of the first three centuries, from Ignatius to Origen, and published it as early as 325 A.D. It may be found in his History (III, xxv; VII, xxv) and also in his work entitled Demonstratio Evangelica.

Another evidence of the genuineness of the canonical books of the N. T. is found in the early versions. The Peshito Syriac translation was made about 175 A.D. and the Old Latin (Itala) about the same time. The two Egyptian versions were made about 250 A.D. and the Aethiopic about 350 A.D.

ment of its leaders. Their decisions approved themselves to the mind and conscience of the whole Church."— BICKNELL, *The Thirty-Nine Articles*, p. 182. As the Old Testament canon was not closed until the Spirit of inspiration was withdrawn, so when the time was fully come, we may believe that the same Spirit closed the volume of the New Testament.

The Apocrypha and Pseudepigrapha. As previously stated, the Jewish canon was regarded as complete by about 100 B.C. However edifying books continued to be written, and were widely used and quoted, but were not regarded as on the same plane with the canonical Scriptures. But this was true only in Palestine. The Hellenistic Jews, especially those of Alexandria took an entirely different attitude. They not only adopted a different arrangement of the books but included among them many later writings, these for the most part being the books now regarded as apocryphal. Thus the early Christian Church as it extended its borders beyond Palestine, found itself confronted with a greater and lesser canon. Since many of these were uninformed, the great body of the Church went on using the Greek Bible and the Alexandrian canon. But Jerome and other learned men who understood the Hebrew language recognized that there was a narrower and truer canon. This Jerome accepted and defended. He was opposed by Augustine, through whose influence in the Councils of Hippo (393 A.D.) and of Carthage (397 A.D.), the apocryphal books were declared to be canonical Scripture, and were thereafter quoted as such by later writers.

The word *Apocrypha*, which came to be applied to the extra-canonical books in the second century, has a number of different meanings. Originally it meant "hidden," and referred to either a secret origin or a secret authority. But the idea of an esoteric teaching was repugnant to the spirit of Christianity, and soon came to mean heretical or spurious. As used by Jerome, however, it simply meant noncanonical. It is in this sense that the Apocrypha is now understood. Protestantism rejected the Apocrypha and accepted the Jewish rather than the Alexandrian canon, the Jewish Scriptures rather than the Septuagint.

The Pseudepigrapha as the name implies was a collection of spurious writings outside both the canonical Scriptures and the Apocryphal books, and never having had any reception in the Jewish or Christian Church. Athanasius, as did the earlier church fathers, distinguished between the canonical (ὁμολογούμενα), those worthy of being read, though not canonical, (ἀντιλογόμενα), and the fictitious works of heretics (νόθα). In the first class he placed the twenty-two Hebrew books which make the Jewish canon, in the second, what we call the Apocrypha, and in the third, the *pseudepigrapha*. The Greek Church retains the same order.

What is commonly called the New Testament Apocrypha is a collection of spurious writings, which were never published in connection with the canonical Scriptures. They were, however, in part at least, gathered

Enoch Pond in his *Lectures on Christian Theology* gives the following arguments against the inspiration of the apocryphal books. (1) They are not found in the Hebrew Bible. They were written originally not in Hebrew but in Greek—a language which was not common among the Jews perhaps not known among them, until after the Old Testament was closed. (2) These apocryphal books have never been received into the sacred canon of the Jews. They are ancient Jewish writings but have never been regarded by that people as inspired. (3) The apocryphal books are never quoted or referred to in the New Testament as possessing any divine authority. (4) The internal evidence is decisive. (5) The writer of the Maccabees disclaims inspiration. He says, "I will here make an end of my narrative. If I have done well, it is what I desired; but if slenderly and meanly, it is what I could attain unto."

As internal evidence against the apocryphal books, Pond cites the following: "They inculcate false doctrine, and a false and unchristian morality. In the Second of the Maccabees we read, "It is a holy and wholesome thought to pray for the dead, that they may be loosed from their sins (12:44-45). The writer of the same book both justifies and commends suicide, "When he was ready to be taken, he fell upon his own sword, choosing to die nobly, rather than fall into the hands of the wicked" (14:41, 42). In several places in the Apocrypha, atonement and justification are represented as being secured by works. "Whoso honoreth his father, maketh atonement for his sin" (Ecclus. 3:3). "Alms doth deliver from death, and shall purge away all sin" (Tobit 12:9).—Pond, *Lect. Chr. Th.*, p. 48.

The addition of Baruch and the Epistle of Jeremiah by Origen and others was occasioned by their being appended to the genuine writings of that prophet in the MSS of the Septuagint. This too will account for the fact that Ambrose, Augustine, and others after them, in the Latin Church, who used the Septuagint, spoke of the apocryphal books as canonical, because they were placed with the canonical books, as being in the same language.—Summers, *Syst. Th.*, I, pp. 503, 504.

up and published under the title "Apocryphal Books of the New Testament." There is no evidence that can be claimed for them as inspired writings, and they have never been accepted by the Church as any part of the Scriptures.

Later History of the Canon. As may be inferred from our discussion of the Apocrypha, the question of the canon was for a long time an open and perplexing one in the mediæval Church. In 1441 A.D. the Council of Florence passed a decree which declared most of the apocryphal books to be canonical. At the time of the Reformation when the lines were being drawn so closely between the Roman Catholic Church and Protestantism, the Council of Trent in 1546 abolished all differences between the books and declared them all canonical. This action being taken by a council reputedly few in number and in opposition to former catalogues, attempts were made by some of the later Romanist theologians to soften the position by distinguishing between Proto-canonical and Deuterocanonical books, or a higher and a lower canon. The Greek Church, after many attempts to separate the apocryphal books from the canon, finally adopted the Apocrypha as canonical at a Jerusalem Synod under Dositheus in 1672 A.D. Protestantism universally rejected the Apocrypha as canonical. Luther, however, admitted the apocrypha as valuable for edification, but the Swiss Reformers were more rigorous in their rejection. The English Church is conciliatory and

The books of the Apocrypha and Pseudepigrapha are classified in various ways. The following is the usual classification:

The Old Testament Apocrypha: I Esdras, II Esdras, Tobit, Judith, Additions to Esther, Wisdom of Solomon, Ecclesiasticus (or Wisdom of Sirach), Baruch, Epistle of Jeremy, Song of the Three Children, The Story of Susana, Bel and the Dragon, The Prayer of Manasses, I-II-III-IV Maccabees.

The New Testament Apocrypha: The Gospel of the Birth of Mary, The Protevangelium of James, The Gospel of the Infancy, the Gospel of Nicodemus (or Acts of Pilate), The Acts of Paul and Thecla.

The Pseudepigrapha: The Book of Jubilees, The Letter of Aristeas, The Books of Adam and Eve, The Martyrdom of Isaiah, I Enoch (Ethiopic), The Testaments of the Twelve Patriarchs, The Sibylline Oracles, The Assumption of Moses, II Enoch (or the Book of the Secrets of Enoch, Slavonic), II Baruch (or the Syriac Apocalypse of Baruch), III Baruch (or the Greek Apocalypse of Baruch), The Psalms of Solomon, Pirke Aboth, the Story of Ahikar, and The Fragments of a Zadokite Work.

regards as fully canonical, only those books of whose authority there was never any doubt, but admits public reading of some parts of the Apocrypha. The earlier Arminians adopted both the canonical books and the Apocrypha as Scripture, but the Methodist bodies everywhere, in common with the Westminster Confession, wholly rejected the apocryphal books as canonical.

THE CANON AS A RULE OF FAITH

The objective canon of Scripture in the sense of the accepted and approved connection of writings, becomes in turn the rule of faith in its application to the Christian Church. Here we define the objective canon as including the canonical books of both the Old and the New Testament, exclusive of the apocryphal books. These latter we regard on the human plane as comparable with other uninspired writings. They are of value from the historical standpoint, and their content in most instances, is edifying. We judge them as to their worth solely on the plane of human effort and ability, and in no sense view them as a rule of faith. The New Testament, however, declares itself as the consummation of Scripture, filling out or completing the revelation made through the Old Testament. This brings us directly to one of the earliest problems of the primitive church—that of the relation between the Old and the New Testament.

ARTICLE VI of the English Church is as follows: Holy Scripture containeth all things necessary to salvation; so that whatsoever is not read therein, nor may be proved thereby, is not to be required of any man, that it should be believed as an Article of Faith, or be thought requisite necessary to salvation. (Here follows a list of the canonical books.) All the books of the New Testament, as they are commonly received, we do receive and account them Canonical. And the other books (as Hierome saith) the Church doth read for example of life and instruction of manners; but yet doth it not apply them to establish any doctrine. (Here follows a list of the apocryphal books.)

Mr. Wesley in arranging the Twenty-Five Articles of Methodism uses the Sixth Article of the *Anglican Confession*, but omits all reference to the apocryphal books. He also substituted the names "The Book of Ezra" and "The Book of Nehemiah" for the I and II Books of Esdras as they are called in the Anglican Confession. In the last sentence, he omits the word "them" before "canonical."

ARTICLE IV. Church of the Nazarene: "We believe in the plenary inspiration of the Holy Scriptures by which we understand the sixty-six books of the Old and New Testament, given by divine inspiration, inerrantly revealing the will of God concerning us in all things necessary to our salvation; so that whatever is not contained therein is not to be enjoined as an article of faith."

The Relation of the Old Testament to the New Testament. One of the first problems to rise in the early Church was that of its relation to Jewish Law. The Jews themselves were reluctant to give up any portion of their regulations, and the Gentiles were loath to receive them. Then, too, the historical perspective, having as yet little or no meaning to the Church, the backwardness of certain parts of the Old Testament constituted a real difficulty for the Christian conscience. It was on this ground of unchristian morality that Marcion and his adherents rejected the Old Testament. The problem became acute when the Apostle Paul declared that it was not necessary for the Gentiles to become Jews before becoming Christians. His Epistle to the Galatians is his declaration of independence as it concerns Judaism in itself. This rough but strong statement is given to the Church in its polished and perfected form in the Epistle to the Romans. The great apostle likewise declared his independence of paganism, in a like rugged and strong epistle—that to the Colossians. This we have in its finished form in the Epistle to the Ephesians. The controversy became so acute, that a council of the elders was called at Jerusalem, over which the Apostle James presided. The Pharisees demanded that the Gentiles be circumcised and keep the law of Moses. Peter, arguing from his experience at the household of Cornelius, and Paul and Barnabas citing the miracles and wonders which had been wrought of God, James rendered the final verdict in these words: *Wherefore my sentence is, that we trouble not them, which from among the Gentiles are turned to God; but that we write unto them, that they abstain from pollutions of idols, and from fornication, and from things strangled, and from blood. For Moses of old time hath in every city them that preach him, being read in the synagogues every sabbath day* (Acts 15:19-21). This was a victory for the liberal party, but the problem has been persistent in every succeeding age of the Church.

At the opening of the Reformation Period, the problem came to the front again. Here it took a twofold form

—that of minifying the Old Testament on the one hand, and an attempt to enforce the minute Jewish ceremonial regulations on the other. The earliest attempt in the English Church to settle this problem was the TEN ARTI-CLES of 1536, which passed rapidly through other statements and was given a more definite expression in the FORTY-TWO ARTICLES of 1553. The present ARTICLE VII of the Anglican Confession was formed by Archbishop Parker out of two of the earlier articles of 1553, and was directed against Romanism on the one hand, and the errors of the Anabaptists on the other. This represents, not only the conclusions of English Protestantism, but is in accord with all Protestantism. As finally settled, the solution took the form of three declarations. *First,* the Old Testament was not to be considered contrary to the New Testament, but to be regarded as an earlier and preparatory stage for Christianity. We are to view the Old Testament as a progressive unfolding of God's revealed will, and that at each stage men and their actions are to be judged in accordance with the accepted standards of their times and in harmony with the amount of divine light accorded them. *Second,* God's promises to the Jews carried with them, not only promises of material blessing, but of spiritual light and salvation. They were not therefore to be regarded as "transitory," but as revelations on various levels and in varying degrees, of the one Messianic hope which found its perfect fulfillment in Christ (Cf. Heb. 1:1). *Third,* the question of the relation of the Church to Jewish Law was solved, by making a distinction between civil and ceremonial law on the one hand, and moral law on the other. This is admittedly a radical distinction, for to the Jew every part of the law was equally

ARTICLE VII, Anglican Confession: The Old Testament is not contrary to the New, for both in the Old and New Testaments everlasting life is offered to mankind by Christ, who is the only Mediator between God and man, being both God and man. Wherefore they are not to be heard, which feign that the old Fathers did look for only transitory promises. Although the Law given from God by Moses, as touching ceremonies and rites, do not bind Christian men, nor the Civil Precepts thereof ought of necessity to be received in any commonwealth; yet notwithstanding, no Christian man whatsoever is free from the obedience of the Commandments which are called Moral.

sacred. Nor could it have been made unless our Lord himself had first abrogated that part of it which belonged solely to the earlier economy. Thus that which was in Judaism as a logical accident and necessary to its earlier expression, is to be superseded by other and more spiritual forms of expression, though through all there abides the truth eternal. His direct statement as to His own relation of superiority to the law and his avowed purpose of lifting it to higher forms of expression (Cf. Matt. 5: 38, 39, 43, 44); his assertion of lordship over even the Sabbath (Cf. Mark 2: 28); and his references to the new cloth and the old garment (Mark 2: 21, 22) and the new wine and the old wineskins, are sufficient proof that He anticipated new and higher forms of expression, for the truth to be revealed through the Holy Spirit. The Council of Jerusalem (*ca.* A.D. 48) claimed the specific direction of the Holy Ghost, which Jesus had promised should be given as a Spirit of truth (Acts 15: 28); and the decision was so definite as to what was to be retained, that there should be no doubt as to its intended abrogation. To this also, St. Paul's epistles to the *Galatians* and to the *Romans* bear direct evidence, declaring that the ritual and ceremonial law was abolished by One who had the authority so to do.

This may be summed up as follows: The civil portions of the Law belonged to Israel as a nation. Since Christianity was regarded as a religion of universal import, these civil restrictions could not possibly be binding upon the Church. The new and spiritual Israel demanded new and universal laws, for in Christ *there is neither Jew nor Greek, there is neither bond nor free, there is neither male nor female; for ye are all one in Christ Jesus* (Gal. 3: 28). This new law must be applicable to all nations, all peoples, all degrees of civilization and culture, and without distinction as to sex. It can therefore be nothing less than the law of faith (Cf. Rom. 3: 21-28). Likewise, also, the ceremonial rites found their offices in the proper instruction of those who observed them. They admittedly pointed forward to Christ as their perfect fulfilment. Hence St. Paul argues that *when we were children, were in bondage under the elements of the world; but when the fulness of the time was come, God sent forth his Son, made of a woman, made under the law, to redeem them that were under the law, that we might receive the adoption of sons* (Gal. 4: 3-5). *Wherefore the law was our schoolmaster to bring us unto Christ, that we might be justified by faith. But after that faith is come, we are no longer under a schoolmaster* (Gal. 3: 24, 25).

As respects the moral law, Christ did not abolish it, but declared his intention to deepen and vitalize it. And this He did because as such, the moral law is God's will for all men, and not necessarily entangled with the accidents of religious ceremonies or civil obligations. It belongs to the nature of man—is the law of His true being and could not be abrogated without the destruction of the human in its higher spiritual aspects. Then again the Christian is inspired by the new law of love as an inner impulsive power, and this exceeds a forced obedience to an outwardly imposed law. Hence there are many injunctions in the Scriptures, exhorting men to walk worthy of their profession by loving obedience to the moral law (Cf. Rom. 13: 9, Eph. 6: 2, James 2: 10).

EVIDENCES OF THE RULE OF FAITH

Having given in brief, the evidences which support the claims of the several books of the Bible to canonicity, we must now make mention of those which are urged in favor of the Scriptures as the authoritative rule of faith and practice in the Church. These evidences properly belong to the field of Apologetics, which on account of its wide range of research and investigation is now generally regarded as a separate branch of theological science. Due to the assaults of infidelity in the past, and the attacks of destructive criticism in modern times, this field is peculiarly difficult. It should demand the attention of only those more mature students who have had the proper scholastic preparation for this work, and who in addition have access to the literature of modern research. This literature will be found in the numerous Introductions to Biblical Science, the various histories of the Canon and the general field of Apologetics. It is evident that the limited scope of this work prevents any extended treatment of the subject. Furthermore, we deem the objections of unbelief as of little worth to the student of theology generally. They do not usually arise from honest intellectual inquiry, but from an evil heart of unbelief. They are always short-lived, and therefore frequently replaced by newer and equally contradictory hypotheses. The development of modern historical research, and the recent discoveries in philology and archæology, have in each instance served to strengthen and confirm the faith of the Church in the authenticity of the sacred Scriptures. Again, we have endeavored in our previous discussion of the Scriptures, to show that their life is not bound up solely with historical evidences, but is to be found also in the *testimonium Spiritus Sancti,* or the inner witness of the Holy Spirit. The Spirit dwelling within the hearts of true believers through the atoning work of Jesus Christ, is found to be the same Spirit who breathes in the pages of the Holy Scriptures. Hence the strongest evidence for the authority of the Scriptures is to be found in the fact that the Spirit of Inspiration, to whom we are indebted for the authorship of the Bible, is Himself the Divine Witness to its genuineness and authenticity.

Classification of Evidences. The evidences offered in support of the claims of the Bible as the authoritative rule of faith and practice in the church, are usually classified as External, Internal and Collateral. External evidences are so-called because they are regarded as external to the Bible, such as miracle and prophecy. These we have previously treated in connection with the subject of Revelation. Internal evidences are those found within the book itself and consists in the arguments for the genuineness, authenticity and integrity of the Holy Scriptures. By Collateral evidences are meant those miscellaneous matters which cannot be properly classified as either External or Internal evidences, and yet are of sufficient importance to demand attention. Here are usually classified such evidences as the rapid expansion of Christianity during the first three centuries, and the beneficial influences of Christianity upon mankind wherever accepted. Reference is sometimes made also to presumptive evidences, by which are meant those arguments which tend to dispose the mind toward the presentation of other evidences. The evidences are further classified as Rational and Authenticating. By a Rational argument is meant the endeavor to convince the mind of the truth of the proposition presented. It has to do with the truth or falsity of a proposition. By an Authenticating argument is meant an attempt to prove that the teacher is divinely commissioned, and may have no further bearing upon the truth of the proposition itself. However, if the claims of the teacher to divine inspiration can be supported by an authenticating argument, this is at least presumptive evidence that the doctrines taught are likewise divinely inspired and therefore true.

In substantiation of the claims of the Old Testament to genuineness and authenticity we may mention: (1) *The Antiquity of the Old Testament.* Josephus quotes such writers as Manetho and Apollonius as agreeing that Moses was the leader of the Hebrew people when they left Egypt. Strabo, Pliny, Tacitus, Juvenal and others mention Moses; and Justin Martyr affirms that nearly all of the ancient historians, poets, philosophers and lawgivers refer to him as the leader of Israel and the founder of the Jewish state. (2) *The Septuagint.* The Old Testament was translated into Greek for the use of the Alexandrian Jews about 287 B.C. This translation is known as the Septuagint and is proof positive that the Pentateuch existed at that time. But it must be admitted that if the Pentateuch existed at that date, it must

Older works on Apologetics. Cf. Nelson, *The Cause and Cure of Infidelity;* William Lee, *The Inspiration of Holy Scripture: Its Nature and Proof;* Rawlinson, *The Historical Evidences of the Truth of the Scripture Records;* Gleig, *The Most Wonderful Book in the World* (New Ed. 1915); Horne, *Introduction to the Holy Scriptures.* Cf. also works on evidences by Paley, Whately, McIlvaine, Conybeare, Cudworth and Lardner.

have existed also in the days of Ezra (c. 536 B.C.), for the circumstances of the Jews in their captivity were such as to preclude its authorship between these two dates. Furthermore, Hebrew ceased to be the living language of the people soon after the time of their captivity, and after that date all important documents appear in either Greek or Chaldee. Both Ezra and Nehemiah mention "the law of Moses" (Ezra 3: 2, Neh. 8: 1), which at the request of the people, was brought forth and read by Ezra before the whole congregation of Israel. (3) *The Samaritan Pentateuch*. In our discussion of the Canon we mentioned the two extant copies of the law of Moses, one received by the Jews, the other by the Samaritans. It is evident that these were both taken from the same original which must therefore, have existed previous to the divided kingdom, this claim being substantiated by the magnificent temple of Solomon and the elaborated ritual which attached to its services. From Moses to David, about four centuries, the circumstances of the period were such as to preclude any possibility of its authorship. When, therefore, it is declared that Joshua

On the Mosaic authorship of the Pentateuch, the following works will be found helpful: Green, *The Higher Criticism of the Pentateuch* (1895), *The Unity of the Book of Genesis* (1895); Bissell, *The Pentateuch: Its Origin and Structure* (1885); Naville, *The Higher Criticism in Relation to the Pentateuch* (1923); Clay, *The Origin of Biblical Traditions* (1923); Griffith, *The Problem of Deuteronomy* (1911) and *The Exodus in the Light of Archæology* (1923); MacDill, *Mosaic Authorship of the Pentateuch;* Finn, *The Author of the Pentateuch* (1931); Pilter, *The Pentateuch: A Historical Record* (1928); Orr, *The Problem of the Old Testament* (1911); Wiener, *The Origin of the Pentateuch* (1910), *Pentateuchal Studies* (1912); McKim, *The Problem of the Pentateuch* (1906); Bartlett, *The Veracity of the Hexateuch* (1897).

The works on Archæology are numerous. There are some very late books on this subject. Ramsay, *The Bearing of Recent Discovery on the Trustworthiness of the New Testament;* Barton, *Archæology and the Bible* (Sixth Ed. 1933); Clay, *Light on the Old Testament from Babel* (1906); Conder, *The Tel el Amarna Tablets; The Bible and the East;* and *The Hittites and Their Language;* Davies, *The Codes of Hammurabi and Moses* (1905); Grimme, *The Law of Hammurabi and Moses* (translated by Pilter); Kyle, *The Deciding Voice of the Monuments* (1921); *Moses and the Monuments* (1920); *The Problem of the Pentateuch* (1920); Naville, *The Discovery of the Book of the Law Under Josiah* (1911); *Archæology and the Old Testament* (1913); Price, *The Monuments and the Old Testament* (1925); Sayce, *The Higher Criticism and the Monuments; The Hittites; Fresh Light from the Ancient Monuments;* Tompkins, *The Life and Times of Joseph in the Light of Egyptian Lore;* Urquhart, *Archæology's Solution of Old Testament Problems* (1906).

wrote the book which bears his name (Joshua 24: 26), and which appears to have been an addition to a previous volume known as the "Book of the Law," or the "Book of the Law of Moses" (Deut. 31: 24-26), there is no sound reason for denying the Mosaic authorship of the Pentateuch. As to whether Moses had access to previous documents, or whether his inspiration was of the nature of a "vision hypothesis" is a matter of conjecture. St. Luke clearly states that he used historical material in preparing the book which bears his name, and yet the inspiration of this book has never been called in question. That the Pentateuch was compiled by redactors from previously written documents as affirmed by those who hold to the modern "documentary hypothesis" does not appear to be substantiated by the facts. (4) *Archaeological Discoveries.* Objections were formerly made to the Mosaic authorship of the Pentateuch, on the grounds that writing was not yet invented in the time of Moses, and that the moral standards of the decalogue were far in advance of his time. Both of these objections have been disproved by the discovery of the *Code of Hammurabi* at Susa, Persia, probably the Shushan of the Book of Esther. The date of this Code is about 2250 B.C. It proves conclusively that writing was in vogue at least a thousand years before the time of Moses. It contains two hundred forty-eight laws formulated by the king of Babylon, some of them remarkably like those given by Moses on Mount Sinai, and answers all objections against the moral standards existing in the time of Moses. It has been abundantly proved, however, that the Mosaic Code was not borrowed from the Babylonians. The *Tel el Amarna Tablets* were found in 1887 and contained cuneiform inscriptions dating back to about 1400 B.C. These tablets represent conditions in Egypt precisely as they are related in Genesis and Exodus, and thus corroborate the testimony as to the Mosaic authorship of the Pentateuch. Another discovery which has

For further study Cf. Spencer, *Did Moses Write the Pentateuch After All?* (1901); Finn, *The Mosaic Authorship of the Pentateuch;* Thomas, *The Organic Unity of the Pentateuch* (1904).

confirmed the truth of the Pentateuch, is that of the Hittites. Until recently critics have discredited the biblical statements concerning this ancient and powerful people, but the discoveries of archæology have confirmed the biblical accounts, and added another proof to the authenticity of the Scriptures. One of the most outstanding evidences of archæology, however, is the discovery of the city of Pithom, where in some parts of the storechambers there are bricks made with straw, others with stubble, and some without straw but bound together with sticks. This is in exact accordance with the biblical account of the Hebrews during their bondage in Egypt.

Genuineness and Authenticity of the Scriptures. By *genuineness* as used in this connection, we understand a reference solely to authorship. A book is genuine when it is the production of the author whose name it bears. The term is frequently confused with *authenticity* which refers not to the authorship of a book but to the truth of its content. In this sense a book may be genuine without being authentic, or authentic without being genuine. There is, however, confusion as to the use of the term in theology and various writers attach different meanings to the words in question. It is admittedly difficult to sharply distinguish between the two in any discussion of scriptural evidences, for if a book is not written by the author it acknowledges, then not only is the question of its genuineness involved but that of its authenticity as well. For this reason it is a common practice with many theologians to treat both subjects under one head.

The authenticity of the New Testament has been

Later works on General Apologetics: Cf. Fisher, *Grounds of Theistic and Christian Belief* (1911); Ingram, *Reasons for Faith and Other Contributions to Christian Evidences* (1910-1914); McGarvey, *Evidences of Christianity* (1912); Cairns, *The Reasonableness of the Christian Faith;* Bissell, *The Historic Origin of the Bible* (1889) Lindberg, *Apologetics: A System of Christian Evidences* (1917); Luthardt, *Fundamental Moral and Saving Truths of Christianity* (3 vols.); Rishell, *The Foundations of the Christian Faith* (1899); Wright, *Scientific Aspects of Christian Evidences* (1906); Wells, *Why We Believe the Bible* (1910); Stewart, *Handbook of Christian Evidences;* Row, *A Manual of Christian Evidences;* Ebrard, *Christian Apologetics or the Scientific Vindication of Christianity* (3 Vols.); Christlieb, *Modern Doubt and Christian Belief* (2nd Ed. 1874); Robertson, *The Bible at the Bar* (1934); Shiner, *The Battle of Beliefs* (1931); Short, *The Bible and Modern Research* (1932), previously discussed and we need not repeat the arguments here. It is sufficient to summarize these arguments as follows: (1) There are quotations from the New Testament found in the writings of the earliest fathers, dating back to the first century and immediately following, such as Clement, Ignatius, Polycarp, Justin Martyr and Irenæus. (2) There is the testimony of the opponents of Christianity such as Celsus in the second century, Porphyry and Hierocles in the third and Julian in the fourth century, all of whom bear witness to the existence of the New Testament in their day. (3) There are the early catalogues of the books of the New Testament. The earliest of these was that of Origen (c. 210 A.D.) which lists all of the books of the New Testament except James and Jude and these are mentioned elsewhere in his writings. (4) The Roman historians whose antiquity has never been questioned bear witness to Christ and early Christianity. Suetonius mentions Christ by name, *Judæos impulsore Christo assidue tumultantes Roma expulit* (Edit. Var., p. 544); while Tacitus mentions Pilate as procurator of Judea, and refers to Christ as the Founder of the sect of Christians. (*Auctor nominis ejus Christus, qui Tiberio imperitante, per procuratoreum Pontium Pilatum supplicio affectus erat.—Annal., 1, 5.*) (5) The style of the books in each case is suited to the age and circumstances of the reputed writer, and the characteristic differences are evidence that the work was not that of one person but of many. (6) The character of the writers is evidence in favor of the authenticity of their writings. They were holy men and incapable of forgery or deception. There is a straight-

For further reading cf. Mullins, *Why Is Christianity True?* Stearns *The Evidences of Christian Experience* (1890); Wright, *Scientific Aspects of Christian Evidences* (1906); Kreitzmann, *The New Testament in the Light of a Believer's Research* (1934); Marston, *New Bible Evidence* (1934); Robertson, *Luke the Historian in the Light of Research* (1920); Machen, *The Origin of Paul's Religion* (1921); Noesgen, *The New Testament and the Pentateuch* (1905); Watson, *Defenders of the Faith: The Christian Apologists of the Second and Third Centuries* (1899); Carrington, *Christian Apologetics in the Second Century* (1921); Cobern, *The New Archæological Discoveries and Their Bearing on the New Testament* (1917); Ramsay, *Was Christ Born in Bethlehem? The Bearing of Recent Discoveries on the Trustworthiness of the New Testament.*

forwardness and frankness about these writers which impostors could not well counterfeit. (7) The writers refer to incidents, persons and places, which can be confirmed by history, and which an impostor would overlook or conceal. They are characterized by an artless simplicity, and relate even those things which no writers of less integrity would mention. It has been truthfully said that in the New Testament we have stronger evidence for the genuineness and authenticity of the books which compose it, than is afforded the books of any other class, sacred or profane.

The Integrity of the Scriptures. Have the sacred books, even though divinely inspired, been transmitted to us in an uncorrupted manner? May we be confident that we are in possession of the truth of the original text? By the integrity of the Scriptures we mean that they have been kept intact and free from essential error, so that we may be assured of the truth originally given by the inspired authors. Here again we must present only a brief summary of the evidences for the integrity of the Scriptures. (1) There is no evidence that the Scriptures have been corrupted. The burden of proof is upon the objectors. Nor need we have any fear as to the result of careful investigation. No proof has ever yet been furnished of essential alterations, and it is certain that

Wakefield sums up the evidences from the credibility of the writers as follows: (1) They were men of strict and exemplary virtue. (2) They were in circumstances certainly to know the truth of what they relate. (3) The apostles were not influenced by worldly interests. (4) Their testimony was in the highest degree circumstantial.—WAKEFIELD, *Christian Theology*, pp. 68-71.

Pond gives the following as the laws of valid testimony: (1) There must be a competent number of witnesses. (2) These witnesses must have had the capacity and the means of forming a correct judgment. (3) They must be persons of unexceptionable moral character. (4) They must be disinterested. (5) Their testimony must be given in plain terms, and must be, on all essential points, a concurrent testimony. (6) It must be of such a nature that the witnesses, if they have falsified, are open to detection. (7) It must be, not contradicted, but (so far as might reasonably be expected) confirmed, by other evidence. (8) It must be followed up, on the part of the witnesses, by a correspondent, consistent course of action. Dr. Pond applies these laws to the Scriptures in an argument of peculiar insight and strength. "Christianity may yet be assailed," he says, "but it will come out of every new trial, as it has out of every previous one, strengthened in its evidences, and not weakened; victorious, and not vanquished."—Cf. POND, *Christian Theology*, pp. 97-105.

none can be furnished in the future. (2) There were strong motives for preserving the Old Testament on the part of the Jews. Besides the high veneration in which their sacred books were held, these books contained the articles of their religious faith and the laws of their land. The antagonism which existed between the Jews and the Samaritans would forbid any mutilation of the Pentateuch of which each nation possessed a copy. (3) The multiplication of copies and their wide diffusion by the Levites as early as the times of the Judges and Kings (Deut. 31: 11) tended to prevent the alteration of the text. The public reading of the Scriptures in the synagogues every Sabbath day also preserved their purity. In addition to this, the Jews were jealous of their Scriptures and enacted a law making one guilty of inexpiable sin who should presume to make the slightest alteration. (4) The exceeding care of the Jewish copyists would likewise reduce to a minimum any errors in transcribing. They used such further precautions against alterations as ascertaining the number of letters and the middle sections of the several books. (5) In the case of the New Testament there is the agreement of the ancient manuscripts. The chief collators of the New Testament were Erasmus, the editors of the Complutensian and London Polyglots and individual biblical scholars such as Bengel, Wetstein, Griesbach, Matthæi, Schols, Kennicott and De Rossi. Dr. Kennicott examined six hundred and fifteen manuscripts and De Rossi collated seven hundred and thirty-one more making thirteen hundred and forty-six in all. The testimony of Dr. Kennicott was that he had "found many variations, and some grammatical errors; but not one of which af-

The Jewish copyists were at some periods, excessively, I had almost said superstitiously, exact. They noted the verses where something was supposed to be forgotten, the words which they believed to be changed, and the letters which they regarded as superfluous. They ascertained the middle letter of the Pentateuch, the middle clause and letter of each book, and how many times each letter of the alphabet occurs in all the Hebrew Scriptures. Thus Aleph, they tell us, occurs 42,377 times; Beth, 32,218 times. I mention these facts to show the excessive care and particularity of these ancient copyists, and how unlikely it is that any considerable change could occur under their hands. —POND, *Christian Theology*, p. 89.

fected, in the smallest degree, any article of faith and practice." (6) The numerous quotations from the New Testament found in the writings of the Fathers, not only prove the authenticity of the Scriptures as previously mentioned, but the integrity of the text as well. (7) Closely allied with these are the various helps which have served to preserve the original text. For the Old Testament there are the Targums, the Talmud and the Septuagint. For the New Testament there are the various translations. Here we may mention the *Peshito,* or Syriac version (c. 150 A.D.); the *Itala,* or old Latin version (c. 160 A.D.); the *Vulgate* or Jerome's translation (latter part of the fourth century; the *Coptic* (or old Egyptian), the *Ethiopic* and the *Gothic,* all of the fourth century and the *Armenian* translation of the fifth century. These translations and recensions confirm both the authenticity and the integrity of the New Testament. Dr. Philip Schaff says that "in the absence of the autographs, we must depend upon copies or secondary sources. But these are fortunately, far more numerous and trustworthy for the Greek New Testament than for any ancient classic."

The *Targums* are Hebrew paraphrases of the Old Testament, the word *Targum* meaning "interpretation." The *Talmud* is a commentary on the Old Testament, the word *Talmud* meaning "instruction." The Talmud is composed of two parts, the *Mishna* which is the text itself in either Babylonian or Palestinian, and the *Gemara* which is the commentary on the text. These helps are an aid in understanding the text and preserving it. The *Septuagint* is the Greek translation of the Old Testament made in Egypt for the Alexandrian Jews about 287 B.C. though the date is sometimes placed at 280 B.C. and by others at 250 B.C.

PART II. THE DOCTRINE OF THE FATHER

CHAPTER IX

THE EXISTENCE AND NATURE OF GOD

The first task of theology is to establish and unfold the doctrine of God. The existence of God is a fundamental concept in religion, and therefore a determinative factor in theological thought. The nature ascribed to God gives color to the entire system. To fail here is to fail in the whole compass of truth. Theology, however, can hardly be expected to furnish a demonstrative proof of God's existence, for belief does not rise altogether from logical arguments. The existence of God is a first truth, and must logically precede and condition all observation and reasoning. Men reach a conviction on this subject apart from scientific discussion. To the great mass of men the theistic arguments are unknown, and to many others they do not carry the conviction of certainty. These arguments will therefore be presented as confirmatory proofs of the existence of God, and will be useful in showing the approach of the human mind in its attempt to grasp and explain its belief in the Divine Existence. It must also be borne in mind, that the best apologetic is a clear statement of the doctrines we would establish. Once the Christian position is clearly understood, many of the objections urged against it become irrelevant. We must, then, seek for other causes which have made belief in God a general and persistent idea among men.

Definition of God. Since the mind must define by limiting the object of its thought, it is evident that the human mind can never form an adequate conception of God or properly define His being. Only the infinite can comprehend the Infinite. This philosophical conclusion finds its support in the New Testament, which reveals God as *dwelling in the light that no man can approach unto; whom no man hath seen, nor can see* (I Tim. 6: 16). The nearest approach to a definition is the *I AM THAT I*

AM of the Old Testament (Exod. 3:14) which asserts His existence with no attempt at proof, and further implies that His essence can be known only to Himself. God, therefore, can be known to us only through a revelation of Himself, and while these manifestations are imperfect, due to our limited capacity, they are, in so far as comprehended by us, actual knowledge, which the mind attributes to God as possessed in an infinite degree. Since our conception of the attributes is likewise in a degree indefinite, they may not in this sense be regarded as a definition; but on the other hand, in so far as they furnish a comprehensive statement of the attributes as revealed in Scripture, they may very properly be considered a definition of God.

God is a Spirit, holy in nature and attributes, absolute in reality, infinite in efficiency, perfect in personality, and thereby the ultimate ground, adequate cause and sufficient reason for all finite existence. In the words of our own creed, "We believe in one eternally existent, infinite God, Sovereign of the universe. That He only is God, creative and administrative, holy in nature, attributes, and purpose. That He, as God, is Triune in essential being, revealed as Father, Son, and Holy Spirit" (*Manual*, p. 25, Art. I). The *Thirty-nine Articles* of the Church of England define God as follows: "There is but one living and true God, everlasting, without body, parts or passions; of infinite power, wisdom, and goodness; the Maker and Preserver of all things both visible and invisible. And in the unity of this Godhead there be three Persons, of one substance, power and eternity; the Father, the Son, and the Holy Ghost" (Article I). John Wesley revised the Anglican Confession for the Methodist Episcopal Church of America, reducing the *Thirty-nine Articles* to what is commonly known as the *Twenty-five Articles*. However, he made no change in Article I except to change the word "be" to "are" in the second part. But in 1786 the Bishops of the Conference omitted the word "passions," so that the Methodist statement reads, "without body or parts." The Anglican statement is one of the original articles of 1553 and its language is very similar to that of the Augsburg Confession. The Westminster Catechism defines God as "A Spirit, infinite, eternal, and unchangeable in His being, power, holiness, justice, goodness and truth."

The definitions of God given by the theologians of the Christian Church differ widely. Dr. Charles Hodge approves the Westminster statement, but Dr. John Miley holds that "personality is the deepest truth in the conception of God and with this should be combined the perfection of his personal attributes." Hence he defines God as "an eternal personal Being, of absolute knowledge, power and goodness." Dr. A. H. Strong's definition is "the infinite and perfect Spirit in whom all things have their source, support and end." Calovius defines God as *essentia spiritualis infinita;* Ebrard as "the eternal source of all that is temporal," Kahnis as "the infinite Spirit"; while Andrew Fuller thinks of God as "the first cause and last end of all things." Martensen says, "God is a Person, that is, He is the self-centralized absolute, the eternal fundamental Being, which knows itself as center—as the I AM in the midst of its infinite glory, which is conscious of being the Lord of this glory." Calderwood defines God as "an infinite Being, who is subject to no restrictive conditions." Henry B. Smith says, "God is a Spirit, absolute, personal, holy, infinite and eternal in His being and attributes, the ground and cause of the universe." Hase defines God as "the absolute personality who out of free love is the cause of the universe"; while Van Oosterzee says, "We speak of Him, not simply as the totality of all being, but as the self-existent One, who unconditionally is and would be, though all beyond Himself should be altogether nonexistent."

Philosophical Conception of God. The term *God* has a different meaning in philosophy from that which attaches to it in religion. In religion, the term *God* as Absolute Personality is interpreted to mean that He possesses in infinite perfection all that constitutes personality in finite beings. In philosophy, the term is a synonym for the Absolute in the sense of ultimate reality, whether conceived as personal or impersonal. The term *Absolute* is not scriptural and not necessarily religious. It has come into current use in modern times only, and is used to express abstract thought concerning the ultimate nature of reality. Aristotle defines God as "the first ground of all being, the Divine Spirit, which unmoved, moves all." The conception of God here is static, an "Unmoved Mover." Perhaps the highest definition in pagan antiquity is that of Plato who says, "God is the eternal mind, the cause of good in nature." Kant defines God as "a Being who by His understanding and will is the cause of nature; a Being who has all rights and no duties; the supreme perfection in substance, the all-obligating Being, author of a universe under moral law; the moral author of the world; an intelligence infinite in every respect." Hegel, whose absolute idealism was the outgrowth of the Kantian philosophy, defines God as "the Absolute Spirit, the pure, essential Being that makes Himself Object to himself; absolute holiness; absolute power, wisdom, goodness, justice." To Spinoza, God is "the absolute universal Substance; the real Cause of all and every existence; the alone, actual, and unconditioned Being, not only Cause of all being, but itself all being, of which every special existence is only a modification." This is a pantheistic definition. When Calvin defined God as "an infinite and spiritual essence," and Luther held to a similar definition, it must be borne in mind, that in the sixteenth century during which they wrote, the pantheistic discussion had not sprung up. Now it is necessary to qualify such abstract statements by including the term personality, which is essential to the Christian conception of God.

In proportion as man's thought approaches maturity, the religious and philosophical conceptions of God tend to become more and more identified. The Spirit of Holiness and the Spirit of Truth are identical, and tend to lead to a rational statement of religious experience. This tendency toward the identification of thought and experience is not an arbitrary matter, but the consequence of a unity of life which combines both philosophic and religious interests in one person. It may be studied in religions and philosophies other than Christianity. With the broader and deeper insights of maturity, man comes to realize that God must be Master of the world if He is to satisfy the religious needs of men; while the philosopher finds that the universe can have no explanation without accounting for the facts of ethical and religious life. Scripture makes this clear in the statement that Christ is not only the Head of the Church, but the Head of all things to the Church (Eph. 1: 22).

In any comprehensive discussion of the doctrine of God, it is obvious that the subject must be considered in its two main branches, *first*, the more general idea of the existence of God as an object of human thought and knowledge; and *second*, the more specific revelation of His nature and attributes. The first is the idea of God in its philosophical aspects, and is commonly known as Theism; the second is the idea of God as found in religion, and commonly treated as Theology, in the narrower sense of the term. These two conceptions cannot be kept entirely apart, but they may be distinguished in a broad way, as God's revelation *in* man as to his constitution and nature; and His revelation *to* man as a free and responsible person. The first is metaphysical, the second is ethical.

The Christian Conception of God. Before taking up the discussion of these two aspects of the Supreme Being, it may be well to notice a third phase of the subject in a preliminary way—the unity of the philosophical and religious aspects of God as revealed in the historical Christ. The Christian conception of God is a conviction that the ultimate Personality of religion and the Absolute of philosophy find their highest expression in Jesus Christ; and that in His Person and work we have the deepest possible insight into the nature and purpose of God. *He that hath seen me hath seen the Father,* is Jesus' enunciation of this great truth (John 14: 9). Stated theocentrically, Christ does not only reveal God, God reveals Himself through Jesus Christ. When theology starts with any conception of God lower than that which is revealed in and through Jesus Christ, says Dickie, it is always difficult to lift that conception to a standard which is fully and consistently Christian. Christian theology must therefore in a large measure be Christo-centric, molding its conceptions in the fullness of Him who is *the effulgence of the Father's glory and the express image of his person* (Heb. 1:3). It is this conception which has expressed itself theologically in the great doctrines of the Incarnation and the Trinity, and which marks the fundamental distinction between the Christian view of God, and that found in other forms of theistic belief.

The Christian idea of God unites in itself historically three fundamental elements which may be traced to a greater or lesser extent in their processes of development. The first is the concept of personality, which forms the basis of the religion of Israel, and was revealed directly to the covenant people by the Spirit himself. The second is the concept of the absolute, indirectly revealed through the search of the human mind after truth. It reaches its noblest expression in the philosophy of the Greeks. Since the Greek language was ordained of the Spirit to be the medium through which the New Testament should be given to the world, its expression was determined largely by the philosophical concepts which characterized that language. This philosophical expression is given the sanction of Divine Revelation in the Logos doctrine as set forth in the Prologue to the Fourth Gospel. In these few verses (John 1:1-18) the inspired writer has lifted out of the mazes of Greek thought, the true concept of Christ as the Logos, and in one of the most remarkable philosophical statements ever uttered, has given us divine insight into the relation existing between the revelation of God in nature and His revelation through the Spirit. The third constituent element is to be found in the interpretation of both personality and absoluteness in terms of the revelation of God in Christ. Christianity contends that in Christ is to be found at once, the explanation of the true nature of ultimate reality as sought by philosophy, and the supreme revelation of the personal God in His character and attributes, as demanded by religion.

THE EXISTENCE OF GOD

Among the older theologians, the philosophical aspects of the doctrine of God were commonly treated under the head of *Theism*. By this is meant a belief in a personal God, Creator and Preserver of all things, who is at once immanent in creation, and transcendent, or above and separate from it. Opposed to this view may be mentioned *Deism* which maintains the personality of God, but denies His immanence in creation and His providential sovereignty of the universe. It is an overemphasis upon the separateness of God from His created works, and historically has denied the Scriptures as a Divine revelation. *Pantheism* on the other hand is an overemphasis upon the relation of God to the universe, and stresses His immanence to the disparagement of His transcendence. In breaking down the distinction between God and creation, pantheism in contradistinction to Theism, denies the personality of God. Philosophical Theism, with its various theories concerning the nature and proofs of God's existence, has in some sense been the most barren department of theological thought. And yet the Scriptures give us some ground for this philosophical approach by their emphasis upon the revelation of God in nature and the constitution of man. St. Paul asserts that *the invisible things of him from the creation of the world are clearly seen, being understood by the things that are made, even his eternal power and Godhead; so that they are without excuse* (Rom. 1:20). The existence of God as we have shown, is a fundamental presupposition, not only of the Christian religion, but of all religion in its higher forms. It is not a conviction to be reached by discursive reason, and does not therefore depend upon demonstration. This conviction is real and potent, is innate in man and tends to become more and more explicit. The existence of God must therefore be regarded both as an innate idea in the limited sense of this term, and as a truth demonstrating itself to reason. According to the former, it is a necessary element in man's consciousness. It is like the atmosphere. We cannot see it, and yet we cannot see without it. According to the latter, it becomes necessary to arrange the elements of consciousness into a system of confirmatory arguments, such as shall justify the claims of reason. We shall therefore treat this subject of the Existence of God, *first,* as to the Origin of the Idea of God in Intuition; and *second,* as a Confirmatory Revelation of God.

ORIGIN OF THE IDEA OF GOD IN INTUITION

God alone can reveal Himself to man. This He has done in a primary revelation found in the nature and constitution of man, and secondarily, by the direct revelation of Himself through the Spirit to the consciousness of men. The first finds its culmination in the Incarnation, or the Word made flesh; while the second has its source in the Glorified Christ, as the foundation for the revelation of God through the Spirit. The term "innate" is therefore applied to our primary knowledge of God. Since this term has been the source of much speculation and debate in philosophy, it may be well to use instead, the term rational intuition. By intuition we mean that power which the mind has of immediate insight into truth. Intuitive truths are self-evident and are usually regarded as above logical proof. There are some truths, however, which are intuitional in a portion of their content, and yet acquired in an experimental or logical manner. Such is that of the existence of God, which is intuitive as an immediate datum of the moral and religious consciousness, and yet a truth to be demonstrated to reason. When, therefore, we speak of the idea of God as being intuitive, we do not mean that it is a first truth written upon the soul prior to consciousness; this would be to make the soul a material substance; nor is it actual knowledge which the soul finds itself in possession of at

By intuition we mean that ability of the soul to receive knowledge independently of the five senses though not contrary to them.—PAUL HILL.

birth; nor is it an idea imprinted upon the mind which may be developed apart from the law of observation and experience. It does mean that in the constitution and nature of man there is a capacity for the knowledge of God which responds in an intuitive manner to revealed truth, comparable to that in which the mind of man responds to the outer world. The Word by whom all things were created, is not only the principle of intelligence and order in the universe, but the mediatory ground, also, of man's intuitive knowledge of God. Thus we bring together three important factors in the knowledge of God, *first,* intuitive reason as the power of immediate insight into truth, which as a consequence of creation through the Divine Word, endows men with a capacity for the knowledge of God; *second,* revelation,

There are some faculties of mind which determine the modes of our ideas. Some we obtain through sense-perception. Sense-experience underlies all such perception. We cannot in this mode reach the idea of God. Many of our ideas are obtained through the logical reason. They are warranted inferences from verified facts or deductions from self-evident principles. Through the same faculty we receive many ideas, with a conviction of their truth, on the ground of human testimony. There are also intuitive truths, immediate cognitions of the primary reason. The conviction of truth in these ideas comes with their intuitive cognition. Through what mode may the idea of God be obtained? Not through sense-perception, as previously stated. Beyond this it is not necessarily limited to any one mental mode: not to the intuitive faculty, because it may be a product of the logical reason or a communication of revelation to the logical reason; nor to this mode, because it may be an immediate truth of the primary reason. . . . . The idea of God as a sense or conviction of this existence is a product of the intuitive faculty. There is an intuitive faculty of the mind, the faculty of immediate insight into truth. Thorough analysis as surely finds such a faculty as it finds the other well-known faculties, such as the presentative, the representative and the logical. To surrender these distinctions of faculty is to abandon psychology. To hold others on the ground of such distinctions is to admit an intuitive faculty.—MILEY, *Systematic Theology,* I, pp. 60, 62.

A. A. Hodge in speaking of the innateness of the idea of God says, "It is not innate in the sense either that man is born with a correct idea of God perfectly developed, or that, independently of instruction, any man can, in the development of his natural powers alone, arrive at a correct knowledge of God. . . . . . On the other hand, independently of all instruction, a sense of dependence and of moral accountability is natural to man. These logically involve the being of God, and when the intellectual and moral character of an individual or race is in any degree developed, these invariably suggest the idea and induce the belief of a God. Thus man is as universally a religious as he is a rational being. And whenever the existence and character of God as providential and moral ruler is offered as fact, then every human soul responds to it as true, seen in its own self-evidencing light, in the absence of all formal demonstration."—A. A. HODGE, *Outlines of Theology,* pp. 12, 13.

or the Spirit's universal presentation of truth to intuitive reason, through the revealing activity of the Divine Word. *This is the true Light, which lighteth every man that cometh into the world* (John 1:9); and *third,* as a consequence of the union of the two previous factors, the universal and necessary idea of God. Human nature, therefore, is such that it necessarily develops the idea of God, through the revelation of the truth by the Spirit, in much the same manner as it develops a knowledge of the world through the data of the senses. This consciousness may be perverted by moral unlikeness to God, even as that of the outward world may be perverted by a false philosophy. The fact that the idea of God assumes so many forms, is proof at once of its intuitive nature on the one hand, and of its perversion on the other—this perversion being due to the withdrawal of the Spirit of holiness occasioned by sin. In support of the intuitive nature of the idea of God as thus set forth, we offer, *first,* the testimony of Scripture; and *second,* the universal experience of men.

The existence of God, God alone can reveal. He has wrought this supreme truth into the constitution of human nature as its Creator. Scripture, which never proves the being of the Supreme, appeals to this consciousness; it also gives the reason for its disturbance, and thus by antipication obviates the force of every argument against it. . . . . All processes of this argument rest finally on the analysis of that original consciousness of God which is the birthright of man as a creature: hence they are derived, *first,* from an appeal to the nature of the human spirit itself; *second,* from a consideration of the relation of the human mind to the phenomena of the universe; and *third,* from the universal Theism of the race as the result of both. . . . The simplest form of the argument is to be sought in the moral constitution of man, which in reason or conscience proclaims the existence of a Supreme Lawgiver, and in its desires and aspirations the existence of a Supreme Object for communion with whom it was made. These are elements of our nature and not the result of education; they are primary, intuitive, and universal; refusing at the outset all argument upon their origin. If conscience is the moral consciousness—its only sound definition—it as much implies a spiritual world into which man is born as consciousness generally implies the natural world. If it is the reason or heart or central personality of man it gives testimony, supreme in the soul, to a Power who rules in righteousness and hates iniquity. The rational law of our nature is its moral law. It points to a Holy Governor, whom it suggests or to whom it appeals, above the visible world nothing in which is capable of exciting its emotions. And the universal feeling of dependence on a Being or a Person higher than ourselves reinforces this argument: the same heart in man which trembles before an Authority above him yearns to be able to trust in Him. This may be called the moral demonstration.—Pope, *Compend, Christian Theology,* I, pp. 234, 235, 236.

The Testimony of Scripture. The Scriptures everywhere assume that there is in man's nature the consciousness of a Supreme Being, upon whom he depends
and to whom he is responsible. It makes an appeal to the
law written in their hearts, and also to the sense of dependence upon God as the source and satisfaction of
all their desires, *if haply they might feel after him, and
find him* (Acts 17: 27). It is in God that *we live, and
move, and have our being. . . . . For we are also his offspring* (Acts 17: 28). The prologue to the Fourth Gospel is explicit in its teachings upon this subject, where
the eternal Logos is declared to be *the true light, which
lighteth every man that cometh into the world* (John 1:
1-18). The only atheism which is recognized in the Scriptures is a practical atheism which grows out of a reprobate mind. Sin has obscured the truth in human nature
and the Scriptures charge men with not desiring to retain
the knowledge of God. It is the fool who has said in
his heart, *There is no God*—that is, there is no God for
me (Cf. Rom. 1: 28, Psalm 14: 1, Eph. 2: 12). Of great
significance also is the fact that the written revelation
begins with the words, *In the beginning God,* and assumes without attempt to prove the existence of God.
The Christian scholar may, therefore, confidently rest
in the fact that God has so laid this fundamental evidence in the nature and constitution of man, that He has
nowhere left Himself without a witness. Even the Greek
philosopher Plato could say that God holds the soul
by its roots—he does not need to demonstrate to the
soul the fact of His existence. He must therefore declare explicitly as does the Scripture, that *the invisible*

The Scripture "certainly declares this at least, that the very life of
the dependent creature is bound up with the idea of its Independent
Source, the very thought of God in man's mind—to anticipate a future
argument—assumes that God is. It goes higher still, if possible. It declares that the eternal Logos or Word is *the true light which lighteth
every man that cometh into the world.* And this precedes, in order of
time and thought, that higher revelation which follows: *No man hath
seen God at any time; the only begotten Son, which is in the bosom of
the Father, he hath declared him* (John 1:18). He is Himself the manifestation of the invisible God, but only as revealing Himself to a preparatory consciousness in mankind. 'Εκεῖνος ἐξηγήσατο: He hath expounded in
a final exegesis the original text implanted in the universal human nature."—POPE, *Compend. Christian Theology,* I, p. 235.

things of him from the creation of the world are clearly seen, being understood by the things that are made, even his eternal power and Godhead; so that they are without excuse (Rom. 1: 20).

The Universal Experience of Men. An intuitive or first truth must be characterized by universality and necessity. If then the idea of God is intuitive, it should be corroborated by an appeal to the universal experience of mankind, and this is the testimony of those whose investigations have enriched the fields of anthropology and comparative religions. In addition to the instances already cited in our discussion of the science of religion, we may mention also Max Mueller who after painstaking and discriminating research concerning the origin and growth of religion states, that "as soon as man becomes conscious of himself as distinct from all other things and persons, he at the same time becomes conscious of a higher self; a power without which he feels that neither he nor anything else would have any life or reality." This is the first sense of the Godhead, the *sensus numinus* as it has been called; for it is a *sensus*, an immediate perception, not the result of reasoning or generalizing, but an intuition as irreversible as the impression of our senses. In receiving it we are passive, at least as passive as receiving from above the image of the sun or any other sensible impression. This *sensus numinus* is the source of all religion. It is that without which no religion true or false is possible (MAX MUELLER, *Science of Language*, p. 145). In his reference to the worship of the lower forms of religion he says, "Not the visible sun, moon and stars are invoked, but something else that cannot be seen." While there have been races which at first appeared to be without any form of religion, closer observation and a better understanding of the varying forms of religious practices, have shown that no tribe is without an object of worship. "The statement that there are nations or tribes which possess no religion," says Tiele, "rests either upon inaccurate observations or on a confusion of ideas. No tribe or nation has yet been met with destitute of belief in any higher beings, and travelers who asserted their existence have been afterwards refuted by facts. It is legitimate, therefore, to call religion, in its most general sense, a universal phenomenon of humanity" (TIELE, *Outlines of the History of Religion*, p. 6). This agreement among individuals, tribes and nations, widely separated in time and place would appear to be sufficient evidence as to the universality of the idea of God. It may assume a thousand forms, but these diverse and imperfectly developed ideas can be accounted for only as perversion of an intuitive conviction common to all men. Washington Gladden once said, "A man may escape from his shadow by going into the dark; but if he comes under the light of the sun, the shadow is there." A man may be so mentally undisciplined that he does not recognize these ideas; but let him learn the use of his reason, let him reflect on his own mental processes and he will know that they are necessary ideas.

The universality of the idea of God leads immediately to its acceptance as a necessary idea. By a necessary idea we mean any intuition which springs directly and immediately from the constitution of the human mind, and which under proper conditions must of necessity so spring. This only can account for the persistence of the idea of God, without which it could never have been perpetuated. "Neither a primitive revelation, nor the logical reason, nor both together could account for the persistence and universality of the idea of God without a moral and religious nature in man to which the idea is native" (MILEY, *Systematic Theology*, I, p. 70). We may carry the argument one step farther, and insist that our intuitions give us objective truth. By a process of negative reason, we may argue that to deny this is to deny the validity of all mental processes. To distrust its intuitions is to lead immediately to a distrust in the interpretation of sense-perceptions through which our knowledge of the external world is mediated. To hold otherwise is to land in agnosticism. But man's mental faculties are trustworthy. His rational intuitions are absolute truth, and the intuition of God, universal and necessary in the experience of the race, finds its only sufficient explanation in the truth of His existence.

CONFIRMATORY REVELATIONS OF GOD

Since the time when English empiricism was led into thorough-going skepticism by Hume, and the famous *Critique* of Immanuel Kant played such an important part in the discussion, the historic arguments for the existence of God have been persistently attacked by both the opponents and the defenders of the theistic position. There are some theists who hold that the existence of God being a first truth, is the logical *prius* of all other knowledge, and must therefore be impossible of demonstration. God must be intuited, it is said, from the necessity of His relations; such as, the Infinite as the correlative of the finite; Absolute Being in contradistinction to dependence; Overmaster or Lord in the nature of law; and Creative Reason as furnishing the guaranty

"The word intuition is a convenient term for stating the fact that the mind on certain occasions from its own inherent energy gives rise to certain thoughts." By an accommodation of language such thoughts are themselves called intuitions; the power the mind has of giving rise to such thoughts is called the intuitive faculty. The same idea is sometimes expressed by the terms, the nature, or the constitution of the mind, that is to say, the mind is conceived of as a somewhat whose nature is to give rise to thoughts when the proper occasion occurs. The same thing is intended when it is said of a class of ideas that they are innate, not that the ideas are in the minds of infants at birth, but that ideas are born in the mind when the conditions of their birth occur. Now, it must be manifest that an inquiry after the genesis of thought must in all cases in the last resort be referred to the nature of the mind itself; for example, in any instance of perception, if we inquire, How came the mind to be in possession of the idea, suppose of color, as white or black? The usual answer is, By the sense of sight; but this answer is not complete, for it may still be inquired, How does sight give such ideas? and the answer must be, It is of the nature of the mind to be so impressed when the organs of sight are brought into exercise. . . . . The affirmation that the idea of God is intuitive, is an affirmation that the idea arises in the mind precisely in the same way as do ideas of time, space, substance, and all others of that class of thoughts. Again, man comes into being in a condition of absolute dependence, and some apprehensions of this dependence must, from the nature of the case, be among the earliest ideas in consciousness. Arising out of this sense of dependence inseparably connected with it, is a sense of obligation. Obligation is an apprehension not only of somewhat as due, but also of somewhat as due to Someone, and that One him upon whom we are dependent. In a word, it would seem evident from the obvious facts of the case, that the sense of dependence and obligation, of which all men are apprehensive from the earliest moments of conscious thought, are by them intuitively referred to an infinite intelligent first cause."—RAYMOND, *Systematic Theology*, I, pp. 248-252.

and basis of human reason. It is necessary, therefore, at the outset, to state in what sense the word proof is used in reference to the divine existence. Ulrici maintains that "the proofs for the existence of God coincide with the grounds for belief in God; they are simply the real grounds for belief, established and expounded in a scientific manner. If there be no such proofs, there are also no such grounds—if possible at all, can be no proper belief, but an arbitrary, self-made, subjective opinion. It must sink to the level of mere illusion." If this be true, then it follows that the proofs of God's existence must be simply confirmatory revelations, the manifestations by which He makes Himself known in consciousness and the external world.

As confirmatory revelations, it is evident that the great theistic arguments must be something less than the full Christian view. There is a limit to their power

"Belief in God is by no means the necessary product of demonstration. As old as humanity itself, it was not at first produced by reasoning, but rather in its most primitive form preceded all reasoning. No one has ever begun to feel convinced of this truth merely because it had been demonstrated to him in a strictly logical manner. Men would hardly, indeed, have given themselves the trouble to seek for proofs for this conviction, had it not with irresistible power forced itself, as it were, on their innermost consciousness. Everywhere do we discover this belief, even where no proof has ever been yet heard of; and it will last even where the weak sides of all known proofs are by no means ignored. Belief in God is consequently no result, but, on the contrary, a starting-point for human thinking on invisible things—a postulate of our whole rational and moral nature, but no result of a universally recognized syllogism.—VAN OOSTERZEE, Chr. Dogm., p. 239.

But Christian dogmatics ought not from its standpoint to overlook the importance of other so-called proofs for the existence of God; much less to make common cause with those who speak with a certain contempt thereof, as a fruit of defective reasoning and foolish imagination. On the contrary, it must and will deplore the levity with which the assertion, in itself true, that God's existence cannot be proved (demonstrated), is frequently repeated, understood, and applied in a way which as much as possible plays into the hands of unbelief and skepticism. "Modern theology, which so readily gives up the proofs for the existence of God, abandons thereby not only its own position as a science; but also, in principle, annihilates faith, and the religion of which it is the theology."—ULRICI. It is true, there is not a single proof against which objections more or less serious might not be, and have been, adduced. All bear the unequivocal traces of the limitation of human thought. . . . . But yet they remain highly commendable, as more or less successful endeavors, not only to bring into satisfactory clearness the utterances of the innermost consciousness, but also to justify them to oneself and others as highly reasonable"—Cf. POPE, Compend. Christian Theology, pp. 233, 234, 236.

of demonstration, and indeed they are more properly regarded in this light, as probable rather than demonstrative arguments. But in either case they require the enforcement of the Holy Spirit's influence as divine credentials, and must in every case derive their strength from the further revelation of God as to His own essence and perfections.

While the earliest objections to the arguments were urged on the basis of being formally invalid from the syllogistic point of view, involving the logical fallacy of assuming that which they profess to prove, later criticism points out that even when carried out to a logical conclusion, they yield a result that is not fully Christian. It should be kept in mind that the period of the Middle Ages in which the schoolmen developed the theistic arguments, was characterized by an emphasis upon the antithesis between reason and revelation. Reason or Natural Theology must be supplemented by Revelation. Originally the theistic arguments were designed to prove that the Christian idea of God was impossible to Natural Theology or Reason, and must be supplied by the Scripture or Revelation. Their function was to show that reason revealed some things about God, but not sufficent for the knowledge of salvation. The rational method was supplemented by authority. But with the changed attitude toward reason and revelation, and the tendency to regard life as a unity, experience becomes the dominant factor in the knowledge of God and must supply the distinctly Christian content.

The sharp distinction between reason and revelation made by the schoolmen, gave rise further, to the two great methods of approach which have played such an important part in this department of theological thought. The first is the method of philosophy, which seeks to establish the existence of God solely from the standpoint of human reason, and thus apart from divine revelation. The second is the method of authority and makes its appeal to the Scriptures, more especially to miracle and prophecy. Both have been historically important, and together they make up the traditional arguments for theism. The method of the older theology, therefore, both Catholic and Protestant, began with the formal and abstract arguments of reason, and filled in from revelation the distinctly Christian content. Dr. Dickie says, that in the first instance this scheme was superimposed upon Christian theology from Greek philosophy, and that it dominated all formal theology for at least seventeen hundred years.

The tendency, therefore, in theology has been to substitute a rationalistic conception of God for the personal revelation of God through the Spirit. The impression has been made that by examination of the evidences for the existence of God, as found in human consciousness and in the external world, man may attain to a spiritual and saving knowledge of God. In the Church of Rome this is held *de fido,* that is, it is heresy not to hold it. But rightly understood there is both a spiritual and a historical value attaching to these arguments. While in some sense they may be regarded as invalid syllogistically, they are of profound significance otherwise. First, they indicate the general starting point for the development of the idea of God, which primarily dwells in the human mind. All the processes of the arguments it will

As we come to the positive theistic argument, it will not be amiss to guard against certain errors respecting its functions. It will be rating the practical worth of the argument much too high to suppose that it affords the whole ground or incentive to theistic belief. Constitutional impulse is prior to syllogisms. The needs of the emotional, the æsthetic, and the moral nature stimulate to thought and unite with intellectual needs to beget and to keep alive the idea of a supernatural and overruling power. The history of the race pays too large tribute to the force, persistency, and universality of this idea to allow the supposition of its adventitious origin. . . . . The function of formal argumentation, therefore, can be only supplementary. The basis of theistic faith is always at hand before philosophy or theology begins to set its proofs in order.— SHELDON, *Sys. Chr. Doct.,* pp. 53, 54.

It would be an overvaluation of theistic argumentation to suppose that it is competent, in the strict sense of the term, to demonstrate the existence of a Divine Person. Demonstration proper belongs to the sphere of ideal quantities and relations, where the data are thus and so by hypothesis, and no account needs to be taken of any uncertainties and imperfections of observation or experience. It cannot, therefore, apply to the sphere of objective reality. In this domain, an overwhelming preponderance of grounds in favor of a particular conclusion is the most that can be attained. This suffices for practical needs, and speculation becomes intemperate when it asks for more, whether in physical science or in theology.—SHELDON, *Syst. Chr. Doct.,* p. 54.

be found, rest ultimately, on the analysis of the original consciousness of God which is the birthright of every creature. We mention this in anticipation of a later discussion concerning the knowledge of God, *i.e.*, that there is a vast difference between *knowing God* and *knowing about God*. Secondary knowledge, such as is given in the arguments, can never lead to a direct knowledge of God; but once God is known through a spiritual revelation, "this secondary knowledge which comes to us indirectly fills out our mental picture, while our personal knowledge, however slight, gives life and actuality to the whole."

The second value of the arguments, is found in the fact that they mark the various stages of knowledge, the lines along which in all ages man's thoughts have risen to God. They are, according to John Caird, "the unconscious or implicit logic of religion." "The manifold witnesses for God," says Bishop Martensen, "which man finds in and around himself are here reduced to general principles, and the various and intricate ways by which the human mind is brought to God are indicated by the summary results of thought." Both Bishop Martensen and Dr. Pope maintain that man's thought rises to God in two ways, by the contemplation of himself, and by the contemplation of the world. The arguments are classified accordingly—the cosmological and teleological growing out of the nature of the external world, and the ontological and moral from the constitution of the human mind. The arguments which have so greatly influenced the thought of the past, cannot therefore be passed over lightly, even though regarded as confirmative rather than demonstrative proofs. Later it is our purpose to

Though these several arguments do not necessarily conduct the unenlightened to the knowledge of God, yet, given even a hint of the divine existence, reason and nature afford abundant corroboration. It is one thing to make a synthesis of all the teachings of nature and reason and declare, God before unknown, to be the necessary result, and quite another thing, the existence of God being given as a proposition for proof. to gather together the evidences of it. There is no proof that the first feat has ever been accomplished by nation or individual. The discoverer of God, though a greater genius than Euclid or Newton, has not recorded his name in history.—SUMMERS, *Syst. Th.*, p. 69, gather them up and present them in their modern and scientific form.

In the more elaborate treatises on Theism, it is the usual practice to divide the arguments into two classes —the *a priori* and the *a posteriori*. This is a convenient arrangement but not accurate. It is difficult to draw a line and assign the arguments wholly to one class or the other. By *a priori* is meant the proof of fact or effect from the knowledge of existing causes; by *a posteriori* is meant the reasoning from effects to antecedent causes. For our purpose the simpler classification previously mentioned is more appropriate. We shall therefore treat the cosmological and teleological arguments as growing out of the nature of the external world, and the ontological and moral as related to the nature and constitution of the human mind. Dr. William Adams Brown defines these arguments and indicates their purpose in the following manner. *First,* the Cosmological Argument (from change to cause) is the Revelation of God as Power. *Second,* the Teleological Argument (from adaptation to purpose) is the Revelation of God as Design. *Third,* the Ontological Argument (from necessary thought to being) is the Revelation of God as Reality; and *Fourth,* the Moral Argument (from ideal to power adequate to realize it) is the Revelation of God as Right. (Cf. BROWN, *Christian Theology in Outline,* p. 124.)

The Cosmological Argument. The term "cosmological" has been conventionally adopted for this argument because it attempts to account for, or endeavors to explain the cosmos or universe. It is more strictly the "etiological" or causal argument by which the mind reasons from the contingency of phenomena to a First Cause. The argument usually takes two forms — the physical which relies upon facts of the material universe, and the metaphysical which makes its appeal to causation or efficient force. The first or physical argument makes use of two indisputable facts of nature—matter and motion. It is certain that something has existed from eternity, but this cannot have been matter for matter is mutable. But since matter because it is mutable cannot be eternal, so the Creator because He is eternal cannot be either mutable or material. From the point of view of physics, we are therefore shut up to belief in a self-existent, spiritual Creator. The second or metaphysical form of the argument is stated by Johnson as follows: "Every change must have a cause; but the only real cause is a first cause; therefore the ever-changing universe must have had a First Cause. Furthermore, the idea of causation arises in the mind upon the exercise of will. We have a conception of cause only by virtue of the fact that in forming volitions, we ourselves are consciously causes. The First Cause must therefore be conceived by us as Will, that is, a Person."

The Teleological Argument. The presence of design or purpose in the universe has been more or less clearly recognized by men from the beginning. The earliest statement is found in Genesis, *i.e.*, the stars are for light, fruit is for food, and like expressions. The Psalms are replete with arguments for design. The one hundred and fourth Psalm has been called the teleological or design Psalm. This argument has always held an important place among theists. Kant treated it with great respect, and Mill looked upon it as the only argument which had any strength. Christian apologetics has made much of it, often carrying it beyond the limits of sound reasoning. The evolutionists claimed for a time that the famous Watch Argument of Paley was invalid and had completely lost its point. But in LeConte, Drummond and others, the argument reappears in a new form—no longer particular design, but universal design. Kant made objection that "the design argument at best proves an architect only, not a Creator," but this objection loses its force when it is seen that origination and design go together.

The Ontological Argument. The germ of this argument is found in St. Augustine's discussion of the Trinity (*Trinity* VII, iv) where he says, "God is more truly thought than He is described, and exists more truly than He is thought." Dr. Shedd in commenting upon this says, "This is one of those pregnant propositions so characteristic of the Latin Fathers, which compresses a theory into a nutshell. . . . . God's existence is more real than even our conception of Him is for our own mind; and our conception confessedly is a reality in our own consciousness. . . . . The subjective idea of God instead of being more real than God is less real. The 'thing' in this instance has more of existence than the 'thought' of it has." It remained, however, for Anselm to first give construction to the ontological argument in syllogistic form, and with all the modifications to which it has been subjected, perhaps the original statement is still the clearest and strongest. "The idea of perfection includes existence, for that which does not exist will be less than perfect; therefore, since we have the idea of a perfect being, that being must exist for the idea includes his being or he would be less than perfect."

The acute and powerful intellect of Anselm possessed that metaphysical intuition which saw both the heart of the atonement and the heart of divine existence. Gaunilon, a contemporary of Anselm, wrote a tract entitled *"Liber pro Insipiento,"* or "Plea for the Fool," in which he raised an objection to the argument which has been repeated over and over again. He maintained that we have the idea of a tree, but it does not follow from this that there is an actual tree; or we have the idea of a winged lion, but this does not assure us that such a creature exists. But the reply to this argument, and all those of a similar nature is, that the vital point of the argument—that of necessary existence has been entirely overlooked. One idea is of a perfect and necessary

Knapp gives the Anselmic argument in this form: "The most perfect being is possible, and therefore, actually exists; for existence is a reality or perfection, and necessary existence is the highest perfection. Consequently necessary existence must be predicted of the most perfect being.—KNAPP, *Christian Theology,* p. 86.

Miley, quoting from the Proslogium gives the following statement of the argument. "We have the idea of the most perfect Being, a Being than whom a greater or more perfect cannot be conceived. This idea includes and must include actual existence, because actual existence is of the necessary content of the idea of the most perfect. An ideal being, however perfect in conception, cannot answer to the idea of the most perfect Being. This most perfect Being is God. Therefore God must exist."—MILEY, *Systematic Theology,* II, p. 74.

being—the other of an imperfect and contingent being. The idea of a tree is contingent, it may or may not be, and therefore from the idea of the tree it is impossible to prove its objective reality. But with the idea of God there is the element of necessity instead of contingency. If the idea is contingent and implies that a thing may or may not exist, then it does not necessarily follow that the object does exist; but if the idea of the thing implies necessity, or that it must exist, then it does follow that the thing exists.

Descartes apparently came to the same conclusion independently. Beginning by doubting all things possible, he came to the truth, "I think, therefore I am," the *cogito ergo sum* which he could not doubt. From this foundation he passed to a second statement, "I found that the existence of a perfect being was comprised in the idea in the same way in which the equality of the three angles of a triangle are equal to two right angles is comprised in the idea of a triangle, and that consequently it is at least as certain that God the perfect Being exists as any demonstration in geometry can be." (Cf. Descartes, *Method,* p. 240.) The English theologians made much use of this argument in their conflict with the atheism of Hobbes and others. Especially was this true of those theologians who were deeply versed in the writings of Plato and Aristotle, such as Cudworth, Bates, Stillingfleet and Henry More.

Kant objected to the ontological argument on the basis which we have before mentioned—that to think a perfect being by no means involves perfect existence. The modern objections, however, are at the opposite poles to the reasoning of Anselm. He held that objective reality is greater than the inward concept, while exactly the opposite is found in Kant and his followers, *i.e.,* that the object is not so real as the idea of it, and therefore must not be inferred from it. However, the argument may rest on another basis, that of absolute existence as necessary and implied in all existence. God is the substratum of all reality. We do not necessarily give up the argument by rejecting the Anselmic or Cartesian

form of it. "The principle of absolute being," says Dr.
Harris, "exists as a necessary law of thought, a constituent element of reasoning, and a necessary postulate in
all things about Being" (HARRIS, *Self-revelation of
God*, p. 164). Relative existence implies absolute existence; and a relative knowledge, absolute knowledge.
God must be the end as well as the beginning of all
things.

The Moral Argument. The highest revelation of God
is the revelation of right. The tendency of speculative
thought is to turn from nature to man. It is not that
nature has no disclosures to make, but the deeper revelation is through man. Man is in the Divine image; nature is secondary. The argument, however, is but another application of the causal principle—one applied to
the moral instead of the natural world. This world is as
orderly and full of purpose, as the physical, and can
be explained only by a cause of the same nature as itself.
The central fact of the moral realm is conscience; but
conscience does not make moral law. The moral law is
independent of man and unvarying from age to age.
Its laws are inexorable, and its existence not only demands an Author, but the moral realm reveals His character as the friend of righteousness and the enemy of
unrighteousness. It was, therefore, the distinctive service of Immanuel Kant, to present this argument in its
full extent and with great emphasis. He regarded it as
the only sufficient argument for God. "Two things there
are," said Kant, "which produce unceasing wonder—
the starry heavens above and the moral law within."
Kant had three postulates, Freedom, Immortality, God.
In the practical problem of pure reason and the necessary pursuance of the highest good, a connection is postu-
lated between happiness and morality, proportionate to
happiness. Man is to seek the highest good, and therefore the highest good must be possible. We must postulate then, the cause of nature as distinct from nature, and
it is this cause which is able to connect morality with happiness. The highest good cannot exist except God exists
—there must therefore be a highest good because our

moral reason demands it. Some highest good exists, therefore God exists. Duty is a great word with Kant. It implies that there is in the highest good a Being who is the supreme cause of nature, and who is the cause or Author of nature through His intelligence or will—that is, God. As the possibility of the highest good is inseparably connected with it, and it is morally necessary to hold the existence of God, one cannot help wondering why Kant did not find the existence of God *in* the moral law rather than as deduced *from* it. Duty is not something of itself apart from persons, but connected with them and recognized by them. It is because there is a Supreme Person that we recognize a supreme good, a supreme duty, a moral law.

CHAPTER X

THE DIVINE NAMES AND PREDICATES

The progressive revelation of God to man, as found in the Holy Scriptures, has its origin and development in the use of the Divine Names, through which God has communicated in varying degrees, something of the unsearchable mystery which surrounds His being. Two of these names, *Elohim* and *Jehovah* or *Yahweh,* when taken in their Old Testament unity, declare the being of God as absolute and necessary. There are many other names applied to Deity, but these two are supreme and run throughout the entire older period of revelation. Another name, *El Shaddai,* a combination of *El* and *Shaddai;* and *Adonai,* especially when used in the plural with Elohim and Jehovah, are of sufficient importance to demand special attention. All of these names are continued in the New Testament, and find their culmination in the revelation of God in Him, whose name is above *every name that is named, not only in this world, but also in that which is to come* (Eph. 1:21).

THE DIVINE NAMES AND HISTORICAL CRITICISM

It is a significant fact, that while theology has not given to the Divine Names the important place they deserve in the historical unfolding of the idea of God, rationalistic thought has built upon them the "documentary hypothesis," which has occupied so prominent a place in the so-called "Higher Criticism." The beginnings of the rationalistic movement are to be found in Eichorn (1781-1854) and his study of the "fragments of Reimaurus." He attempted to apply the principles of the so-called historical school to ecclesiastical law, and in the preface to his *Introduction to the Old Testament* uses the term "Higher Criticism" to distinguish his position from that of the older theology. In the formulation of the documentary hypothesis, however, it belonged to Jean Astruc (1684-1766), a French physician, to first introduce the terms *Elohist* and *Jehovist* or *Elohistic* and *Jehovistic* as applied to portions of the Old Testament. Reading the Book of Genesis, Astruc was arrested by the fact, which up to that time had been apparently unnoticed, that the first chapter of Genesis uses only the word *Elohim* for "God," while in other sections the word *Jehovah* is as persistently used. In the second and third chapters, the two names are combined, giving rise to a new conception of Deity as *Jehovah-Elohim* or the *"Lord-God."* With the thought in mind that possibly Moses had before him earlier documents, some perhaps dating back to Abraham, and that these had been combined into a single account, he sought to find whether there was a possibility of detecting and separating these documents and assigning them to their original sources. This he attempted to do on the basis that the varying use of terms indicated different writers. It was on this supposition that the modern critical attitude toward the Scriptures was founded.

In the development of the Higher Criticism, both Eichorn and DeWette accepted the theory of Astruc. DeWette (1780-1849) developed the theory further by asserting that the Book of Deuteronomy was not written by the author of the first four books of the Pentateuch; and his *Introduction to the Old Testament* published in 1806 marks one of the epochs in the development of rationalistic criticism. Strauss (1806-1874), Bauer (1792-1860) and the Tubingen School directed their attacks against the New Testament. Vatke published a book in 1836, in which he applied the principles of Hegelian philosophy to the Scriptures. Graf in 1866, advanced the theory that the body of laws found in the middle books of the Pentateuch was a late production, manufactured and placed in its present position after the Babylonian exile. This is commonly known as "the Graffian Hypothesis," and was accepted by Kuenen who published *The Religion of Israel* in 1869-1870, a further step in destructive criticism. It remained, however, for

Julius Wellhausen (1844-1918), by his popular gifts and intellectual acuteness, to secure for this position its wide acceptance in modern theological thought. We have given this brief account of the Higher Criticism, which in its radical and destructive form has so blighted the faith of the Church, in order to show more clearly the distinction between the development of rationalism in its concept of God and His Word, and God's own revelation of Himself through the Divine Names. When it is recalled that the historical perspective underlies the modern critical developments, new significance must be attached to God's appointed means for revealing Himself to His creatures.

Elohim. The first name of God given to us in the Scriptures, and one which pervades all the earlier writings is that of *Elohim.* The derivation of the word is uncertain, but it may be traced to the simple root word meaning *power,* or to the singular form which signifies the *effect of power.* In Genesis 31: 29 Laban says, *It is in the power [El] of my hand to do you hurt.* Moses in predicting the judgments which should come upon Israel if they disobeyed God said, *Thy sons and daughters shall be given to another people . . . . and there shall be no might [El] in thy hand* (Deut. 28: 32) The word *El* is translated "God" in about two hundred twenty-five places in the Authorized Version of the Old Testament, and in every case assumes the power of God used in behalf of His people. It signifies, therefore, that God is the possessor of every form of power. The word is generally used in the plural form in order to express the fullness and glory of the divine powers, and the majesty of Him in whom these powers inhere; but since the name is used with a singular verb, it maintains the monotheistic position without interpreting this in such a rigid manner as to preclude the later Trinitarian conception

As to the English word God, Dr. Adam Clarke says, "It is pure Anglo-Saxon and among our ancestors signifies not only the Divine Being now commonly designated by the word, but also *good;* as in their apprehension it appeared that *God* and *good* were correlative terms. When they thought or spoke of Him, they were doubtless led, from the word itself, to consider Him as the *Good being,* a fountain of infinite benevolence and beneficence toward His creatures."

of God. The name *Elohim* indicates the primary revelation of God as power, through the forces of nature and the constitution of man. As such it is a generic term, which may be and is applied in the Scriptures to the gods of paganism. There is in it also, the basis of the trinal energy as further developed in the revelation of His activity. *In the beginning Elohim created the heaven and the earth . . . . and the Spirit of Elohim moved upon the face of the waters. And Elohim said, Let there be light.* Here there are three distinct movements predicated of God, Elohim, the Spirit of Elohim, and the Word which appears in the formula, *Elohim said.* All are alike active in creation, and mark with some degree of distinctness the beginnings of that which is to become the triune conception of the Godhead, as revealed through Christ. The distinctions have not come into clear view, but the faint streaks of the dawn are discernible, and later unfoldings of the divine revelation make it possible to read into these terms the fullness of the Godhead.

Jehovah or *Yahweh.* The second name in the unfolding revelation of God is *Jehovah* or *Yahweh,* and lifts the concept of God from the mere plane of power to that of personal relationships. Elohim is a generic term; Jehovah is a proper noun-name. It was interpreted by God himself to His servant Moses as I AM, or I AM THAT I AM, expressions which may be equally well rendered as HE WHO IS, or HE WHO IS WHAT HE IS. The name unites in a single concept, what to man is the past, present and future, and as such denotes Absolute Being conjoined with the process of continual becoming, through the historical revelation of Himself to His people. The name may be further interpreted as *He shall cause to be,* and signifies the personal faithfulness of Jehovah to His people. It thus reveals the spirituality of God's purpose for men, and the increased importance which attaches to individual and personal relationships. It brings into clearer light the transcendence of God, and lifts Him above the forces of nature out of which the ethnic religions develop. It brings God to the plane of spiritual relationships, made known only through supernatural revelation.

The emphasis upon the historical process of revelation, as found in the name of Jehovah, finds its warrant in both the Scriptures and the history of the human race—especially in its relation to the Messianic promise. There can be no true conception of the relation of the Old Testament to the New, of the mission of Moses and of Christ, or of the relation between the written Word and the Personal Word, without a recognition of the divine method of a progressive revelation unfolding in the processes of history. Only from the genetic viewpoint will the revelation of God given at *sundry times and in divers manners* be found to form parts of a well-articulated whole. There is a false position oftentimes assumed, in regard to the relation existing between the Scriptures as the Word of God, and Christ as the Personal Word. The written Word is given a false autonomy by a failure to view it as a spiritual utterance. It thus becomes the letter which kills, rather than the spirit which gives life. This is the source of much which is little short of Bible worship, as over against the spiritual knowledge of Christ. The Bible is thus made the end instead of the means, the object of reverence in itself instead of the reverence which grows out of its use as a means of revealing the Personal Word. So also, this method of interpretation fails to discern the generic difference between Moses and Christ, and therefore to recognize the difference between the preliminary and the final revelation. Assuming that the Old and New Testaments move on the same plane of revelation, theologians have been tempted to set the one over against the other. When Christ said, *the law saith, but I say unto you,* He was not disparaging, much less contradicting the truths of the Old Testament, but He did admit that they contained but the lower stages of the divine revelation, and that they were to be carried to their perfection through a fuller and more perfect revelation. To fail to recognize the genetic processes of history, is to fail to see the Old and New Testaments in their relation to each other, or to understand the relation existing between the written and the Personal Word.

The Abrahamic Covenant introduced a new idea in the historical process of revelation, a truer and more satisfying fellowship between God and man, because effected by supernatural spiritual forces. Its inception is found in the protevangelium, spoken by God to man at the gates of Paradise, the initial promise of personal redemption. *The seed of the woman shall bruise the serpent's head.* This could come into the clearer light of the Abrahamic Covenant only through the name of Jehovah. Elohim signified the intuitive revelation of God through the forces of nature and the constitution of man, and reaches its height in what may be termed a knowledge *about* God. It is something short of personal fellowship. It signifies the immanence of God out of which pantheism grows, and which gives rise to the ethnic religions. But it is only through Jehovah or the revelation of God as a Person, that knowledge can deepen into fellowship and ethical relationships be established. This higher knowledge and fellowship initiated by the Abrahamic Covenant, takes the form of a promise in which Jehovah becomes the God of Abraham, of Isaac and of Jacob, and their seed after them from generation to generation. This covenant, however, is something more than a mere compact between two parties on the basis of certain stipulated agreements; it is rather of the nature of an institution, and Abraham with his posterity become mutually members. It differs from natural intuition in that it is a supernatural revelation, as the etymology of the word covenant would seem to indicate, *con,* with, and *venire,* to come, a divine advent, a special coming of Jehovah to His people. It differs also from the more external teaching about God, in that it is a spiritual bestowment, a personal fellowship which necessitates the knowledge of God in individual experience. It emphasizes further the transcendence of God and man, and in so far constitutes the covenant an ethical and spiritual institution, a household of faith.

El Shaddai. While the two supreme names applied to God in the Old Testament are *Elohim* and *Jehovah,* there are many variations and combinations of these, one of the more important being *El Shaddai* or *God Almighty.* Other names similar to this are the *Living God* (Job 5: 17) the *Most High* (Gen. 14: 18), the *Lord,* or the *Lord God of Hosts* (Jer. 5: 14). The word *Shaddai* is generally derived from terms meaning "powerful," or "mighty." *El Shaddai* is frequently found as a name for God in the patriarchal accounts and in Job. The passages in which it occurs are seen specially to reveal God as the Bountiful Giver. Parkhurst in his Lexicon defines the name *Shaddai* as "one of the divine titles, meaning the power or Shedder-forth, that is of blessings temporal and spiritual." It is also defined as "Nourisher" or "Strength-giver," or in a secondary sense, the Satisfier who pours Himself into believing lives. God therefore becomes the spiritual Nourisher or Satisfier of His people. It was first spoken to Abraham (Gen. 17:1), and is the figure which God has chosen to express the nature of His Almightiness—not of force or power, but that of never-failing love which freely gives itself for those whom He has redeemed. In the process of revelation, this aspect of God comes to its final expression in the Spirit of love—the Comforter, who is the promise of the Father and the gift of the risen and exalted Christ.

Adonai. The name *Adonai* is in the plural form and when applied to God is used as a *pluralis excellentiæ* to express possession and sovereign dominion. It means

Field in his *Handbook of Christian Theology* gives the following names and their uses (p. 10):

1. *Elohim,* "adorable," "strong." This name is usually plural or used with plural adjuncts. The Christian Fathers held this to indicate a plurality of persons in the Godhead—a belief which appears to be well founded.

2. *Jehovah* (or Yahveh) translated "Lord" and printed in capitals in the Authorized Version, "Self-existent"; "the Being"; "I Am"; "I Am That I Am" (Exodus 3:14). This name is never used except when applied to the Divine Being.

3. *El-Shaddai* or *Shaddai,* "The Strong"; "The Mighty One"; "Almighty"; "All-sufficient."

4. *Adoni,* or *Adon,* "Lord"; "Supporter"; "Judge"; "Master."

5. *El-Elyon,* "The Most High"; "The Supreme."

6. *Elyeh,* "I Am"; "I Will Be."

Lord or Master and is translated in the Greek Κύριος, a term very frequently applied to Christ. The word *Adonai* is frequently conjoined with the two original names *Elohim* and *Jehovah,* since it denotes His dominion and lordship in a way which the word Jehovah does not. The word Jehovah is from the Hebrew word *to be,* and denotes self-existence and unchangeableness. Since it was regarded as the incommunicable name of God, the Jews held it in such superstitious reverence that they refused to pronounce it, always substituting in their reading the word *Adonai* or *Lord.* Adonai is used with Elohim in the Psalms and is found in such expressions as "my God and my Lord" (Psalm 35:23) and "O Lord my God" (Psalm 38:15). The testimony of Thomas, "My Lord and my God" (John 20:28) represents the combined use of the terms in the New Testament.

Elohim-Jehovah. The words Elohim and Jehovah are frequently united in the Scriptures, and when so used express both the generic idea and the personal nature of God. As united, these names are a protest against Polytheism on the one hand, and Pantheism on the other. Each denotes the soleness, the necessity and the infinity of the Divine Being, and each is connected with man and the creature in a manner which demands the most definite personality. Furthermore, there is contained in the divine names a revelation of the God of

This double name expresses clearly all that Pantheism has labored in vain to express during the course of its many evolutions; but forever precludes the error into which Pantheism has fallen. It avows an infinite fullness of life and possibility in the eternal essence; but assigns all to the controlling will of a Person. The Scripture scarcely ever approaches the notion of an abstract entity; it invariably makes both Elohim and Jehovah the subjects of endless predicates and predicative ascriptions. *In him we live, and move, and have our being* (Acts 17:28); in Him, a Person to be sought unto and found. In fact, the personality of God, as a Spirit of self-conscious and self-determining and independent individuality, is as deeply stamped upon His revelation of Himself as is His existence. We are created in His image; our Archetype has in eternal reality the being which we possess as shadows of Him; He has in eternal truth the personality which we know to be our own characteristic, though we hold it in fealty from Him. *Thy God* is the Divine Word; *my God,* the human response, through the pages of revelation. No subtilty of modern philosophy has ever equalled the definition of the absolute I AM; the English words give the right meaning of the original only when it lays the stress upon the AM for the essential being, and I for the personality of that being."—POPE, *Compend. Christian Theology,* I, pp. 253, 254, creation, and a revelation of the God of redemption; and when the name *El Shaddai* is used, there is given also the nature of the relation of God to His redeemed people. In these names, therefore, is veiled the fuller revelation of the Triune name, which found expression in God as the Father, Jesus Christ the Son as the incarnate Word, and the Holy Spirit as the Paraclete or Comforter. It is significant that all the Greek representatives of the four Hebrew names, *Elohim, Jehovah, Shaddai* and *Adonai* are grouped together in our Lord's introduction of Himself to the churches in His risen and exalted state. *I am Alpha and Omega, the beginning and the ending, saith the Lord, which is, and which was, and which is to come, the Almighty* (Rev. 1: 8).

In addition to the names of God which express His essence or essential nature, such as those above mentioned, there are also names which are used in an attributive and relative sense. Attributive names are those which express some attribute of God, such as the "Omnipotent," or the "Eternal." Relative terms are drawn from the relations which God bears to men, such as the "King of kings" or "Lord of lords." Our Lord in the prayer which He taught His disciples uses the term "Name" in a comprehensive sense to express all that God is to men—the prayer *Hallowed be thy name* meaning the hallowing or making holy of all that belongs to God in His relations with men. St. John especially, uses attributive names such as *God is light* and *God is love* (I John 1: 5; 4: 16), which combine the nature of God with His attributes, and form a natural transition to our study of the Divine Essence and Perfections.

THE DIVINE ESSENCE AND PERFECTIONS

God's revelation of Himself as declared in His Essential Names, gives us a conception of His being and nature. Some of these names refer especially to the Eternal Essence, some to the Divine Existence, and some to God as Substance clothed with attributes. But it must be remembered that there are other methods, also, by which God has presented Himself to the thought of His creatures, and to these we must now give attention. Of God the Scriptures predicate, *first,* that He is Spirit (John 4:24); *second,* that He is light (I John 1:5); and *third,* that He is love (I John 4:8). These predicates may not be called definitions in the strict use of that term, but they are presentations of certain fundamental aspects of God. God is *Spirit* (Πνεῦμα ὁ Θεός, not a Spirit—John 4:24) and this indicates a self-moving, efficient, animating principle. It embraces the unity and life-motion of the creative activity, and is referred to as *vita absoluta,* i.e., underived, eternal life (John 5:26, 11:25, I John 5:20). It includes, therefore, both the idea of substantiality and of personality. God is *Light* (Φῶς, the self-manifesting and intuitional principle—I John 1:5). According to the Logos theory, this is the Eternal Reason, in which Spirit becomes objective to itself, and God is revealed to Himself (John 1:1, I Tim. 6:16, Heb. 1:3). God is *Love* (ὁ Θεὸς ἀγάπη ἐστίν, I John 4:8, ὁ Θεὸς ἀγάπη ἐστίν 4:16). This refers to the self-completing, self-sufficing and self-satisfying principle, the τὸ τέλος or Perfect One referred to in Matthew's Gospel (Matt. 5:48). Spirit, Reason, Love are thus the simplest and most fundamental elements in the Christian conception of God. And as in the human consciousness of the indivisible *Ego,* is the unity and coherence of reason, feeling and power, is the exact arresting point of psychological science, beyond which it is impossible to go; so also in the Absolute Being, the identity of Reason, Power and Love is the arresting point of theological science, beyond which nothing can be known.

It is evident, therefore, that God can be known only through His self-revelation, after the same manner that man may either reveal himself or hide his inmost thoughts and feelings within himself. But he has power to reveal himself to others, and this power lies in the fact that there is a common principle of intelligence in man, a reason with both intuitive and discursive powers. But we must not stop here. This intelligent principle of reason and order in man is also in the created universe, through which man is afforded a medium of communication—that of the bodily nexus—by which man understands and knows the world, and by means of which he understands and communicates with others. This principle must be carried into the divine nature itself, to the Eternal Logos or the Word through whom God not only created all things, but through whom also He constituted man a personal and intelligent being. It is for this reason, that John in his marvelous Prologue relates the Incarnate Christ to the Eternal Word of God. He first declares the deity of the Word in its eternal aspects —*In the beginning was the Word, and the Word was with God, and the Word was God* (John 1:1). He then relates Christ to the Creative Word—*All things were made by him; and without him was not any thing made that was made* (John 1:3); and follows immediately with the statement, *In him was life; and the life was the light of men* (John 1:4). Here then it is evident that as the human Ego is related to both nature and man; the Divine Logos is related to both Creation and human personality. Both nature and man in some sense partake of the Logos, nature receiving its substantiality and order; man his personal consciousness. Thus there is established between man and God a means of communication as evident as that between man and man. It is evident, also, why the Apostle John felt it necessary not only to identify the Incarnate Christ with the Divine and Eternal Order, but to link Him likewise with creation as its principle of substantiality and order, and with man as his inner light and life. Christ therefore became the revealing power of God, and incarnate by the Holy Ghost in His infinite efficiency, became also the enabling power of redemption.

The doctrine of God is commonly treated under the three main divisions of *Being, Attributes* and *Trinity.* Before taking up the immediate study of this subject, however, it will be necessary to give some consideration to the technical terms which will be used in the discussion, such as Substance and Essence, Attribute and Predicate, Subsistence and Hypostasis.

Substance and Essence. While the changed view-point of modern thought has rendered obsolete many of the positions worked out with such minuteness of detail by the schoolmen, their distinctions as to substance, essence, attribute and relation are not without value in a discussion of the essential nature of God; nor could the development of the trinitarian doctrine be understood without careful attention to such terms as person, hypostasis, property and subsistence. If for no other reason we may allow a pedagogical value to the discussion of these terms, which must be taken into account in any historical approach to these great doctrines. There is scriptural justification, also, for the application of the term substance to God, as found in the name which He applies to Himself—the *I AM* (Exodus 3:14), or *HE WHO IS* as applied to Him in the Apocalypse (Rev. 1:4). God is spoken of further as having a nature (Gal. 4:8, II Peter 1:4), and Godhead is attributed to Him (Rom. 1:20, Col. 2:9). The Scriptures teach that God as the infinite and eternal Spirit has real and substantial existence, and is not a mere idea of the intellect. They assert that He has objective existence apart from man, and is not the result of a subjectivising tendency which would make God the creature of human experience, deny the existence of the self as an entity, and reduce theology to a mere branch of functional psychology.

The term *essence* is derived from *esse*, to be, and denotes energetic being. *Substance* is from *substare*, and signifies latent potentiality of being. The term *essence* when used of God denotes the sum total of His perfections; while the term substance refers to the underlying ground of His infinite activities. The first is active in form, the second passive; the one conveys the idea of spirituality, the other may be applied to material things. We do not speak of material essence but of material substance. In addition to these two terms the Latins used another, *subsistence,* in their discussions of the Trinity—a term which is the equivalent of hypostasis or person. This term more precisely denotes a distinction within the ultimate substance, rather than the substance *(substantia)* itself.

Essence and Attribute. The relation of substance or essence to attribute, has been the ground of much discussion in both philosophy and theology. Does substance underlie attributes, or are attributes simply the unfolding of the essence—that is, are the two things different or identical? This is merely a theological statement of the philosophical problem of noumena and phenomena, appearance and reality. It is evident, therefore, that the manner in which the term attribute is defined, determines largely the manner in which it is used in its application to the doctrine of God. Dickie defines the attributes as those "qualities which belong to and constitute the Divine Essence or Nature." Cocker states that in every conception of an attribute, the Divine Essence is, in some mode or other, supposed. He therefore defines attribute as "a conception of the unconditioned Being under some relation to our consciousness." Shedd regards the attributes as "modes either of the relation, or of the operation of the Divine essence" which is entirely in harmony with his Platonic realism as unfolded in his Augustinian-Edwardean idea of God as the Absolute Being. At the other extreme is the definition of H. B. Smith who holds that an attribute is "any conception which is necessary to the explicit idea of God, any distinctive conception which cannot be resolved into any other." This definition is accepted by both William Adams Brown, and Albert C. Knudson. Similar to this is the position of Olin A. Curtis whose definition of an attribute is "any characteristic which we must ascribe to God to express what He really is."

Attribute and Predicate. It is necessary that a careful distinction be made between attributes and predi-

The attributes of God are those distinguishing characteristics of the divine nature which are inseparable from the idea of God and which constitute the basis and ground for His various manifestations to His creatures. We call them attributes, because we are compelled to attribute them to God as fundamental qualities or powers of His being, in order to give rational account of certain facts constant in God's self-revelation.—A. H. STRONG, *Systematic Theology,* I, p. 244.

cates. A predicate is anything that may be affirmed or predicated of God, such as sovereignty, creatorship or like affirmations which do not attribute to God essential qualities or distinguishing characteristics. Predicate is the wider term and includes all the attributes, but the converse is not true. Predicates may change, but attributes are unchangeable. Varying predicates are, therefore, based upon unvarying attributes.

In the application of philosophical terms to the idea of God, it is evident that He must be thought of by us as under the categories of Being, Attribute and Relation. Without these fundamental categories we cannot think at all. Dr. Cocker has pointed out, we think very truly, that we cannot think of God as the unconditioned Being, conditioning Himself, without conceiving of Him as *Reality, Efficiency* and *Personality*. These constitute the conception of the Divine Essence whereby it is what it is. When we think of the attributes of such a Being, we must think of them as *Absolute, Infinite* and *Perfect*. And when we think of the relations of God to finite existence and finite consciousness, we regard Him as *Ground, Cause* and *Reason* of all dependent being. He combines these into one categorical scheme of thought and gives us this outline.

BEING (Essentia)	REALITY	EFFICIENCY	PERSONALITY
ATTRIBUTES (Related Essence)	ABSOLUTE	INFINITE	PERFECT
RELATION (Free Determination)	GROUND	CAUSE	REASON OR END

Thus in Absolute Reality we have the ultimate Ground; in the Infinite Efficiency we have the adequate cause; and in the Perfect Personality we have the sufficient reason or final cause of all existence (COCKER, *Theistic Conception of the World,* pp. 41ff.) In our discussion of God we shall then, consider Him in His threefold relation to the created universe as its Ground, its Cause and its End. This gives us a logical classification for our material and we shall, therefore, treat the subject under discussion as Absolute Reality, Infinite Efficiency and Perfect Personality.

CHAPTER XI

GOD AS ABSOLUTE REALITY

In our introductory study of the theological and philosophical definitions of God, a preliminary statement was made to the effect that the ultimate Personality of religion and the Absolute of philosophy find together their highest expression in Jesus Christ; and that in His Person and work, we have the deepest possible insight into the nature and purpose of God. As indicated, also, the Christian concept, historically considered, is a blending of the Hebrew conception as expressed in the Old Testament prophets, with that held by the Greeks, as expressed in their language, through which in the providence of God, most if not all of the books of the New Testament were given to the Christian Church. This gave rise immediately to a conflict of ideas concerning the nature of God as Absolute, due to the attempt to express the higher concepts of divine revelation through the lower concepts of a language which fell short of the full Christian content. The Hebrew conception of God was that of a transcendent Being, powerful, holy, righteous and hence personal. He was regarded as the Creator of all things, was One and was Perfect. Judaism developed a true monotheism. In the Christian concept, the Jewish monotheistic element was carried over, with the added concept of a further revelation through Christ and the Holy Spirit. The Greek concept of God had a long period of development before it came into contact with Christianity, and was not at that time a unity. From nature-gods, through nature itself, it had developed toward a philosophical theism. The concept of Plato was dynamic; while that of Aristotle was static. To Plato, God was the *Idea of the Good,* or as expressed in modern terminology, the *Ideal,* this Ideal being the supreme Reality of the Universe. To Aristotle, God was the *Prime Mover* of the universe, but Himself the *Unmoved Mover.*

The Stoics regarded God in a pantheistic manner as a sort of quasi-material, the *Soul of the Universe*. To the Epicureans, the gods were transcendent and aloof from the affairs of men. The Neo-Platonists held to an agnostic idea, which has been the ground of much modern agnosticism. To them God was absolutely transcendent, and therefore impassible, beyond all predicates, but mediated through His Mind in a series of emanations. The mystery religions each had its own *Kyrios* or Lord, but these were regarded more in the sense of the Lord of a religion or cult, than the God of the universe. They were finite beings rather than Infinite.

Christianity entered the world at a time when it was under the sway of Deism on the one hand and Pantheism on the other; and these necessitated a consideration of the problem of immanence and transcendence. In addition, there were the ethical questions of sin and grace which were vitally related to those of immanence and transcendence, whether considered in reference to creation or providence. The Greek and Roman philosophies clashed very early with the Christian conception. *Certain philosophers of the Epicureans and Stoics encountered* the Apostle Paul (Acts 17:18) in the market place at Athens, which garnished the occasion for his great address on Mars' Hill (Acts 17:22-31). From these false philosophies there arose the Colossian Heresy, a form of gnosticism against which St. Paul directed his Epistle to the Colossians. St. John, also, in his first epistle, attacks the same heresy. Perhaps Christian doctrine was never subjected to a severer test than in the early centuries of the Church, especially in the period immediately preceding the time of Augustine. Mithraism, Gnosticism, Manichæism, and Neo-Platonism all combined to rob the Church of the simplicity of its conception of God, as the Father of our Lord Jesus Christ. It was for this reason that St. Paul warned the Colossians against *philosophy and vain deceit* (Col. 2:8), and cautioned Timothy to beware of the *oppositions of science falsely so called* (I Tim. 6:20). But the apologists of the church had a keen insight as to the fundamentals of the faith, and gave themselves to the propagation of a right idea of God, upon which, they saw, hinged all other doctrines. They took the position that God was related historically to the covenant people of the Old Testament, that He was related spiritually to the Church of the New Testament, and creatively to the world apart from the Church. Furthermore, they removed all the mythological elements which clung to the Aryan conceptions of God, maintained the Christian idea of God as pure spirituality, and denied reality to all heathen deities. The Christian concept of God, therefore, became one of unity, spirituality and absoluteness, which they consistently maintained against pagan philosophy from without, and heretical opinions from within.

THE ORIGIN OF THE ABSOLUTE

The term *absolute* is the creation of modern philosophy, but the fact of absoluteness is an age old problem. No chapter in ancient philosophy carries with it more pathos than the sincere but blind groping after truth on the part of earnest but unenlightened men. The Ionians sought for a first principle, a *prima materia* which should explain the origin and unity of the created universe. Thales found it in water, Anaximenes in air, and Anaximander, reaching a somewhat loftier plane, found it in the Infinite. Then followed the "Being" of Parmenides, the "atoms" of Democritus, and a foregleam of that which was to follow in the "nous" or "reason" of Anaxagoras. Ancient thought on the plane of materialism could rise no higher, and was followed as a consequence by a period of skepticism. Out of this confusion Greek thought was led by Socrates to a higher level, that of the moral nature of the universe. On this new plane, Greek philosophy reached its supreme heights in the mysticism of Plato and the logic of Aristotle. It could advance no farther, and again sank into decline. At the time of Christ, Greek philosophy was groping about on the plane of primitive religion expressed in philosophical terms. St. Paul seems to have had this in mind, when after referring to the "unknown God" in his Athenian address, he declared that God in His sovereignty over the nations had appointed the bounds of their habitation, *that they should seek the Lord,* by which we are to understand an intellectual pursuit of truth; *if haply they might feel after him,* that is in the moral pressure upon the consciences of men; *and find him, though he be not far from every one of us: for in him we live, and move, and have our being; as certain also of your own poets have said, For we are also his offspring* (Acts 17: 24-28). *Whom therefore ye ignorantly worship,* he triumphantly exclaims, *him declare I unto you* (Acts 17: 23). Thus to the intellectual gropings of unenlightened men, and to the moral pressure upon conscience, St. Paul adds another factor — spiritual illumination — which comes through the redemptive religion of the Lord Jesus Christ, and brings men's gropings and pressures to full fruition in finding God. In one divinely inspired and illuminating grasp, therefore, St. Paul combines both the *creatura* and *natura* aspects of God—both the personal transcendence of the Hebrews, and the immanence of the Greeks. In this authoritative address is given the Christian concept of God. The attempt to harmonize the diverse elements gave rise to great problems which in every age have perplexed theology, but even more so, science and philosophy. The apostle had a deep insight into the different tempers of mind exhibited by the Jew and the Greek when he wrote that *we preach Christ crucified, unto the Jews,* with their scientific temper of mind, *a stumblingblock; and unto the Greeks,* with their philosophical temper of mind, *foolishness; but unto them which are called, both Jews and Greeks, Christ the power of God, and the wisdom of God* (I Cor. 1: 23, 24).

It is a broadening and heartening thought that God who revealed Himself to the Jews in a more objective manner, revealed Himself in a measure also to the Gentiles, through their search after truth. The limit of this seeking seems to have been set by the Apostle Paul, as the knowledge of *his eternal power and Godhead.* Beyond this it cannot go, for the true knowledge of God is at once ethical and spiritual. The redemptive aspect is involved. There was, therefore, as we have indicated, a period of skepticism in Greek thought at the time of Christ. The fullness of time in which Jesus came, seems to have applied not only to the Jews but to the Gentile world as well. It is significant that a company of Greeks came to the disciples and said, *Sir, we would see Jesus* (John 12:21). Greek thought with its search after truth through intellectual acumen and moral pressure had broken down, and the vague, unsatisfied longings of their hearts, in connection with the providences of God, had brought them to Jesus. The answer which Jesus gave them is significant also, and will receive fuller treatment in our discussion of the knowledge of God. *Except a corn of wheat fall into the ground and die,* He said, *it abideth alone: but if it die, it bringeth forth much fruit* (John 12:24). The hindering cause does not lie in the failure of the intellectual grasp, or even in the lack of moral pressure, He said, but in the sense of sin which brings a moral and ethical unlikeness to God, and thereby destroys the true basis for personal and spiritual knowledge. There must, therefore, be a death to the sinful nature, and the infusion of a new life, before there can be spiritual comprehension. In the redemptive Christ all the seeming contradictions of life find their principle of unity. Here the Jewish idea of sin as transgression finds forgiveness, and the Jewish mission is thereby fulfilled. Here the Greek conception of sin as a "missing of the mark" or failure, finds its completion in Jesus. This then is the prophetic vision of Christ, *a light to lighten the Gentiles, and the glory of thy people Israel* (Luke 2:32).

In this brief historical sketch, we have reviewed the various philosophical concepts of God regarded as the Absolute. The Jews held to the idea of a transcendent God. Because of their belief in creation through the Divine Word, they never regarded God as apart from all relations, and were thereby preserved from an agnostic position. However, when brought into contact with Greek philosophy at Alexandria, Philo and the Neo-Platonists carried the idea of transcendence to such ex-

treme lengths that it issued in agnosticism. They were
therefore, under the necessity of superseding the idea of
creation, and consequently posited a series of emanations
in order to account for the world. From this false philosophy there arose the several gnostic sects, which exerted an unwholesome influence in the church. But
Greek philosophy on the whole was pantheistic. That
is, it regarded God as the Absolute, not apart from all
relations but inclusive of all such relations. The difficulty of the agnostic position concerning the Absolute,
lay in its failure to relate God to the universe; the weakness of pantheism lay in its failure to distinguish God
from the universe. Christianity, and therefore Christian philosophy, took a mediating position. It maintained that God as Absolute is neither apart from relations on the one hand, nor inclusive of relations on the
other. It maintains that the Absolute is independent
Self-existence. As such it is capable of existing apart
from all external relations, or of entering into free relations with created beings, either in an outward and
transcendent manner, or an inward and immanent manner. Christian philosophy maintains that to hold less
than this, is to limit and thereby destroy any true conception of the Absolute. We turn our attention now to
an investigation from the Christian viewpoint, of the
various theories of the Absolute which have been current in modern philosophy.

The New Platonists taught that the original ground and source of
all things was simple being, without life or consciousness; of which
absolutely nothing could be known, beyond that it is. They assumed an
unknown quantity, of which nothing can be predicated. The pseudo-
Dionysius called this original ground of all things God, and taught that
God was mere being without attributes of any kind, not only unknowable by man, but of whom there was nothing to be known, as absolute
being is in the language of modern philosophy—Nothing; nothing in
itself, yet nevertheless the δύναμις τῶν πάντων or (cause of all things).
The universe proceeds from primal being, not by any exercise of conscious power or will, but by a process of emanation. . . . . The primary
emanations from the ground of all being, which the heathen called
gods; the New Platonists, spirits or intelligences; and the Gnostics,
æons; the pseudo-Dionysius called angels. These he divided into three
triads: (1) thrones, cherubim, and seraphim; (2) powers, lordships,
authorities; (3) angels, archangels, principalities."—HODGE, Systematic
Theology, I, pp. 71, 72. (Cf. Col. 1:16).

MODERN PHILOSOPHICAL CONCEPTS OF THE ABSOLUTE

Modern philosophy has interpreted the term "Absolute" in three different ways. *First,* it has interpreted it to mean that which is entirely unrelated. This position of necessity issues in Agnosticism which maintains that the Absolute is unknowable. *Second,* at the other extreme, it has been interpreted to mean the totality of all things, or that Being which embraces the universe as a whole. This is Pantheism. It was against these positions in their ancient forms that the Apostle Paul reasoned on Mars' Hill, and they are no less anti-Christian in their modern philosophical forms. *Third,* the Absolute has been interpreted as meaning that which is independent or self-existent. On this theory, the Absolute is not necessarily apart from all relations, but these relations are free and the existence of the absolute is not dependent upon them. This is the position of Theism. Christianity is theistic, and it is only within the third classification that the Christian viewpoint is to be found. The distinctive feature of the Christian system is, that its revelation is made through a Person and not through the barren abstractions of philosophy.

While Christianity is based upon the theistic conception of the Absolute, it endeavors to guard the truth in the first and second classifications without allowing it to be perverted into Agnosticism on the one hand or Pantheism on the other. In the first, there is the thought of transcendence. Christianity has always maintained that God is incomprehensible as transcending the limits of human knowledge, but it denies Agnosticism in that it insists that its knowledge of God is true within the limits of finite conception. In the second, there is the thought of divine immanence, which if the idea of personality be persistently held can never become pantheistic. Both immanence and transcendence belong to the Christian conception of God, but it denies both Pantheism and Agnosticism. Since these forms of modern philosophy furnish nonbiblical conceptions of God, they must be given further consideration and refutation.

Theism has also been attacked in modern times by the so-called "Anti-Theistical Theories," and of these we must later make brief mention.

Agnosticism. This is the negative theory of the Unknowable, and while in the case of Herbert Spencer it was made to apply equally to the ultimate of science and that of religion, the theory has assumed its most definite form in the denial of the possibility of any true knowledge of God. It is the outgrowth of phenomenalism and is closely connected with the skepticism of Hume, but has been accepted also in some instances by those who rest their doctrine of the Infinite and the Absolute on the limitation of human intelligence. Three stages may be noted in the development of agnosticism, preceding its fuller and perhaps final culmination in the theory of Naturalistic Evolution. The first stage is usually attributed to Kant, whose philosophy is admittedly due to that of Locke and Hume, for its inspiration if not its content. Kant's *Critical Philosophy* was an attempt to ascertain to what extent knowledge is given in experience, and how much of it is due to the mind's own contribution. This latter was understood not in the sense of actual knowledge, but as the necessary forms which determined the possibilities of knowledge. He therefore attributed all our knowledge to three cognitive faculties, the sensory, the understanding, and the reason. The sensory gives us the perceptions of the phenomena of understanding, a more elaborated knowledge grouped under the categories of quantity, quality, relation and modality; while the reason gives us those ideas which are regulative of the system of our knowledge— the soul, the universe and God. When Kant speaks of knowledge ending with reason, he regards the reason as the faculty or principle which regulates the understanding, and consequently as the highest reach of human intelligence. The matter of knowledge is phenomenal and comes through the senses; the form is supplied by the mind itself; and therefore the categories and the ideas, space and time, the soul, the universe and God are only regulative of mental procedure and do not furnish the knowledge of real existences. The basis for agnosticism, however, is found only in his *Critique of Pure Reason*. In his *Critique of Practical Reason,* he stresses the categorical imperative of moral law and establishes his doctrine of the existence of God, as based upon faith rather than reason.

The second stage is found in the philosophy of Sir William Hamilton and that of Henry Longueville Mansel. Hamilton maintained that "the mind can conceive, and consequently can know, only the limited and conditionally limited. The unconditionally limited, whether the Infinite or the Absolute, cannot positively be construed to the mind; they can be conceived only by thinking away from, or abstractions of those very conditions under which thought itself is realized; consequently the notion of the unconditioned is only negative—the negative of the conceivable itself" (HAMILTON, *Discussions on Philosophy,* p. 13). Dean Mansel of St. Paul's (1820-1871) accepted the philosophy of Hamilton and sought to apply it as an apologetic in theology. This he did in his famous Bampton Lectures, delivered at Oxford under the title of *The Limits of Religious Thought.* Instead, however, of appealing to the theologians, his lecture afforded a stimulus to agnosticism. His argument, borrowed from Hamilton, stated that to think is to condition, and therefore the unconditioned cannot be an object of thought, thus excluding the whole range of revealed truth concerning God, as beyond the pale of logic. The third stage is found in the philosophy of John Stuart Mill, who in his *Examination of Hamilton's Philosophy* carried out the implications of Hamilton, and denied that we have "an intuitive knowledge of God." "Whatever relates to God," he says, "I hold to be a matter of inference; I would add, of inference *a posteriori.*" While accepting the philosophy of Hamilton, his criticism was, that Hamilton did not rigidly carry out his agnostic principles and treat the Absolute as an unmeaning abstraction. This brings us to a consideration of the agnosticism of Huxley and Spencer, the immediate precursors of the doctrine of evolution as advanced by Darwin.

Thomas E. Huxley (1825-1895) based his agnostic philosophy upon Hume and Kant, while Herbert Spencer (1820-1903) starts from Hamilton's *Philosophy of the Unconditioned,* and Mansel's *Limits of Religious Thought.* Huxley boasted that he invented the term "agnostic" in order to designate his mental attitude toward the many problems which remained for him unsolved. "It is an ill-omened invention," declares Dr. Harris, for the word etymologically denotes the negation of all knowledge, and is synonymous with universal skepticism. Perhaps he builded better than he knew; for the way of thinking to which he applied the name necessarily involves skepticism as its ultimate, logical issue." Hume was the great protagonist of Huxley's philosophy, and he makes it clear that his positions are but an application of Hume's theory of knowledge. "In the business of life," says Huxley, "we constantly take the most serious action upon evidence of an utterly insufficient character. But it is surely plain that faith is not entitled to dispense with ratiocination, because ratiocination cannot dispense with faith as a starting point; and that because we are too often obliged by the pressure of events to act on very bad evidence, it does not follow that it is proper to act on such evidence when the pressure is absent." Here the agnostic principle is directed toward the destruction of all religious belief. Rishell points out that in the course of investigation this form of agnosticism undergoes a complete change. It quietly substitutes "I do not believe" for "I do not know." What right has agnosticism in the realm of belief? But it draws a practical conclusion from "I do not believe" and says, "I will not act." If it had remained agnosticism it might have acted in spite of its lack of knowledge. But its "I do not believe" is a complete annihilation of all impulse to action. The difference between agnosticism in this form, and atheism is almost, if not wholly, in name (RISHELL, *Foundations of the Christian Faith,* p. 62). Huxley's agnosticism differs from that of Spencer, and is more in accord with the principles of Comte's Positivism.

Herbert Spencer as an Evolutionist carried the doctrine of Hamilton and Mansel one step farther, and professed belief in "an Absolute that transcends not only human knowledge, but human conception." He wrote his *First Principles of a New System of Philosophy* in an attempt to discover a basis for the reconciliation of science and religion. He endeavors, therefore, to show that the ultimate ideas of both science and religion lie in a great mystery behind all things and are identical. "If religion and science are to be reconciled," he says, "the basis of reconciliation must be this deepest, widest and most certain of all facts; that the Power which the universe manifests to us is utterly inscrutable" (Cf. *First Principles*, chapters 2, 3). The agnosticism of Spencer is not a thorough-going denial of all knowledge, for it recognizes not only man's knowledge of the universe, but an absolute Being, which as an omnipresent Power reveals itself through all the phenomena of the universe. The fallacy of this type of agnosticism comes out more clearly in its treatment of symbolic conceptions and the relativity of knowledge, and we may add, its antitheistic character as well. "When instead of things whose attributes can be tolerably united in a single state of consciousness, we have to deal with things whose attributes are too vast or numerous to be united, we must," he says, "either drop in thought part of their attributes, or else not think of them at all; either form a more or less symbolic conception or no conception." "We are led," he then continues, "to deal with our symbolic conceptions as though they are actual ones, not only because we cannot clearly separate the two, but also because in a majority of cases, the first serve our purposes nearly or quite as well as the last—are simply abbreviated signs we substitute for those more elaborate signs which are our equivalent for real objects. . . . . Thus we open the door to some which profess to stand for known things, but which really stand for things which cannot be known in any way" (*First Principles*, pp. 28, 29). Then, without any ground in either science or religion, he proceeds to include all ultimate ideas of both science and religion in the class of the Unknown, and by analysis attempts to show that the Reality behind the appearances is and must ever be unknown. All knowledge with him is relative, that is, a knowledge of relations, but never reaching the finality of things. From this viewpoint there can be no knowledge of the world-ground upon which all finite things depend, nor can God as the Absolute, the Infinite, or the First Cause be known. Against this agnostic theory, theism maintains that while man's knowledge of God is inadequate, it is yet positive and not merely a negative abstraction.

Wherein does the fallacy of Agnosticism lie? *First,* it lies in the attempt to develop the Absolute from a mere *a priori* idea. From the presupposition that the Absolute is entirely unrelated, the unlimited, the unconditioned or the independent, nothing can be developed but a series of negations without positive content. This is the type of thought represented by Hamilton and Mansel. *Second,* not only is it impossible to unfold a doctrine of the Absolute from an *a priori* idea, but in some types of agnosticism there is a false conception of this *a priori* idea. It is defined as that which is apart from all relations and hence "unknowable." The error here lies in assuming that the absolute is unrelated. The Absolute is not indeed conditioned by the universe as a necessary relation, but it does condition the universe, and is therefore not apart from all relation. This sometimes takes the form of Kant's thing-in-itself, and sometimes is an attempt to resolve the universal into indeterminate qualities, but both lead immediately to agnosticism. *Third,* in the assumption that all definition limits, and therefore if known and defined, the Absolute would cease to be the Absolute,

Spencer objects to the position taken by Hamilton and Mansel, which he thinks calls in question the impossibility of affirming the positive existence of anything beyond phenomena, whereas for him there is what he defines as "a Power, the First Cause, absolute and infinite, and capable of manifesting itself," and insists that "its positive existence is a necessary datum of consciousness; that so long as consciousness continues we cannot for an instant rid it of this datum; and that thus the belief which this datum constitutes has a higher warrant than any other whatever.—*First Principles*, p. 98.

and the Infinite become finite. The argument of Dr. Harris against this position so dominant in modern philosophy is, we think, unanswerable, and is thus stated: "The maxim that all definition limits is pertinent to a logical general notion or a mathematical sum total, not to a concrete being. The arguments of agnostics are conclusive as to the false ideas of the Absolute which they hold, but have no force against our knowledge of the real Absolute or unconditioned Being, whose existence the universe reveals. But the more powers it reveals, the more determined it is. There are fewer beings like it; fewer in the class designated by the general name. The increased determinateness, which restricts the logical general notion to fewer beings, greatens the beings. And when we come to the absolute Being, which is one and reveals itself in all the powers of the universe, it is the Being at once the most determinate and greatest of all. It is not necessary that the Absolute be everything to prevent its being limited by that which it is not. The existence of finite beings dependent on absolute Being is no limitation of the Absolute. On the contrary, if the absolute Being could not manifest itself in finite beings dependent on itself, that inability would be a limitation of it" (HARRIS, *Self-revelaton of God,* pp. 175, 176).

Pantheism. As a philosophical theory of the universe, Pantheism reduces all being to a single essence or substance. It derives its name from ἐν καὶ πᾶν, or the One and the All, and seems to have been first used by Xenophanes, the Greek philosopher, about the sixth century B.C. It has appeared in many forms. The common substance which composes the universe may be regarded as matter, and hence we have materialistic pantheism. Or, it may regard the universal substance or ground of the universe as thought, in which case we have idealistic pantheism, its most common form philosophically. Only, however, as pantheism makes God the sole substance, does it acquire the significance which the name implies. As such, the theory holds that God is not outside and beyond the universe, but that he is the universe. He exists only in it, and apart from it has no existence. He is the Soul, Reason and Spirit of the world. The natural world is his body in which he comes to expression. God is everything—the sum total of all being. It is evident that Pantheism occupies a middle ground between Materialism, which identifies God with Nature; and Theism which holds to a belief in God as a self-conscious Being, a Person, infinite and eternal who created the world and sustains it by His power.

Pantheism is closely related to polytheism as found among the ethnic religions. The two seem so dissimilar that this relationship is often overlooked. Just as the Greek religion held that in addition to the Olympian gods, there were innumerable demigods, as nymphs and naiads peopling all nature; so the Greek philosopher saw in all nature a manifestation of Deity. Pantheism and polytheism are therefore but two forms of the same fundamental belief, the first seeking in a philosophical manner for unity amidst individual phenomena, and the latter stopping short with personifications of them. It is for this reason, that pantheism, both religious and philosophical, is always found closely associated with polytheistic forms of religion.

Disregarding the religious fallacies of pantheism, which we reserve for a later paragraph, pantheism as a theory of the Absolute in relation to the world-ground is scientifically untenable. *First,* it is built upon assumptions which are not only unproved but incapable of proof. As Materialism is built upon the supposition of the eternity of matter, so Spinoza who is the pattern for modern day pantheism, builds upon the supposition of a universal substance which he identifies with God. He does not investigate this idea of God. He substitutes, instead, a mere logical universal in which are embraced all individual notions; but he fails to see that this is merely a subjective idea, not a real existence. This confusion of thought with existence, this merely imagined unity of ideas in our consciousness with the actually existing objective order, is the fallacy which underlies most modern thought concerning the nature of the Absolute. "I have," says Spinoza, "opinions as to God and nature entirely different from those which modern Christians are wont to vindicate. To my mind God is the immanent, and not the transcendent Cause of all things; that is, the totality of finite objects is posited in the Essence of God, and not in His Will. Nature considered *per se,* is one with the essence of God." *Second,* Pantheism fails to account for the origin of cosmical matter. Since the world and God are regarded as of identical essence, it is inconceivable that He could call it into existence out of its former nothingness. Spinoza attempts an explanation on the basis of a *natura naturans,* or a "begetting nature" which from eternity is constantly begetting and bringing forth mundane phenomena (*natura naturata*). In order to account for this eternal fullness of life, Spinoza maintains that begotten nature reacts upon the begetting nature, and thus a harmony is established. Against such absurdities, the biblical idea of creation as a miracle must appear far more reasonable. *Third,* Pantheism fails to realize its idea of the Infinite, because the Infinite always has its actuality in the finite. The action of the universe is a perpetual evolving of the

"If we demand the origin of the actual world, that is of 'begotten nature' we are told that 'begetting nature' is the ultimate cause; and if we demand the origin of the latter, we are again referred to 'begotten nature,' that is, to the very fact of which we seek an explanation."— CHRISTLIEB, *Mod. Doubt and Chr. Belief,* p. 116.

The utter erroneousness of pantheism is manifest in this, that the monism which it maintains determines all finite existences to be mere modes of the one infinite substance, mere phenomena without any reality of being in themselves. The physical universe becomes unsubstantial as in the extremist form of idealism. Mind becomes equally unreal. Neither can be thus dismissed from the realm of substantial existence. In the physical universe there is a very real being. Not all is mere appearance. And every personal mind has its own consciousness the absolute proof of being in itself. Personal mind is not a mere phenomenon. The monism of Pantheism is utterly false in doctrine.— MILEY, *Systematic Theology,* I, pp. 115, 116.

Pantheism as surely as materialism would, if carried out to its logical results, destroy all thought. It begins with the contradiction of the fundamental facts of consciousness. If we do not know that we exist as personal and free agents we know nothing. For to deny this is to deny the ego, in contradistinction from which alone we know the non-ego. So that both the self and the not-self are struck down at a single blow. But if we are so grossly deceived in the primary facts of consciousness, in those things which are most accessible to thought, how can we trust our conclusions in matters more remote.—RISHELL, *Foundations of the Christian Faith,* p. 102.

absolute Substance into its various modes of existence, but never producing effects *ad extra,* outside of or beyond itself. It is therefore an eternal process of becoming, and the God which it would reveal is perpetually hidden. *Fourth,* Pantheism denies the personality of God. It is under the necessity, therefore, of explaining how personality can proceed from an impersonal Substance. Pantheism maintains that God is free in the sense that there are no external constraints. But freedom to choose is denied Him because He must unfold according to the nature of His essential being. What He does, He does because of what He is and not because He wills to do so. Intelligence is thus denied God in the only sense of the word which is known to us. Pantheism regards man and other finite beings as but a mode of God's existence, embracing the only two attributes known to us—thought and extension. The mind of man is essentially a portion of the divine thought, while the body is the object of the mind. These are related to each other, not because of their essential unity but because they are regarded as twofold aspects of the same substance. But while Spinoza denies self-determination and free will to man, he does not deny that he possesses self-consciousness. The question immediately arises, "How can this self-consciousness proceed from the Soul of the world, if God does not Himself possess it? How can God create or communicate that which He does not possess? Here pantheism must ever break down from its own inherent weakness. The Absolute of pantheism is not a true Absolute because it is deficient at the point of personality. It is this restriction which denies to pantheism on its own assumptions, the use of the term Absolute.

The relation of pantheism to religion has already been anticipated. Religion presupposes a personal God,

There is even a form of Pantheism, or rather of semi-Pantheism, in which the personality of God is to some extent preserved, which looks upon the world as an efflux from Deity, and hence as being of His essence, but not co-extensive with Him. Thus, for instance, the doctrine of the emanations in the Indian Vedas. But here too, the personality of God is dangerously comprised by the necessity of the natural process in which these emanations take place. Cf. CHRISTLIEB, *Modern Doubt and Christian Belief,* p. 163.

who is not only endowed with intelligence and power, but with all moral excellence. Pantheism identifies God with the universe. It denies to Him personality, free will or moral attributes. He is the Soul or Reason of the world, and all nature His body which must unfold according to the law of necessity. The idea of creation then as a free act of will must be given up and emanation substituted in its place. Belief in miracles and a superintending providence must likewise be given up. Since pantheism makes man a phenomenon only, or a mere mode of the infinite, there can be in him no free will and hence no sense of responsibility. Sin and guilt become, therefore, mere figments of the imagination. Furthermore, since God is all, that which appears to be evil must be regarded as Good. The sinful acts and passions of men become, in this theory, as much the acts and states of God as those which are righteous and holy. Again, pantheism destroys belief in individual immortality by merging it with the life of the universe. Without a personal God there can be no object worthy of reverence or worship, no place for prayer and providence, no object of adoration and love. Pantheism by identifying God with the universe excludes all personal relations, and thereby destroys the foundations of both morality and religion.

Theism. The third form under which philosophy conceives the Absolute is theistic, as over against the agnostic

In conceiving of God, the choice before a pantheist lies between alternatives from which no genius has yet devised a real escape. God, the pantheist must assert, is literally everything; God is the whole material and spiritual universe; he is humanity in all its manifestations; he is by inclusion every moral and immoral agent; and every form and exaggeration of moral evil, no less than every variety of moral excellence and beauty, is part of the all-pervading, all-comprehending movement of his universal life. If this revolting blasphemy be declined, then the God of pantheism must be the barest abstraction of abstract being; he must, as with the Alexandrian thinkers, be so exaggerated an abstraction as to transcend existence itself; he must be conceived of as utterly unreal, lifeless, nonexistent; while the only real beings are these finite and determinate forms of existence whereof "nature" is composed. This dilemma haunts all the historical transformations of pantheism, in Europe as in the East, today as two thousand years ago. Pantheism must either assert that its God is the one only existing being whose existence absorbs and is identified with the universe and humanity; or else it must admit that He is the rarest and most unreal of conceivable abstractions; in plain terms, that he is no being at all.—LIDDON, *Bampton Lectures.*

and pantheistic positions. Here the Absolute is conceived, not as entirely unrelated, nor again as the sum total of all existence, but simply as independent or self-existent. Under this third class erroneous opinions have also arisen, such as *Materialism* which regards matter as the ultimate ground of the world; or *Idealism* in some of its many forms which make thought ultimate, but these belong properly to the subject of "Antitheistic Theories." The distinguishing feature of theism, as it concerns these theories, is its belief in the world ground as personal. But can the Absolute of philosophy be identified with the Christian conception of God? Christianity affirms that it can. It insists that the philosophy which would prevent this is false; but it concedes, also, that theism has itself frequently misconstrued the Christian idea of God. To mature thought they must be identical. We are dealing, however, not primarily with the personality of God—this must be a later argument, but with God as the Absolute in the sense of the world ground. Christianity maintains that the world ground is personal; that God is the ground of all finite being and rational intelligence. Reason is seen to be universal, and the Absolute becomes the ultimate in thought and rela-

By the term "world ground" we mean the basic reality of the world. Materialism regards this basic reality as "matter"; Idealism as "thought"; and the modern Personalistic philosophies as "personal."

Theism means the existence of a personal God, Creator, Preserver and Ruler of all things. Deism equally means the personality of God and also His creative work, but denies His providence in the sense of theism. These terms were formerly used in much the same sense, but since early in the last century deism has mostly been used in a sense opposed to the Scriptures as a divine revelation, and to a divine providence. Such is now its distinction from theism. Pantheism differs from theism in the denial of the divine personality. With this denial, pantheism can mean no proper work of creation or providence. The philosophic agnosticism which posits the Infinite as the ground of finite existence, but denies its personality, is in this denial quite at one with pantheism. The distinction of theism from these several opposing terms sets its own meaning in the clearer light.—MILEY, *Systematic Theology*, I, p. 57.

Julius Kaftan favors the use of the term Absolute in theology. However, he maintains that it should be used, not merely in its etymological sense, but from the meaning it has acquired by its use in language. "We should never forget," he says, "that by the expression, 'God is the absolute,' we do not mean to make a fundamental affirmation as to the essence of God, but simply an expression of the significance the idea of God has for us."—KAFTAN, *Dogmatics*, p. 162.

tions. All the ultimate realities such as the True, the Right, the Perfect and the Good center in the Absolute, where all relations have their ground and beyond which they cannot go. If viewed otherwise, Dr. Harris points out that "no rational conclusion would be possible, no scientific observation would be trustworthy, no scientific system could be verified, science would be disintegrated, and all knowledge crumbled into isolated and illusive impressions. Hence God is essential to the reality of all knowledge as well as all being. We cannot think Him away; for without the assumption explicit or implied of His existence, all ratiocinated thought becomes empty and cannot conclude in knowledge. If thought rests ultimately on zero all its creations and conclusions must be zero" (HARRIS, *Self-revelation of God*, p. 227).

THE ABSOLUTE AND THE IDEA OF GOD

We have shown that theism must rest upon a conception of the Absolute as independent or self-existent, and that it is this position which distinguishes it from Agnosticism and Pantheism. But theism is also personal, as over against certain philosophical theories which in opposition to theism regard the world-ground as impersonal. Such is the philosophy of Materialism which regards matter as the ultimate reality, or some of the many forms of Monism or Idealism which conceive of the world-ground as of the nature of thought. These equally with Agnosticism and the older Pantheism must be regarded as antitheistic. Since, however, the same arguments may be urged against them as in the case of pantheism we need here only to make brief mention of these antitheistical theories.

The teaching of Scripture concerning God is based on the theistic conception, that, namely, which holds fast at once His supramundane and His intramundane character; the one in virtue of His nature and essence, the other of His will and power. For while Theism, on the one hand, regards the Theos as a personal Being, and so as essentially distinct from the whole created universe and from man, it is no less careful, on the other hand, to present Him as the ever-living and working One in His immediate personal relationship to man and the universe by the doctrine of a universal Divine Providence.—CHRISTLIEB, *Modern Doubt and Christian Belief*, p. 210.

Antitheistical Theories. There are three theories
which have been advanced in modern times in opposition to theism, and these have been peculiarly subversive
of the Christian conception of God. (1) *Atheism.* This is
a negative term and is a direct denial of the conception
of God as held by theism. In its application, however, it
has always been used in a more or less relative sense.
The Greek word originally meant a denial of the Greek
conception of God. Hence the pagans accused the Christians of being atheists, and Socrates was condemned by
the Athenians on the same charge. Atheism was held in
disrepute by the ancient Greeks and was considered synonymous with wickedness. Christlieb points out that
this view after having appeared sporadically for ages,
first assumed the character of a system—if indeed it be
worthy of the name—in the train of French materialism.
La Mettrie, for instance, pronounced the belief in the
existence of God to be as groundless as it was unprofit-
able. This tendency penetrated the mass of the French
people during the "reign of terror" under the Convention, when the "Herbertists" laid it down as a principle
"That the King of heaven must be dethroned just as
the kings of earth." In more recent times, Feuerbach
argued for atheism as follows: "There is no God; it is
as clear as the sun, and as evident as the day that there
is no God, and still more, that there can be none, for if
there were a God, then there must be one; He would be
necessary. But now if there is no God, then there can
be no God; therefore there is no God. There is no God
because there cannot be any." This is the type of reasoning used to substantiate the claims of atheism. The most

"If atheism is true, then man is out of harmony with truth." This
is an anomaly, and how are we to account for it? Atheism says there
is no God—no supernatural first cause; but man has within him the intuitive conviction that there is a God, and this conviction is as universal as the family of man. If man is the offspring of chance, or if he
is evolved from some lower order of being, it is strange indeed that he
should be so completely "out of harmony with truth." It would seem
most reasonable that whatever caused him to exist would impress upon
his nature the truth. But if atheism is true, then that which caused man
to be is untrustworthy, for it impressed upon his consciousness the conviction that there is a God—some being or beings superior to himself.—
WEAVER, *Christian Theology*, p. 11.

simple and direct refutation of this false and unworthy position, says a modern apologist, is the fact that a direct certainty of God exists in our mind. "We do not merely believe that there is a God, but we know it in virtue of an ideal cognition consisting in an immediate act of faith in human consciousness." (2) *Materialism*. This is a form of philosophy which gives priority to matter as the ground of the universe, and ignores the distinction between mind and matter. According to this theory all the phenomena of the universe, whether physical or mental are to be regarded as functions of matter. Materialism was first given systematic form by Epicurus (342-271 B.C.). In the history of modern philosophy, Materialism is represented by La Mettrie and Von Holback who are usually classed as materialistic atheists by Buchner, Voght, Mollschott, Strechner, Feuerbach and others. This theory asserts (1) that matter is eternal; (2) that matter and force have built up the universe apart from any personal Creator; (3) that the soul is material and mortal; (4) that a fixed code of morals is impossible, and (5) that religion as commonly understood is unessential. The weakness of Materialism is its inability to account for mind and its manifestations. (3) *Idealism*. By this we mean those monistic philoso-

Christlieb describes in the following graphic paragraph, the reign of terror during the French Revolution when atheism was in the ascendancy. "Encouraged by the abjuration of Christianity on the part of the Bishop of Paris and his priests, they came before the Convention with a petition for the abrogation of Christianity, and the institution of a worship of Reason, presenting the wife of one of their colleagues as the Goddess of Reason. Clad in white garments and a sky-blue mantle, with the red cap on her head and a pike in her hand, they placed her on a fantastically ornamented car, and conducted her, surrounded by crowds of bacchanalian dancers, to the "Temple of Reason," as they were pleased to rename the Cathedral of Notre Dame. There she was seated on the high altar, and amidst profound obeisances, frantic speeches, and frivolous songs, divine honors were paid to her—a scandal which was immediately imitated in several thousand churches in the country. Who does not see from this what abysses are opened before a nation when atheism once gains ground in it!—Christlieb, *Mod. Doubt and Chr. Belief*, p. 139.

Foster mentions three types of atheism: (1) dogmatic atheism, which denies that any God exists; (2) skeptical atheism, which doubts that any God exists; (3) critical atheism, which says that if a God exists there is no evidence of it. It is doubtful if there have ever been any thorough-going atheists of the first class. The third type is closely akin to agnosticism.

phies which have succeeded to the place formerly held by the older materialism, such as Idealistic Monism and Materialistic Monism. These regard matter as a product of force, rather than force as a property of matter. Materialistic Monism was advocated by August Florel and Ernst Haeckel. Florel taught that the brain and the soul were one, the soul having its material aspect and the brain its psychical aspect. Psychology and brain physiology therefore were but two aspects of the same thing. Haeckel in a similar manner maintained that what we call the soul is but the sum of the physiological process of the brain. Idealistic Monism as represented by Hoffding holds that there is one substance which works in both spirit and matter but denies any interaction between them. It advocates rather a parallelism between the activity of consciousness and the functions of the nervous system. In addition to these theories there is an extreme idealism which holds that the sensitive and cognitive mind alone is real and that the phenomena of the material world are but modifications of mind. Whether Atheism, Materialism or Monism be advanced as an explanation of the universe, all equally fail before the intuitive and universal conviction of mankind that there is a God and that He alone is the Creator and Preserver of all things.

Modern Disintegration of the Idea of God. From the time of Augustine to that of Descartes and Spinoza, there was but little change in the common concept of God. Beginning with Descartes, and especially with Spinoza, we have a new cycle of thought which gave emphasis to the philosophical concepts of God, and consequently affected religious beliefs. While each of the modern philosophical definitions contain some fundamental truth, none of them reach the sublime heights of the Christian conception of God. (1) Descartes held to the idea of God as supreme Substance; (2) Spinoza to an All-Substance; (3) Leibnitz to a Chief Monad in a universe of monads; (4) Kant to the idea of a Moral Governor; (5) Herbert Spencer to an Unknowable Ultimate Reality, sometimes mentioned as "The Infinite and

Eternal Energy from which all things proceed"; (6) Hegel, the Absolute Mind; (7) Fichte, the Social Ego; (8) H. G. Wells, the Veiled Being; (9) Höffding, the Principle of the Conservation of Value; (10) Bergson, the Life Force, his favorite term being Vital Impetus; (11) A. N. Whitehead, the "Integral Impetus" or the Principle of Concretion; while (12) William James, H. G. Wells and others advanced anew the idea of a Finite God. It will be seen that these philosophical conceptions are only partial, and can in nowise satisfy the religious nature of man, which demands an object of worship as well as an explanation of the universe.

Basic Ideas of God. The numerous ideas of God advanced by modern philosophers may be classified in three main groups, insofar as they stress one of the following basic elements in the definition of God: *First*, God is regarded as the source of all Reality, generally expressed in terms of creatorship. This may be called the cosmic idea of God. *Second*, there is the conception of God as the Ideal, or the sum of all Values, all Goodness and all Perfection. Murray calls this theory the "focus of all hypostatized values," while Galsworthy regards it as "the sum of altruism in man." This is the idealistic aspect of God. *Third*, there is that which conceives of God as a Supreme Being or an Independent Entity. This is primarily the religious conception as over against the philosophical concepts mentioned above. In its scope it may reach from the lowest conception of God held by the primitive religions, to the highest Christian concept of the Triune God.

The first or cosmic aspect affirms that God must be to us at least as real as physical things or human persons. This argument is based upon the nature of consciousness, in which is to be found the idea of dependence. However free we may be as moral persons, we are aware in consciousness that this freedom is limited. We are therefore ultimately dependent upon an independent Being, and this Being the cosmic philosophers call God. The idea, however, is one of bare existence only, and tells us nothing of the content of this Being. Hoffding saw that not only must the sense of dependence be included in religion, but the sense of values also. These values we may believe are to be found in moral personality. God, therefore, is the conservator of values and consequently of persons. The second or idealistic aspect of God is that which views the supreme Being as the Ideal, or that which comprises truth, beauty and goodness. These ideals are regarded as having absolute or divine authority, so that truth is the divine word and duty the divine law. When religion is regarded as aspiration, the Ideal takes on new significance. The Idealistic philosophers maintain that this ideal does not exist as a necessity, but subsists in a transcendent manner as a progressively permanent Reality. But it has been found difficult to harmonize Absolute Reality with a transcendent Idea which is eternally becoming, without a unifying concept of moral will. This leads directly to the third aspect of God as an independent Entity, a Personal Being. If God be characterized by personality, He may be absolutely Ideal in character and yet His perfect will may still be unrealized in the objective world. As a Personal Being, He may be trusted and worshiped, while leaving at the same time a place for the moral imperative, which calls upon man to share in the task and the prayer which our Lord taught His disciples, *Thy kingdom come. Thy will be done in earth, as it is in heaven* (Matt. 6: 10).

CHAPTER XII

GOD AS INFINITE EFFICIENCY

We have pointed out that the Absolute as the world ground must be identical with the God of religion. But in viewing God as the Absolute, we have seen that the finite, whether in Being or knowledge, must rest in Him. What, then, is the character of the relations which He bears to the universe of finite things? Are they dependent upon him in a merely logical order, or do they emanate from his being as the Neo-Platonist would maintain? The theistic conception of God as personal, necessitates a belief in will as in intellect, and must therefore account for efficiency as well as absoluteness. It must regard God as the source as well as the ground of reality. While it is generally assumed that God stands in relation to the world as Creator, this truth needs to be given proper emphasis, as being a necessary and characteristic feature of the Christian idea of the universe. Unless the universe depends upon God as a world-ground, it cannot be the pliant instrument of his infinite efficiency.

Modern Speculative Theism. The necessity of the causal relations of God to the universe, is shown by the various theories of modern theistic speculation. This type of theism differs from the older deism in its conception of the relation of God to the world, mainly in its emphasis upon immanence rather than transcendence. It developed as a reaction to the barrenness of the speculations concerning the Absolute as transcendent and unknowable, and is represented by such writers as Theodore Parker and James Martineau. Specifically stated, God is not to be identified with the world as in pantheism, but yet is so far one with it that His activity is rigidly confined within it and limited to the course of nature. The energy displayed in the world is the divine immanence revealing itself in the realm of both matter and mind, but in each according to its own laws. The theory has all the effect, therefore, in its consequences, as that of ancient Stoicism. It denies creative activity to God in the sense of a volitional act, and limits human freedom to a mere expression of the inner divine activity. These theists, however, guard carefully against pantheism in their insistence upon the distinctness of God from the world. Theodore Parker says, "If God be infinite, then He must be immanent, perfectly and totally present in nature and in spirit. Thus there is no point, no atom of matter, but God is there; no point of spirit, and no atom of soul, but God is there. And yet finite matter and finite spirit do not exhaust God. He transcends the world of matter and of spirit, and in virtue of that transcendence continually makes the world of matter fairer, and the world of spirit wiser. So there is really a progress in the manifestation of God, not a progress in God the manifesting. In thought you may annihilate the world of matter and of man; but you do not thereby in thought annihilate the Infinite God, or subtract anything from the existence of God. In thought you may double the world of matter and of man; but in so doing you do not in thought double the Being of the Infinite God; that remains the same as before. That is what I mean when I say that God is infinite, and transcends matter and spirit, and is different in kind from the finite universe" (PARKER, *Works*, XI, p. 108). This form of theism, while closely related to pantheism must be classed with the older Deism. Delitzsch sums up the two positions in this statement, "While speculative theism in a one-sided manner emphasizes the immanence of God, the older deism emphasized with equal one-sidedness His transcendence. The former makes God the active ground of the world development according to natural law, which is dependent on Him, He in turn being dependent on it; the latter placed Him above the *perpetuum mobile* of the universe, and made Him a mere spectator of human history; both agreeing in the opinion that there is no need or room for a supernatural incursion of God into the natural course of development, and refusing to recognize in Christ a new creative beginning and all that goes along with that" (DELITZSCH, *Christian Apologetics*, p. 157). Bruce says that the distinction may be made more vivid to the imagination by representing the immanent Deity as *imprisoned* within the world, and the transcendent Deity as *banished* to the outside of the world (Cf. BRUCE, *Apologetics*, p. 135). Hence, in carrying out the above statement in a truly Christian sense, Dr. Parker carries out the implications of his theory by a denial of the miraculous. "No whim in God, therefore no miracle in nature. The law of nature represents the modes of God himself, who is the only true cause and the only true power, and as He is infinite, unchangeably perfect, and perfectly unchangeable, His mode of action is therefore constant and universal, so that there can be no such thing as a violation of God's constant mode of action" (PARKER, *Works*, XI, p. 114). It may readily be seen, therefore, that it is possible to regard the personal God as the Absolute in the sense of the world-ground, and deny to Him the Christian conception of volitional activity in the world, as it affects both creation and providence. It is for this reason that we must stress the infinite efficiency of the Spirit, if we are to maintain the Christian conception of the personality of God.

THE IDEA OF A FINITE GOD

The attempt to harmonize the Absolute of philosophy with the God of religion, has given rise to various theories which have as their basis the idea of a finite

If "God were simply living Nature," says Dorner, "not being Master of Himself, and therefore not being truly Almighty, because He is not another than Himself, He might create, but He could only work Himself out and produce Himself by physical necessity. All Cosmogony would thus be Theogony. On the contrary, if His Nature is the servant of His Will, then without prejudice to His original power or His Omnipotence, there will remain a place for the world, and that a free world, by virtue of which alone is reciprocal action possible between God and it, and in which the Law of Causality finds its perfection anew. God cannot, it is true, be limited from without, but can be conditioned only by Himself; but if He is Almighty, by virtue of His Omnipotence, and without limitation of it, He can freely determine to condition His action by causalities in the world He has formed, upon whom He bestows the possibility of free determination. A more thorough statement can be admitted only in the higher categories of the divine idea, and especially of the ethical attributes of God."—DORNER, *System of Christian Doctrine*, p. 261.

God. It is frequently assumed that such a reconciliation of thought is impossible, and that religious belief
must rest upon the basis of the ethical and religious feelings. Master Eckhart (1260-1329), the noted German
mystic, made a distinction between the Godhead and
God; and Dean Inge, who follows him in this particular,
asserts that "the God of religion is not the Absolute, but
the highest form under which the Absolute can manifest
Himself to finite creatures" (INGE, *Personal Idealism
and Mysticism,* pp. 13, 14). The theory of a finite God is
not a product of modern thought, but strikes its roots
deep in both Greek philosophy and Greek religion. The
Greeks had their pantheon in which one god while supreme was yet but one among many. Plato identified
God with the Idea of the Good, but at the same time admitted other ideas equally self-existent and eternal. To
Aristotle, God was the "unmoved Mover" absolutely independent of the world, but to him the world was equally
self-existent and eternal. In modern times, the idea of
a finite God is closely associated with the skepticism of
David Hume, but was given more definite form in the
philosophy of John Stuart Mill. Here the motive is not so
much ontological as ethical, and arises from the attempt
to harmonize belief in the infinite goodness of God with
the problem of existent evil. Hume held that it is impossible "to reconcile any mixture of evil in the universe
with infinite attributes." He adopts, therefore, the idea
of a finite God in order to account for evil, which he
thinks lies outside and beyond the God of religion as we
know Him. On this theory, infinity is not necessary to
creatorship, but "benevolence regulated by wisdom,
and limited by necessity, may produce just such a world
as at present." Mill is equally specific in denying the
possibility of "reconciling infinite benevolence and jus-

That God is finite rather than infinite roots back into Greek philosophy. To Plato God was the supreme Idea or Good, but there were
other ideas equally self-existent, like the heavenly bodies in relation to
the sun; and besides, He is not the author of all things; God is not the
author of evil but of good only (*Republic,* Bk. II, p. 380). Aristotle
conceived of God as a perfect self-consciousness, whose being was absolutely independent of the world which was, equally with God, self-
existent and eternal.—WINDELBAND, *History of Philosophy,* p. 689.

tice with infinite power in the Creator of such a world as this." The idea of finiteness has assumed different forms. *First,* there is the agnostic idea represented in modern times by Samuel Butler and H. G. Wells, which maintains that there is an unrevealed Reality back of the God of religion and which called the latter into existence. This theory is closely related to the Gnosticism and Neo-Platonism of the first Christian century, against which St. Paul warned the Colossians, and St. John wrote his First Epistle. *Second,* there is the idea of a finite God which is embraced in the community theory of the Absolute. Both Dr. Rashdall and Dr. A. E. Taylor hold that the Absolute is not to be identified with God, but must include God in a wider community of other consciousness. "The Ultimate Being is a single power," says Dr. Rashdall, "manifested in a plurality of consciousness, one consciousness which is omniscient and eternal, and many consciousnesses which are of limited knowledge, which having a beginning, and some of which, it is possible, or probable, have an end." *Third,* and closely related to the preceding is the idea of a growing or developing God. This is represented in the philosophy of Henri Bergson and his followers, and also by William James in his *Pluralistic Universe* and his *Varieties of Religious Experience.* With Bergson, philosophers appear to be undecided as to whether he believes in the growth of the totality of the universe, or whether he restricts it to that portion known as the phenomenal realm. William James, however, makes it very clear that he regards the growth of the universe as a whole, which to him, with his pluralistic conception, is an aggregate rather than an organism. Since finite individuals grow by drawing upon their environment, he regards God as "having an environment, being in time and working out a history just like ourselves." *Fourth,* we may mention the theory of Horace Bushnell which is set forth in his work entitled, "God in Christ," and is usually regarded as one of the earliest attempts in this country to prove the finiteness of God. The theory is directly related to the agnosticism of Hume, and is an attempt to bridge the chasm between an Absolute, inconceivable and unrevealed, and the God of religion, not by reasoned argument, but by the sense of religious need. "My heart wants the Father," he says, "my heart wants the Son, my heart wants the Holy Ghost!" Hence he conceives of the philosophical Absolute by an inner generative power, coming forth in a dramatic impersonation, giving us the God of religion and presenting Himself under a threefold aspect, that of Father, Son and Holy Spirit, each of which is finite. Dr. Bushnell maintained that in so far as the Absolute is unrevealed, it is wholly negligible and has the value only of Zero. *Fifth*, we may mention what is usually classed as a theory of a finite God, but which in reality amounts to a redefinition of the Absolute to conform to the theistic doctrine of God. Bishop Francis J. McConnell argues that the so-called "unlimited" idea of God as expressed in the Absolute of philosophy is in reality more limited than the Christian idea of God. He charges the abstract theologians as limiting God in that they tend to empty the idea of all concrete content, and so impoverish the idea of God by limiting Him to bare abstractions. In much the same strain, Dr. E. S. Brightman suggests that there is in God what he calls a "Given" which as a retarding factor needs to be overcome. This "Given" is something akin to sensation in man, and accounts for the irrational elements in creation and their consequences in suffering.

GOD AND THE UNIVERSE

Having indicated the positions of modern speculative theism concerning God's causal relation to the world, and having pointed out also, some of the attempts to harmonize the absolute of philosophy with the God of religion, we must now treat more directly of God's volitional relation to the world, reserving for a later chapter the various theories advanced to account for the nature of creation.

The church was forced very early to attempt an explanation of the universe in its relation to God. The current philosophy of the Stoics and Neo-Platonists made it necessary for the Church to present a Christian view of God and the world. The immediate occasion for this, was the development of the heretical sects commonly known as gnostics. These varied widely, but their theories are generally classified as Eastern or Syrian Gnosticism, and Western or Alexandrian Gnosticism. Representatives of the former were Saturninus of Antioch, Bardesanes of Edessa, Marcion of Sinope and Tatian of Assyria. These were all of the second century and are sometimes known as Anti-Judaistic Gnostics. Representatives of the latter were Basilides and Valentinus, frequently known as Judaizing Gnostics. The various sects of Gnosticism had these things in common: (1) They all agreed that the world did not proceed immediately from the Supreme Being. In this they were agnostic despite their name. Valentinus regarded the Supreme being as the unfathomable Abyss, and Basilides as the Unnamable. (2) They related the world to God by the process of emanation. (3) The world proceeding from the essence of God was therefore of like essence with Him. In this they were pantheists. (4) They believed in the eternity of both spirit and matter, good and evil, light and darkness, and were therefore dualists. The distinction between pantheism and dualism may be stated thus: Pantheism holds that God is in all things in the sense that God is all; Dualism holds that God moves in all things either as its soul, or the harmonizer of its discords. Agnosticism and Pantheism have been previously considered in connection with the idea of God as the absolute; attention must now be given to the dualistic theories which have been advanced in opposition to God's Infinite Efficiency.

Syrian Gnosticism was characterized by its emphasis upon emanation, and was in general more dualistic than that of Alexandria. It was a theory of the universe which maintained that the world was not created by a divine fiat, but was the consequence of the flowing forth of the divine essence, which with each succeeding æon gradually deteriorated until it became matter. Their

favorite illustration was that of the light, which proceeding from the sun is the most intense when nearest
its source but decreases in intensity as it recedes until it
is lost in darkness. The dual principles of light and
darkness were eternal. The emanating æons bridged
the chasm between the Infinite and the finite, between
good and evil. Gnosticism under the guise of a Christian philosophy made its influence felt in the churches
of Asia, especially at Colosse, and for this reason is
sometimes known as the Colossian Heresy. When,
therefore, St. Paul in his Epistle to this church declares
that *by him were all things created, that are in heaven,
and that are in earth, visible and invisible, whether they
be thrones, or dominions, or principalities, or powers:
all things were created by him, and for him* (Col. 1:16)
he is using similar if not the exact terminology which
the Gnostics applied to the emanating æons.

Alexandrian Gnosticism was more philosophical in
its character, and its dualism more deeply veiled. In
Valentinus and Basilides efforts were made to transcend
dualism, and motives from both emanation and evolution are often strangely mingled. Gnosticism was the
rationalism of the early church and closely related to
Neo-Platonism. God is the unknown, the unfathomable, the Abyss (Βυθός). With him there is a pleroma
(πλήρωμα) or spiritual world (κόσμος νοήματος), composed of a system of æons which unfold the dark and
mysterious Depth. Besides this spiritual world, matter as
an eternal principle exists in the form of the κένωμα,
or empty void, which appears to be a logical otherness,
or a nonexistent existence. This unintelligent force
God endowed with a portion of His own intelligence
(νοῦς), so that it becomes the Demiurgus or world-
soul. The bridge between the pleroma (πλήρωμα)
and kenoma (κένωμα) is made by the last emanation, or
wisdom (σοφία). Thus God is not Himself even the
framer of the world. This is the work of the Demiurgus
or world-soul, which pervades the visible universe and
constitutes it one living animated whole.

Against Gnosticism in all forms, the Church reacted, and sought to employ instead, the ethical view of free, creative action. It held fast to the idea of personality as belonging to the Original Being, and consequently conceived of the world as proceeding from God, not by the physical or logical necessity of His unfolding essence, but as an act of will. It regarded it, therefore, not as an eternal process, but as a fact that had occurred once for all. It conceived also of the world as mediated through the Divine Word (λόγος), in whom the transcendence and immanence of God as separate potencies remain united, the Logos or God within the world, furnishing a resting-place for the God without the world. Hence St. John sweeps away with a single stroke all thought of emanations and declares that *In the beginning was the Word,* [ἐν ἀρχῇ ἦν ὁ λόγος] *and the Word was with God, and the Word was God* (John 1:1). It was the Word that bridged the chasm between the Infinite and the finite, between God and the world. This Word was creative. *All things were made by him.* This statement is in the emphatic form—(οὐδὲ ἓν ὃ γέγονεν) "without it was done not even one, that has been done." Furthermore, this Word is the pleroma (πληρώματος αὐτοῦ). *Of his fulness have all we received, and grace for grace* (χάριν ἀντὶ χάριτος or favor upon favor) (John 1:16). Thus the Logos is both creative and redemptive, and Christ is the Mediator in both nature and grace. St. Paul likewise warns us against vain philosophy (Col. 2:8) and science falsely so-called (I Tim. 6:20), having in mind, doubtless, the gnostic tendencies which were pressing for

Reason demands for the universe unity of dependence on some common original ground or cause, unity of order and law, of common intelligibility and significance, and of rational end; and theism meets and satisfies these demands. It presents, as the absolute ground or cause from which all things originate, the absolute Reason, self-exerting and self-directing. In the last analysis of physical force, science always finds a power transcending it and suggestive of will-power. In all its explorations of nature and its explanations of it by natural laws, it carries us into sight of the mystery of the infinite which no natural law can explain. . . . . The constitution of the physical system is the archetypal thought of God expressed in it. Its invariable factual sequences which are called the laws of nature and constitute its uniformity and continuity, are accordant with the truths, laws, ideals and ends which are eternal in the absolute Reason.—HARRIS, *Self-revelation of God,* pp. 288ff.

recognition in the Church. To him, Christ *is the image of the invisible God, the first born of every creature; for by him were all things created. And he is before all things, and by him all things consist,* or "He precedes all things and in him all things have been permanently placed" (Col. 1:15, 17). St. Paul also has his pleroma doctrine, and we might add, his avatar doctrine also. The pleroma finds expression in the words, *For it pleased the Father that in him should all fulness dwell,* (πᾶν τὸ πλήρωμα κατοικῆσαι or the whole fullness should dwell). To the Gnostic teaching concerning light and darkness as eternal principles of good and evil, and the whole bewildering attempt to bridge the chasm between them, both philosophically and religiously, St. Paul gives answer in a hymn of praise, *Giving thanks unto the Father, which hath made us meet to be partakers of the inheritance of the saints in light; who hath delivered us from the power of darkness, and hath translated us into the kingdom of his dear Son: in whom we have redemption through his blood, even the forgiveness of sins* (Col. 1:12-14).

We have considered this subject at some length, in order to present the Christian idea of God in His creative aspect. We need not give attention to those philosophies, which from the time of Gnosticism to the present have sought to explain God's relation to the world without a Mediator; nor to those which, ignoring the Divine Word, have substituted in His stead a series of impersonal emanations. Pantheism without the mediation of the Logos or Word resolves the world into God; materialism on the other hand confines God to the realm of matter or falls into atheism. The more modern monistic philosophies are usually but thinly veiled pantheism, and rightly deserve the name of "facile monism." Pluralism apparently gives up any attempt at unity. Against all these theories Christianity posits the Infinite Efficiency of Absolute Personality. It sees creation as the result of a creative fiat, and finds its unity in the *Logos* as the Eternal Word. The will, however, as here used is something more than mere choice or volition, it is thought or purpose, it is reason or end.

This St. Paul states specifically in his Epistle to the Ephesians. He speaks first of *the good pleasure of his will* (τὴν εὐδοκίαν τοῦ θελήματος αὐτοῦ) or benevolent affection of His will (Eph. 1: 5); then of *the mystery of his will according to the good pleasure which he hath purposed in himself,* (προέθετο ἐν αὐτῷ or according to his own benevolent design, which He had previously purposed in Himself) (Eph. 1: 9); and lastly of *the purpose of him who worketh all things after the counsel of his own will* (βουλὴν τοῦ θελήματος αὐτοῦ or who effectuates or is operating according to the counsel, purpose or design, of His own will) (Eph. 1: 11). Here, then, according to the Christian view, the world is created by the Infinite Efficiency of God, divine love being the originating cause, the divine will the efficient cause, and the divine Word the instrumental cause.

The sublime doctrine of the relation of the Eternal Son to the creature is the only secret of the continuity which is taught, the only bridge between the Creator and the creature. He is the Mediator—if such a use of the term may be allowed—between the Infinite and the finite, between God and the creature. . . . . St. Paul contradicts the Gnostic speculations as to the Demiurgus; the entire pleroma of the Godhead, and not an emanation, dwelt in Him and did not descend upon Him bodily, and not in semblance. And He who was the *First begotten before every creature,* was such as the 'Αρχή or Beginning, in Whom and through Whom creation began. *By him were all things created:* as if in Him the Absolute God, or the Father, originated creaturely existence, upholds it and administers it; by an incarnation before the Incarnation. We cannot conceive how the creaturely universe should have this specific relation to the Son, and how in Him the Infinite became finite, before God became flesh; but we must receive the mystery and adore it. Our Lord was the Firstborn of the new creation when He began its life in Himself; and He is the First begotten, or beginning of the creation of God which had its origin in Him.—Pope, *Compend. Chr. Th.,* I, pp. 384, 385.

CHAPTER XIII

GOD AS PERFECT PERSONALITY

We have considered God as the Absolute in the sense of the ground of all reality, and as the Infinite in the sense of efficiency; it remains now for us to consider God as Perfect Personality, *first*, in the sense of a completion or perfecting of the two previous aspects; and *second*, as furnishing the reason or purpose of all things. The Christian conception of God must therefore include the idea of Absolute Reality as the ground of existence, His Infinite Efficiency as its cause, and His Perfect Personality as the reason or end of all things.

We have seen that false conceptions of the Absolute and the Infinite have led to grievous errors respecting the true nature of God, so also a false conception of personality has led many to maintain that there is an inconsistency in ascribing personality and personal attributes to the Absolute and the Infinite. One of the outstanding problems of modern philosophy and theology, therefore, is this question of personality. At no point perhaps have philosophy and theology had such a direct contact, nor has philosophy done more to shape the theological conceptions of God, than in these conflicts which have arisen over the being and nature of God.

Origin and Meaning of the Term. The idea of personality has been dominant in thought from the earliest times, but by a strange coincidence the word itself came into use only in modern times. The earliest Greek conceptions of the Deity were personal even if polytheistic, but the attributes of goodness and truth were not applied to them. Far earlier than this was the Hebrew conception of a personal God, with all the attributes which we ascribe to human personality. It was Boethius, however, in the earlier part of the sixth century who gave the definition of personality which has been current in the church until modern times. This definition is, *Persona est naturæ rationalis individua substantia,* or a "person is the individual subsistence of a rational nature." A person then, was characterized in a twofold way—an individual as being separate and distinct from others; and a common rational nature of which each individual was a partaker.

Thomas Aquinas in his *Summa Theologica* defines a person as "that which is most perfect in all nature, as subsisting in rational nature." He argues then, "that the term *person* may be applied to God, since His essence contains in itself all perfection, but not in the same way it is given to His creatures, but in a more excellent way, as other names that are given to creatures are ascribed *via eminentiæ* to God." It is evident that St. Thomas is thinking more of personality as being *in* God than as applied *to* God. The Trinitarian controversies had been carried on under the prevailing influence of Platonic Realism, and the tendency was to subordinate the individual to the universal. This was noticeable in the earlier Greek concepts of religion. The gods of the polytheistic pantheon were too personal, in the sense that their finiteness was subversive of their universality. The word "person," therefore, was thought of in the sense in which we commonly use it in its application to the Trinity, while the unity of God was expressed by the word "substance" or "essence." Thus we have the Greek word *hypostasis* and the Latin word *substantia* which as the equivalent of *hypostasis* should, to be more exact, have been translated *subsistence,* instead of *substance,* the former denoting a distinction within the ultimate substance, rather than the substance itself. Thus God was personal in the sense of the Trinitarian distinctions, but to the ultimate and unitary being of God the more abstract term of *essence* or *substance* was applied. This failure to apply the term "person" to the whole being of God gave rise to the modern controversies between philosophy and theology concerning the nature of personality; and further, to controversies within theology itself respecting the nature of the Trinity. Out of these has come a firmer and wider grasp of the meaning of personality. It is seen to apply now, not only to the hypostatic distinctions of the Trinity, but to the whole conception of God as both Unity and Trinity. It has proved to be the ultimate reality, through which alone the Absolute can be understood. The world-ground is therefore personal, and the infinite efficiency of the first cause is likewise personal. Reserving the trinal nature of God for a later discussion, we shall trace the development of this wider concept of personality, presenting *first*, the Psychological Argument from the nature of self-consciousness, and *second*, the Metaphysical Argument from the nature of personality itself. The first argument is stated in the most able manner by Dr. William G. Shedd in his *Dogmatic Theology;* the second is best represented by Lotze in his discussion of the nature of personality.

The Psychological Argument for Personality. Personality is marked by self-consciousness and self-decision. Dr. Olin A. Curtis in his *Christian Faith* defines it as "the power of self-grasp, self-estimate, and self-decision," or more concisely "the power of self-conscious decision." Consciousness implies the duality of subject and object —a subject to know and an object to be known. Without this, consciousness is impossible. Self-consciousness is a higher form of consciousness, in which the subject and object are identified. The duality remains but the human spirit, in the act of self-cognition furnishes both subject and object in one being or substance. It has the power of setting itself over against itself, and thereby duplicating its own unity as subject and object. Man, therefore, not only thinks, feels and wills, but he knows that he thinks, feels and wills. It is this power of self-consciousness and determination that constitutes him a personal being. Dr. Shedd states the position as follows: Self-consciousness is (1) the power which a rational spirit or mind has of making itself its own object; and (2) of knowing that it has done so. If the first step is taken, and not the second, there is consciousness but not self-consciousness; because the subject would not, in this case, know that the object is the self. And the second step cannot be taken, if the first has not been. These two acts of a rational spirit, or mind, involve three distinctions in it, or modes of it. The whole mind as a subject contemplates the very same whole mind as an object. Here are two distinctions or modes of mind. And the very same whole mind also perceives that the contemplating subject and the contemplating object are one and the same essence or being. Here are three modes of one mind, each distinct from the others, yet all three going to make up the one *self-conscious spirit*. Unless there were these two acts and the three resulting distinctions, there would be no self-knowledge. Mere singleness, a mere subject without an object, is incompatible with self-consciousness. And mere duality would yield only consciousness, not self-consciousness. Consciousness is dual; self-consciousness is trinal (Cf. SHEDD, *Dogmatic Theology*, I, p. 183ff). Self-consciousness, being the most perfect form of consciousness, is applicable to God as the Supreme Being or Perfect Personality. But we must make a distinction here. Man has both consciousness and self-consciousness. By consciousness he is related to the objective world through sentiency. There is in him the sensuous consciousness of the animal and the blind agencies of physical appetite. The animal is impressed by external objects which are no part of itself, but apparently is never impressed by itself. It experiences heat and cold, pleasure and pain, but cannot duplicate its own unity and thus become aware of the subject which experiences them. An animal is not a person and cannot have self-consciousness. Man has this sentient consciousness also, but it differs in this respect, that it is capable of being scrutinized and converted into self-consciousness. On this lower plane, man may think, but he does not think of what he thinks; or he may feel, and not direct his attention to the character and quality of those feelings. It is one of the effects of conviction by the Holy Spirit," says Dr. Shedd, "to convert consciousness into self-consciousness. Conviction of sin is the consciousness of self as the guilty author of sin. It is forcing the man to say, 'I know that I have thus felt, and thus thought, and thus acted.' The truth and the Spirit of God bring sinners to self-knowledge and self-consciousness, from out of a state of mere consciousness" (SHEDD, *Christian Dogmatics*, I, p. 180). Dr. Olin A. Curtis emphasizes this same fact but gives more attention to the volitional than to the intellectual and affectional aspects of personality. He regards self-decision as the most important feature of the entire personal process because it is the culmination. "Whenever we will anything, supremely conscious of self, that volition is self-decision." "Whenever a man sees himself out there," he says, "as an existing, isolated, peculiar individual, and then in the flash of that vision of self, wills anything, that volition is self-decision. The person first makes himself the clear, full objective of his own thought, and then makes that definite point of his person the original initiative of his choice. And so the significance of self-decision becomes tremendous because the decision is charged with the conception, with the entire valuation, which the man has of himself" (CURTIS, *Christian Faith*, pp. 23, 24).

Self-consciousness belongs to God. It is evident, however, that God like man cannot have consciousness apart from self-consciousness. *First,* sentiency cannot be attributed to God. God is Spirit (John 4:24). According to the creedal statement He is "without body, parts, or passions." Here a sharp distinction is made between spirit and matter. Matter has bodily form, and must have parts and passions. A body is divisible and therefore capable of being destroyed. A body is capable of passions in the etymological sense of the term, that is, it can be wrought upon from without by material substances. Spirit being a unity can have no parts and is therefore indestructible. God as the Absolute Spirit is a unity and therefore can stand in no passive and organic relations to that which is not Himself. When the creed states that He is without "passions" it means that He is not operated upon or moved from the outside, but that all His activity is self-determined. The divine movement is all from within, that is, *ab intra* as over against *ab extra*. His personal decisions are always self-decisions of the highest possible type. His knowledge and affections are always the expression of His infinite and eternal worth. *Second,* there can be no growth or development of consciousness in God. Man comes to self-consciousness gradually through the increasing complexity of the relationships existing between the self and the objective world. As he develops physically from infancy to manhood, so he must develop in his mental and moral life. Like the Word incarnate, he increases in wisdom and stature, and like Him he should increase in favor with God and man. We cannot think of God as having blind and unreflecting mental processes. His reason is not discursive but intuitive. His is ever "self-conscious, self-contemplating, self-knowing and self-communing." He is indeed cognizant of the universe which He created, but this knowledge is not mediated through the senses as in man, and consequently is never partial or imperfect. Here we hear the breaking of the great deep on the infinite and eternal shores of God's omnipresence, His omniscience and His omnipotence.

The Metaphysical Nature of Personality. We have presented some of the psychological aspects of personality as found in the nature of self-consciousness; we must now consider more carefully its metaphysical characteristics. Pantheistic thought asserts that personality cannot be conceived without finite limitations. For this reason it has always objected to the application of the term personality to God. Personality according to the Hegelians and Neo-Hegelians consists in the contraposition of self to another object, a nonego by which it is limited. This limitation of the self by the cosmical ego is the cause of consciousness reflecting upon itself, thus giving rise to self-consciousness or personality. Infinite personality, then, according to this type of thought would be a contradiction in terms. But does personality depend upon this limitation? Theists reply in the negative. They maintain that this limitation may be the occasion but not the cause of personality. The root of personality lies in

6296<

its nature before there is any contraposition to other
subjects, and consists in the peculiar constitution of the
subject as a finite spirit. The contraposition, therefore,
is not the essence of personality, but only an inherent
consequence of its nature.

The philosophical argument of the Hegelians against
the Personality of God has been ably met on philosophical grounds by Hermann Lotze (1817-1881), whose
writings have profoundly influenced theology. His
chief works bearing upon this are the *Microcosmos* and
his class lectures on the *Philosophy of Religion*. Lotze
approaches the subject of personality from the opposite
angle, affirming that perfect personality belongs to God
only, and that the necessity finite personality has of
thinking itself over against a not-self is due to the limitation of finiteness rather than personality. He begins
his argument by an analysis of personality which he finds
yields two features, *first*, that the subject possesses an
image of cognition or representation of what it is, by
which it distinguishes itself from others; and *second*,
that this image is unique, in that it cannot be contrasted
with any other image in the same sense, that the other
image may be contrasted with a third. The uniqueness
and distinctness of this image he holds to be fundamental
to personality. While our knowledge of personality may
come from experience in the sense of mental development, it is not merely the orderly arrangement of ideas
according to some system, but the ego standing in direct
opposition to every nonego. Thus he finds that self-
consciousness always implies the existence of a fundamental self-feeling which is its most essential element.
Lotze also denies that personality is occasioned by the
ego's activity being "reflected" back from a nonego.
This he asserts is a "mere supplement of thought devoid of all basis." Such a process he says, would not
distinguish the "I" from "thou" or "he," our own personality from that of others. This distinction, he maintains, is not effected by means of pure ideation, but by
the power of the self to combine its experiencing of feeling with its ideas. It is this combination that enables us

to distinguish a personal state as our own. "The smallest capability for the experience of feeling," he says, "is sufficient to distinguish the one who experiences it from the external world, but the highest intellectuality apart from this capability, will not be able to apprehend itself as an ego over against a nonego. This is to say, once again, that personality presupposes feeling or self-feeling and cannot be subsequent intellectual construction only."

Lotze in denying limitation as the essence of personality, lays a firm foundation for belief in the personality of God. "What justification is there," he asks, "for attributing the term personality to its incomplete form in man, and grudging it to the Deity completely endowed with it?" Finiteness, then, according to Lotze, is the limitation rather than the expression of personality, and only in the infinite is there the truest and highest personality. "So little, therefore, is the idea of God's personality contradicted by His infinite greatness and perfection," says Christlieb, "that, on the contrary, it is precisely by reason of them that He must be personal" (CHRISTLIEB, *Modern Doubt and Christian Belief*, p. 170).

There are two factors in human self-knowledge: (1) a direct feeling of self; and (2) a conception of self or of the powers and properties of self. This conception of self is developed, but the feeling of self is present from the beginning. The child has little or no conception of itself, but it has the liveliest experience of itself. This experience of self is quite independent of all antithesis of subject and object, and is underived. But allowing all that can be claimed for the development of our self-consciousness, it does not lie in the notion of self-consciousness that it must be developed. An eternal self is metaphysically as possible as an eternal not-self. To say that because our self-consciousness is developed all self-consciousness must be developed, is just as rational as to say that all being must have a beginning because we have. It is to transfer to the independent all the limitations of the finite, which is the very thing the pantheist claims to abhor.—BOWNE, *Studies in Theism*, p. 274.

Not a few hints are given us in the human range that mind is intrinsically the power of initiation, the original spring of energy. Accordingly it is no speculative rashness to conceive that the infinite mind, notwithstanding the absence of external stimulus, may be alive, energetic, inclusive of all loftiest feelings and purposes, and thus have abundant means of self-consciousness. Indeed, there is good reason for concluding with Lotze that complete self-consciousness, or personality in the highest sense, can be predicated of the infinite alone.—SHELDON, *System of Christian Doctrine*, p. 37.

We must draw our argument for the personality of God to a close. We have seen that the infinity of God, instead of placing Him outside the reach of human knowledge as agnosticism declares; or denying to Him personality as pantheism maintains, is instead, the very presupposition of His personality. And further, the idea of the Absolute can be maintained only as it posits an absolute Subject, that is, the absolute Personality. Thus the Absolute instead of being a contradiction of person-

Lotze gathers up the results of this investigation in the following propositions: (1) Selfhood, the essence of all personality, does not depend upon any opposition that either has happened or is happening of the Ego to the Non-Ego, but it consists in an immediate self-existence which constitutes the basis of the possibility of that contrast wherever it appears. Self-consciousness is the elucidation of this self-existence which is brought about by means of knowledge, and even this is by no means necessarily bound up with the distinction of the Ego from the Non-Ego, which is substantially opposed to it. (2) In the nature of the finite mind as such, is to be found the reason why the development of its personal consciousness can take place only through the influences of that cosmic whole which the finite being itself is not, that is, through stimulation coming from the Non-Ego, not because it needs the contrast with something alien in order to have self-existence, but because in this respect, as in every other, it does not contain in itself the conditions of its existence. We do not find this limitation in the going of the Infinite: hence for it alone is there possible a self-existence, which needs neither to be initiated nor to be continuously developed by something not itself, but which maintains itself within itself with spontaneous action that is eternal and had no beginning. (3) Perfect Personality is in God only, to all finite minds there is allotted but a pale copy thereof: the finiteness of the finite is not a producing condition of this Personality, but a limit and a hindrance of its development. (For further study cf. RELTON, Christology, pp. 166, 167.)

If I do not mistake, the whole system of this reasoning rests upon an error common to skepticism and pantheism, which formerly misled, and still deceives, many a superior mind. This error consists in maintaining that every determination is a negation. Omnis determinatio negatio est, says Hamilton after Spinoza. Nothing can be falser or more arbitrary than this principle. It arises from the confusion of two things essentially different, namely, the limits of a being, and its determinate and constitutive characteristics. I am an intelligent being, and my intelligence is limited; these are two facts equally certain. The possession of intelligence is the constitutive characteristic of my being, which distinguishes me from the brute being. The limitation imposed on my intellect, which can see only a small number of truths at a time, is my limit, and this is what distinguishes me from the Absolute Being, from the Perfect Intelligence which sees all truth at a single glance. That which constitutes my imperfection is not, certainly, my being intelligent; therein, on the contrary, lies the strength, the richness, and the dignity of my being. What constitutes my weakness and my nothingness is that this intelligence is inclosed in a narrow circle. Thus, inasmuch as I am intelligent, I participate in being and perfection; inasmuch as I am intelligent only within certain limits, I am imperfect.—
SAISSET, Modern Pantheism, Vol. II, pp. 69-72.

ality, can be explained only in the light of personality. The self-consciousness of the Absolute Personality does not need to limit itself by a not-self outside. God created the universe and gave it the position it holds, so that if we consider it a limitation in any sense of the word, it must be a self-limitation. This necessarily involves a belief in freedom. If we deny to God the freedom to create a world of finite existence apart from Himself, this very limitation would be a denial of His absoluteness. Thus the Christian concept of God preserves it from pantheism. On the other hand, it is maintained that one person can be distinguished from another, only by the multiplicity of powers which characterize him. Thus agnosticism holds that the Absolute, being by abstraction outside the realm of attributes, cannot be known. The Christian concept of God is that these powers are not abstracted from personality, but function in it as a unity instead of a multiplicity. Knowledge, feeling and will may be distinguished in finite personality, and exercised in some degree of independence, but this is not true of the Absolute Personality. Personal powers may correspond to certain objective distinctions in God, but it is His whole being that knows and feels and wills, and this in such a manner that their exercise does not break the absolute unity of His being. But apart from the philosophical significance of the term personality as applied to God, there is a religious significance to the term. As a personal Being, self-conscious and free, God stands in ethical and spiritual relations to mankind. As personal, God is Absolute reality in relation to the ground of all existence; as Infinite Efficiency, He is the Cause of all existence; so also as Perfect Personality, He is the reason or purpose of all existence.

PERSONALITY AS THE FINAL CAUSE OF FINITE EXISTENCE

We have shown that Perfect Personality is the completion of the process, which includes the concept of the Absolute as the ground of all reality, and the Infinite as the cause of all finite existence. We must now show that there is a sufficient reason or final cause of the universe, and this we find in Perfect Personality also. So far we have dealt mainly with the philosophical aspects of absoluteness, infinity and personality. But the term personality has a richer content than that given to it by metaphysics alone. To self-consciousness must be added self-determination. Perfect Personality involves perfection of intellect, feeling and will. There is therefore within the cosmos itself, a teleology or purpose which is derived from its Author. Dr. Dorner has shown that Spirit expresses something positive, a peculiar Being transcending Nature and its categories, which is not merely in degree of higher worth than all finite good things, but which is also the absolute final end. In this higher something, or in God as Spirit, the principles will be found of all those ideas of which the world forms the mere finite manifestation or type, the principles of Measure, Design and Order, of Beauty and Harmony. God, as Spirit is the original seat of the "eternal truths"; they have in Him their absolute being. . . . . For how can absolute Being, which is to be necessarily thought of as the real and original possibility, both of existing things and of knowledge, be such a possibility if it is not essentially spiritual? (Cf. DORNER, *System of Christian Doctrine,* p. 284). God as Perfect Personality satisfies, therefore, the religious nature of man, not only in its intellectual aspects, but in its moral and ethical demands as well.

Nature and the Personal Spirit. Perfect Personality lies only in the realm of spirit. Spirit, therefore, must give meaning to nature. The spiritual sphere is the only sufficient explanation of nature, without which its contradictions for rational thought must ever remain an unsolved riddle. "It is no tragic accident," says Dorner, "that without exception, every individual thing or every natural good passes away. It lies in the nature of the case." Nature must be permeated by the spiritual sphere, so that all its processes are taken up and made subservient to higher ends. This is the argument of St. Paul in his First Epistle to the Corinthians. *There is,* he says, *a natural body, and there is a spiritual body. And so it is written, The first man Adam was made a living soul; the last Adam was made a quickening spirit. Howbeit that was not first which is spiritual, but that which is natural; and afterward that which is spiritual. The first man is of the earth, earthy: the second man is the Lord from heaven. As is the earthy, such are they also that are earthy: and as is the heavenly, such are they also that are heavenly. And as we have borne the image of the earthy, we shall also bear the image of the heavenly* (I Cor. 15: 44-49). Here it is clearly declared that the end of nature is the spiritual, and that it is inherent in Christianity as a philosophy of life, that the natural must be spiritualized, that nature must be made to serve spiritual ends. The transient nature of finite existence, or the consumption of nature, is not therefore irrational, since it serves a permanent purpose and comes to fuller expression in something higher than the finite, thus serving an infinite end.

Personality and Its Positive Spiritual Content. But the spiritual realm not only transcends nature and becomes its end in a general way, there is a positive content to the term Spirit. It signifies not merely a higher degree of worth than nature, but a unique, personal being, transcending nature and its categories, and is in itself the Sufficient Reason of nature, its absolute and final end. It was Athanasius (296-373), the great champion of the Trinitarian conception of God who declared that "he who contemplates Creation rightly is contemplating also the Word who framed it, and through him begins to apprehend the Father" (ATHANASIUS, *Discourse Against the Arians,* I, p. 12). Here we approach the deep and unfathomable mystery of the adorable Trinity. But it is impossible to discuss the question of Perfect Personality without anticipating the distinctly Christian conception of God as Trinal Spirit or Triune Being. Why are the principles of truth, right, beauty and harmony in the world? Do they not force us immediately to the belief that there is a principle of order in the world? And can there be order without wisdom? And can wisdom be less than personal? Here we have reached the inspired declaration of the Prologue to the Fourth Gospel: *In the beginning was the Word, and the Word was with God, and the Word was God. The same was in the beginning with God. All things were made by him; and without him was not anything made that was made* (John 1:1-3). Here it is specifically stated that the world was created by the Word, that is, according to a rational order, and after principles absolute in the personal Word which later became incarnate in Christ. It was just because the *Logos* was personal and creative, that Christ became the Redemptive Person. In Him was manifested the fullness of grace and truth. It is then in God as Spirit, that we must find the original seat of mercy and truth, strength and beauty (Psalm 96:6). It is in the *Logos* as the Eternal Word that they have their absolute and unoriginated being. These principles did not originate in will; they are true in themselves and are therefore eternal within His essence as Spirit. They are the categories which presuppose Divine Intelligence. Whether finite or absolute, there can be no true end apart from intelligence, nor can there be either beauty or harmony without it. Only as there is a synthesis of the mind within nature and the mind within man can there be any understanding of nature by man, or any communication of man with man. It is because of the eternal Logos which precedes and underlies the very structure of creation, constituting it a cosmos and not a chaos, that we have our world of order and beauty. And further still, it is because the Christian conception of the Logos given us by St. John is both personal and creative, that we are preserved from pantheism, which on the one hand would merge everything into God, or on the other, regard the world as an emergence or emanation from God. St. Paul in his address on Mars' Hill declared to the Athenians that God is not *worshipped with men's hands, as though he needed any thing, seeing he giveth to all life, and breath, and all things;* and passing directly from the creative aspect, he presents the ethical as the great goal of human personality, *that they should seek the Lord, if haply they might feel after him, and find him, though he be not far from every one of us; for in him we live, and move, and have our being* (Acts 17:25-28). A firm grasp upon the fact of personality forever prevents thought from becoming pantheistic.

THE PRINCIPLES OF RATIONAL INTUITION

What are these absolute principles, eternal in the Godhead and peculiarly the property of the Divine Logos, which form the archetypal ideas of the world, the rational principles of order in the universe? The ancient philosophers expressed these norms in the familiar classification of the true, the beautiful and the good. Dr. Samuel Harris in his *Philosophical Basis of Theism* (p. 180ff) thinks this classification inadequate. Starting with Kant's questions, "What can I know? What shall I do? What may I hope?" he divides the last into two; which he finds to be "What may I become?" and "What may I acquire and enjoy?" He thus finds four norms instead of three, which he regards as ultimate realities, known through rational intuition. These are (1) the *true*, which is the rational standard or norm of what a man may know; (2) the *right*, which is the norm of human activity; (3) the *perfect*, which is the norm of what a man may become; and (4) the *good*, which is the norm of what a man may acquire and enjoy. A brief discussion of these will give us some idea of the richness of Perfect Personality, which forms the

That the goal of the universe is spiritual and is to be found in Perfect Personality is given definite and beautiful expression in these words of St. Paul: *Then cometh the end, when he shall have delivered up the kingdom to God, even the Father; when he shall have put down all rule and all authority and power. For he must reign, till he hath put all enemies under his feet. The last enemy that shall be destroyed is death. For he hath put all things under his feet. But when he saith all things are put under him, it is manifest that he is excepted which did put all things under him. And when all things shall be subdued . . . . then shall the Son himself be subject unto him that put all things under him, that God may be all in all* (I Cor. 15:24-28). *Behold I shew you a mystery; We shall not all sleep, but we shall all be changed, in a moment, in the twinkling of an eye, at the last trump: for the trumpet shall sound, and the dead shall be raised incorruptible, and we shall be changed. For this corruptible must put on incorruption, and this mortal shall put on immortality* (I Cor. 15:51-53). This is the lively hope unto which we have been begotten again by the resurrection of Jesus Christ from the dead (I Peter. 1:3).

spiritual goal of finite human beings and the supreme end of all things.

The First Ultimate Is the True. By the "true" we mean those universal truths or primitive principles of the mind which regulate all knowing. These truths of the reason have objective reality as principles or laws of things, in that they are the constituent elements in absolute reason. There can be no truth apart from the reality of the world-ground, just as there can be no laws of nature apart from the Author or Creator. "By truth," says Dr. Strong, "we mean that attribute of the divine nature in virtue of which God's being and God's knowledge eternally conform to each other" (STRONG, *Systematic Theology,* I, p. 260). Thus as a Divine Perfection we must regard truth as an absolute correspondence of revelation with reality. Dr. Samuel Harris approves of Plato's position in regard to archetypal ideas, when touched, as he says by Christian theism. These archetypal ideas of the true, the right, the perfect and the good exist eternally and archetypally in God the Supreme Reason. These and all other forms and ideals compatible with them were in the mind of God as an ideal universe before they came to existence in the physical universe as we now perceive it. To these He gives expression in time and space, and under other limitations of finite beings. He also created men as finite rational beings which in their normal development come not only to know themselves, but to know themselves in the light of Another, and thus arises the moral and ethical system in which God gives expression to even higher archetypal thoughts.

Truth as it is applicable to God is usually classified as verity, veracity and faithfulness or fidelity. The two latter may be considered attributes in that they represent transitive truth manifested to His creatures. The former must be regarded as immanent truth, and not merely an active attribute. It is the exact correspondence of the Divine Nature with the ideal of absolute perfection. While this ideal can be only partially comprehended by finite beings, it is fully known to God in all its excellence, and to this supreme excellence His whole nature corresponds. It is in this aspect that the Scriptures call Him the true God, as indicated in the following references: *And this is life eternal, that they might know thee the only true God, and Jesus Christ, whom thou has sent* (John 17:3). Since truth is reality revealed, Jesus is the Truth because in Him are revealed the hidden qualities of God. This is given further statement in I John 5:20 where the writer declares that *We know that the Son of God is come, and hath given us an understanding, that we may know him that is true, and we are in him that is true, even in his Son Jesus Christ. This is the true God, and eternal life.* In both of these passages the word ἀληθινόν is used which describes God as genuine or real as distinguished from ἀληθής, a term used to express the veracity or truthfulness of God. When, therefore, our Lord speaks of himself as the Truth, He means not merely that He is the truthful One, but that He is the Truth and the source of truth. His truth is that of being and not merely that of expression (Cf. also II Chron. 15:3, Jer. 10:10, I Thess. 1:9, Rev. 3:7).

As to the veracity and faithfulness of God, the Scriptures abound in both references and illustrations. Since God's knowledge is perfect He cannot be mistaken; since He is holy there can be no disposition to deceive; and since His resources are infinite He is under no necessity of failure. His law being a transcript of His nature is unchangeable and exactly adapted to the character and condition of His people. It becomes, therefore, the ground of adoration and praise. *Thy righteousness is an everlasting righteousness, and thy law is the truth. Thy word is true from the beginning: and every one of thy righteous judgments endureth forever* (Psalm 119:142, 160). The Scripture writers delight in meditating upon the faithfulness of God as the foundation for faith and hope and love. If God were not true in all

All truth among men, whether mathematical, logical, moral or religious, is to be regarded as having its foundation in this immanent truth of the divine nature and as disclosing facts in the being of God.—STRONG, *Syst. Th.,* I, p. 261.

His promises and faithful in all His engagements, religion would be impossible. Hence we have such references as the following: *God is not a man, that he should lie; neither the son of man, that he should repent: hath he said, and shall he not do it? or hath he spoken, and shall he not make it good?* (Num. 23:19). *He is a Rock, his work is perfect: for all his ways are judgment: a God of truth, and without iniquity, just and right is he* (Deut. 32:4). *Thy truth reacheth unto the clouds* (Psalm 108: 4). *The truth of the Lord endureth forever* (Psalm 117: 2). *Thy faithfulness is unto all generations* (Psalm 119: 90). In the New Testament we have such references as the following: *God is faithful, by whom ye were called unto the fellowship of his Son Jesus Christ our Lord* (I Cor. 1:9). *If we believe not, yet he abideth faithful: he cannot deny himself* (II Tim. 2:13). *Every good gift and every perfect gift is from above, and cometh down from the Father of lights, with whom is no variableness, neither shadow of turning* (Jas. 1:17). Other references must be reserved for treatment in relation to the specific attributes of God.

The Second Ultimate Is the Right. Here the principles of rational intuition are known as laws, in that they are regulative of energy or power. These apply in every realm—the physical, the moral and the spiritual. The term right is used to express conformity of action to the principles of reason regarded as law. This is applicable to both intellect and will. By the term "ought" is meant the action of a free rational being in response to the demands of reason. Law in its bare intellectual form is merely observed sequences, and as it concerns physical power is conformity of action to the laws of the physical realm. In duty, however, a new reality arises which must be considered in relation to free will and thus becomes moral law. Like the other intuitions of reason this law is operative in a practical way before it is formulated in thought. As man reflects, he comes to see that whatever he knows as true in the reason, becomes a law of action. Hence there develops a sense of oughtness, and duty takes on a new and intense meaning. He sees himself under an overmaster or Lord, and in conscience he knows himself along with, or in the light of, Another. Kant in his *Metaphysics of Morals* represents conscience as conducting a case before a court and gives his conclusion in these words: "Now that he who is accused by conscience should be figured to be just the same person as the judge, is an absurd representation of a tribunal; since in such an event the accuser would always lose his suit. Conscience must, therefore, represent itself always some one other than itself as Judge, unless it is to arrive at a contradiction with itself." He finds, also, that conformity or lack of conformity to the law as right results in two conflicting types of character. To the one he applies the term virtue and to the other vice. More remotely, however, he finds the one to be holy and the other sinful, and this in direct relation to the Overmaster, known and felt in conscience. God as Perfect Personality must, therefore, be both holy and righteous, and as such demands both holiness and righteousness in His subjects. "Holiness," says William Newton Clarke, "is the glorious fullness of God's moral excellence, held as a principle of His own action and the standard for His creatures" (CLARKE, *Outline of Christian Theology*, p. 89).

The Third Ultimate Is the Perfect. By perfection is meant the correspondence of outward action with the inner rational standard. When the mind imagines a perfect object, that creation of the imagination is called an ideal. Ideals, therefore, are not obtained by imitation, or the copying of observed objects, but are creations of the mind itself. Beauty and harmony are not dependent upon material altogether, but may be pure spiritual images. Beauty is primarily and originally pure form. It does not arise from matter, but is a form impressed upon matter. Material things as we find them in nature become beautiful through the interworking of these forms. Furthermore, this formative principle must be capable of being fixed in thought, not merely as outward law of beauty or harmony, but as a principle of the Essence itself. The law of the beautiful, of harmony and order, of perfection must therefore belong to the nature of God and be a part of the absolute Essence. As God is the Supreme Being, or the Being of beings, so His perfection is a supreme perfection, or a perfection of all perfections. It belongs therefore to God to impress the stamp of His own being upon all the divine works, and consequently His works are perfect. It was for this reason that Augustine loved to think of God as primary beauty and harmony. "God," he says, "is lovely as the beautiful, for we can only love the beautiful; but the truly beautiful is the supersensuous, is immutable truth." As applied to God, perfection is usually regarded in theology as the principle of harmony which unifies and consummates all the divine attributes, thus preventing the sacrifice of one attribute to another, and bringing each one to its supreme manifestation. Perfection in God is not the combination of many qualities, but only, "the undivided glory of the several rays of the divine character." It is the harmony of absolute freedom from inner contradictions. Beauty is therefore directly connected with holiness, and we are commanded to *worship the Lord in the beauty of holiness* (Psalm 96: 9. Cf. I Chron. 16: 29, Psalm 29: 2, II Chron. 20: 21, Psalm 110: 3).

But the Divine Life as perfect, is not merely one of freedom from inner contradictions, it is also one of positive content. It is filled with inner divine potentialities, and all these potencies are in harmonious equilibrium. It becomes, therefore, essentially a Self-purpose. The Scriptures recognize this beauty and harmony which characterize the Divine Perfection, as it recognizes truth and righteousness as belonging to the Divine Nature. The psalmist declared that *Out of Zion, the perfection of beauty, God hath shined* (Psalm 50: 2); and again, *Thou art clothed with honour and majesty. Who coverest thyself with light as with a garment: who stretchest out the heavens like a curtain* (Psalm 104: 1-3). When Jesus in His Sermon on the Mount enjoined upon His disciples the principles of perfection, saying, *Be ye therefore perfect, even as your Father which is in heaven is perfect* (Matt. 5: 48), He could have referred to nothing short of that freedom from inner contradictions which constitutes a holy being, and the possession of those positive potencies which in harmony with the divine nature stamped themselves in beauty upon all His works. The perfection He enjoins upon His disciples is not the absolute perfection of the Divine Being, but that in human personality which corresponds to the divine nature. It is the deliverance of the soul from the inner contradictions brought about by sin, or inherited depravity, and its restoration to purity of heart and simplicity of purpose. And, furthermore, this perfection implies in man as it does in God, a correspondence between the outer activities of life and the inner harmony of being. Perfection in this sense is intensely ethical, in that it includes both inner holiness and outward righteousness. It is the fulfillment of *the oath which he sware to our father Abraham, That he would grant unto us, that we being delivered out of the hand of our enemies might serve him without fear, in holiness and righteousness before him, all the days of our life* (Luke 1: 73-75).

The Fourth Ultimate Is the Good. The good is the last and highest in the series of ultimates which constitute the norms of finite human existence. In its ultimate and absolute sense, our Lord applies the term to God only, *there is none good but one, that is God* (Matt. 19: 17). In this sense it is to be interpreted as the divine sentiment which wills the good of all creatures as such. Thus there is seen to be a distinction between the perfect in the sense of a conformity to the norms of truth and right, and the good in the sense of the useful. A thing may be either a means to something else, or it may be an end in itself. In the former sense, its value is estimated only in relation to that other thing and not for its own sake. This determines it as useful. "The fitting, the useful, the convenient, depend on something else," says Augustine, and "cannot be judged by themselves, but only according to that relation to something else." On the other hand, a thing may be willed for its own sake instead of another, and through its own inner harmony and beauty become an end in itself or a good. It should be observed that the good as the highest in the series of norms involves each of the others in an order of precedence and dependence. Truth in itself appears to be foundational and presupposes no truth, and right is such, only by conformity to truth as a law of action. The perfect presupposes both the ideas of truth and right; while the good not only involves the experiences of joy and sorrow, but presupposes the true, the right and the perfect as the norm or standard by which to discriminate the sources of joy and the pursuit of pleasures worthy of a rational being. The good is then the rational.

The good, therefore, is the rational end or object of acquisition, possession and enjoyment. It presupposes the true, the right and the perfect; it is that in which they culminate. Here we come to the province of ethics, and the necessary investigation of the realm of ends, which shall constitute a full and sufficient reason for life itself. It is this reality known by reason, which opens to knowledge the whole sphere of teleology or final causes. But while the good may be defined as that which has rational worth, the question arises immediately, "What is this good? What is it which has in itself some worth as estimated by reason; which is everywhere and always worthy of human acquisition and possession, and everywhere and always worthy to be the source of happiness to a rational being?" This Harris defines as "the perfection of his being; his consequent harmony with himself, with God the Supreme Reason, and with the constitution of the universe; and the happiness necessarily resulting" (HARRIS, *Self-revelation of God*, p. 271).

Harris uses the term *good* as synonymous with well-being. The occasion in experience on which the idea of good and evil arises is some feeling impelling to exertion for some end or reacting in joy or sorrow, pleasure or pain. If man were never impelled by any motive to action and were incapable of enjoyment or suffering, he could have no idea of good and evil. If it were possible to conceive of a being as pure reason and nothing else, we could not conceive of that being as a subject of good and evil; for the being would never experience the impulse of any motive nor be affected by any feeling.—HARRIS, *Philosophical Basis of Theism*, p. 256.

It will be seen, then, that perfect personality is not only the highest philosophical concept of the Divine Being, but it becomes also the supreme end of finite existence. The essential good is primarily the perfection of the being in personality. The good is itself the realization of the truths, laws and ideals of reason. In so far as man attains the perfection of his own being, he attains the end which reason declares to have true worth. This is an end worthy of pursuit and acquisition, not only for ourselves but for all moral beings. The steps in this process of development must begin in the acquisition of a right moral character. Character begins in choice, and from thenceforth the will is a charactered will. Each succeeding choice develops, confirms or modifies this character. The moral law requires of its subjects, love to God as supreme, and love to our neighbor equally with ourselves. Love is therefore the fulfilling of the law. It is the essential germ of all right character.

But the good not only includes harmony within the individual person, in the sense of a character unified and motivated by perfect love, it includes also the perfection of all the powers and susceptibilities of the person progressively unfolding according to the law of love. This tends toward the discipline, development and refinement of the individual, but implies also a correspondence of finite reason with the Supreme Reason, the finite will with the infinite will of God. Holiness, as we have pointed out, is "the glorious fullness of God's moral excellence, held as the principle of His own action and the standard for His creatures," and therefore the Supreme Good for all of God's creatures. Furthermore, we must regard harmony with God's universe as involved in this Supreme Good. The universe, both physical and spiritual, is the expression of the archetypal ideas of God, and was brought into existence through the Divine Word or Logos (John 1:3). The individual cannot work out his own good apart from the universe. He belongs to a universal system of which God is the Author, and in which His wisdom and His love are evermore coming to harmonious expression. His well-being consists in a proper and harmonious adjustment to the system of which he is a part, and which was designed by the Supreme Reason for his progressive good. Here is the deep and profound meaning of the words, *All things work together for good to them that love God, to them who are the called according to his purpose* (Rom. 8: 28). Then again, the good must include happiness. This follows as a consequence of the perfection of the person and his harmony with God and the universe. Happiness can have no separate existence. It is always inseparable from that in which it has its source. Thus joy springs out of right character and action and is inseparable from it. This is the meaning of Jesus who said to His sorrowing disciples, *I will see you again, and your heart shall rejoice, and your joy no man taketh from you* (John 16: 22). The personal, therefore, must ever be the true end or object of acquisition, possession or enjoyment. It is only in personality that the ideas of the true, the right and the perfect culminate. God as Perfect Personality is the only worthy object of human choice, and love to God the fulfilling of the law. With perfect love to God and man, the soul must forever unfold in the light of this Supreme Good, and at every stage of its progress will embrace enlarged conceptions of the true, and the right, the perfect and the good.

THE CHRISTIAN CONCEPTION OF GOD

In our discussion of the Divine Names and Predicates, we pointed out in a preliminary manner, some of the Scripture predicates of God as used by our Lord and His apostles. Among these were the terms *Spirit, Life, Light* and *Love*. Having now presented the philosophical aspects of God as the Absolute, the Infinite and the Personal; and having shown the necessity of a personal God to meet the ethical and religious demands of finite personality, we turn from philosophy to discuss the religious concept of God. Christianity holds that the true concept of God is that which Christ revealed, or more specifically, which God himself revealed through Christ. We shall therefore endeavor to fill up in some

measure the outline already presented, by a further discussion of Christ's concept of God, enlarged and interpreted by those additional concepts given by Him to the
apostles through the inspiration of the Holy Spirit.

God Is Spirit. In a revealing statement our Lord declares that *God is a Spirit: and they that worship him
must worship him in spirit and in truth* (John 4:24).
Perhaps the passage should be more truly translated as
"Spirit" and not "a Spirit." Doubtless the statement is
intended to affirm the personality and religious value of
God, and not primarily the mere philosophical essence as
it is sometimes used. God is Spirit, an infinite Spirit; man
is spirit, a finite spirit, but there is a common relationship so that "Spirit may with spirit meet"; and this possibility of spiritual communion is the basis of true worship. St. Paul emphasizes the aspect of spirit in his First
Epistle to the Corinthians. Of the Spirit of God he affirms, *the Spirit searcheth all things, yea, the deep
things of God.* Of the human spirit he says, *For what
man knoweth the things of a man, save the spirit of man
which is in him? even so the things of God knoweth no
man, but the Spirit of God. Now we have received, not
the spirit of the world, but the spirit which is of God;
that we might know the things that are freely given to
us of God* (I Cor. 2:11, 12).

It is sometimes objected that our Lord's declaration
concerning the nature of God cannot be called a definition of God. Christlieb, however, affirms that we have
here "the most profound definition of Scripture as to
the nature of God, a definition to the sublimity of which
the presentiments and longings of no heathen people
ever rose, although the truth of them directly forces
itself on the reason and the conscience. . . . . Man has
spirit, God is Spirit. In Him the Spirit does not form
merely a portion of His being; but the whole substance
of His nature, His peculiar self is Spirit. Here we
have the idea of God in His inner perfection, just as the
names Elohim and Jehovah tell us mainly of His external position. As Spirit, God is the eternal, self-de-
pendent brightness and truth, absolute knowledge, the

intelligent principle of all forces whose glance penetrates into everything, and produces light and truth in all directions" (CHRISTLIEB, *Modern Doubt and Christian Belief*, p. 221).

God as Spirit Is Life. Of God the Scriptures predicate not only that He exists but that He lives. *The Father hath life in himself; so hath he given to the Son to have life in himself* (John 5:26). Of Himself Jesus declared, *I am the way, the truth, and the life* (John 14:6). This life which exists absolutely in the Father, is mediated to the Church through Jesus as the bread from heaven. *As the living Father hath sent me, and I live by the Father: so he that eateth me, even he shall live by me. This is that bread which came down from heaven: not as your fathers did eat manna, and are dead: he that eateth of this bread shall live for ever* (John 6:57, 58). St. John affirms also of the eternal Logos, that *in him was life; and the life was the light of men* (John 1:4); while St. Paul in his discussion of the redemptive mission of Christ testifies that *the law of the Spirit of life in Christ Jesus hath made me free from the law of sin and death* (Rom. 8:2). We are to understand by the term "life" as here used, not only the *ens* which denotes simple reality or being, but organized life, an organism including the fullness of truth, order, proportion, harmony and beauty. The Scriptures give us no warrant for thinking of God as mere Being in repose. Neither may He be regarded as merely thought or ideal. "As absolute Life," says Dorner, "He has a pleroma ($\pi\lambda\acute{\eta}\rho\omega\mu\alpha$), a world of real forces in Himself. He bears within Him an inexhaustible spring, by virtue of which He is Life eternally streaming forth, but also eternally streaming back into Himself. Still He is not to be defined as transient Life; He is before everything essentially Absolute Life; He neither empties nor loses Himself in His vital activity. He is a sea of self-revolving life; an infinite fullness of force moves, so to speak, and undulates therein. . . . . The life of God is expressed in an especially picturesque manner, in that vision of Ezekiel (Ezekiel 1: cf. Rev. 4) where the theme is Living Beings, who are not angels, but who belong to the throne of God or to His manifestation. They are united with the symbols of wheels which lift of themselves and move freely on all sides, because in them there is a spirit of life, of forcibly revolving life, which flashes to and fro. The wheels point to the circular movement of life: (Cf. James 3: 6, the course or 'wheel' of nature) they are sown with a thousand eyes, to express that space is everywhere equally present to them; whilst the wings signify the life which moves freely on all sides. But it is to be considered that in Ezekiel this life and motion of the powers of life do not exhaust the description of the theophany. All this, the cherubim with the living wheels, merely forms, so to speak, the chariot, the base for the living God, is the mere forecourt of the divine sphere—the innermost circle is reserved for God as living Spirit (Ezek. 1: 26). If we approach from the side of the world, this heavenly fullness of life may already appear to be the Godhead or God. But later on, when we are in possession of the Divine Personality, that fullness will be a predicate of God, a mere substratum, so to say, of His Personality. As absolute Life, He is absolutely exalted above passivity or dimunition and transitoriness, as well as above increase. He has absolute Sufficiency in Himself, for He has Life in Himself" (John 5: 26 cf. 1: 3) (DORNER, *System of Christian Doctrine*, I, pp. 259, 260). As absolute Life, God is Perfect Personality. Life is in some sense the substratum in which the attributes inhere. The necessary powers of personal spirit are not attributes, but the essence of the Being who possesses the attributes. Life may thus in some sense be indefinable, but it is known in consciousness as thought, feeling and will, and therefore the source of all reason, emotion and self-directed activity. In God thought is creative, His affections perfect and His activity infinitely free and powerful.

The references to the "Living God" are many, both in the Old Testament and in the New. The following is but a partial list: I Sam. 17:36, II Kings 19:4, Psalms 42:2, 84:2, Jer. 10:10, 23:36, Acts 14:3, I Tim. 6:16, 3:15, 4:10, II Cor. 3:3, 6:16, Rom. 9:26, Heb. 10:31, Rev. 2:8, 7:2, 22:13, Cf. also John 6:63, 69, Matt. 22:32.

God as Spirit Is Light. Another fundamental property of Spirit, as set forth by St. John, is that of Light or
Absolute Truth. The apostle uses the term in its most
general sense, not "a light," but "light." "God is light,"
says Meyer, "so also all light outside of Him is the radia-
tion of His nature." God as Absolute Personality is
luminous with truth. In Him is no darkness at all. Hence
the possibility of falsehood and error is excluded. Light
is revealing, and the supreme revelation of God in Christ
becomes the firm basis of the Christian religion, in both
its objective and subjective subsistence. But the contrast between natural light and darkness is but the symbol of a deeper contrast between holiness and sin.
Isaiah uses both terms in a related sense prophetically,
*And the light of Israel shall be for a fire, and his Holy
One for a flame: and it shall burn and devour his thorns
and his briers in one day* (Isa. 10:17). Light is therefore the outshining or effulgence of the Father's intrinsically holy nature, for the natural and the moral
in God must be regarded as one. "Holiness is the hidden glory," as one writer expresses it, and "glory the
manifested holiness of God." This is the conception of
God as revealed in Christ according to the author of
the Epistle to the Hebrews. *Who being the brightness
of his glory, and the express image of his person,* affirms
that Christ is the full objectification of God's inner glory;
and upholding all things by the word of his power,
relates Him as the Divine Son to the whole creative process; while the last clause identifies Him with God's redemptive purpose, *when he had by himself purged our
sin, sat down on the right hand of the Majesty on high*
(Heb. 1:3). St. Paul also in a single verse of great
depth and comprehensiveness, uses the term light as a
miraculous consequence of the Divine Word, to express
the spiritual transformation in the hearts of men. *For
God, who commanded the light to shine out of darkness,
hath shined in our hearts, to give the light of the knowledge of the glory of God in the face of Jesus Christ*
(II Cor. 4:6). Here the terms light, knowledge, and
glory are identified or at least used in a closely related

sense, and all shining in the face of Jesus Christ as God's supreme revelation of Himself to the world.

There are two doctrines of primary significance in the Christian system, which arise immediately from the conception of light as absolute holiness and truth. *First,* there is the negative conception of moral depravity as the absence of spiritual light. This results in ignorance of God and His relations to the world and to man. But this absence of light is such, because of personal freedom asserting itself in contradiction to God. It is a voluntary shutting out of the light with its illuminating and healing influences. But this contradiction of God is also a self-contradiction, that is, it is a violation of the immanent law of God in the nature and constitution of man. This perverted activity of personal freedom brings about a false attitude on the part of the human spirit, giving rise to a sphere of inner contradictions characterized by falsehood and ignorance. The self-contradictory state which follows in the intellectual and ethical life, is that in which reigns the deceitfulness of sin as self-perverted personality. It is therefore a state of moral darkness. It is the consequence of a "deprivation" of light, and therefore a state of moral depravity. Original sin as a state is due to original sin as an act, and becomes in turn the state or condition of the natural man out of which springs the transgression of the law of God. St. Paul declares of the heathen, that *even as they did not like to retain God in their knowledge, God gave them over to a reprobate mind* (Rom. 1:28), a state which he in the same epistle calls *the carnal mind* which is *enmity against God: for it is not subject to the law of God, neither indeed can be* (Rom. 8:7). Back of this, the apostle maintains, is the "God of this world," who is not merely the personification of darkness, but a personality, a spirit which embraces within it that moral and spiritual darkness occasioned by the absence of every ray of spiritual light. Satan therefore, as *the god of this world hath blinded the minds of them which believe not, lest the light of the glorious gospel of Christ, who is the image of God, should shine unto them* (II Cor. 4:4).

There is, *second,* the positive content of light which issues from the holiness of God, as over against the negative concept of moral depravity, consequent upon the absence of spiritual light. The Scriptures affirm that *God is light, and in him is no darkness at all* (I John 1: 5). We have seen that Spirit implies not only self-consciousness but self-determination, and the eternally free self-determinations of God must be in accord with His divine nature. His goodness and His holiness being absolute, his self-knowledge and self-determination must be commensurate with the infinitude of His Being. Consequently, down to the depths of His infinite Being, there is no darkness, nothing that is undiscovered, nothing that is unfulfilled, nothing that needs to be brought to completion or perfection. He is the *Father of lights, with whom is no variableness, neither shadow of turning* (Jas. 1: 17). God as light is the inexhaustible fountain of truth, *Who only hath immortality, dwelling in the light which no man can approach unto; whom no man hath seen, nor can see: to whom be honour and power everlasting. Amen* (I Tim. 6: 16).

God as Spirit Is Love. The third fundamental property of Spirit is love. Here again we are indebted to St. John for his clear and strong utterances on this phase of the nature of God. *He that loveth not, knoweth not God; for God is love.* And again, *God is love; and he that dwelleth in love dwelleth in God, and God dwelleth in him* (I John 4: 8, 16). Personality, as we have seen, demands a subject and an object in order to knowledge, and in self-consciousness this subject and object are identified. So also in love there is an equal necessity for subject and object, and also a free and reciprocal relationship between them. In love, the subject and the object are identified with each other, and yet each asserts and maintains a distinct selfhood. Here again we must anticipate the trinal nature of Spirit and the trinitarian distinctions in the Godhead. To the Father primarily belongs life; to the Son light, and to the Spirit love, which is *the bond of perfectness* (Col. 3: 14). Of the Father, the Son declared *Thou lovedst me before the foundation of the world* (John 17:24), and in a statement immediately preceding it, affirms the same love toward the disciples in the words, *and hast loved them, as thou hast loved me* (John 17:23). Here the communion is personal. Not only are the terms Father and Son personal, but the organ of this reciprocal love, the bond of perfectness, is likewise personal. "This unity, this absolute communion of love with love, of the personal subject with the personal object, in the glory of the Divine Life, is," says Gerhart, "the Holy Spirit" (GERHART, *Institutes,* I, p. 447). But love belongs to both the nature and the attributes of God. Here we must consider love as the essence of God only, leaving the discussion of the attribute of love which forms a link between the absolute Godhead, and His manifestation to His creatures, for a later chapter.

CHAPTER XIV

THE ATTRIBUTES OF GOD

We have previously pointed out in our analysis of terms, that there are two groups of definitions applied to the attributes—the one more general and popular, the other more technical and philosophical. The former may well be represented by the definition of Henry B. Smith who holds that "an attribute is any conception which is necessary to the explicit idea of God, any distinctive conception which cannot be resolved into any other." In this sense, the attributes may be regarded as the qualities which belong to and constitute the divine nature. Dr. Pope calls them "the full assemblage of those perfections which God ascribes to himself in His Word; partly as the fuller expansion of His names, and partly as designed to regulate our conception of His character. They are to be distinguished from the properties of the Triune Essence on the one hand; and on the other from the acts by which His relation to His creatures are made known. Hence Dogmatic Theology regards them, first in their unity as perfections manifesting the divine nature; and secondly in their variety as attributes capable of systematic arrangement" (Pope, *Compend. Chr. Th.*, I, p. 287). Quenstedt, the Lutheran theologian (1617-1686), says the *attributes* were so-called because they are attributed to God by our intelligence; and *perfections* because they make up the divine essence. Theology therefore adopts the word *perfections* for these qualities as they are applied to God by Himself; *attributes*, as they are assigned to Him by His creatures.

At the other extreme is the more technical and philosophical definition of Dr. Shedd, who regards the attributes "as modes either of the relation or the operation of the divine essence." They are therefore merely an analytical and closer description of the essence. In support of his position, which is so evidently Platonic, he cites the position of Nitzsch, who says that "every divine attribute is a conception of the idea of God." Here the term "concept" and "idea" are used in the sense of Schelling's philosophy. As the general and undefined idea is reduced to the form of the particular and definite conception, so the general divine essence is contemplated in the particular attribute. The attributes are not parts of the essence, of which this latter is composed. The whole essence is in each attribute, and the attribute in the essence. We must not conceive of the essence as existing by itself, and prior to the attributes, and of the attributes as an addition to it. God is not essence *and* attributes, but *in* attributes. The attributes are essential qualities of God" (SHEDD, *Dogm. Th.*, I, p. 334). Here it is well to point out also, the distinction between hypostasis and attribute. The *Hypostasis* or "Person" as the term is used in reference to the Divine Trinity, is a mode of the *existence* of the essence; while an *attribute* is a mode either of the *relation* or *external operation* of the essence. Over against this *external* operation is the *internal* operation of the essence which refers necessarily to the persons or hypostases and not to the attributes.

There are two questions which must be answered concerning the attributes, and in answering them, the Church has had to guard against two prevalent errors. *First,* are the attributes realities in the divine nature, or are they merely human modes of apprehending God with nothing in the divine essence corresponding to these human conceptions? *Second,* how do we come to know the attributes? As a corollary of this question, do we know God through His attributes; or knowing God, are the attributes merely an analytical and closer description of the essence as suggested above?

The first problem concerns the relation of the attributes to the nature of God—are they realities in the divine essence, or merely human modes of conception? To which we must reply, they are objective and real. They are not merely subjective human conceptions, with nothing objective corresponding to them in the nature of

God. However, this question has been discussed at great length by theologians of a philosophical cast such as Augustine, Thomas Aquinas, William of Occam, and in modern times by Nitzsch and Dorner. Augustine taught that "God is truly called in manifold ways, great, good, wise, blessed, true, and whatsoever other things seem to be said of Him not unworthily; but His greatness is the same as His wisdom; for He is not great by bulk, but by power; and His goodness is the same as His wisdom and His greatness, and His truth the same as all those things; and in Him it is not one thing to be blessed, and another to be great, or wise, or true, or good, or, in a word, to be Himself.—*De Trinitate*, VII, p. 7. The Nominalist Schoolmen of the Middle Ages, William of Occam (c. 1270-1347) and Gabriel Biel (d. 1495) maintained that God had and could have but one quality or attribute, a position which grew out of an attempt to justify the being of God as *ens simplicissimum,* and therefore without distinction of qualities and powers. Thomas Aquinas (1227-1274) on the other hand, marks carefully the distinction between what God is in Himself, and what He is in relation to finite being, defining the attributes as relations corresponding to nothing in God viewed in Himself, but to something not merely thought but objectively real in His relation to the world. This position preserves the unity of God sufficiently against the danger which arises from ascribing to Him a variety of attributes, in that these represent only the undivided essence in its relation to the world. Schleiermacher (1768-1834) follows Augustine (354-430), and states his position in a similar manner. "All attributes which we ascribe to God, are to be taken as denoting not something special in God, but only something special in the manner in which the feeling of dependence is to be related to Him . . . . the divine thinking is the same as the divine will, and omnipotence and omniscience are one and the same" (*Der Christliche Glaube, Eng. Trans.,* p. 474). This overemphasis upon the Absolute has been the bane of both philosophy and theology, and if carried logically to its length, would lead directly into

agnosticism. Martensen states the position truly when
he declares that the attributes are "not human modes
of apprehending God, but God's mode of revealing Himself." Dr. Olin A. Curtis takes practically the same position when he defines an attribute as "any characteristic
which we must ascribe to God to express what He
really is."

The second problem is concerned with the manner in
which we come to know the attributes of God. Like the
former question, much error has been associated with
attempted solutions of the problem. Closely connected
with this is the problem of the knowledge of God. Do
we know God by means of His attributes? Or, knowing
God, do we know the attributes as closer and more explicit analyses of this primary personal knowledge? The
two positions are at opposite extremes, the one making
more prominent the mystical element in knowledge, the
other the rational. Here again, many of the older theologians took the position that we know God through
knowing His attributes. The rationalist in philosophy
and theology seeks to come to a knowledge of God
through the theistic proofs. This he does in a piecemeal
manner by organizing them into a unity. The rationalistic spirit is seen also in certain types of biblical study,
especially that which would merely collate the Scripture
teachings concerning the attributes of God and blend
them into a totality. In both of these instances the seeker
after God can attain nothing more than a "knowledge
about God," never a "knowledge of God." We must
maintain that we come to a personal knowledge of God
in the same manner as we come to a knowledge of finite
human personality. However much we may learn about
a person, we can never be said to have personal knowledge until there is spiritual contact. But having once
made this spiritual contact, everything that we learn or
discover through personal association may be regarded
as personal qualities or human attributes.

So also is our knowledge of God. We gain our idea
of the attributes only by analyzing the personal knowledge of God which has been revealed to us in Christ

through the Spirit. Having this personal knowledge
we may analyze it into more definite and specific forms.
Consequently we must maintain that we know God personally in the unity of His Being, however imperfect
this may be; and the attributes are the analyses of this
total knowledge of God by which He manifests Himself
in nature and in grace. In other words, it is our personal knowledge of God that makes possible a true
knowledge of His attributes, and not a mere rationalistic summing up of the attributes that gives us our
knowledge of God.

It follows, then, that a proper arrangement of these
attributes is of great importance, in bringing the distinctive features of the divine nature to clearest expression. As in each finite person, some trait of character
seems dominant and central, so it is in our finite conceptions of God, though we shall show later, that there can
be no disunity or lack of harmony in the attributes of
God. Philosophy has generally made omniscience or
wisdom the central attribute, although the divine will
has sometimes been advanced as of prime importance.
Augustinianism regarded grace, or condescending love
as central. Calvinism makes justice the central attribute. But none of these fully reproduce Christ's conception of God as Father. If God is Father, holy love must
be supreme and central. Indeed, love is so central, that
the other attributes of personality may be regarded as
love energizing in certain directions. Justice is love in
relation to moral law, omniscience is love exemplifying
wisdom, and omnipresence is love in its universal presence. Holy love must occupy the central place in our
knowledge of God. But we are anticipating our discussion of the moral attributes.

It may be admitted that the doctrine of the attributes
is not quite germane to the simplicity of the Christian
idea of God, and we have previously referred to the
attempt, on the part of theologians to preserve this simplicity from logical disunity. On the other hand, there
is the constant danger of looking upon God as a bundle
of attributes. The present day trends in psychology are

toward the simpler forms of classification. Psychology is not nearly so sure as it was, as to the advisability of marking off the human mind into clearly defined and separate departments. It is the mind as a whole that acts in the unity of personality, and hence the intellectual, the volitional and the emotional aspects must be considered in relation to the mind as a whole. It is better, therefore, to guard against a multiplication of the attributes, and to center the interest in a few fundamental characteristics. This is the position of Dr. Carl Knudson who begins his study with an inquiry concerning the existence of God, and arranges the material following in three chapters dealing with, *first,* the absoluteness; *second,* the personality, and *third,* the goodness of God.

Perhaps the chief value of the study of the attributes lies in the fact that it tends to preserve the idea of God from indefiniteness and corruption. But it must be constantly kept in mind that the attributes can have no existence apart from the nature of God, nor can the being of God have reality apart from its attributes. The attributes are simply the qualities revealed to us, and as such belong to, and are inseparable from personality.

PRINCIPLES OF CLASSIFICATION

One of the simplest forms of classification is the twofold division into absolute and relative attributes, or the *attributa absoluta* and *attributa relativa* of the older theologians. This twofold division is sometimes expressed in other terms, as communicable and incommunicable, transitive and immanent, positive and negative, moral and natural, ethical and metaphysical. Whatever the term used, the principle of classification is the same. Martensen adopts the twofold classification, but rejects the terms absolute and relative as attended with difficulties, since there are no attributes that are not relative or transitive, that is, do not express a relation to the world; nor are there any which are not reflexive, that is, which do not go back to God himself. "We gain a more determinate principle of division," he says, "when we consider the twofold relation which God holds to the world. The relation of God to the world, namely, on the one hand a relation of *unity*, on the other hand, a relation of diversity or *antithesis*. Indeed, our religious life, with all its morals and states, moves between these two poles—that of unity and that of diversity, that of freedom and that of dependence, that of reconciliation and that of separation" (MARTENSEN, *Christian Dogmatics*, p. 93). In his consideration of the attributes, therefore, he finds it necessary to give consideration to the *momenta* of both unity and diversity. On the other hand, Dr. Pope objects to the terms incommunicable and communicable, on the ground that those termed communicable may be similar to the attributes of God, but considered strictly as attributes, they are not communicable. Similarity there may be, but the one belongs to God, and the other to finite human personality.

Another method of classification follows the analogy of human personality. This according to Dr. Miley is the true classification, since the method of science always gives attention to the most determinate factor, which in this instance is personality. "Personality is the most determinate conception of God," he says, and therefore, "the truest, deepest sense in which he can be viewed as the subject of His own attributes." Since man is conscious of the substantiality of his being, and knows that he has a self which is unaffected in its identity by all changes, so also he conceives of the subsistence of God as apart from all phenomena. But man is a person with intellect, feeling and will, and in his consciousness is

The favorite method has been to make a division into two counterpart classes. Hence they are distributed as natural and moral by a distinction which the meaning of neither of these words will allow; both are inappropriate to Deity, and the harshness is not removed if metaphysical and ethical are substituted. The instinctive objection we feel to these terms is not felt to the correlatives of absolute and relative, immanent and transitive, internal and external: these distinctions furnish the right clue and are sound as far as they go; but they do not suggest those special manifestations of God which give their peculiar glory to Christian theology. It is dangerous to speak of positive and negative attributes; for while there is no positive excellence in Deity which does not imply negation or its opposite, the negative ideas of infinity and so forth are really and truly positive. Lastly, when they are classed as communicable and incommunicable, it must be remembered that, as attributes, all are alike incommunicable to the creatures.—POPE, *Compend. Chr. Th.*, I, p. 290.

aware of these three modes of the manifestation of the self. Under this classification God as Absolute Personality is *first*, Absolute Reason or Omniscience; *second*, Absolute Feeling or Goodness, which Dr. Miley interprets as holiness, justice, love, mercy and truth; and *third*, Absolute Will or Omnipotence.

But man is also conscious of his own substantial existence through all the changes of time and space, and this gives rise to the thought of Absolute Existence, and the consequent attributes of aseity or self-subsistence, and immutability or unchangeableness; hence there is omnipresence in relation to space, and eternity in relation to time. These latter give expression to that which is primary and fundamental in the Christian concept of God, and to these the previous classification does not appear to do full justice. Both William Newton Clarke and William Adams Brown take this into consideration, and therefore arrange the attributes as follows: (a) Attributes of personality: spirituality, life and unity; (b) attributes of character: wisdom, love and holiness; (c) attributes of absolutism: omnipresence, omnipotence, omniscience and immutability. The first is primary, the others secondary. With the same emphasis upon personality as a determining factor, another class of theologians think that the truth may be reached in a more direct and simple manner, by following a twofold outline or classification; (a) attributes of absolute personality, including what is usually presented under the term absolute and relative attributes; and (b) attributes of holy love, or the moral attributes. In this class we may mention Luthardt, 1823-1902) Haering and Dickie.

Differing from these and yet with the determining principle of personality as the basis of classification, is another class of theologians who, following Schleiermacher, have stressed more especially the religious demands upon man's nature. Here we have (a) the sense of dependence giving rise to the necessity of the absolute attributes; (b) man's sense of sin, the moral attributes; and (c) the whole consummated by the revelation of love through Jesus Christ. McPherson thinks that the classification under being, understanding, feeling and will is not sufficiently exact, and admits of a very confusing cross division. The correct principle of classification he thinks is that which follows the leading moments in the historical development of the Christian revelation. God's attributes then are His ways of manifesting Himself in the world and to men. They are to be classified therefore according to God's relation, (a) to the natural world; (b) to the moral world apart from redemption; and (c) to the world of grace, or the moral world inclusive of redemption. Here may be classified Alexander Schweizer (1808-1888), Herman Schultz (1836-1903), and F. A. B. Nitzsch (1832-1898).

Having reviewed the various principles of classification, we turn to the threefold method as being the simplest and most practical method for our discussion of the various attributes of God. If the twofold method of absolute and relative attributes be adopted, we are under the necessity of classifying such attributes as omniscience, omnipotence and omnipresence, which imply God's creative relation to the world, with the moral attributes, such as wisdom, justice, love and goodness, by which He administers His government of moral and responsible beings. If on the other hand we accept such a twofold classification as natural and moral, or incommunicable and communicable, we are compelled to classify together, the so-called absolute and relative attributes. This is confusing, in that we must thereby overlook the distinction between God's mode of existence, and His mode of operation. We therefore adopt the

Drury (*Outlines of Doctrinal Theology*, p. 143) thinks the best warranted classification is that given by Dr. Samuel Harris, although previously developed and used in part by others. This classification is as follows:

Divine Attributes......
- Absolute.... Self-existence, Immensity, Eternity
- Personal.... Plentitude, Omnipresence, Divine Sensibility....Love, Holiness, Omnipotence

The subdivisions of love and holiness are not directly given by Dr. Harris but are used by Dr. Drury in his adaptation of the scheme.

threefold method of classification, as being logically the most simple method of arrangement, and at the same time the clearest form of presentation from the pedagogical standpoint. Our outline is as follows:

1. The Absolute Attributes, or those qualities which belong to God apart from His creative work.

II. The Relative Attributes, or those arising out of the relation existing between the Creator and the created, and which of necessity require the creature for their manifestation.

III. The Moral Attributes, or those which belong to the relation between God and the moral beings under His government, more especially as they concern mankind.

THE ABSOLUTE ATTRIBUTES

By the Absolute or Immanent Attributes we mean those qualities which have relation to God's mode of existence, in contradistinction to those which refer to His mode of operation or activity. They must be conceived as far as is possible, apart from any relation to the creature. They are absolute in that they are unlimited by time or space, are independent of all other existence, and perfect in themselves. They have their basis in the fact that God is, in Himself, Absolute Being. They are immanent in that they belong to spirit, and are essential to any right conception of the Divine Nature. They are the attributes of a Personal Being, and may be summed up as spirituality, infinity, eternity, immensity, immutability and perfection.

Watson classifies the attributes as follows: (1) Unity; (2) Spirituality; (3) Eternity; (4) Omnipotence; (5) Omnipresence; (6) Omniscience; (7) Immutability; (8) Wisdom; (9) Goodness; (10) Holiness.

Wakefield: (1) Unity; (2) Spirituality; (3) Eternity; (4) Omnipotence; (5) Omnipresence; (6) Omniscience; (7) Immutability; (8) Wisdom; (9) Truth; (10) Justice; (11) Holiness; (12) Goodness.

Raymond: (1) Unity; (2) Spirituality; (3) Eternity; (4) Immutability; (5) Omnipotence; (6) Omnipresence; (7) Omniscience; (8) Wisdom; (9) Goodness.

Ralston: (1) Unity; (2) Spirituality; (3) Eternity; (4) Omniscience; (5) Wisdom; (6) Omnipotence; (7) Omnipresence; (8) Immutability; (9) Holiness; (10) Truth; (11) Justice; (12) Goodness.

Miley: (1) Omniscience; (2) Divine Sensibility; (3) Omnipotence. Dr. Miley treats Eternity, Unity, Omnipresence and Immutability as predicables but not distinctively attributes.

1. *Spirituality.* This has frequently been regarded as belonging to the essence of God, rather than as an attribute of that essence. This would be true were we using the term in the sense of pure spirit. But even this must be known by its effects, as is implied in the term *pneuma,* which means a breathing forth. Consequently we use the term which most closely approaches pure spirit; and as previously analyzed, this gives aseity or self-subsistence, which is sometimes enlarged to include unity, simplicity and ideality. Viewing spirituality from the standpoint of self-subsistence, there can be no objection to regarding it as an attribute.

By "aseity" (*aseitas*) we mean self-subsistence, or the possession of life in Himself which is independent of all other existence. Man has life in himself but only in communion with the Son (John 6: 53); the Son has life in Himself, but even this is given to Him of the Father (John 5: 26); but the Father alone has it from no one. He has it in Himself precisely because He is the Absolute Person. Aseity, therefore, denotes that the ground of being is in Himself. *God that made the world and all things therein, seeing that he is Lord of heaven and earth, dwelleth not in temples made with hands; neither is worshipped with men's hands, as though he needed any thing, seeing he giveth to all life and breath, and all things* (Acts 17: 24, 25).

It is evident that this truth concerning the independence and self-subsistence of God was not known to the heathen, but was understood by Israel, and declared with clearness and power by the early Church. For this reason Van Oosterzee regards it to a certain extent,

The idea we have of what the Divine Spirit is, is derived from our idea of what the human spirit is; this involves the actual existence of a real entity, a substance, an individual, simple substance, endowed with power to know, to feel and to will, a person conscious of self and not self, capable of moral actions and susceptible of moral character. These elements of being, conceived of as without limitation or defect, with all other known or unknown possible perfections, infinite in degree, make up our idea of God, and this, in the light of our conscious intuitions, confirmed, illustrated and enlarged by revelation, we are confident is, so far as it goes, a true idea; our knowledge of God is at best extremely limited and imperfect, but it is still positive knowledge; of spirituality and consequent self-conscious personality we cannot reasonably doubt.—RAYMOND, *Syst. Th.,* I, p. 314.

as the test of the purity of our conception of God—whether or not it acknowledges this independence without limitation. That philosophy which holds creation to be necessary to the personality of God as a subject, and the world as His object, must necessarily issue in pantheism. Yet from the standpoint of theism it must be recognized, that while the world is not necessary to existence of God as Absolute Personality, as the Highest Love He will have creatures of His own. This is not the self-sufficiency of Stoicism, but Love's inexhaustible fullness of life which can give without the need of receiving.

The term "simplicity" as applied to pure uncompounded spirit, is sometimes referred to as an attribute. Dr. Boyce for instance, treats the first attribute under this head, which he affirms "means more than the spirituality of God, for that includes only that He must be spiritual." However, created spirits may have a composite spiritual nature which includes a spiritual body as well as a spiritual soul, and in this there is no contradiction. But in God spiritual nature must be uncompounded, and His attributes and His nature are in such a manner one, that they are inseparable from each other. Simplicity, therefore, is the unity of the spiritual nature as opposed to form and limitation. The difficulty of this concept to the finite mind, which is under the necessity of thinking in terms of time and space, frequently gives rise to anthropomorphism, although the church has always rejected it. Melito (A.D. 162) is said to have been the

Three of the more essential attributes of God—namely, His self-existence, His eternal existence, and His literal independence—are all involved in the very idea of Him as the first originating cause. Thus, if He is the first cause of all things, then He is in Himself without cause. And if there is no cause of His existence outside of Himself, then He must have the grounds, the elements of existence within Himself; which is but saying that He is self-existent.—POND, *Chr. Th.*, p. 49.

It follows also that God is a simple Being, not only as not composed of different elements, but also as not admitting of the distinction between substance and accidents. Nothing can either be added to, or taken from God. In this view the simplicity, as well as the other attributes of God, are of a higher order than the corresponding attributes of our spiritual nature. The soul of man is a simple substance, but it is subject to change. It can gain and lose knowledge, holiness and power. These are in this view accidents in our substance. But in God they are attributes, essential and immutable.—HODGE, *Syst. Th.*, I, p. 379.

first Christian writer to ascribe a body to God. Tertullian
also ascribed a body or *corpus* to God, and regarded the
soul as material, but this materiality was not that of the
human body. It was as he viewed it, a *tertium quid* or
a different substance from that which we call matter,
and was considered the necessary form of all existence.
Origen opposed this as did the entire Alexandrian
School. Their tendency toward idealization, as has been
pointed out, resulted in a concept of the Deity as mere
negation. Irenæus held that God is not to be compared
to frail men, and yet His love justifies us in using human
phraseology when speaking of Him. In modern times
the Church has expressed clearly its belief in the spirituality and simplicity of God. This statement is found in
Article I of the *Thirty-Nine Articles* as revised by John
Wesley for the American churches and generally known
as the *Twenty-Five Articles* of Methodism. That portion of the Article which refers to the spirituality of
God is as follows: "There is but one living and true
God, everlasting, without body, parts or passions."

The term "passions" in the foregoing statement,
early became a matter of disagreement in the Church and
the bishops of the Conference of 1787 removed it. Originally the word passion referred to passivity, and hence
God, not being a creature of environment and acted
upon from without, the creed denied a passive nature to
Him. But in time the word came to mean an emotion or
a manifestation of feeling. To deny the term passion,
then, seemed to convey the idea that God was devoid of
an affectional nature. Those who held to the former
view, maintained that the references to God as possessed
of emotions were purely metaphorical. Richard Watson,
the theologian of early Methodism, opposed this view.
"It is assumed," he says, "that the nature of God is es-

Nothing of a material or bodily nature can appertain to spirit. Matter
possesses no power of thought or will, and is governed by laws entirely
different from those which prevail in the sphere of spirit. The former is
governed by the law of necessity, the latter by that of freedom. If this is
so, and spirit is wholly unlike matter, it cannot be compounded, and is
therefore simple (Cf. John 4:24). Here belong those texts which teach
that God cannot be represented (Isa. 40:25, Exod. 20:4).—KNAPP, *Chr.
Th.*, p. 98.

sentially different from the spiritual nature of man. This is not the doctrine of Scripture. . . . . The nature of God and the nature of man, are not the same; but they are similar, because they bear many attributes in common, though on the part of the divine nature, in a degree of perfection infinitely exceeding" (WATSON, *Institutes*, I, p. 389). We must therefore conceive of knowledge and love as being the same in God as in man, only in God they are free from all imperfections.

2. *Infinity.* By infinity, we mean that there are no bounds or limits to the Divine Nature. The term applies to God only, and is peculiarly applicable to the personal attributes of wisdom, power and goodness. It is for this reason that the creedal statements, found in the *Thirty-nine Articles* of the Anglican Church and the *Twenty-five Articles* of Methodism, include the words "of infinite power, wisdom and goodness." Modern theologians of the Arminian type, have tended to absorb the doctrine of infinity in the other attributes. Neither Watson, Wakefield, Raymond, Ralston nor Summers mentions it among the attributes. Field mentions it briefly, and Banks treats it as infinite wisdom. Pope alone gives it any extended treatment. On the other hand, the Westminster Catechism defines God as "A Spirit, infinite, eternal, and unchangeable in His being, power, holiness, justice, goodness and truth." Consequently we find the Reformed theologians tending to the opposite extreme of absorbing the other attributes in infinity. Strong makes infinity basic to self-existence, immutability and unity, while Foster considers it the ground of eternity and immensity or omnipresence. Dr. Charles Hodge states that the infinitude of God relative to space is immensity or omnipresence; relative to time, it is eternity. He further regards immensity as that aspect of infinity by which God fills all with His presence, while omnipresence is His infinity viewed in relation to His creatures (Cf. HODGE, *Systematic Theology*, I, pp. 383ff).

The term, "infinity," being negative in form, has sometimes been interpreted to be negative in content.

This leads directly to agnosticism as we have shown in our treatment of that subject. We must, therefore, consider the term infinite as a positive concept in negative form, and as such it applies only to Personal Spirit. It has no meaning when applied extensively to time and space, and its application in this sense leads directly to pantheism. For this reason we must not regard transcendence as mere externality but as a boundless supply from within. In the words of Augustine, "He knows how to be everywhere in His whole Being and to be limited by no place. He knows how to come without departing from the place where He was; He knows how to go away without leaving the place whither He has come (*Ep.* cxxxvii, 4); and again, "He is everywhere in His whole Being, contained by no place, bound by no bond, divisible into no parts, mutable in no respect, filling heaven and earth with the presence of His power (*De Civ. Dei*, vii, 30). Theologians have generally recognized three modes of presence in space. Bodies are in space *circumscriptively*, that is they are bounded by it. Spirits are in space *definitively* as having an *ubi*, *i.e.*, they are not everywhere but only somewhere. God is in space *repletively*, as filling all space. This, however, cannot be considered from the standpoint of extension, for this property applies only to matter. God is above the limitations of space, in that these are not applicable to Him. He is not absent from any portion of space any more than He is present in one portion more than another. Man and nature are everywhere present to Him, for *all things are naked and opened unto the eyes of him with whom we have to do* (Heb. 4: 13). Yet the Christian concept of a Personal God prevents any trend toward pantheism, and clearly distinguishes God from all things in both fact and thought. If it be insisted that infinite Being must include all things, we can only refer again to our treatment of the Absolute. Infinite Spirit, to which only the term can apply, must if it is infinite in any true sense of the term, be able to create finite existences and endow them with free will.

3. *Eternity.* By eternity as an attribute of God, we can mean only that He stands superior to time, free from the temporal distinctions of past and future, and in whose life there can be no succession. This is the sense of those scriptures which speak of the eternity of God, none of which more explicitly set it forth than the revelation of the name I AM THAT I AM. From its first declaration made to Moses (Exod. 3:14) to the final revelation made to St. John in the Apocalypse as that *which is, and which was, and which is to come, the Almighty* (Rev. 1:8), this name not only declares the Aseity or Self-sufficiency but the Eternity of God. Earlier than the revelation to Moses, we are told that *Abraham called there on the name of Jehovah, the everlasting God,* or as it may be translated, the God of eternity (Gen. 21: 33). In Deuteronomy we read that *The eternal God is thy dwelling place, and underneath are the everlasting arms* (Deut. 33:27, R.V.). The psalmist declares that *Before the mountains were brought forth, or ever thou hadst formed the earth and the world, even from everlasting to everlasting, thou art God* (Psalm 90:2); and again, *Thou art the same, and thy years shall have no end* (Psalm 102:27). The Prophet Isaiah is specific in his reference to this attribute. *I am the first and I am the last; and beside me there is no God* (Isa. 44:6); and again, *thus saith the high and lofty One that inhabiteth eternity, whose name is Holy* (Isa. 57:15, Cf. 40:28).

In the New Testament the same idea is expressed, but still in a more or less negative form. St. Paul speaks of *his eternal power and Godhead* (Rom. 1:20). And closely related to this thought mentions *the glory of the uncorruptible God* (Rom. 1:23). In the First Epistle to Timothy, the attribute of eternity is expressed by an

When it is said that God is eternal, the primary idea is, that His existence had no beginning, and will have no end; but evidently the Scripture representations and the philosophic thought involve something more than the mere idea of duration: eternity is regarded as an attribute of God; that is, He is eternal in the sense that it is His nature to exist.— RAYMOND, *Syst. Th.,* I, p. 315.

When considered as without a beginning, the schoolmen spoke of eternity as *a parte ante;* when considered as having no end, it was called *a parte post.* This latter was frequently called immortality, which unlike that of finite creatures was considered necessary.

ascription of praise, *Now unto the King eternal, immortal, invisible, the only wise God, be honour and glory for ever and ever. Amen* (I Tim. 1: 17). Apart from the august name I AM, it is evident that the references just cited carry with them the thought of duration indefinitely extended, but this is due to the fact that finite beings have no other mode of conception. Eternity must therefore be expressed in finite terms although the notion of a timeless being is not wanting. Furthermore, the pure idea of eternity was too abstract to find expression in the earlier ages of the world, and Knapp points out that there was no word to express it in any of the ancient languages. The Hebrews like other nations were compelled to have recourse to circumlocution. To express eternity *a parte ante,* they used the expression, *before the world was;* and for eternity *a parte post,* they said, *when the world shall be no more.*

There are three different senses in which theologians have understood eternity in its relation to time. *First,* as endless duration, according to which time is a sort of existence which is external to God and conditions His existence. This would destroy His unity and likewise prove contradictory to His attribute of unchangeableness or immutability. *Second,* there is the idea of timelessness. As a philosophical theory this dates back to Plato and his timeless flow of ideas. But whether in philosophy or theology, the deepest thinkers of all the ages have seen the impossibility of attributing to God the ideas of time and succession as the conditions under which finite beings must think and act. To do so would indicate that the life of God was in successive parts, which must either be finite or infinite; if infinite, then each part would be equal to the whole, and each would be equal to the other. On the other hand, if the suc-

---

In the Scripture doctrine of God we, however, not only find it asserted that God has no beginning, but that He shall have no end. . . . . No creature can, without contradiction, be supposed to have been from eternity; but even a creature may be supposed to continue to exist forever. Its existence, however, being originally dependent and derived, must continue so. It is not, so to speak, in its nature to live, or it never would have been nonexistent; and what it has not from itself, it has received, and must through every moment of its actual existence receive from its Maker.—WATSON, *Theolog. Institutes.*

cessive parts were finite, then the infinite would be the sum of finite things, and in either case the conclusion would be a *reductio ad absurdum*. *Third,* there is the position that both time and eternity are combined in the divine consciousness. One of two positions has generally been held concerning this relation in the Divine Mind, either that time has no meaning for God and therefore He bears no relation to the temporal order; or, that God's superiority over time is in some way connected with His intervention in time. As the finite self is above the stream of consciousness, without which there could be no knowledge of the temporal flow, so God as the Eternal is above all limitations of time; and it is exactly because of this that time exists or has any meaning. The two ideas of time and eternity are not exclusive. They are, on the other hand, objectively

The question of God's eternity has been a fruitful field for debate among theologians. It resolves itself into this, Is there succession in the divine consciousness? Some affirm, others deny. Those who affirm make eternity to consist in duration or continuance of being; those who deny maintain a *nunc stans* or eternal "Now." Of the former class, Watson says, "Duration as applied to God, is no more than an extension of the idea as applied to ourselves, and to exhort us to conceive of it as something essentially different is to require us to conceive what is inconceivable. Charles Hodge says, "If, therefore, God be a Person, or a thinking Being, He cannot be timeless; there must be succession; one thought or state must follow another. To deny this, it is said, is to deny the personality of God. The dictum, therefore, of the schoolmen, and of the theologians, that eternity precludes succession—that it is a persistent unmoving Now—is according to this repudiated (HODGE, *Syst. Th.,* I, p. 388ff). Dr. Summers criticizes this position advocated by Dr. Dwight as open to serious objection.

The explanation seems to lie in a truer conception of the nature of personality. There is a self which must be supra-temporal to the temporal flow of consciousness, or there could be no conception of this flow. Without an observer outside or above the temporal flow, how could succession be known. So also in man as finite personality, there is an abiding element which constitutes itself one and the same, regardless of the multiplicity of changes in its own consciousness. Now may it not be possible, that those theologians above mentioned which are so insistent upon succession, and who regard eternity as mere duration, are referring rather to the content of consciousness with its multiplicity and change, while those who refer to the *nunc stans* or eternal Now, regard eternity as that which is back of and conditions the idea of succession. Dr. Summers seems to admit this when he says that perhaps the objection to succession in duration arises from confounding it with change in substance. We change by the flow of time; but we can conceive of an essence or substance which does not change, though there is a flow or succession in its duration. Simple duration has nothing to do with mutability or immutability; it is compatible with the former as predicated to us, and with the latter as predicated of God (Cf. SUMMERS, *Syst. Th.,* I. p. 78).

connected. The temporal, of necessity presupposes the eternal; and the eternal is at once the positive ground and the perpetual possibility of the temporal. The movement of the world in time, by which the future becomes the present and the present the past, would immediately cease were it not for the eternal. "The temporal and

Dr. Raymond takes a clear and strong position. Referring to such Scripture citations as Isaiah 44:5 and 57:15, he says, "It is sometimes said that these affirmations so evidently true are equivalent to the affirmation that with God there is no past or future, but from eternity to eternity one eternal now. If this be a denial that God sees things and events in succession, it is objectional; for evidently events occur in succession, and God sees things as they are; not that He is older today than yesterday; nor yet that He is a stagnant ocean, eternally, immutably the subject of one and the same sole consciousness. He apprehends all His intelligent creatures as having a present, a past, and a future, as doing this now and that then. To Himself his own thought, purposes, and plans may be as eternal as Himself; and in this regard perhaps the conception of an eternal now may be valid; but as to all that is not God, it must be conceived that God regards them as existent yesterday, today and tomorrow. Of the truthfulness of the primary thought in respect to eternity of God, namely, that His existence had no beginning and will have no end, and also of the conception of necessary and therefore eternal existence, there can be no reasonable doubt; beyond this, probably silence is wiser than speculation.—RAYMOND, Syst. Th., I, p. 316ff.

Dr. Pope takes a definite position in favor of the nunc stans. He says, "The perfect idea of eternity, as it is in the human mind, cannot tolerate duration or succession of thoughts as necessary to the divine consciousness. And this is the deep perplexity of our human intellect, which, however, must accept the profound meaning of the I AM as teaching an eternal now enfolding and surrounding the successive existence of time. The Personal Jehovah once and once only declared His pure eternity. His name is the only word which human language affords in its poverty to express that thought; such terms as eternal and everlasting have temporal notions clinging to them; and all our phrases go no farther than that the Supreme fills all space and all time, and that He was before them, the very word carrying duration with it. But I AM —before time or space was I AM has in it all the strength of eternity. It is literally the assertion of pure existence, without distinction of past, present or future as measured in time and regulated by motion in space. We must therefore accept this doctrine of God in all its incomprehensibleness, as the only one that satisfies the mind. The Eternal in Himself knows no succession in time any more than He knows circumscription of space; and when He created all things, His being remains as independent of duration as it is independent of locality. (POPE, Compend. Chr. Th., I, p. 295ff). Dr. Pope finds the explanation of his relations between time and eternity in Christ the eternal Logos. "We may dare to say that the Eternal inhabits eternity; and yet in the Son, the Firstborn of every creature, He inhabits time also. As in the incarnation God is manifest in the flesh, so in creation God is manifest in time. And as God will forever be manifest in His incarnate Son, so will He have forever in and through His Son, the Viceregent of created things, a manifestation in time; that is to say in plain words, eternity and time will forever coexist. Something pertaining to time will cease; its change and probation and opportunity. In this sense time will cease to be, but in no other sense than this.—POPE, Compend. Chr. Th., I, p. 298ff.

eternal do not in any way exclude each other," says Rothe. "The opposite of the temporal is the timeless, and therefore originless; the opposite of the eternal is the nonexistent" (ROTHE, *Still Hours*, p. 99). Instead of being opposed to each other, we must regard the eternal as the guaranty of continuity. From the negative point of view, eternity is merely the negation of time, but in the positive sense it is a mode of being which God sustains to time. The truth of eternity in the positive sense, is in some mysterious manner connected with the intuitive idea of God, while the temporal belongs to the intuitive idea of man. We must then hold fast the truth that as in self-consciousness, the self transcends the flow of time and yet recognizes this flow, so God also as the Eternal transcends time, but as the God of His creatures He works out His purposes for them under the law of time which He has Himself created. There is succession in the order of things as they exist; there can be no succession in God's knowledge of them. In dealing with His creatures, therefore, God recognizes them as past, present and future in this succession of existence; or as one theologian has so aptly stated it, God knows the past as past, the present as present and the future as future.

4. *Immensity.* As eternity expresses the contrast with the temporal world in God's mode of existence, so immensity expresses the same contrast with reference to the space world. It is sometimes identified with infinity in opposition to the limitations of space, and is related to omnipresence as transcendence is to immanence. As time is born out of eternity, so space is born out of immensity. Space is objective in that it is an existence mode of man, and subjective in that it is a thought mode of human reason. So also the immensity of infinitude is objective as the mode of the divine existence; and subjective as the order of divine reason. Immensity cannot be conceived as extension of space, as eternity cannot be conceived as the extension of duration. God as Spirit is above all spatial limitations, and it is because of this that such relations have validity.

This attribute is mentioned directly but once in the Bible, in two parallel passages found in I Kings 8:27 and II Chronicles 6:18, *Behold, heaven and the heaven of heavens cannot contain thee; how much less this house which I have built.* There are other passages, however, which indirectly teach the same truth. *Thus saith the Lord, the heaven is my throne, and the earth is my footstool* (Isa. 66:1). *Can any hide himself in secret places that I shall not see him? saith the Lord. Do not I fill heaven and earth? saith the Lord* (Jer. 23:24). *The Lord looked down from heaven upon the children of men, to see if there were any that did understand, and seek God* (Ps. 14:2). As with the other attributes, the appeal of the Scriptures is primarily religious and devotional; and in this instance is designed especially to guard against the danger of unduly localizing our thought of God.

5. *Immutability.* By the immutability of God is meant His changelessness in essence or attribute, purpose or consciousness. Dr. Dickie thinks that this attribute should be included under eternity, and Dr. MacPherson points out, also, that eternity is generally associated with unchangeableness. The two are related in much the same manner as omnipresence is related to immensity. When viewed *ad intra* immutability excludes all development, the process of becoming, any change or possibility of change; when viewed *ad extra*, God is the same after creation as before, the fullness of life and light and love, undiminished by the free outflow in creation. It is opposed, therefore, to pantheism, or to any other form of emanation. "God is immutable," says Rothe, "because His being, in all its changes and modifications, remains constantly true to its own conception. . . . . Seeing that God, at all times and in all His relations with the world, perfectly corresponds to His own idea. He is at all times like Himself, and consequently immutable" (ROTHE, *Still Hours*, p. 102). But there are some limitations. The divine unchangeableness must

Lotze says, "According to the ordinary view space *exists*, and things exist *in it*; according to our view, only things exist, and between them nothing exists, but space exists *in them*" (*Outline Metaphysics*, p. 87).

not be so interpreted as to preclude any movement in the divine life. Immutability is not a rigid sameness of being, but a characteristic of free intelligence. It refers to the essence or attributes of God, and not to His operations in creation and providence, only in so far as these are always in harmony with the immutability of the divine nature. He loves righteousness and hates iniquity. Consequently His moral government is always in harmony with His nature as holy love. He regards a person now with displeasure and now with complacency, according as that person is disobedient or righteous. The Divine immutability is therefore vital to both morality and religion.

The scriptural references to the immutability of God are peculiarly rich and satisfying. The psalmist declares, *Thou art the same, and thy years shall have no end* (Psalm 102: 27) and the author of the Epistle to the Hebrews restates it in the words, *But thou art the same, and thy years shall not fail* (Heb. 1: 12). In the last book of the Old Testament the Prophet Malachi voices this attribute in the words, *For I the Lord change not* (Mal. 3: 6). *Every good gift,* says St. James, *and every perfect gift is from above, and cometh down from the Father of Lights, with whom is no variableness, neither shadow of turning"* (James 1: 17). In Hebrews it is again stated that, *Wherein God, willing more abundantly to shew unto the heirs of promise the immutability of his counsel, confirmed it by an oath; that by two immutable things, in which it was impossible for God to lie, we might have a strong consolation, who have fled for refuge to lay hold upon the hope set before us* (Heb. 6: 17, 18). "This is the perfection," says Dr. Blair,

Most closely connected with this eternity of the Divine Being is the Unchangeableness, in virtue of which every idea of modification in His form of existence is utterly excluded (Mal. 3:6, James 1:17), since He dwells in eternity; so that His perfection just as little admits of increase or diminution. In so far then, it is less accurate to speak of God's nature, since this word, by virtue of its derivation (nature from "nasci") necessarily suggests the idea of a growing or becoming. It is better to speak of the Being of God, as indicating that which in itself from eternity to eternity IS. (Exod. 3:14). What strong consolation flows from a believing acknowledgment thereof, can here only be indicated. Compare the 90th Psalm.—VAN OOSTERZEE, *Chr. Dogm.,* pp. 257, 258.

"which perhaps more than any other distinguishes the divine nature from the human, gives complete energy to all its attributes, and entitles it to the highest adoration. From hence are derived the regular order of nature and the steadfastness of the universe." The Eternal God who revealed Himself as the I AM to Moses, is the I AM of today, "infinite, eternal, unchangeable, in his being, wisdom, power, holiness, justice, goodness, and truth."

6. *Perfection.* By the term perfection is meant that attribute which consummates and harmonizes all the other perfections. It is by virtue of this that God is self-sufficient. Nothing, therefore, is wanting to His being which is needed for His blessedness. His knowledge, His will and His love are not dependent upon the existence of the creature, but find their relations and the infinite scope of their activity in the Persons of the Triune God.

The divine intelligence is immutable, in the sense that it is an eternal, perfect knowledge of all things; but evidently a perfect knowledge of all things is a knowledge of them as they are: possible, as possible; actual, as actual; past, as past; present, as present; and future, as future; necessary events as necessary, and contingent events, as contingent. The phenomena of the divine moral and æsthetic nature are immutably the same, in the sense that they eternally correspond with the inherent nature of their object. God loves invariably that which is excellent, and ever feels aversion to that which is unlovely. He loves righteousness and hates iniquity and punishes the wicked. He is immutable in the principles of His government and is as variable in the application of those principles as are the ever varying objects to which they apply.—RAYMOND, *Syst. Th.*, I, p. 318.

The importance of this attribute is found in its use as a reverent defense of the adorable nature from all that would dishonor it in our thoughts or theological systems. If we sacrifice any one attribute to any other we derogate from the perfection of God who is the Being in whom every attribute has its supreme existence and manifestation. As it belongs essentially to God in Himself, so it impresses its stamp on all the divine works, and must give the law to all our theological views of His character.—POPE, *Compend. Chr. Th.*, I, p. 304.

Strong relates perfection to the moral attributes, making it not quantitative completeness but qualitative excellence. Right action among men presupposes a perfect moral organization, a normal state of intellect, affection and will. So God's activity presupposes a principle of intelligence, of affection, of volition, in His inmost being, and the existence of a worthy object for each of these powers of his nature. But in eternity past there is nothing existing outside or apart from God. He must find, as He does find, the sufficient object of intellect, affection and will, in himself. There is a self-knowing, a self-loving, a self-willing which constitute His absolute perfection. The consideration of the immanent attributes is, therefore, properly concluded with an account of that truth, love, and holiness, which render God entirely sufficient to himself.—STRONG, *Syst. Th.*, I, p. 260.

We must regard this perfection also as a unity, unique and absolute. It is not the combination of the individual perfections, it is not the culmination of a process, it is the ground and source of all other perfection, and it excludes all possibility of defect. God's perfection is simple and unique, excluding all plurality, and is peculiar to Himself. When, therefore, our Lord enjoined upon His disciples, *Be ye therefore perfect, even as your Father which is in heaven is perfect* (Matt. 5:48), He is presenting the Father as the *Summum Bonum* of all spiritual good and the chief end of man's enjoyment and devotion; because as the Perfect One, He comprehends in His own being all that is needed for our own eternal blessedness.

THE RELATIVE OR CAUSAL ATTRIBUTES

In passing from a consideration of the Absolute to the Relative or Causal Attributes, it should be kept in mind that we are not presenting a new class of attributes, but the same perfections in another form and application. We have already sensed the difficulty of attempting to express the Absolute attributes apart from the relative, as for instance, when we speak of immensity or immutability, we are in reality applying to spiritual qualities the language of material things. It is this poverty of language that creates much of the difficulty in both philosophy and theology. If, as Dr. Pope suggests, we change our terms and speak of God as a Personal Spirit, infinite and eternal, ever the same in His nature and mode of being, and not thinking or acting of necessity under the limitations of time and space, we rid ourselves of this anomaly. But in doing so, we create another, this time the relation of personality and infinity. In dwelling upon the Absolute Attributes as we now attempt to bring them within the range of finite operation concerning the creature, we must hold firmly in our thinking to the fact that they form the background of every representation. This will obviate any difficulties which may arise from the use of anthropomorphic language and secure to us the truth, that without God speaking to man in terms which he can comprehend, there can be no science of theology and no religion. In changing from a consideration of the attributes as Absolute to the same attributes as Relative or Casual, we change our point of view from Absoluteness to Efficiency, from Being to Power. Thus the Divine Aseity or Self-sufficiency finds expression in omnipotence or the all-powerfulness of God; while the Divine Immensity considered in relation to space, and eternity in relation to time, with its closely related quality of Immutability, find expression in the omnipresence of God. Omniscience, however, does not appear to be so closely related to the Absolute Attributes as we have considered them, except in what we have summed up as Perfection. It belongs more especially to personality as we understand it in the finite sense, and therefore becomes the logical transition point between the metaphysical attributes considered as a whole, and the ethical attributes which belong to God in His relations with human personality. We shall then present the Relative or Causal Attributes in this order, *first,* Omnipresence, *second,* Omnipotence, *third,* Omniscience, and *fourth,* sum these up in the moral quality of goodness as related to perfection on the one hand, and the ethical attributes on the other.

1. *Omnipresence.* The Divine Immensity as previously considered is the presupposition of the Divine Omnipresence. In the former, God was considered in a

There is another predicate which must be given consideration also, before passing from the absolute to the Relative Attributes, that of the Divine Freedom which we must posit in opposition to pantheism as a sufficient reason why anything not God exists at all. But in ascribing will to God, we have carried our study to a consideration of His spiritual nature in the light of our own as we have not done before. But the Spirit as it applies to God must embrace knowledge, sensibility and will. Personality has its essential factors, self-determination, and self-evaluation. The apostle sums up this idea of will as expressed in purpose and resulting in act in the Epistle to the Ephesians (1:11) *Who worketh all things after the counsel of his own will.* Here we have θελμα or will in exercise; βουλη or determination of that will; and the issue in action as ενεργουντος. It is therefore one of the attributes which with the divine omniscience forms a link between the absolute perfections and those perfections related to the creature. This needs to be understood, for it means that the act of God going toward His creatures is to be sought only in Himself; the will is indeed the necessity of His essence, like the attributes already considered, but it is itself under no necessity.—Pope, *Compend. Chr. Th.,* I, p. 308.

transcendental aspect as being superior to all spatial relations, here God is considered in an immanent aspect, as being present in all space as well as above it. By omnipresence we mean that God is not excluded from anything on the one hand, or included in anything on the other. But this immanence must be regarded as free and not necessitated. The error of pantheism lies in this, that it fails to recognize the truth that God's presence is not restricted to the limits of space; and further, that His immanence in space can be understood only on the presupposition of His transcendence over space. "When, therefore, in harmony with Scripture, we speak of God as commensurable and everywhere present," says Van Oosterzee, "we have to understand this last expression, not in the extensive, but in the dynamical sense, and to be careful to keep ourselves from pantheistical leaven. Not a substantial, but an operative presence of God in every point of His creation must be ascribed to Him. In creating, He has not limited, but most gloriously revealed Himself. With His life-awakening power He is active in all things; but nevertheless is by no means imprisoned in His own work. He embraces, rules, penetrates it, not in the pantheistic, but in the theistic sense of the term" (VAN OOSTERZEE, *Chr. Dogm.*, p. 258). Dr. Miley takes a similar position. He holds that the truth does not lie in the sense of a ubiquitous divine essence, which considered in itself would be without personal attributes, and therefore could not exercise the agency which must ever be a reality of the divine presence (MILEY, *Systematic Theology*, I, pp. 218, 219). So also,

Dr. Knudson treats the attribute of omnipresence as a specification under omnipotence. E. G. Robinson regards omnipresence as a compound of omnipotence and omniscience. Foster considers Immensity and Omnipresence together, regarding them as the same attribute under different aspects. He makes this distinction in that he regards omnipresence as limiting the Divine essence to the bounds of creation, while immensity carries with it the thought that the essence is limitless beyond the bounds of creation. Wakefield defines the Omnipresence or Ubiquity of God as His being everywhere present at the same time.

We are not to conceive of the omnipresence of God, however, as a universal, material extension; so that a part of him is in one place and a part in another; for, being a spirit, God is not divisible into parts. Besides, something more than a part of God is needed here, and everywhere, for the performance of Divine works.—POND, *Chr. Th.*, p. 50.

Thomas Aquinas taught (*Summa Theologica,* p. 8) that "God is in all things, not indeed as a part of their essence, nor as an accident, but as an agent is present to that upon which it works."

There are three ways in which God may be regarded as omnipresent in the universe. *First,* the actual presence of the Deity in every portion of the created universe. *Do not I fill heaven and earth? saith the Lord* (Jer. 23: 24). By this it cannot be meant that the essence of God is extended or diffused in a pantheistic sense, for Spirit is not extended substance. It means rather in the dynamical or spiritual sense as we have just indicated. Nor can He in this sense be absent from any portion of the universe, or from any act of the beings which He has created and still be regarded as omnipresent. Dr. Dickie thinks that this means simply that God is not limited by spatial relations as we are. Dr. Rudolph Otto holds that God's relation to space is not the metaphysical abstraction of omnipresence, but that God is where He wills to be, and that He is not where He does not will to be. Dr. Pope holds that this position with all its inevitable consequences is His absolute, or natural omnipresence. *Second,* by omnipresence is meant the presence of every creature to God, as would seem to be indicated in the statement, *In him we live, and move, and have our being* (Acts 17: 28). Viewed from the practical standpoint, this scripture is intended to impress upon men, that in His presence, every creature lives and moves, every thought is conceived and every deed done, so that nothing is hidden from the eyes of Him with whom we have to do. But it may be viewed in a metaphysical sense also. Creation as a potentiality is to be found in the very depths of the Eternal Being, but it becomes an actuality, only when there is an existence different and separate from that of God in which it lives and moves.

Turretin says, "Bodies are conceived of as existing in space circumscriptively because occupying a certain portion of space, they are bounded by space on every side. Created spirits do not occupy any portion of space, nor are they embraced by any. They are in space definitively as here and not there. God is in space repletively, because in a transcendent manner His essence fills all space."

True it is that everything is filled with God, but not in the pantheistic sense as we have already indicated. In this sense the divine omnipresence means simply that every creature is directly present to God and runs His course before Him. *Third,* by omnipresence is meant the exertion of God's power, which relates it even more closely to the divine activity. *Whither shall I go from thy Spirit? or whither shall I flee from thy presence?* (Ps. 139:7). This scripture when taken with its context indicates that God is present wherever there is a manifestation of His power. In the light of our previous discussion of the unity of God's person, the manifestation of His power is to be understood in connection with His omnipresence—that He is present at every point with His entire being.

One matter further, needs to be considered in our discussion of omnipresence. While God is omnipresent, He must be regarded as standing in different relations to His creatures. "God is present in one way in nature," says Bishop Martensen, "in another way in history; in one way in the Church, in another way in the world; He is not in the same sense, present alike in the hearts of His saints, and in those of the ungodly; in heaven and in hell" (James 4:8) (MARTENSEN, *Chr. Dogm.,* p. 94). Dr. Gerhart takes a similar position, maintaining that the presence of God with the world is determined by the form of receptivity with which each order of creation is endowed by His own free creative word (GERHART, *Institutes,* I, p. 487). With these distinctions before us, we must conclude that the omnipresence of God with finite things must ever be different from His presence with Himself in His glory. When the prophet called upon God to *look down from heaven, and behold from the habitation of thy holiness and of thy glory* (Isa. 63:15) he could but mean that God who is omnipresent everywhere, manifests His glory more peculiarly and brightly in the region which we call heaven than in any other sphere, just as the sun which shines everywhere displays its full splendor only in the firmament. Nothing, therefore, prevents us from think-

ing of heaven as a place higher than the earthly and
material sphere of things, and that it is to this habitation of His presence that Jesus intended to point us, when
He taught us to pray, "Our Father which art in heaven"
(Matt. 6: 9).

While the question of omnipresence has given rise
to many metaphysical problems, the Scriptures are rich
and varied in their teaching on this subject. Furthermore, it is a truth also, which is admitted by common intelligence. The devout always worship Him as a very
present help in time of need. *Am I a God at hand, saith
the Lord, and not a God afar off? Can any hide himself
in secret places that I shall not see him? saith the Lord.
Do not I fill heaven and earth? saith the Lord* (Jer. 23:
23, 24). *For thus saith the high and lofty One that inhabiteth eternity, whose name is Holy; I dwell in the high
and holy place, with him also that is of a contrite and
humble spirit, to revive the spirit of the humble, and to
revive the heart of the contrite ones* (Isa. 57: 15). *Thus
saith the Lord, The heaven is my throne, and the earth
is my footstool* (Isa. 66: 1). *For he looketh to the ends of
the earth, and seeth under the whole heaven* (Job 28:
24). *The Lord looketh from heaven; he beholdeth all the
sons of men. From the place of his habitation he looketh
upon all the inhabitants of the earth* (Psalm 33: 13, 14).
It is such scriptures as these that lead us to a conception
of the value of the divine omnipresence in religious
worship. How it is possible that the Infinite Person
should be everywhere is to the finite mind beyond all
comprehension, and yet whenever God's people draw

It was on this principle that the apostle argued when he disputed
with the learned Athenians. God is *not far from every one of us,* that
is, He is intimately near and present with us; *for in him we live, and
move, and have our being.* If things live, God is in them and gives them
life. If things move, God imparts to them their motion. If things have
being, that being is in God. Every object that meets our eye on the sur-
face of the earth, or in the expanse above us, announces His presence.
By Him the sun shines, the winds blow, the earth is clothed with vegetation, and the tides of the ocean rise and fall. Everywhere He exists in
the fullness of perfection. The universe is a magnificent temple, erected
by His own hands, in which He manifests Himself to His intelligent creatures. The Divine Inhabitant fills it, and every part shines with His
glory.—WAKEFIELD, *Chr. Th.,* p. 150.

near to Him in prayer, they apprehend Him as then and there present in the fullness of His infinite perfections.

2. *Omnipotence*. The omnipotence of God is the ground of all that we call efficiency or causality. It is related to the absolute attribute of Aseity as personality expressed in will, and to the omnipresence of God, as Aseity related to the creature. Being an expression of the divine will, it is also directly and vitally connected with the moral attributes of God. Omnipotence is rightly defined as that perfection of God by virtue of which He is able to do all that He pleases to do. This is the scriptural definition. *There is nothing too hard for thee* (Jer. 32:17). *But our God is in the heavens: he hath done whatsoever he hath pleased* (Psalm 115:3). Both the prophets and the psalmist are discriminating in

Hahn remarks, that from the history of the various opinions which have prevailed respecting the omnipresence of God, it appears that most of the errors have arisen from confounding the ideas of body and substance. In doing this our author has followed the example of Reinhard, Morus, Doederlein and others, who adopted the philosophy of Leibnitz and Wolf. In denying to God a body, and thus avoiding the errors of pantheism, they seemed at the same time unconsciously to deny Him substance, and to transmute Him into an unessential thought, and then to locate Him somewhat beyond the limits of the universe, from whence He looks forth, and exerts His power upon all His works; in which, therefore, He is not otherwise present than by His knowledge and agency. —KNAPP, *Chr. Th.*, p. 106.

Knapp points out that some of the older theologians entertained more than others the scriptural position that both the substantial and efficient presence of God were involved in His omnipresence. The tendency to separate between these two, were it possible, leads to a misplaced emphasis. Thus Dr. Miley sees only in omnipresence the divine efficiency, and tends to minify the notion of an omnipresent divine essence as the necessary ground of omniscience and omnipotence. He maintains that personal agency is for us the only vital reality of this presence. It is to this position that Dr. Hills objects, maintaining that this omnipresence is not to be understood as a mere presence in knowledge and power, but an omnipresence of the divine essence. This, however, is in nowise interpreted in the pantheistic sense (Cf. HILLS, *Fund. Th.*, I, p. 230ff). Dr. Raymond, with his usual comprehensive grasp of truth, gathers up both phases of the truth in the statement, "Such assumptions as are inconsistent with the Bible representations and the common apprehensions must be rejected. For example, if it be affirmed that God is everywhere present by extension or diffusion, so that it may be said that a part of God is here and a part of God there; or if it be said that God is present everywhere solely by His knowledge and His power, such views are to be rejected, since truth requires us to conceive that the divine essence is unlimited as fully and as perfectly as are the divine attributes. God, as to all that is God, is everywhere always; the infinite essence is incapable of division and separation; essence and attribute, immutably inseparable, fill immensity; all of God everywhere is a truth cognized both by piety and sound philosophy."—RAYMOND, *Syst. Th.*, I, p. 328.

their thought, limiting God's power to that which is in conformity with His good pleasure. He can do all, not perhaps in the abstract as appertaining to that which is contrary to His nature and will, but all that He wills to do. Whatever is impossible to Him, is not such because of a limitation of His power but solely because His nature makes it so, in the same sense that His holiness is incompatible with sin. Tertullian says, "For God to will is to be able, and not to will is not to be able." With the exception, therefore of that which is contrary to His nature, nothing exists for Him of which the realization surpasses the power.

The Scriptures throughout abound in expressions which declare the infinite power of God. From the earliest time God revealed Himself to Abraham saying, *I am the Almighty God; walk before me and be thou perfect* (Gen. 17:1); and this is followed by the declaration, *I appeared unto Abraham, unto Isaac, and unto*

Proceeding from this principle, we may dwell on a few important inferences. (I) The omnipotence of God is the ground and secret of all efficiency, or what we call causality. No argument, however specious, can rob us of the indestructible conviction that there is such a power in the nature of things as we call cause; that there is a connection between events which is more than sequence. As in regard to almost every attribute of God, but in this case with more than usual distinctness we perceive in ourselves the finite reflection of the Infinite. We are conscious of producing effects as ourselves their cause. From that, remembering two things, we rise to the Divine Omnipotence. (II) The range of our direct causation is exceedingly limited: very decisive so far as it extends, it soon reaches its term. In the interior economy of our spiritual nature it is comparatively great; in the government of our bodily constitution less; in our action upon others it has decreased rapidly; and in our action upon external nature it is gone. . . . . (III) All power in us is derived from Him: He is the absolute source of all causation. It is not simply that He can do all things; but all things that are done are done by the operation of causes that owe their efficiency to Him, though in many cases the efficiency is contrary to His will.—POPE, *Compend. Chr. Th.*, I, pp. 311, 312.

In explanation of the foregoing paradox, Dr. Pope says, "In the infinite wisdom of God things contrary to His will in one sense are permitted by His will in another. This leads up to the original mystery that the Almighty created beings capable of falling from Him; and down again to the present mystery that omnipotence sustains in being creatures opposing His authority; and then forward to the same mystery in its consummate form that omnipotence will preserve in being, not indeed active rebels against His authority, but spirits separated from Himself. It is the solemn peculiarity of this attribute, in common with wisdom and goodness, that it is traversed and thwarted, so to speak, by the creatures that owe to it their origin. But the same three attributes are conspicuous in the redeeming economy.—POPE, *Compend. Chr. Th.*, I, p. 313.

Jacob, as God Almighty (Exod. 6: 3, R.V.). The Psalms
with their devotional richness, make much of the all-
powerfulness of God. *God hath spoken once; twice have
I heard this; that power belongeth unto God* (Psalm
62: 11). *Let all the earth fear the Lord: let all the
inhabitants of the world stand in awe of him. For he
spake, and it was done; he commanded, and it stood fast*
(Psalm 33: 8, 9). The Prophet Jeremiah declares that
*He hath made the earth by his power, he hath estab-
lished the world by his wisdom . . . . when he uttereth his
voice, there is a tumult of waters in the heavens, and he
causeth the vapors to ascend from the ends of the earth;
he maketh lightnings for the rain, and bringeth forth the
wind out of his treasuries* (Jer. 10: 12, 13, R.V.).

The New Testament is equally explicit in its teaching concerning the omnipotence of God, but here the religious significance is even more marked than in the Old
Testament. It is well understood that in the Greek
creeds the word *pantokrator* (παντοκράτωρ), translated
into the Latin as *omnipotens*, means the all-governing;
and it is in this sense that it is largely used by the New
Testament writers. In its application to the work of
salvation, Jesus declared that *with men this is impossible; but with God all things are possible* (Matt. 19: 26).
Referring to God's preserving and protective power as
exerted toward His people, Jesus said to the Jews in
Solomon's porch, *My Father, which gave them me, is
greater than all; and no man is able to pluck them out of
my Father's hand* (John 10: 29). The Apostle Paul in a
reference to Abraham, speaks of God *who quickeneth
the dead, and calleth those things which be not as though
they were* (Rom. 4: 17). Later in an ascription of praise
he says, *Now unto him that is able to do exceeding
abundantly above all that we ask or think, according to
the power that worketh in us, unto him be glory in the
church by Christ Jesus throughout all ages, world without end. Amen* (Eph. 3: 20, 21). The last book of the
New Testament gives us a vision of God as the *Alpha
and Omega, the beginning and the ending . . . . which is,
and which was, and which is to come, the Almighty* (Rev.

1:8). And again, *Thou art worthy, O Lord, to receive glory and honour and power: for thou hast created all things, and for thy pleasure they are and were created* (Rev. 4:11). Thus the attribute of omnipotence is made the basis on the one hand, for deep and abiding religious adoration; and on the other, is the ground and firm support for quiet trust and assurance.

It is evident that even omnipotence must be conditioned by God's wisdom and goodness. William Newton Clarke points out that it is easy to fall into the error of regarding omnipotence as the ability to do everything that can be thought, but divine power must always operate in harmony with the divine nature. He cannot do anything contrary to His divine will, this would be irrational, and contradictory to Himself. It was this that occasioned in Van Oosterzee the contention that Sovereignty must be regarded as an attribute of God, and this in an unlimited sense (VAN OOSTERZEE, *Chr. Dogm.*, p. 263ff). William Adams Brown defines omnipotence as God's ability to do all things which His character and purpose may suggest (BROWN, *Th. in Outline*, p. 116). This, says Dr. Charles Hodge, is all we need to know on this subject, were it not for the vain attempts of theologians to reconcile these simple and sublime truths of the Bible with their philosophical speculations.

There are several deductions of importance that should be mentioned here. (1) Theologians have generally made a distinction between the mediate and immediate, an ordaining and an ordained manner in which the power of God is manifested. To this difference in the manifestation of power, the term *potestas absoluta* is applied to the absolute power which creates all things at first; and *potestas ordinata* to the government through secondary laws. The immediate exertion of power in

God cannot do that which is repugnant to any of His perfections. He cannot lie, or deceive, or deny Himself, for to do so would be injurious to His truth. He cannot love sin, for this would be inconsistent with His holiness. He cannot punish the innocent, for this would destroy His goodness. This, however, is not a physical, but a moral impossibility, and is, therefore, no limitation of omnipotence; but to ascribe a power to God which is inconsistent with the rectitude of His nature, is not to magnify, but to abase Him.—WAKEFIELD, *Chr. Th.*, pp. 148, 149.

this sense would be the *potestas absoluta,* while the mediate exercise of that power would be the *potestas ordinata.* The first would be ordaining or absolute; the second ordained or relative. This distinction makes clear the difference between the supreme creative power of God, and the economical exercise of that power for the benefit of His creatures. (2) Modern empirical philosophy which denies cause as that to which an effect is due, and makes it consist solely in that which uniformly precedes it, destroys thereby the idea of power, and finds no place for the omnipotence of God. This was the doctrine of causation advanced by Hume, Kant, Brown, Mill and in some sense by Hamilton; and it is this idea which lies at the foundation of Comte's Positive Philosophy. (3) Dr. Miley calls attention to an important distinction between the elective and the executive agency of the divine will. The choice of an end, he points out, is not necessarily its producing cause, otherwise the effect must be instant upon the choice. This would deny to God the possibility of a plan or purpose and destroy all future effectuation by the causal energy of His personal will (Cf. MILEY, *Syst. Th.,* I, p. 213). God as a personal Being is free to determine His own plans by the elective agency of His will, and to perfect them by the executive agency of that same will. This is the meaning of the apostolic declaration that He worketh all things after the counsel of his own will. (Eph. 1: 11.)

As previously indicated, there is no doctrine more important in religious value than that of the divine omnipotence. It led our Lord courageously to the cross, in the confidence that through the omnipotence of God, His cause would triumph even over death, the last enemy.

Concerning the distinction between *potentia absoluta* and *potentia ordinata* as he expresses these terms, Dr. Charles Hodge says, "This distinction is important, as it draws the line between the natural and the supernatural, between what is due to the operation of natural causes, sustained and guided by the providential efficiency of God, and what is due to the immediate exercise of His power. This distinction indeed, is rejected by modern philosophy." Modern philosophy holds that God in creating and sustaining the world, does it as a whole. Nothing is therefore isolated and consequently there are no individual acts, but only a general efficiency on the part of God. Nothing is referred to His immediate agency. Everything is natural, and hence both miracles and special providences are rejected. (Cf. HODGE, *Syst. Th.,* I, p. 410.)

It has given courage to the saints of all ages, and in spite of discouragement and apparent defeat, has caused them to be more than conquerors.

3. *Omniscience.* By omniscience is meant the perfect knowledge which God has of Himself and of all things. It is the infinite perfection of that which in us we call knowledge. Consequently we read that *His understanding is infinite* (Psalm 147:5). God understands and knows the hearts of men. Nothing is hidden from Him. He sees things as they are, in both their causes and ends. The teaching of the Scriptures concerning this attribute is, as in the case of those which we have previously discussed, made the basis of religious values. The Prophet Isaiah expressly assigns an insight into all futurity, as marking the distinction between Jehovah and false gods. *Shew the things that are to come hereafter, that we may know that ye are gods;* (Isa. 41:23) and again, *Behold, the former things are come to pass, and new things do I declare; before they spring forth I tell you of them* (Isa. 42:9). Ezekiel takes a like position. *Thus have ye said, O house of Israel: for I know the things that come into your mind, every one of them* (Ezek. 11:5). In I Chronicles 28:9 David enjoins obedience upon Solomon, declaring that *the Lord searcheth all hearts, and understandeth all the imaginations of the thoughts.* Again he seems overwhelmed with the thought that He *knowest my downsitting and mine uprising, thou understandest my thought afar off......For there is not a word in my tongue, but, lo, O Lord, thou knowest it altogether..... Such knowledge is too wonderful for me; it is high, I cannot attain unto it* (Psalm 139:2-6 and entire Psalm). The New Testa-

Dr. Raymond says of the Scripture representations of divine power, that they are "incomparable in their perspicuity and their sublimity; perspicuous because written by the inspiration of the Almighty, who alone can comprehend the measure of His power; and sublime because the thing described is itself the perfection of sublimity. These are not the invented words of a poetic fancy, but the words of truth and soberness, literally presenting the thought intended.—RAYMOND, *Syst. Th.*, I, p. 320ff.

Foster affirms that aside from the first chapter of Genesis, perhaps the finest description of physical omnipotence is the description found in Job, chapter thirty-eight.

ment presents this attribute with even greater clearness. The Apostle James in speaking to the Council at Jerusalem uses the expression, *Known unto God are all his works from the beginning of the world* (Acts 15: 18). St. Paul uses foreknowledge in conjunction with predestination, *For whom he did foreknow, he also did predestinate to be conformed to the image of his Son, that he might be the firstborn among many brethren* (Rom. 8: 29. Cf. also Eph. 1: 4, 5). Conformable to this are the words of St. Peter, *Elect according to the foreknowledge of God the Father, through sanctification of the Spirit, unto obedience and sprinkling of the blood of Jesus Christ* (I Peter 1: 2).

The attribute of omniscience occupies a critical and important place in theology. There is something about it peculiarly perplexing, even more so than the attribute of omnipotence. As omnipotence cannot be considered apart from the attributes of wisdom and knowledge, so omniscience seems to bear even a closer relation if possible to the unique and Divine Personality. It does in fact, furnish the transitional point between the relative and moral attributes, although we must sum up the former in a consideration of goodness, which as an attribute of God, may in some sense be included in either classification. In the New Testament citations of the preceding paragraph, it has been shown that the attribute of omniscience has, for the most part been considered in relation to the moral government of God. This gives rise to two problems; (I) the question of the divine knowledge of contingent events, commonly known as foreknowledge. This subject is frequently discussed under the head of nescience and prescience, the former being a denial of foreknowledge in God, the latter its affirmation. (II) The question concerning the relation which exists between foreknowledge and predestination.

(I) The question of the divine foreknowledge has been the occasion of much speculation. Its importance lies in the fact that it is closely connected with predestination, which as the ground for a type of redemptive theory, forms the subject of our next paragraph. The question of the reality of the divine knowledge has been held in the following forms. (1) Pantheism denies the divine knowledge in the sense of omniscience, for the Divine Being in the pantheistic sense is a coming to consciousness only through finite creatures, and therefore can never be infinite. (2) Divine foreknowledge has been denied by some Christian theologians on the ground of a *nunc stans* or eternal now in the consciousness of God. Thus Augustine says, "What is prescience but the knowledge of future things? What can be future to God, who transcends all time? But of the knowledge He has of things themselves, they are not to Him future, but present, and consequently it cannot be called prescience but knowledge." (3) Both the Arminian and Calvinistic theologians hold to the *scientia necessaria,* or the knowledge that God has of Himself, and *scientia libera,* or the free knowledge which God has of persons and things outside of Himself. However, they differ as to the ground of this foreknowledge, the Arminians generally maintaining that God has a knowledge of pure contingency, while the Calvinistic theologians connect it with the decrees which God has purposed in Himself. (4) There is a mediating position commonly known as *scientia media* or a knowledge of the hypothetical. This theory was advanced by the Jesuits, Molina, Fonseca, Suarez and other distinguished theologians of this order, who were opposed to the predestinarianism of the Jansenists. It was accepted by the Arminian theologians, Limborch and Curcellæus, and by a number of the Lutheran divines. Pope states that it has been generally accepted by all antipredestinarian theologians. The Calvinists were generally opposed to it. Van Oosterzee defines the three positions as follows: "The divine knowledge," he says, "is divided into a natural knowledge, which He has of Himself; and a so-called free knowledge, which He has of all that exists beyond Himself. And then again, from these two is further distinguished the conditional knowledge (*Scientia media* or *hypothetica*), by virtue of which He is exactly acquainted, not only with all which will happen, but also with all which would or would not happen under certain nonexistent conditions—the so-called *futuribile*. That this last also is known to God, will certainly not be denied: it is simply an insignificant part of that great whole which lies naked and open before Him." His conclusion is that whether knowledge be free or conditional, "absolutely nothing is excluded from the divine knowledge."

(II) Our second question is concerned with the relation which exists between foreknowledge and predestination. Three positions are taken in theology: (1) The Arminian position holds that the power of contrary choice is a constituent element of human freedom, and that foreknowledge must refer to free acts and therefore to pure contingency. Both Limborch and Curcellæus maintain that God's ability to know is not to be judged by human standards, but that He foresees the necessary as coming to pass in a necessary way, and the contingent as occurring contingently (CURCELLÆUS, II, 6; LIMBORCH, II, 8). "It is not the divine foreknowledge that conditions what takes place," says Dr. Pope, "but what takes place conditions the divine foreknowledge. We have seen again and again that the God of eternity has condescended to be the God of time, with its past, present and future. Instead of saying with the schoolmen that to God there is only an eternal now, it were better to say that to God as absolute essence there is the eternal now, and also to God as related to the creature there is the process of succession. Predestination must have its rights; all that God wills to do is foredetermined. But what human freedom accomplishes, God can only foreknow; otherwise freedom is no longer freedom" (POPE, *Compend. Chr. Th.*, I, p. 318ff). Dr. Sheldon says that this theory should rather be called the Catholic than the Arminian, since it was the current theory in the pre-Reformation Church from the apostolic age onward. It has in general been held by both the Lutheran and Anglican divines, and is still the dominant theory in the Greek and Roman Catholic churches (Cf. SHELDON, *Syst. Chr. Doct.*, p. 173). (2) The Calvinistic position identifies foreknowledge and foreordination, maintaining that the divine decrees are the ground for the occurrence of all events, including the voluntary actions of men. On this theory, foreknowlege depends upon the certainty of the decrees, and is not strictly a knowledge of contingent events. "He foresees future events," says Calvin, "only in consequence of His decree that they should happen" (CALVIN, *Institutes*, Bk. III, Chapt. 23). Turretin takes the same position. "The reason is," he says, "that the foreknowledge of God follows His decree, and as the decree cannot be changed, so neither can His knowledge be subject to mistake" (TURRETIN, *Inst. Locus III, Quæst.* 12). Cocceius after identifying foreknowledge with the divine agency, makes a place for second causes. "God foresees from eternity what is to take place," he says, "because nothing is to take place without the agency of God." Then follows the statement, that "What He sees as hereafter to come to pass, He sees in the decree, by which either He summons events to take place, or by which He has decided to supply to the sinning creature the concursus of the first cause, without which the second is not able to act" (COCCEIUS, *Summa Theol.*, Chapt. X). Dr. Charles Hodge thinks that the difficulty vanishes when a distinction is made between the certainty of an act and the mode of its occurrence. (3) The Socinian position denies that God has any foreknowledge of contingent events. Both Faustus Socinus and Johannes Crell maintained that the contingent is in its very nature unknowable, and that therefore it is no more derogatory to exclude prescience from the omniscience of God than it is to exclude from omnipotence the power to do those things which are contradictory to the divine nature. This theory was advanced in an attempt to harmonize foreknowledge and freedom. At a

William Newton Clarke attempts an explanation similar to that of Pope by maintaining a twofold aspect of omniscience, a knowledge of the universe as it exists eternally as His own idea, and a knowledge of that universe as existing in time and space, and therefore as a perpetual process of becoming. This goes back to the Logos idea of a pleroma. Dr. Clarke offers this as an explanation as to how God may have at once a foreknowledge of things as under the temporal order and a simultaneous knowledge in the eternal order (Cf. CLARKE, *Outline of Chr. Th.*, p. 82).

later time Dr. Adam Clarke advanced the peculiar view that God *can* know all future events but does not *choose* to do so. This view was never accepted by the Methodist theologians. Rothe and Martensen have in a measure reasserted the Socinian theory, the latter maintaining a conditional foreknowledge. "The actual alone," he says, "which is in and for itself rational and necessary, can be the subject of an unconditional foreknowledge, the actual which is not this, cannot be so; it can only be foreknown as possible, as eventual." Again, he says, that events "in so far as these are conditioned by the freedom of the creature, can only be the subject of a conditional foreknowledge; *i.e.*, they can only be foreknown as possibilities, as Futurabilia, but not as realities, because other possibilities may actually take place" (Cf. MARTENSEN, *Chr. Dogm.*, pp. 218, 219). It is evident that here the original Socinian position is considerably modified. In other statements in this section (Sec. 116) the reformed tendencies are in evidence, and appear in contrast to the strict Lutheranism of the greater portion of his valuable work.

The Arminian position, as has been pointed out, is in reality the Catholic view of the Church, and is the only one which can be consistently maintained in harmony with the great doctrines of salvation. Both the earlier Arminians and the later Wesleyans have substantiated their positions with lengthy and logical arguments. Perhaps the best known of these arguments in favor of divine prescience is that of Richard Watson in his *Theological Institutes* (I, p. 365ff). Wakefield asserts, that the position which holds that certain pre-

"This whole difficulty," says Hodge, "arises out of the assumption that contingency is essential to free agency. If an act may be certain as to its occurrence, and yet free as to the mode of its occurrence, the difficulty vanishes. That free acts may be absolutely certain, is plain, because they have in a multitude of cases been predicted. It was certain that the acts of Christ would be holy, yet they were free. The continued holiness of the saints in heaven is certain, and yet they are perfectly free. The foreknowledge of God is inconsistent with a false theory of free agency, but not with the true doctrine on that subject. After Augustine, the common way of meeting the difficulty of reconciling foreknowledge with liberty, was to represent it as merely subjective. The distinction between knowledge and foreknowledge is only in us" —HODGE, *Syst. Th.*, I, p. 401.

science destroys contingency, is a mere sophism. Dr.
Raymond with no little zeal declares that "with the exception of atheists, pantheists, positivists, and that class
of thinkers who have discussed the absolute and the infinite in a way to philosophize themselves into a profession of total ignorance, and into a conviction that the
knowledge of God is impossible, all men regarded the infinite First Cause as not only absolute and infinite, but
also a Person possessing intelligence and free will, and
especially regard His intelligence as without limitation.
In the common apprehension, God has a perfect knowledge of all that is or can be; all existence and all events,
the actual and the possible, the present, the past and the
future" (RAYMOND, *Syst. Th.*, I, p. 330).

4. *Wisdom.* As a divine attribute wisdom is closely
related to and dependent upon omniscience, but is usually given separate treatment by Arminian theologians.

Knapp states the argument as follows: "The foreknowledge of God,
which is contended for, invades the freedom of the will in man and
other moral beings. For if God foreknows all things, and is infallible
in His knowledge, whatever He knows must take place, is therefore
necessary, and no longer dependent on the freedom of man. But this
argument is fallacious; for man does not perform one action, or another
because it was foreknown by God; but God foreknew the action, because man in the exercise of his free will would perform it."—KNAPP,
Chr. Th., p. 104.

Watson's great argument may be summarized as follows: "The
great fallacy in the argument that the certain prescience of a moral
action destroys its contingent nature, lies in supposing that contingency
and certainty are the opposites of each other. . . . . If, however, the
term contingent in this controversy has any definite meaning at all, as
applied to the moral actions of men, it must mean their freedom and
stands opposed not to certainty, but to necessity. . . . . Free actions foreknown will not, therefore, cease to be contingent. But how stands the
case as to their certainty? Precisely on the same ground. The certainty of a necessary action foreknown, does not result from the knowledge of the action, but from the operation of the necessitating cause;
and in like manner, the certainty of a free action does not result from
the knowledge of it, which is no cause at all, but from the voluntary
cause, that is, the determination of the will. It alters not the case in
the least to say that the voluntary action might have been otherwise.
Had it been otherwise, the knowledge of it would have been otherwise; but as the will which gives birth to the action, is not dependent
upon the previous knowledge of God, but the knowledge of the action
upon foresight of the choice of the will, neither the will nor the act is
controlled by knowledge, and the action though foreseen, is still free
and contingent. The foreknowledge of God then has no influence upon
either the freedom or the certainty of actions, for this plain reason, that
it is knowledge and not influence; and actions may be certainly foreknown, without their being rendered necessary by that foreknowledge.—
WATSON, *Institutes*, I, pp. 379ff.

Dr. Summers, however, treats omniscience as comprehended under the attribute of Wisdom. Wakefield defines the wisdom of God as "that attribute of His nature by which He knows and orders all things for the promotion of His glory and the good of His creatures" (Cf. WAKEFIELD, *Chr. Th.*, p. 159). While wisdom and knowledge are closely related, the distinction is clear. Knowledge is the apprehension of things as they are, and wisdom is the adaptation of this knowledge to certain ends. As knowledge is necessary to wisdom, so omniscience in God is necessary to His infinite wisdom. The Scriptures are peculiarly rich in their references to the religious value of the divine wisdom and to this we shall give our attention.

Job declares that *With him is wisdom and strength; he hath counsel and understanding* (Job 12:13), and again, *He is mighty in strength and wisdom* (Job 36:5). The psalmist exclaims, *O Lord, how manifold are thy works! in wisdom hast thou made them all: the earth is full of thy riches* (Psalm 104:24). *The Lord by wisdom hath founded the earth; by understanding hath he established the heavens* (Prov. 3:19). *Daniel answered and said, Blessed be the name of God for ever and ever: for wisdom and might are his* (Dan. 2:20). The New Testament is equally rich in its praise of this divine attribute. *O the depth of the riches both of the wisdom and knowledge of God! how unsearchable are his judgments, and his ways past finding out* (Rom. 11:33). The Apostle Paul in his refutation of the Gnostic tendencies, declares that Christ is *the power of God and the wisdom of God* (I Cor. 1:24); again, that He is *made unto us wisdom,*

Richard Watson gives the following marks of wisdom: (1) The first character of wisdom is to act for worthy ends. To act with design is a sufficient character of intelligence; but wisdom is the fit and proper exercise of the understanding. (2) It is another mark of wisdom when the process by which any work is accomplished is simple, and many effects are produced from one or a few elements. "When every several effort has a particular separate cause, this gives no pleasure to the spectators, as not discovering contrivance; but that work is beheld with admiration and delight as the result of deep counsel, which is complicated in its parts, and yet simple in its operation, when a great variety of effects are seen to arise from one principle operating uniformly (ABERNATHY on *Attributes*). (Cf. WATSON, *Institutes*, I, p. 405ff.)

and righteousness, and sanctification, and redemption
(I Cor. 1: 30). This is a reference to the Logos or the
Divine Word, which in the Old Testament was personified as Wisdom. *The Lord possessed me in the beginning of his way, before his works of old. I was set up
from everlasting, from the beginning, or ever the earth
was. . . . . Then I was by him, as one brought up with
him: and I was daily his delight, rejoicing always before
him* (Prov. 8: 22, 23, 30). This wisdom became the incarnate Word, which was in the beginning with God and
was God (Cf. John 1: 1). *Now unto the King eternal, immortal, invisible, the only wise God, be honour and glory
for ever and ever. Amen* (I Tim. 1: 17).

5. *Goodness.* The goodness of God is that attribute
by reason of which God wills the happiness of His creatures. Perfection as we have shown, is the absolute excellence which God has in Himself; goodness is that excellence which moves God to impart being and life to
finite things apart from His divine essence, and to communicate to them such gifts as they have capacity to receive. Goodness is generally expressed by the Hebrew
word *chesedh*, and by the Greek words ἀγαθοσύνη or
χρηστότης and such like terms. The goodness of God
ad intra belongs to the Holy Trinity, in which the Blessed
Three eternally communicate to each other their infinite
richness. In this sense, goodness is eternal and necessary. The goodness of God *ad extra* is voluntary, and
refers primarily to His benevolence which may be defined as that disposition which seeks to promote the
happiness of His creatures. Schouppe defines it as "the
constant will of God to communicate felicity to His creatures, according to their conditions and His own wisdom."It is related to love, but love is limited to respon-
sive persons or to those capable of reciprocation, while
goodness applies to the whole creation. *Not a sparrow is
forgotten before God* (Luke 12: 6). The word is applied
to the whole creation in the dawn of its existence. *And
God saw every thing that he had made, and, behold, it
was very good* (Gen. 1: 31). The positive declarations of
Scripture concerning the goodness of God are numerous

and convincing. God said to Moses, *I will make all my goodness pass before thee* (Exod. 33:19); and again, *The Lord God, merciful and gracious, longsuffering, and abundant in goodness and truth* (Exod. 34:6). The psalmist seems to take delight in meditating upon the goodness of God. *Surely goodness and mercy shall follow me all the days of my life: and I will dwell in the house of the Lord for ever* (Psalm 23:6). *I had fainted, unless I had believed to see the goodness of the Lord in the land of the living* (Psalm 27:13). *O how great is thy goodness, which thou hast laid up for them that fear thee* (Psalm 31:19). *The goodness of God endureth continually* (Psalm 52:1). *They shall abundantly utter the memory of thy great goodness, and shall sing of thy righteousness* (Psalm 145:7). Isaiah mentions the great goodness toward the house of Israel (Isa. 63:7) and Zechariah voices the exclamation, *For how great is his goodness, and how great is his beauty!* (Zech. 9:17). In the New Testament the Apostle Paul speaks of the goodness of God as leading to repentance (Rom. 2:4); and in the same epistle mentions the goodness and severity of God as apparently the constituent elements of the divine holiness (Rom. 22:22). In Gal. 5:22 and Eph. 5:9 goodness is mentioned as a fruit of the spirit.

It is common in this connection to append a theodicy, or at least to give the subject some consideration. By *theodicy* is meant the vindication of God's wisdom and goodness in the creation and government of the world. Within the sacred canon, the Book of Job may be said to be the theodicy of the Old Testament. In true philosophical form, the first work of importance on this subject in modern times was that of Leibnitz (1747); and closely following were the works of Benedict (1822), Von Schaden (1842), Maret (1857), and Young, *Evil and Good* (1861). Dr. Summers gives a chapter to this important subject (Cf. SUMMERS, *Syst. Th.*, I, pp. 122-146). Dr. Pope treats the subject briefly, introducing it as follows: "But the tremendous difficulty arises that evil exists. The goodness of God is the attribute which this fact most directly confronts: not His love, which

does not emerge in its glory from the ground of His
lovingkindness until sin already exists; not His holiness, which likewise implies the existence of what He
forever rejects; not His wisdom, which has its grand-
est illustration in its making evil subservient to His de-
signs. But it is forever argued that a Creator of unbounded benevolence and power, must, or might, or
ought to have prevented the origination of evil. There
are only two possible solutions of this profound difficulty.
Either the desperate expedient must be adopted of re-
nouncing a supreme God altogether; a solution which is
really no solution, for atheism solves nothing but dis-
solves all. Or, accepting the testimony of God himself,
we must bow before an unfathomable mystery, and seek
our refuge in the harmony of the divine attributes (Cf.
POPE, *Compend. Chr. Th.*, I, p. 322). Probably no better
solution has ever been offered than that of John Wesley.
"Why is sin in the world? Because man was created in
the image of God; because he is not mere matter, a clod
of earth, a lump of clay, without sense or understanding,
but a spirit like his Creator; a being endued not only
with sense and understanding, but also with a will ex-
erting itself in various affections. To crown all the rest,
he was endued with liberty, a power of directing his own
affections and actions, a capacity of determining himself, or of choosing good and evil. Indeed, had not man
been endued with this, all the rest would have been of
no use. Had he not been a free as well as an intelligent
being, his understanding would have been as incapable
of holiness or any other kind of virtue, as a tree or a
block of marble. And having this power, a power of

Watson gives an interesting and helpful discussion of this subject
in that he gives the older viewpoint, with rather extended excerpts from
Paley's *Natural Theology,* King's *Origin of Evil,* Gisborne's *Testimony
of Natural Philosophy to Christianity,* and Scott's *Remarks on the Refutation of Calvinism.* The tone of the apology is to place nature in a better
light than is commonly done by those who viewing it under the curse
and consequences of sin, find in it nothing of good.

In recent times, *The Philosophy of the Christian Religion,* by A. M.
Fairbairn, Principal of Mansfield College, Oxford, is a sincere and
reverent attempt to present a true philosophy of the Christian religion.
Whatever the judgment which may be formed as to his conclusions, all
will admit that for scholarship and candor, the book is of a high order.

choosing good and evil, he chose the latter, he chose evil. Thus 'sin entered into the world.' " (WESLEY, *Sermons*).

THE MORAL ATTRIBUTES

The moral attributes of God relate to His government over free and intelligent creatures. Since moral bonds are essential to the existence and perpetuity of society, the knowledge of God must ever be a determining factor in the community life of men. Clear views of the divine nature are indispensable to both stability and progress. There is abundant proof from history that society is ultimately dependent upon the strength of its moral bonds, and when these are relaxed or decay, the social structure collapses. There is a marked difference also between the metaphysical attributes and the ethical in this, that while both may in a measure be comprehended by finite reason, the latter depend more particularly upon a common experience. Man being made in the image of God, may as a rational being comprehend within the limits of his finiteness, the natural attributes of God; but man having fallen into sin lacks the subjective basis for the perception of God's moral and spiritual character. It is only the pure in heart who see God. God's holiness forbids the approach of sinful man. There is no meeting place, no common basis for understanding. It is evident, therefore, that only through the mediatorship of Jesus Christ can man become a partaker of the divine nature, and hence come to know in the deepest and truest sense His holiness and His love. It is at this point of the moral attributes of God, that natural revelation is most defective. Man cannot rest satisfied with it. To no inconsiderable extent, the errors in theology have grown out of the confused notions of God which are consequent upon it. Our question then is, "What is the nature and character of God made known to us through this redemptive revelation?" Herein lies the importance of this department of theology.

We need first of all to remind ourselves that the term *personality,* as we have used it in its application to God, conveys the idea of a richer content than that given to it by metaphysics alone. It embraces not only self-consciousness but self-determination. It involves the perfection of reason, power and love, and has, therefore, not only metaphysical existence but ethical and moral quality. Every objection urged against ascribing a Nature to the Divine Being, rests upon a false and unreal conception of the absolute. The arguments for the existence of God presuppose His ethical character, in order to account for the moral nature of man. But to ascribe a moral nature to God carries with it something more than merely ethical distinctions. It means that moral feeling must be co-ordinated with perfect knowledge and unlimited power. It means, further, that the Divine Will must give perfect expression to that which constitutes His Being, so that He wills that holiness which forms the essential quality of His nature. It follows, then, that the moral nature of God is not merely a quiescent state, but active with infinite intensity in the free and unlimited range of His personal powers. If in the metaphysical realm we may speak of the existence of God under the twofold distinction of essence and attribute, we may also with equal propriety in the realm of God's moral government, observe the distinction between the divine nature and the moral attributes; and if we may regard the metaphysical attributes as inhering in the essence of God and expressive of it; so we may regard the moral attributes as inhering in a Divine Nature or Moral Character, to which likewise they give expression.

All the perfections of God as manifested in His moral government may be resolved into two—His holiness and His love. These in their essence and relation can be understood only through a proper analysis of the nature of personal life. It is a characteristic of personality to mark itself off as separate and distinct from all other existences, personal or otherwise, in what is commonly known as self-grasp or self-affirmation. But it likewise belongs to personality to reveal and impart itself. If, then, we view the ethical nature of God from this standpoint of self-grasp or self-affirmation, we have the concept of divine holiness; if we view it from the standpoint of self-impartation or self-communication, we have the concept of divine love. We may with perfect propriety say, therefore, that the nature of God consists in holy love, but in this statement we neither identify nor confuse the terms.

Holiness as Nature or Attribute. Theologians have greatly differed in their positions concerning the holiness of God. Three positions may be and are taken concerning this subject: *first,* it may be regarded as one attribute alongside of and co-ordinate with other attributes; *second,* it may be regarded as the sum total of all the attributes; and *third,* it may be regarded not as an attribute, but as a nature, of which the attributes are the expression. "The holiness of God," says Wakefield, "is commonly regarded as an attribute distinct from His other perfections; but this we think, is a mistake. Holiness is a complex term, and denotes not so much a particular attribute, as that general character of God which results from all his moral perfections. The holiness of man is not a distinct quality from his virtuous disposition, but signifies the state of his mind and heart as influenced by these. When we proceed to analyze his holiness, or to show in what it consists, we say that he is a devout man, a man of integrity, a man faithful to all his engagements and conscientious in all his relative duties, a man who abhors sin and loves righteousness. In like manner, the holiness of God is not, and cannot be, something different from the moral perfections of his nature, but is a general term under which all these perfections are comprehended" (WAKEFIELD, *Christian Theology,* p. 168). This is similar to the position of Dr. Dick who held that holiness was not a particular attribute, but "the general character of God as resulting from His moral attributes" (DICK, *Theology,* I, p. 274). Dr. Wardlaw defines holiness as "the union of all the attributes, as pure white light is the union of all the colored rays of the spectrum" (WARDLAW, *Systematic Theology,* I, p. 619). Dr. Strong regards holiness as the fundamental attribute of God. Veracity and faithfulness he regards as transitive truth; mercy and goodness as transitive love; and justice and righteousness as transitive holiness. To this position Dr. Dickie objects, refusing to classify either love or holiness as distinct attributes. To make either holiness or love fundamental would, he thinks, either subordinate the one to the other, or formally countenance a dualistic conception of the divine nature, as if love and holiness were opposed to each other. To him, the love of God is holy and the holiness of God loving. For this reason he maintains that Dr. Strong's position falls short of the full statement of Christian truth. Dr. Pope takes the dual position just mentioned, but to him, holiness and love as attributes are co-ordinate with each other, "two ascendencies in their yet not fully explained union and harmony." They therefore become the foundation for two classes of prominent attributes, justice, righteousness and truth belonging to God's holiness, and grace and its related attributes to His love (Cf. DICKIE, *Organism of Christian Truth*, p. 94; POPE, *Compendium of Christian Theology*, I, p. 329). Dr. Sheldon takes a position similar to that of Dr. Dickie, maintaining that the ethical nature of God is best expressed in the phrase, *holy love,* or with nearly equal propriety, *loving righteousness.* He recognizes, however, the distinction between them which Dr. Pope indicates, and holds that holiness may not be subsumed under love, nor love under righteousness, but are to be regarded as terms of a couplet which stand for closely related and perfectly harmonious perfections (SHELDON, *Syst. of Chr. Doct.,* p. 184). Dr. Summers treats holiness under the head of goodness, which he regards as both essential and relative. Essential goodness he defines as holiness (SUMMERS, *Systematic Theology,* I, p. 98). In this connection, also, we may refer briefly to those theologians who attach the idea of holiness to some faculty of personality such as the will or the affections. Those theologians who make *will* the highest expression of personality commonly treat holiness in relation to it. Thus Dr. Fairchild holds that holiness or virtue is a benevolent regard for the good. This is a voluntary attitude, a state of will, a simple exercise, not changed in its character by changing perceptions or feelings (FAIRCHILD, *Elements of Theology*, p. 127). Dr. Foster likewise defines holiness as an attribute of the divine will, but in so doing is not to be understood as limiting it to the volitions. The will itself is holy. "All his self-determinations are holy, whether we conceive of them as eternal or temporal. If God is a person, we cannot conceive of Him as thinking, without first conceiving of Him as one who wills to think. If we speak of His thoughts as holy, it is because we regard them as the expression of His eternally holy will. If we regard His very essence as holy, as indeed we must, it is because we must at the same time regard it as personal essence; and we regard it as an eternally personal essence because it exists eternally as an essence *willing*. This *will* is the form of an immanent, and of course, conscious preference" (FOSTER, *Christian Theology*, p. 227). Dr. Miley, on the other hand, relates holiness more closely to the divine sentiency, affirming that there is a truth of moral feeling in God which is deeper than the more definite distinctions of mode, the moral feeling which is intrinsic to the holiness of the divine nature (MILEY, *Systematic Theology*, I, p. 199). From this brief review of the various positions held, it is evident that holiness occupies a central position of importance in the moral government of God; and that when it is limited to one faculty in contradistinction to others, it is only because this particular faculty is regarded as supreme in personal life.

We may say then, that holiness belongs to the essential nature of God in a deeper and more profound sense than merely as one attribute among others. If it be objected that holiness could not be known were it of the essence and not of the attributes, we may refer the reader to our discussion of the absolute. It was indicated that the term is used in three different senses, *first,* as that which is entirely unrelated, which leads directly to agnosticism; *second,* as the totality of all relations, which leads to pantheism; and *third,* as that which is independent and self-existent. This is the theistic and Christian position. The Christian maintains that his knowledge of God is limited but that it is true so far as it goes; and that this knowledge to any degree or extent is due solely to the self-revelation of God. This is as true of the ethical as of the metaphysical nature of God. God can be known only as He reveals Himself through the eternal Son and the ever blessed Spirit. And this knowledge of God which comes through the mystical contact of Spirit with spirit, is unfolded to the understanding in an ever deepening and widening concept of the moral attributes. We are not, however, averse to the position of Dr. Pope, who holds that the two divine perfections, holiness and love, may be called the moral nature of God; and that these two are the only terms which unite in one the attributes and the essence of God (Cf. POPE, *Compend. Chr. Th.,* I, p. 331). As essence, these constitute the moral nature of God; as attributes they are the revelation of this nature through the economy of divine grace.

The moral attributes differ in a peculiar sense from the natural attributes, in that they cannot be understood without that subjective character in man which corresponds to the moral nature of God, and therefore cannot be separated from the redemptive work of Christ. The perfect revelation of God's holiness is found in the incarnate Son of whom it is written, *Thou hast loved righteousness, and hated iniquity; therefore God, even thy God, hath anointed thee with the oil of gladness above thy fellows* (Heb. 1:9). Holiness, then, is primarily that disposition which is back of all the attributes—a disposition or a nature which manifests itself in a love for righteousness and in a hatred for iniquity. It is holy love. But as previously indicated, holiness belongs to the self-affirmation of personality, rather than self-impartation; and self-affirmation is always deeper and more fundamental than self-manifestation. That

God is the synthesis of all good by virtue of His very being; He is perfection, both metaphysical and ethical.—KUBEL.

which severs God from the creaturely nature, even apart from sin, that by which the soleness and integrity of His being is maintained, is holiness. Nor must this idea of separateness be forgotten or overlooked. Holiness is not merely synonymous with perfection generally, nor can it be interpreted as communicative goodness, an indefinite flowing over of love into man's nature apart from moral distinctions. Holy love demands a community of persons, each separate and distinct, and the purity of the love depends upon the strict regard which is paid to the limits which separate one from the other. Holiness in the ethical aspect of the Divine Being is characterized by the separateness of God in essence from all other beings. It belongs to the integrity of His being rather than to His relationships. Holiness is immanent and essential to the very idea of God. Love indeed has its seat in the free relations of the persons of the Divine Trinity, but holiness belongs to the necessary relationships. Holiness is therefore more fundamental in some sense than love, at least it must be given logical priority, though love may occupy the more exalted sphere. "The kingdom of love," says Martensen, "is established on the foundation of holiness. Holiness is the principle that guards the eternal distinction between the Creator and the creature, between God and man, in the union effected between them; it preserves the divine dignity and majesty from being infringed by the divine love; it eternally excludes everything evil and impure from the divine nature. The Christian mind knows nothing of a love without holiness" (MARTENSEN, *Christian Dogmatics*, p. 99ff).

We may further refer in this connection to the trisagion found in Isaiah 6:3, *Holy, holy, holy, is the Lord of hosts,* and also in Rev. 4:8 where the "living creatures" corresponding to the seraphim of Isaiah, rest not day nor night saying, *Holy, holy, holy, Lord God Almighty, which was, and is, and is to come.* The Church has always maintained that this threefold ascription refers to the Divine Trinity, and therefore that holiness belongs equally to the Father, the Son and the ever blessed Spirit. The glory which by Isaiah is ascribed to the Lord of Hosts, is by St. John ascribed to the Son (John 12: 41) and by St. Paul to the Holy Spirit (Acts 28: 25, 26). If we may be permitted to refer again to our discussion of the Christian conception of God, we found there as basic to this concept, the statement of our Lord that *God is a Spirit* (John 4: 24), and this was further interpreted by the New Testament writers as *life* (John 5: 26), *light* (I John 1: 5) and *love* (I John 4: 8). In the Trinity, therefore, life is peculiarly the property of the Father, Light of the Son, and Love of the Spirit. But basic and fundamental to each is ascribed a nature characterized as holy, and the threefold ascription of adoration and praise is not on the ground of life or light or love, but of holiness. We may say, then, that holiness in the Father is the mystery of life, separate, distinct and unoriginated; holiness in the Son is light, which down to the depths of His infinite being, reveals no darkness, nothing undiscovered, nothing unfulfilled, nothing which needs to be brought to perfection; holiness in the Spirit is the disclosure of love which exists between the Father and the Son, and is by St. Paul called the bond of perfectness. In the Father, holiness is original and underived, in the Son holiness is revealed, and in the Spirit holiness is imparted. It is therefore not by mere chance that we find the expression *partakers of the divine nature* (II Peter 1: 4), associated with *partakers of his holiness* (Heb. 12: 10); and *partakers of the glory* (I Peter 5: 1) with *partakers of Christ* (Heb. 3: 14) and *of the Holy Ghost* (Heb. 6: 4). These distinctions must be further considered as "The Biblical Concept of Holiness" and "The Concept of Divine Love."

The Biblical Concept of Holiness. The term *holiness* has had a long and complex history. In the religion of Israel it first appears as expressive of the nature of God in Exodus 15: 11, *Who is like unto thee, O Lord, among the gods? who is like unto thee, glorious in holiness, fearful in praises, doing wonders.* It occurs in the same relation for the last time in Revelation 15: 4, *Who shall not fear thee, O Lord, and glorify thy name? for thou*

*only art holy; for all nations shall come and worship be-
fore thee; for thy judgments are made manifest.* It is
significant also, that the term first occurs as a revelation of Jehovah to His chosen people in His redemptive
relation, and not in His revelation of Himself as Creator.
This fact marks it as the ground of His ethical character
in the moral government of a free and responsible people. The word indeed occurs in Genesis, but there it is
associated with the perfection of the works of God. *And
God blessed the seventh day, and sanctified it; because
that in it he had rested from all his work which God
created and made* (Gen. 2:3). While the idea of perfection stands out more prominently, there is even here
the idea of separateness. Holiness attaches to the day because of the presence of God. God's resting place, or
the place of His abiding presence is holy. Later the same
idea attaches to the house of God, concerning which the
psalmist declares, *Holiness becometh thine house, O
Lord, for ever* (Psalm 93:5). The idea of separation in
order to possession attaches to both the day and the
house. The day is set apart or devoted as a memorial of
the finished creation. It is holy, because it is separated in
devotion to God, and thus becoming peculiarly His possession, He rests or abides in it. Of the house it is written,
*Let them make me a sanctuary; that I may dwell among
them* (Exod. 25:8). We may say, then, that even at this
early date the two ideas of separation and possession attach to the word holiness. Both of these qualities come
into clearer light with the Abrahamic covenant, and are
set forth in their perfection by the redemptive Trinity in
the New Covenant. Following the suggestion of the trisagion we shall consider the term holiness in its threefold aspect as it relates to the Father, the Son and the
Holy Spirit.

Holiness as it relates to the Father, expresses the perfection of moral excellence which in Him exists unoriginated and underived. It is therefore *first,* the
ground of reverence and adoration. *Who shall not fear
thee, O Lord, and glorify thy name?* (Rev. 15:4). It
was because of this resplendent glory that the psalm-

ist exclaimed, *Holy and reverend is his name* (Psalm 111:9). Here the idea is suggestive of majesty. This is true also of the passage *his holy arm hath gotten him the victory,* and again, *Exalt the Lord our God, and worship at his holy hill; for the Lord our God is holy* (Psalm 99:9). *Second,* holiness is the standard of all moral goodness. It is in this connection that the concept of holiness held by William Newton Clarke is peculiarly appropriate. As previously indicated, he regards holiness as the glorious fullness of God's moral excellence, held as the principle of His own action and the standard for His creatures (CLARKE, *An Outline of Christian Theology,* p. 89). Here it is evident that holiness is not only the inward character of God as perfect goodness, but consistency with this character as a standard for His own activity; and further, it is a requirement for His morally responsible creatures. It is for this reason that we have the injunction, *Be ye holy, for I am holy* (I Peter 1:13). Holiness demands character, consistency and requirement. The character of God as holy could not be such unless it possessed all moral goodness. It is the sum of all excellencies, not as a mathematical total but as a nature which includes every perfection, not one of which could be diminished without destroying His holiness. In God's consistency with His perfections, we have the action of the will to which holiness is sometimes ascribed. But perfect character demands perfect conduct, and for this reason His perfect freedom must be in perfect harmony with His character. During the scholastic period the question was frequently debated, as to whether God willed the good because it was good, or whether it was good because He willed it. Thomas Aquinas held to the former position, and Duns Scotus

The God whose glory filled the temple, and revealed only the unholiness of all who approached Him, nevertheless bade the unholy draw near to be sanctified. Was it then by the rays of His holiness shining upon and around them? Most assuredly not. The mystery of this paradox, that the attribute which separated God from sinners and Himself, is solved only by the system of sacrificial expiation typifying the great atonement, which through a satisfaction offered to the divine righteousness opened the fellowship of love between God and man.—POPE, *Compend. Chr. Th.,* I, p. 334.

to the latter. But the question is a meaningless one, for God's holiness is not determined by something outside of Him but within Him. He cannot contradict Himself and is therefore morally incapable of that which does not truly express His nature as holy. He cannot make evil good without ceasing to be God. By omnipotence in God we mean that He is not limited by anything outside of Himself, but we do insist that He is limited by His own divine nature or character. He cannot will anything contrary to His nature or in anywise be untrue to Himself. *Third*, and closely related to the foregoing, holiness as the standard of goodness is eternally opposed to sin. Consequently we read *Thou art of purer eyes than to behold evil, and canst not look upon iniquity* (Hab. 1:13), and again, *Who is able to stand before this holy Lord God?* (I Sam. 6:20). Holiness is therefore not only the standard of all good, but as such must necessarily include the repulsion of all evil. It is evident that this aspect of the divine nature comes into clearer light by contrast, and it may be as Dr. Pope suggests, that it is always "displayed against the dark background of sin." This brings us to a discussion of holiness as related to the redemptive work of Christ.

Holiness as it relates to the Son is found in both His revealing and redemptive mission. Holiness in God can be known only by those who like Him are holy. It is for this reason, as we have previously indicated, that He says, *Be ye holy, for I am holy* (I Peter 1:16). Holiness repels every approach of defilement. It is evident, therefore, that the holiness of God may be known by sinful man only through an economy of divine grace. It

The well-known query: Is the good good because God wills it? or does God will it because it is good? is not properly put. The question is not as to God's willing, but as to His essence. The good is good for the simple reason that it is an outflow, a self-manifestation, of God Himself. This answers the question also as to the ground of right. Right is God; a creature does right when it harmonizes with God—that is, when it fulfills the divinely fixed end of its being. The definitions of the divine holiness and righteousness are of the same character. God's holiness is that attribute in virtue of which He takes His own absolutely perfect self as the norm of his entire activity. His holiness as revealed to man, and as revealing to man God's purpose in creating him, constitute God's and man's righteousness."—SUMMERS, *Systematic Theology*, p. 99.

is this conception which underlies and gives significance to the ritualistic system of Judaism, as preparatory to the redemptive work of Christ. The idea of sacrifice in the Scriptures carries with it the thought of uncleanness in the offerer, who by a propitiatory act must be cleansed or made holy. The love of the Father finds its highest expression in the gift of His Son, but this gift is specifically declared to be a propitiatory offering for sin. By it man may be made holy and again enter into fellowship with the Father. *Herein is love, not that we loved God, but that he loved us, and sent his Son to be the propitiation for our sins* (I John 4:10). Thus love made the offering or propitiation for sin which holiness required. (The word "to be" is better omitted. Love sent the Son the propitiation for our sins, *i.e.*, already a propitiation, the Lamb slain from the foundation of the world.) The same thought underlies the familiar text, *For God so loved the world, that he gave his only begotten Son, that whosoever believeth in him should not perish, but have everlasting life* (John 3:16). Here the love of God rests upon His divine holiness as an immutable basis. It was this alone which required and made possible the stupendous exhibition of divine love. If love sent the Son, it was His holiness that demanded the sacrifice—*our God is a consuming fire* (Heb. 12:29). Sanctification is not by an effusion of love, but by the sprinkling of blood. *Wherefore Jesus also, that he might sanctify the people with his own blood, suffered without the gate. Let us go forth therefore unto him without the camp, bearing his reproach* (Heb. 13:12, 13). Holiness and love in the nature of God assume the form of righteousness and grace in the redemptive economy. For this reason it is declared that the righteousness of God is revealed *from faith to faith* (Rom. 1:17); while from the standpoint of divine love, St. Paul declares that *the grace of God that bringeth salvation hath appeared to all men* (Titus 2:11).

Holiness as it relates to the Spirit is holiness imparted or made accessible to men. It is through the Spirit that we became "partakers of the divine nature." Hence the term "Holy Spirit" affirms not only the nature of the Spirit as in Himself holy, but declares also that it is His office and work to make men holy. Holiness and love thus appear to be closely conjoined if not identified in the Holy Spirit. He is at once the Spirit of holiness and the Spirit of love. The distinction, however, remains, and must be given due consideration. For this reason we must not overlook the distinctions made by our Lord in His high priestly prayer: *I have declared unto them thy name, and will declare it; that the love wherewith thou hast loved me may be in them, and I in them* (John 17: 26). Here is a revelation of both the holiness and love of God which is to be imparted or communicated through the Spirit. The "name" or nature must be declared before the love can be manifested. The Spirit by His hallowing act must identify man with the sanctifying blood of Christ, the propitiatory offering, before there can be any free inflow of divine love. There must be a partaking of His holiness before there can be the fullness of His love. Hence to be partakers of the divine nature is to share in both His holiness and His love. This is further set forth in the declaration, *I in them, and thou in me, that they may be made perfect in one; and that the world may know that thou hast sent me, and hast loved them, as thou hast loved me* (John 17: 23). St. Peter approaches this truth differently from St. Paul or even St. John. *Elect according to the foreknowledge of God the Father, through sanctification of the Spirit, unto obedience and sprinkling of the blood of Jesus Christ* (I Peter 1: 2); and again, *Seeing ye have purified your souls in obeying the truth through the Spirit unto unfeigned love of the brethren, see that ye love one another with a pure heart fervently* (I Peter 1: 22). We may say then that our partaking of the divine holiness is by the sanctification of the Spirit; while our partaking of the divine love is explained to be *because he hath given us of his Spirit*. While the act of the Holy Spirit in sanctification must ever precede logically that communication of Himself by which "the love of God is shed abroad in our hearts," yet in human experience the two may be said to be concomitant (Cf. Rom. 5:5 and I John 4:13).

The Concept of Divine Love. In our discussion of the holiness of God we found it necessary to mention briefly the nature of divine love. This subject, however, is of such vast importance both to religion and to theology, that it now demands further consideration, *first* as to its origin; *second* as to its nature; and *third* as to its relation to holiness. We may say then, (1) that *love has its origin* in the triunity of God. In the mysterious intercommunion of the Father and the Son, love is the bond of union. Thus St. Paul characterizes charity or divine love as the "bond of perfectness" (Col. 3:14). While the more extended treatment of this subject belongs to the following chapter we must at this point call attention to the personal nature of this relationship. The communion of the Father and the Son is vital and real, as between a personal subject and a personal object. But not only are the terms Father and Son personal, the organ of reciprocal interaction and intercommunion must likewise be personal. The bond of union which exists between the Father and the Son as personal Beings, and furnishes both the condition and ground of communion, is the personal Holy Ghost, the Third Person of the Trinity. And this absolute intercommunion and reciprocity of love, demands the equality and consubstantiality of the Holy Spirit with that of the Father and Son, "the glory equal, the majesty co-eternal." It is for this reason that He is called the Spirit of communion in the apostolic benedictions, *The grace of the Lord Jesus Christ, and the love of God, and the communion of the Holy Ghost, be with you all* (II Cor. 13:14). The Father loves the Son and is in turn loved by the Son, and the bond of love which is the ground of communion is the Holy Spirit. We may then regard love as the moral or ethical expression of the Divine Unity, and therefore the focal point of all the moral attributes. Here is displayed the profound truth that *God is love; and he that dwelleth in love dwelleth in God, and God in him* (I John 4:16). We may also, on the authority of the sacred Scriptures, confidently believe that the Triune God exists eternally in the sphere of love; that this love gave Jesus Christ our Lord as a propitiation for sin; and that it is into this holy fellowship of divine love that His finite creatures are to be received through the gift of the Holy Spirit. It was for this reason that our Lord in the fulfillment of His mission concluded His high priestly prayer with the words, *I have declared unto them thy name, and will declare it; that the love wherewith thou hast loved me may be in them, and I in them* (John 17:26).

We must consider (2) *the Nature of Divine Love.* Schleiermacher defines love as "that attribute in virtue of which God communicates Himself"; Dr. Francis J. Hall, as "the attribute by reason of which God wills a personal fellowship with Himself of those who are holy or capable of being made so" (HALL, *Theological Outlines*, p. 89); while William Newton Clarke whose definitions are always concise and clear, regards it as "God's desire to impart Himself and all good to other beings, and to possess them for His own spiritual fellowship" (CLARKE, *Outline of Christian Theology*, p. 95). From these definitions, it is evident that there are at least three essential principles in love—self-communication, fellowship, and a desire to possess the object loved. Referring again to our characterization of holiness as the self-affirming aspect of God's nature as holy love, we insisted that holiness is not merely self-affirmed purity in the negative sense of the term, but includes also a positive delight or complacency in the right. Here we see these qualities reappearing in a new light within love itself. Love must come to expression in the twofold desire to possess other beings for Himself, and to

Julius Mueller in his doctrine of the Trinity states that "Its inmost significance is that God has in Himself the eternal and wholly adequate object of His love, independent of all relation to the world. *Thou lovedst me before the foundation of the world* (John 17:24). This requires alike the unity of the essence, and the distinctness of the Persons. For without the distinction of Persons, without an I and Thou, there could be no love. Again, without the unity of the essence there would follow from the love of God a necessary relation to an essence distinct from God. Both are therefore implied in what is said of the Logos in the beginning of St. John's Gospel."—MUELLER, *The Chr. Doct. of Sin*, II, p. 136ff.

impart to them Himself and all other good. It is frequently pointed out that the self-sacrificing mother who gives herself for her child, is the one whose longing for the answering love of the child is most deep and inextinguishable. However great the self-surrender and sacrifice of love, it is always accompanied by the desire for reciprocation. But in the very devotion of a mother to her son, that mother affirms her distinct personality. The self-surrender and the self-assertion must be equal, nor can either increase without the other if love is to be maintained. If self-assertion is not accompanied by its equivalent in self-surrender, we have not love but selfishness under the guise of love; if self-surrender be not balanced by self-assertion, we have not love but weakness. As love develops, it grows richer in self-sacrificing, and increases its desire for possession of the object loved. When therefore St. John declares that *We love him, because he first loved us* (I John 4:19) he is giving voice to that reciprocal love which delights the heart of God. From the standpoint of divine love, it is well also to remember that without God man is an orphan; without man, God is bereaved.

One of the outstanding contributions to modern theology will be found in Ritschl's analysis of love (Cf. RITSCHL, *Justification and Reconciliation*, p. 277ff). After defining love as "will, aiming either at the appropriation of an object, or at the enrichment of its existence, because moved by a feeling of its worth," he enumerates several conditions necessary to its existence. We may summarize these briefly as follows: (1) It is necessary that the objects loved should be of like nature

Dr. Pope states that if we take the words, *Thou lovedst me before the foundation of the world,* and connect them with those which immediately precede, *and thou hast loved them, as thou hast loved me,* and these again with the assurance, *as the Father hath loved me, so have I loved you,* and these once more with the command, *that ye love one another, as I have loved you,* it will appear how perfect is the identity in kind between the finite and infinite love, between the reflection in us and the reality in the essential Trinity, and how profound is the meaning of those words, "Love is of God," a form of expression used of no other grace. "Thus," he says, "we may boldly repeat that more glorious things are spoken of the divine perfection of love than of any other."—POPE, *Compend. Chr. Th.,* pp. 344, 345.

to the subject which loves, that is, persons. To speak of love for things or animals, is to degrade the conception of love beneath its proper meaning. (2) Love implies a will which is constant in its aim. If objects change, we may have fancies but cannot have love. (3) Love aims at the promotion of another's personal end, whether known or conjectured. Nor is love interested merely in those things which are accidental, it estimates everything which concerns the other by its bearing on the character of the loved one. Love desires either to promote, to maintain, and through sympathetic interest to enjoy the individuality of the character acquired by the others, or to assist him in securing those blessings which are necessary to insure the attainment of his personal ideal. (4) If love is to be a constant attitude of will, and if the appropriation and the promotion of the other's interests and ideals are not to diverge but to coincide in each act, then the will of the person who loves must take up the other's personal interests and make them a part of his own. Love continually strives to appropriate the other personality, regarding this as a task necessary to his own conscious individuality. This characteristic implies that the will as love does not give itself up for the other's sake.

We must consider (3) the *Relation of Holiness to Love.* We have all along carefully guarded against any confusion of these terms, and therefore the question is forced upon us as to the relation which the one bears to the other. If the nature of God as holy love is, from the standpoint of self-affirmation to be defined as holy, and from the standpoint of self-communication to be interpreted as love, then holiness and love are equally of the essence of God. Holiness is considered fundamental solely from logical priority, for self-affirmation must al-

Ritschl's application of these principles is vitiated by two things, (1) he makes love to lie solely in the will, and therefore views the love of God as will without emotional content; (2) his lack of a proper conception of the Trinity makes it impossible for him to furnish any true ground for either love or holiness. He fails to see that God's love is primarily directed to the Son and only secondarily toward the Christian community, and consequently ignores the immanent or essential Trinity.

ways precede self-communication. Holiness and love in God are related in much the same manner as integrity and generosity in man. Holiness demands not only a nature, but a nature consistent with itself. Since that nature is in its out-goings always love, then holiness in God requires that He always act out of pure love. Hence in the first Christian Council at Jerusalem, St. Peter says concerning the Gentiles that *God, which knoweth the hearts, bare them witness, giving them the Holy Ghost, even as he did unto us; and put no difference between us and them, purifying their hearts by faith* (Acts 15:8, 9); and in his general epistle, *Seeing ye have purified your souls in obeying the truth through the Spirit unto unfeigned love of the brethren, see that ye love one another with a pure heart fervently* (I Peter 1:22). If, on the other hand, we view the nature of God from the standpoint of love or self-communication, then it is God's nature to impart Himself and that self is holy. Holiness must always act according to love, and love must always win its object to holiness. We may say then with Dr. Clarke, that love is in fact the desire to impart holiness, and this desire is satisfied only when the beings whom it seeks are rendered holy (Cf. CLARKE, *Outlines Chr. Th.*, p. 100). Consequently we read that *God commendeth his love toward us, in that, while we were yet sinners, Christ died for us* (Rom. 5:8); and again, *Herein is love, not that we loved God, but that he loved us, and sent his Son to be the propitiation for our sins* (I John 4:10).

There is, however, a danger here which we must not fail to take into consideration. Dr. Strong defines holiness as self-affirming purity, and in virtue of this attribute of His nature, God eternally wills and maintains His own moral excellence. This purity is not only negative, but positive, not only the absence of all moral stain, but complacency in all moral good. Hence in God's moral nature as necessary acting, there are the two elements of willing and being, but the passive logically precedes the active, and *being* comes before *willing*. God *is* pure before He *wills* purity. God is holy in that

His nature is the source and standard of right. Holiness furnishes the norm for love and therefore must be superior to it. God is not holy because He loves, but loves because He is holy. Dr. Strong thus preserves the distinction between holiness and love and makes holiness logically prior to it. In all this he is true and strong. But he goes farther, he makes holiness fundamental, in that it is a necessity of the divine nature while love is voluntary. For this reason, justice as transitive holiness must be exercised, while mercy as transitive love is optional. Hence God was under no obligation to provide a redemption for sinners. Thus there is laid the basis for the Calvinistic concept of divine grace which finds its logical issue in election and predestination. The same position is taken by Dr. Shedd who states that God can apply the salvation after He has wrought it out to whomsoever He will (Cf. SHEDD, *Discourses and Essays*, p. 277ff). Dr. G. B. Stevens in his review of Dr. Strong's *Philosophy and Religion* states that this view underlies the whole soteriology of this author's *Systematic Theology* as it does that of Dr. Shedd's *Dogmatic Theology* (Cf. STEVENS, *Johannine Theology*, pp. 285, 286). Dr. Pope avoids this error and states the true Arminian view when, as we have previously indicated, he takes the position that holiness and love are the two perfections which together may be called the nature of God, and that these are the only two terms which unite in one the attributes and essence (Cf. POPE, *Compend. Chr. Th.*, I, p. 331). Both holiness and love belong to the divine essence as well as to the attributes and cannot be separated except in thought. Justice, therefore, can never be necessary and mercy optional, but are always conjoined; and in the redemptive economy, holiness and mercy are supreme.

It may be well also, to note at this time the close connection existing between holiness and perfect love, between purity and perfection. These qualities are all strangely blended in the divine nature. We have already shown that God could not be love if He were not holy. Love being the impulse to give all, then perfect love in its highest degree can exist only as it has all to give. If He were not perfect it could not be said of Him, *God is love.* Thus perfection and perfect love are inseparably conjoined. Nor can there be perfect love in the creature unless to the measure of his capacity he gives his all. But, on the other hand, love desires to possess another in fellowship, a fellowship which demands the highest good of the object loved. There must be no touch of selfishness, else it would not be pure love. Purity is, therefore, love free from all defilement, and the self-affirmation of this purity is holiness.

Two other subjects are closely connected with this concept of divine love, the idea of blessedness, and the idea of wrath. These demand only brief mention at this time. (1) *The Idea of Blessedness.* This subject is rarely mentioned in the general works on theology, yet the word itself was frequently on the lips of our Lord (Cf. Matt. 5: 3-11, 11: 6, 13: 16, 25: 34, Luke 11: 28, John 20: 29). Bishop Martensen defines blessedness as a term "expressive of a life which is complete in itself," and further describes it as "the reflection of the rays of love back on God, after passing through His kingdom" (MARTENSEN, *Chr. Dogm.*, p. 101). The word is frequently translated happiness, but this is too weak to convey the full meaning of the original term. However, it is so translated in the words, *I think myself happy, king Agrippa* (Acts 26: 2). The term may be said to convey the delight which God has in the reciprocation of His love on the part of His creatures, and this delight He communicates to those who respond to His love. It is closely akin to the peace and joy which Christ communicates to His disciples apart from the happiness which arises from favorable circumstances. *Peace I leave with you, my peace I give unto you: not as the world giveth, give I unto you* (John 14: 27); and again, *These things have I spoken unto you, that my joy might remain in you, and that your joy might be full* (John 15: 11). Blessedness is closely akin also to the *rest of faith* (Heb. 4: 3) or the *keeping of the sabbath* (Heb. 4: 9), but the idea of rest must be sharply distinguished from the *eudaimonia* or idle enjoyment attributed to the gods of paganism. (2) *The Idea of Divine Wrath.* There are two positions which have been taken in the church concerning the subject of divine wrath. The common view is that wrath is not incompatible with divine love, and this has the support of the Scriptures. Speculative theologians, in order to avoid the difficulties which attach to this subject, have sought to explain it as a mere mode of human speech without any reality in the nature of God. The common view was contested very early in the Church, due doubtless to the influence of pagan philosophy. The Neo-Platonists and the Stoics with their pantheistic views of God and the world, held that God could not be subject to any emotion, for this necessitated passivity. Wrath, therefore, was impossible to God. To this position Lactantius (c. 320 A.D.) objected, maintaining that God must be capable of just resentment or His character would be imperfect. Augustine seems to reveal the influence of philosophy in his own thought when he identifies the wrath of God with the sentence which He pronounces against sin. "God's anger does not inflame His mind," he says, "nor disturb His unchangeable tranquillity." During the Deistical Period in England when divine love was reduced to complacent indulgence, Bishop Butler met the arguments of the Deists in his sermons on *Resentment* and *The Love of God,* which are usually regarded as the English classics on this subject. Ritschl, whose analysis of love we have already cited, attempted a mediating position, maintaining that wrath in God was purely eschatological, and consisted in the final sentence against sin which He would pronounce at the end of the world.

The Christian position generally, is that wrath is but the obverse side of love and necessary to the perfection of the Divine Personality, or even to love itself. God revealed Himself in Jesus Christ as loving righteousness and hating iniquity; and the hatred of iniquity is as essential to Perfect Personality as the love of righteousness. Divine wrath, therefore, must be regarded as the hatred of iniquity, and is in some proper sense the same emotion which exercised towards righteousness is known as divine love.

As the concept of holiness has developed through an age-long process of history, so love also had its historical development. The two are always associated in the Scriptures. It is interesting to note, however, that in the earlier history of the chosen people, the idea of holiness seems to precede that of love. The divine majesty is essential to adoration, and adoration to love. Holiness is ever the guardian of love, excluding every approach of evil. Thus we have the concept of God as *glorious in holiness, fearful in praises, doing wonders* (Exod. 15:11). While the aspect of holiness here is that of separation, a *jealous God, visiting the iniquity of the fathers upon the children,* there is immediately following, the declaration that He shews *mercy unto thousands* of them that love Him and keep His commandments (Exodus 20:6). At a later period in the progressive unfolding of divine grace, the revelation of love precedes that of holiness. *The Lord passed by before him, and proclaimed, The Lord, The Lord God, merciful and gracious, longsuffering, and abundant in goodness and truth* (Exod. 34:6). It is only in the Word incarnate that the supreme revelation of God's holiness and His love is to be found. Christ was the holy One. He loved righteousness and hated iniquity. He was also the revelation of the Father's love. *For God so loved the world, that he gave his only begotten Son, that whosoever believeth in him should not perish, but have everlasting life* (John 3:16). Here we begin to sound the depths of the mystery of the atoning work of our Lord Jesus Christ. Here do we find for the first time an identification of love with the very Being of God. St. John makes bold to speak it, *God is love* (I John 4:8).

The nature of God as holy love exhibits itself in two great branches of the moral attributes—the one corresponding more nearly to the idea of holiness, the other to that of love. From the aspect of the divine holiness we may mention; (1) justice or righteousness, which though sometimes given separate treatment are usually considered together; and (2) truth, which divides itself into veracity and faithfulness. From the aspect of divine love, we may mention, mercy, benevolence, long-suffering, compassion, and all those qualities which are generally known as the fruit of the Spirit.

Justice and Righteousness. Dr. Strong regards justice and righteousness as transitive holiness, by which he means that the treatment of His creatures always conforms to the purity or holiness of His nature. While closely related, justice and righteousness may be distinguished from each other, and both from holiness. The term holiness applies to the nature or essence of God as such, while righteousness is His standard of activity in conformity to that nature. This refers both to Himself and to His creatures. Justice may be said to be the counterpart of God's righteousness but is sometimes identified with it. Righteousness is the foundation of the divine law, justice the administration of that law. When we regard God as the author of our moral nature, we conceive of Him as holy; when we think of that nature as the standard of action, we conceive of Him as righteous; when we think of Him as administering that law in the bestowment of rewards and penalties, we conceive of Him as just. Justice is sometimes considered in the wider sense of *justitia interna,* or moral excellence, and sometimes in the narrower sense as *justitia externa,* or moral rectitude. A further division of the term is (1) *Legislative Justice* which determines the moral duty of man and defines the consequences in rewards or penalties; and (2) *Judicial Justice,* sometimes known

This sentiment or feeling in God, originating and directing the economy of redemption, was not fully revealed until the Lord himself revealed it. And when revealed, it is reserved for one service: to preside over the cross and the recovery of mankind. No record or register of the Divine Perfections, related to the created universe as such, contains that of love. His goodness and His loving-kindness are often alluded to as the nearest approach to the attribute that is never turned toward any but the objects of redeeming love. But at length the set time came for the new revelation, or at least the fuller revelation, of the attribute that governs all the rest: that which to adopt St. James' word, is the *royal law* in God as in man.—Pope, *Compendium of Christian Theology,* I, pp. 345ff.

as *Distributive Justice*, by which God renders to all men according to their works. The justice by which He rewards the obedient is sometimes known as *remunerative justice*, while that by which He punishes the guilty is *retributive* or *vindictive justice*. But whether as legislator or judge, God is eternally just.

In the following scripture references no distinction is made between the terms justice and righteousness. The careful student of this subject will be impressed with the many and various ways in which these attributes are combined. *The judgments of the Lord are true and righteous altogether* (Psalm 19:9). *Justice and judgment are the habitation of thy throne: mercy and truth shall go before thy face* (Psalm 89:14). *There is no God else beside me; a just God and a Saviour; there is none beside me* (Isa. 45:21). *The just Lord is in the midst thereof; he will not do iniquity* (Zeph. 3:5). *Who will render to every man according to his deeds* (Rom. 2:6). *Great and marvellous are thy works, Lord God Almighty; just and true are thy ways* (Rev. 15:3).

Dr. Strong takes the position that neither justice nor righteousness can bestow rewards, in that obedience is due to God and therefore no creature can claim a reward for that which he justly owes. Dr. Pope takes a more scriptural position, insisting that while all that is praiseworthy in human nature is of God, either by prevenient grace or the renewing of the Spirit, there can be no mention of merit except as the word is used in divine condescension. Nevertheless, He who crowns the work of His own hands in glorifying the sanctified believer, constantly speaks of his own works of faith as a matter of reward. *God is not unrighteous to forget your work and labour of love* (Heb. 6:10). *Is God unrighteous who taketh vengeance? (I speak as a man) God forbid: for then how shall God judge the world?* (Rom. 3:5, 6). (Cf. STRONG, *Syst. Th.*, I, p. 293 and POPE, *Compend. Chr. Th.*, I, p. 341.) The rewards of God's judicial or distributive justice are, therefore, according to St. Paul, to be reckoned not of debt but of grace (Rom. 4:4). The last day is, by the same apostle, called the *revelation of the righteous judgment of God* (Rom. 2: 5). We may therefore with confidence believe that the punishment of evil doers, will be at once an infliction of the divine judgment and the consequences of the treasuring up of wrath against the day of wrath. And we may equally assure ourselves that the rewards of the righteous will be at once the decision of a Just Judge, and the fruitage of their own sowing in righteousness.

Truth. This perfection, like justice or righteousness, is closely related to holiness. It is commonly treated from the twofold aspect of veracity and faithfulness. (1) By veracity is meant that all God's manifestations to His creatures, whether natural or supernatural, are in strict conformity to His own divine nature. Thus when the Scriptures speak of the "true" God, the intention is to distinguish Him from the false gods of the heathen; but when they mention Him as the "God of truth," they intend to convey the idea of His veracity. (2) By faithfulness is meant God's fulfillment of His promises, whether these promises are given directly by His Word, or whether they are indirectly implied in the constitution and nature of man.

The Bible abounds with references to both God's veracity and His faithfulness. (1) As to His veracity, the psalmist declares *Thou hast redeemed me, O Lord God of truth* (Psalm 31: 5); *The truth of the Lord endureth forever* (Psalm 117: 2); *The sum of thy word is truth* (Psalm 119: 160, R.V.); and further refers to God as He *which keepeth truth forever* (Psalm 146: 6). The references to truth in the New Testament are equally specific. *Jesus saith unto him, I am the way, the truth, and the life; no man cometh unto the Father, but by me* (John 14: 6). In His high priestly prayer Jesus says, *Sanctify them through thy truth; thy word is truth* (John 17: 17). Here the first clause evidently refers to the faithfulness of God, but this is grounded in His veracity—thy word is truth. St. Paul in his description of the heathen, asserts that *they changed the truth of God into a lie, and worshipped and served the creature more than the Creator* (Rom. 1: 25); and again, *let God be*

true, but every man a liar (Rom. 3:4). The author of
the Epistle to the Hebrews declares that *it is impossible
for God to lie* (Heb. 6:18), while St. John affirms that
*it is the Spirit that beareth witness, because the Spirit is
truth* (I John 5:6). (2) The references to God's faithfulness are equally definite. *He is the Rock, his work is perfect: for all his ways are judgment: a God of truth and
without iniquity, just and right is he* (Deut. 32:4). *The
grass withereth, the flower fadeth; but the word of our
God shall stand forever* (Isa. 40:8). Jesus declared
that *one jot or one tittle shall in no wise pass from the
law, till all be fulfilled* (Matt. 5:18); and again, *He
that hath received his testimony hath set to his seal that
God is true* (John 3:33). The Epistles refer frequently
to the faithfulness of God in the redemptive economy. St.
Paul's prayer for the perfected holiness of believers is
accompanied by the testimony, *Faithful is he that calleth
you, who also will do it* (I Thess. 5:24). In another
prayer for the encouragement of believers, the same
apostle says, *But the Lord is faithful, who shall stablish
you, and keep you from evil* (II Thess. 3:3). St. John
likewise testifies to the faithfulness of God in the work
of salvation. *If we confess our sins, he is faithful and
just to forgive us our sins, and to cleanse us from all unrighteousness* (I John 1:9).

Grace and Its Related Attributes. As justice and
righteousness may be regarded as transitive holiness, so
grace and its related attributes, such as mercy, compassion, longsuffering and forbearance, may with equal
propriety be regarded as transitive love. Thus the love
of God is given different names in accordance with the
different relations which He bears to His creatures and
their condition. Most prominent among these terms,
and peculiarly applicable to the entire redemptive economy is the word grace. It is found in its various deriva-
tives in the following texts: *And all bare him witness,
and wondered at the gracious words which proceeded out
of his mouth* (Luke 4:22). *Let your speech be alway
with grace* (Col. 4:6). *By whom also we have access
by faith into this grace wherein we stand, and rejoice in*

hope of the glory of God (Rom. 5:2). *Thou therefore, my son, be strong in the grace that is in Christ Jesus* (II Tim. 2:1, Cf. also I Peter 5:12, II Peter 3:18). It is frequently used in the benedictions at the close of the epistles. *The grace of our Lord Jesus Christ be with you* (Rom. 16:20, Cf. I Cor. 16:23, II Cor. 13:13, Gal. 6:18, Eph. 6:24). The word is used in the sense of showing favor or giving pleasure in Acts 24:27, and in the sense of alms in II Cor. 8:19.

As grace is unmerited favor exercised toward the unworthy and sinful, so mercy (ἔλεος) is love exercised toward the miserable, and includes both pity and compassion. *Jesus was moved with compassion* (ἐσπλαγχνίσθη, pity or compassion) (Matt. 9:36). Forbearance is love in the deferring or abating of punishment. Like longsuffering it pertains to God's education of men through divine grace. *Or despisest thou the riches of his goodness* [χρηστότητος] *and forbearance* [ἀνοχῆς] *and longsuffering* [μακροθυμίας patience or longsuffering]; *not knowing that the goodness* [χρηστὸν] *of God leadeth thee to repentance* (Rom. 2:4, Cf. also Rom. 9:22). When the love of God is used in respect to men generally, it is known as kindness or philanthropy, and comes from the Greek word φιλανθρωπία (benevolence, kindness or philanthropy). *But after that the kindness* [χρηστότης or goodness] *and love* [φιλανθρωπία or love to man] *of God our Saviour toward man appeared* (Titus 3:4). The word δικαιοσύνης (translated righteousness, Rom. 4:11, Heb. 5:13) is frequently used in the sense of benevolence, as are also the words ἀγαθωσύνη (translated goodness, Gal. 5:22, II Thess. 1:11, Eph. 5:9, Rom. 15:14), and χρηστότης (translated good, Rom. 3:12, kindness, II Cor. 6:6, Gal. 5:22). Here we find the attribute of goodness filling a place in the moral as well as the relative attributes and forming a transition between them.

The grace of God is universal and impartial. He gives to His creatures as much good as it is their capacity to receive. This seems to be the principle according to which He dispenses His favors. *The Lord is good to all;*

and his tender mercies are over all his works (Psalm
145:9). *For as the heaven is high above the earth, so
great is his mercy toward them that fear him* (Psalm
103:11). *But thou, O Lord, art a God full of compassion, and gracious, longsuffering, and plenteous in mercy
and truth* (Psalm 86:15). The grace of God is unmerited and gratuitous. *Now to him that worketh is
the reward not reckoned of grace, but of debt. But to
him that worketh not, but believeth on him that justi-
fieth the ungodly, his faith is counted for righteousness*
(Rom. 4:4).

We have given an extended treatment of the attributes of God, *first,* because the delineation of these perfections in their harmony and proportion is the glory of
theology; and *second,* because the heresies which have
brought the greatest dissension in the Church, have
grown out of an unworthy or perverted notion of the
divine attributes. We may, then, profitably close this
discussion with a summary of the attributes given to us
by Augustine in a passage of great beauty. "Most merciful, yet most just; most hidden, yet most present; most
beautiful, yet most strong; stable, yet incomprehensible;
unchangeable, yet changing all things; never new, never
old; renewing all things, yet bringing age upon the
proud, though they know it not; ever at work, ever at
rest; gathering, yet lacking nothing; supporting and
filling and protecting; creating and nourishing and ma-
turing; seeking, yet having all things. Thou lovest, yet
Thou art not moved by passion; Thou art jealous, yet
Thou art free from anxiety; Thou repentest, yet Thou
dost not grieve; Thou art angry, yet Thou art calm;
Thou changest the works, yet the design Thou dost not
change; Thou receivest again what Thou dost find, yet
Thou hast never lost; Thou art never in need, yet Thou
rejoicest in gains; Thou art never covetous, yet Thou
exactest usury" (Cf. AUGUSTINE, *Confessions,* i:4).

CHAPTER XV

THE TRINITY

The evangelical doctrine of the Trinity affirms that the Godhead is one substance, and that in this one substance there is a trinality of persons. Perhaps the simplest statement of this truth is found in the Nicene Creed which declares "There is but one living and true God. . . . . And in the unity of this Godhead there be Three Persons, of one substance, power and eternity: the Father, the Son, and the Holy Ghost." The doctrine of the Trinity is one of the deepest and most sacred in the Christian system. Stearns points out that St. Augustine in beginning one of the books in his treatise on the Trinity breathes the following prayer: "I pray to our Lord God himself, of whom we ought always to think worthily, in praise of whom blessing is at all times rendered, and whom no speech is sufficient to declare, that He will grant me both help for understanding and explaining that which I design, and pardon if in anything I offend" (*De Trinitate,* v. i, 1) . Whether or not God would have revealed Himself as Trinity, if man had continued sinless, we need not inquire. We do know that it is in the mystery of redemption that this truth comes into clear vision. Reason may have suspected it, but only in the redemptive Christ has it been made visible. Nor can we enter into this most sacred sanctuary of the Christian faith by way of human knowledge, but only through Christ who is the Way as well as the Truth and the Life.

The Experiential Basis of the Doctrine. The doctrine of the Trinity is in the Bible as humid air. The cool wave of reflection through which the church passed, condensed its thought and precipitated what all along had been in solution. While there are philosophical views of the Trinity, yet philosophical analysis probably never could have produced, and certainly did not produce it.

It arose as an expression of experience, and that too, of an experience which was complex and rich. The doctrine is an attempt at simplification, stating and summarizing briefly what is given more at length in the New Testament. It was religion before it was theology, and in order to be effective must again become in each of us, religion as well as theology.

The doctrine of the Trinity is not, therefore, a merely theoretical or speculative one. It is intensely practical. With it is bound up our eternal salvation. It is revealed historically in close connection with redemption, and not merely as an abstract metaphysical or theological conception. God the Father sent His Son into the world to redeem us; God the Son became incarnate in order to save us; and the Holy Spirit applies the redemptive work to our souls. The Trinity, therefore, is vitally involved in the work of redemption, and it is from this practical and religious aspect of the doctrine that the truth must be approached. Because of its bearing on human conduct and destiny, it has been necessary to define it metaphysically in order to prevent its perversion by speculative thought. The doctrine, while receiving contributions from the various systems and types of philosophy, does not owe its origin to any of them, and can never be fully explained by them.

The experience of the apostles and early disciples was intensely religious, rich, luxuriant and all-compelling. The Epistles of St. Paul which form an open gateway to the thought and life of the New Testament, reveal a full-fledged organized religion, a Church living in the ardent belief that Christ as the divinely glorified Son of God, was giving His life to it by the Holy Spirit. But later Judaism into which this new religion came was also a fully organized religion, aflame with faith in one God, the revealed law of God, and the coming of the kingdom of God. It held at least some belief also, in a Messiah who should be connected with the Spirit of the Lord, and by this means inaugurate the new kingdom. What happened between these two viewpoints must furnish the clue to a solution of the problem. *First,* Jesus had appeared in a ministry like that of the old prophets, had later been recognized as the Messiah by some of His disciples, had then claimed the title at Jerusalem, was then regarded with religious awe by His disciples, discredited and put to death by the rulers, leaving behind Him an utterly discouraged and desolate following. *Second,* there had followed immediately many appearances of Jesus risen and glorified, and these had turned the testimony of the disciples into one of triumphant joy. *Third,* after a brief period of tarrying in Jerusalem, there had been the bestowal of the Holy Spirit according to promise; and this had issued in confident and successful missionary effort. These facts were sufficient to bridge the gap, and accounted for the success of the gospel ministry through a continuation of the mystical presence of Christ in the Church. Increasing attention was of necessity given to Christ in the thought of the Church. He was proved to be the Messiah by the resurrection from the dead, and the bestowal of the Divine Spirit. Hence He was invoked in prayer, and without sharp personal distinctions was called God.

THE SCRIPTURAL DEVELOPMENT OF THE DOCTRINE

It is to the sacred Scriptures we must turn, as a foundation for our faith in both the unity and triunity of God. As God can be known only through His self-revelation, so also the Trinitarian distinctions which relate to the inner life of the Godhead can be known in no other way (Cf. I Cor. 2: 10-12).

The Unity of God. That the Lord our God is one Lord, is a truth asserted or implied throughout the entire body of Scripture. In earliest times the Israelite confessed his faith as he does now in the words, *Hear, O Israel: The Lord our God is one Lord* (Deut. 6:4). In the midst of the most seductive forms of polytheism, it was necessary that the Israelite be thoroughly instructed in the divine unity. The first and fundamental commandment therefore was, *Thou shalt have no other gods before me* (Exod. 20:3). Hence we find such statements as *the Lord he is God; there is none else beside him* (Deut. 4:35. Cf. also I Kings 8:60). Of Jehovah Isaiah says, *I am the Lord: that is my name: and my glory will I not give to another, neither my praise to graven images* (Isa. 42:8; and again, *I am the first, and I am the last; and beside me there is no God* (Isa. 44:6). *Is there a God beside me? yea, there is no God; I know not any* (Isa. 44:8). In the New Testament we find the same explicit statements. *And Jesus answered him, The first of all the commandments is, Hear, O Israel; The Lord our God is one Lord* (Mark 12:29). *And this is life eternal, that they might know thee the only true God, and Jesus Christ, whom thou hast sent* (John 17:3). *Is he the God of the Jews only? is he not also of the Gentiles? Yes, of the Gentiles also* (Rom. 3:29). *There is none other God but one. For though there be that are called gods, whether in heaven or in earth (as there be gods many, and lords many,) but to us there is but one God, the Father, of whom are all things, and we in him; and one Lord Jesus Christ, by whom are all things, and we by him* (I Cor. 8:4-6). *Now a mediator is not a mediator of one, but God is one* (Gal. 3:20). (Cf. also I Tim. 1:17, 2:5 and James 2:19.)

The Triunity of God. That God is equally regarded as a Trinity is also clear from the Scriptures. The proof is usually drawn from the theophany at the time of Christ's baptism; and from the fact that in the Scriptures, divine names, divine attributes, divine works and divine worship are ascribed respectively to the Father, to the Son, and to the Holy Spirit. The baptismal formula is the fundamental text, in which two Persons are united with the Father, in a manner not elsewhere found in the Scriptures. *Go ye therefore, and teach all nations, baptizing them in the name of the Father, and of the Son, and of the Holy Ghost* (Matt. 28:19). Closely associated with the baptismal formula are the benedictions which link together the three names of Deity. *The grace of the Lord Jesus Christ, and the love of God, and the communion of the Holy Ghost, be with you all. Amen* (II

Cor. 13:14); and the gifts of the Spirit also as in I Cor. 12:4-6, *Now there are diversities of gifts, but the same Spirit. And there are differences of administrations, but the same Lord. And there are diversities of operations, but it is the same God which worketh all in all.* Since those who acknowledge the existence of a personal God never question His Fatherhood, it is evident that the question concerning the Trinity resolves itself into the proof of the Deity of the Son and the Holy Spirit.

The Old Testament Conception. There has been much discussion in theology as to whether or not the Old Testament gives us a revelation of the Trinity. Among the older dogmatists, Quenstedt maintained that since this doctrine is necessary for salvation, it must have been clearly taught in the Old Testament and known to the Old Testament saints. Calovius likewise taught that the doctrine is explicit in the Old Testament, and found fault with Calixtus for teaching that it was only implicitly there. Modern thought, however, seems to favor the position of Calixtus. Dr. Stump, a Lutheran theologian of the present time, breaks with the thought of the older dogmatists of his church, and asserts that the doctrine of the Trinity is not explicitly taught in the Old Testament, that it is a New Testament truth and could not be known until revealed in Christ, that the Jews never found it there, and had we no revelation but that contained in the Old Testament we should be in ignorance of the doctrine (STUMP, *The Christian Faith,* pp. 47, 48). We may safely take the position that the doctrine of the Trinity, like all other New Testament truths, was contained in germ in the Old Testament; but only with the revelation of God in Christ could it come to full development. In the clear light of the Christian dis-

The doctrine of the Trinity, like every other, had in the mystery of the divine education in the Church, its slow development. Remembering the law, that the progress of Old Testament doctrine must be traced in the light of the New Testament, we can discern throughout the ancient records a preintimation of the Three-One, ready to be revealed in the last time. No word of ancient record is to be studied as standing alone; but according to the analogy of faith, which is no other than the one truth that reigns in the organic whole of Scripture.—POPE, *Compendium of Christian Theology,* I, p. 260.

pensation, there are many passages in the Old Testament which are seen to contain implicitly the doctrine of the Trinity. These intimations are found in references to the plural use of the names of God, the Angel of Jehovah, the Aaronic Benediction, the Trisagion, the use of the terms Word and Wisdom, and the descriptions of the Messiah.

The use of the plural names to designate Deity is frequent in the sacred Scriptures. This is sometimes attributed to the sense of majesty, much as the plural pronouns are used editorially at the present time. Theologians, however, in every age, have asserted that it is impossible to explain the use of the plural rather than singular nouns, unless there be a plurality of persons in the Godhead. Hence there is an allusion to the doctrine of the Trinity, which in the progress of revelation was afterward to be clearly revealed. This plural use is found in the opening sentence of Genesis, where it is stated that *In the beginning God* [*i.e., Elohim* or the Gods] *created the heavens and the earth* (Gen. 1:1). This is found again in verse 26. *And God said, Let us make man in our image, after our likeness,* and also in Gen. 3:22, *And the Lord said, Behold, the man is become as one of us.* Wakefield says that the plural is preferred even when the design is to assert, in the most solemn manner, the unity of God. Thus, *Hear, O Israel, the Lord* [*Elohaynu,* our Gods] *is one Lord* (Deut. 6:4). Nor is the plural restricted simply to the divine names. It applies to other terms which refer to the Divine Being. *If I be a Father* [*Adonim,* Masters] *where is my fear?* (Mal. 1:6). *Remember* [*Eth Boreka,* thy Creators] *in the days of thy youth* (Eccles. 12:1). *For thy maker* [*Boalaik Osaik,* thy Makers] *is thy husband* (Isa. 54:5). (Cf. WAKEFIELD, *Christian Theology,* p. 182). The *Angel of Jehovah* as used from Genesis to Malachi is another expression which contains implicitly the thought of the Trinity. The "Angel" is the Messenger or manifestation of God, which although separated from God is nevertheless identified with Him. While the phrase is sometimes used to denote a human messenger and at other times a created angel, it is with these few exceptions used to designate the pre-incarnate Logos. His manifestations in angelic or human form, preshadowed His appearance in the flesh. In one instance (Exodus 23: 20, 21) there is a reference to Jehovah, to the Angel of Jehovah and to the Spirit, the latter being found in the expression, *My name is in him*. The word Angel is sometimes used with the plural Elohim. The Aaronic Benediction uses the word *Jehovah* in a threefold sense. *Jehovah bless thee, and keep thee; Jehovah make his face to shine upon thee, and be gracious unto thee; Jehovah lift up his countenance upon thee, and give thee peace* (Numbers 6: 24-27). The three members of this form may be said to correspond to the "love of the Father," "the grace of the Lord Jesus Christ," and the "communion of the Holy Ghost" (Cf. II Cor. 13: 14).

Closely related to this is the *Trisagion* or threefold use of the word "holy" in the act of adoration. As the inner place of the Jewish sanctuary was known as the "Holy of Holies" we may understand this to mean the Holy Place of the Holy Ones. Here it was that the seraphim veiled their faces and cried one to another and said, *Holy, holy, holy, is the Lord of hosts* (Isa. 6: 3). This is an act of adoration in which the term holy is used equally and appropriately of each of the Persons in the adorable Trinity and is answered from the more excellent glory in the same language of plurality. *Also I heard the voice of the Lord, saying, Whom shall I send, and who will go for us?* (Isa. 6: 8). It is interesting to note the Trinitarian treatment of this scripture by the New Testament writers, St. John and St. Paul. The term "Lord of Hosts" is everywhere acknowledged as a reference to the Father. St. John regarded the vision as referring to Christ the Son when he wrote, *These things said Esaias, when he saw his glory and spake of him* (John 12: 41). In the previous verse reference is made to the futility of the mission as committed to Isaiah the prophet (Cf. John 12: 39, 40 and Isa. 6: 9-11), a prophecy which St. Paul attributes to the Holy Spirit. *Well spake the Holy Ghost by Esaias the prophet unto our fathers, Saying, Go unto this people, and say, Hearing ye shall hear, and shall not understand; and seeing ye shall see, and not perceive* (Acts 28:25, 26). Here then the Trisagion is by later Scripture regarded as a reference to the Trinity. The descriptions of the Messiah found in the Old Testament refer implicitly to the Trinity also, but these will be considered in a later paragraph. It is sufficient to mention but two of them here. Isaiah in referring to the Messiah says, *And now the Lord God, and his Spirit, hath sent me* (Isa. 48:16) words manifestly spoken by the Messiah who declares Himself to be sent by the *Lord God* and his Spirit. The second reference is similar and is found in Haggai 2:4-7, *I am with you, saith the Lord of hosts: according to the word that I covenanted with you when ye came out of Egypt, so my Spirit remaineth among you; fear ye not. For thus saith the Lord of hosts; . . . . I will shake all nations, and the Desire of all nations shall come.* Here there is a threefold reference to the *Lord of hosts,* his Spirit, and the Messiah as the *Desire of all nations.*

The Son and the Spirit in the Old Testament. There is no direct and immediate foreannouncement of the Son in the Old Testament, because the Fatherhood of God was not as such revealed. Both the Fatherhood and the Sonship are New Testament revelations and the one waited for the other. But the idea of sonship permeates the entire Old Testament Scriptures, from the first verse of Genesis to the last verse of Malachi. Occasional mention of the Son may be admitted also. We have already indicated that intimations of the Second Person of the Trinity are to be found first of all in such expressions as "the Angel of Jehovah," "the Word or Wisdom," and the descriptions of the Messiah. The "Angel of the Lord" refers directly to the eternal Logos, who while distinct from Jehovah is yet Jehovah himself. *And the angel of the Lord called unto Abraham out of heaven the second time, and said, By myself have I sworn, saith the Lord* (Gen. 22:15, 16). Here the "angel of the Lord" is clearly identified with Jehovah. It was the "angel of the Lord" who called to Moses out of the burning bush and said, *I am the God of thy father, the God of Abraham, the God of Isaac, and the God of Jacob. And Moses hid his face; for he was afraid to look upon God* (Exod. 3:6). (Cf. also, Gen. 16:9-11; Gen. 48:14; Exod. 23:20, 21; Judges 13:20-22). The second intimation of the Divine Sonship is found in the use of the terms "Word" and "Wisdom," which express in a clearer manner the Divine Logos which was to become incarnate in the likeness of men. The "Word" appears in veiled form in the third verse of Genesis. *And God said, Let there be light: and there was light* (Gen. 1:3). The word "said" is the first intimation of the Logos or Word. This appears in clearer form in the personification of Wisdom found in the eighth chapter of Proverbs, and a portion of the ninth. Here Lady Wisdom appears in contrast with Madame Folly (Prov. 9:13-18). *Doth not wisdom cry? . . . . The Lord possessed me in the beginning of his way, before his works of old. . . . . Then was I by him, as one brought up with him: and I was daily his delight, rejoicing always before him* (Prov. 8:1, 22, 30). We may say, therefore, that the Word appears at first in abstract form, then as personified, and later as *the Word made flesh* (John 1:1-18). It is in the descriptions of the Messiah that we find the clearest vision of the Second Person of the Trinity as the Divine Son. *For unto us a child is born, unto us a son is given: and the government shall be upon his shoulder: and his name shall be called Wonderful, Counsellor, The mighty God, the Everlasting Father, The Prince of Peace* (Isa. 9:6).

Throughout the Gospels, from Gabriel's testimony to the angel greater than he, downwards, there is no question that the Jehovah-Angel is Jehovah himself, and that Jehovah himself reappears in the name Lord, very often though not exclusively. Not Esaias alone, but all the Old Testament writers, *saw his glory and spake of him* (John 12:41). But the uncreated minister of Jehovah's will is not generally in the Old Testament foreannounced as the Son, any more than Jehovah is revealed as the Father. This, however, is not quite wanting. The link that connects the Angel of the Face in the ancient with the Son in the later Scripture is threefold. He is in the Psalms and Prophecy termed the Son expressly, the Word or Oracle of God or hypostatised Wisdom; and He is called *Adonai* or Lord, the Mighty God. But these more occasional testimonies flow into a general representation of the future Messiah; and as such they must be reserved for the fuller exhibition of the Mediatorial Trinity, and the Person of Christ.—POPE, *Compendium of Christian Theology,* I, p. 263.

*But thou, Bethlehem Ephratah, though thou be little
among the thousands of Judah, yet out of thee shall he
come forth unto me that is to be ruler in Israel: whose
goings forth have been from of old, from everlasting*
(Micah 5:2). *Thy throne, O God, is for ever and ever:
the sceptre of thy kingdom is a right sceptre. Thou lovest
righteousness and hatest wickedness: Therefore God, thy
God, hath anointed thee with the oil of gladness above
thy fellows* (Psalm 45:6, 7. Cf. Heb. 1:8, 9). *Behold, I
will send my messenger, and he shall prepare the way
before me: and the Lord, whom ye seek, shall suddenly
come to his temple, even the messenger of the covenant,
whom ye delight in: behold, he shall come, saith the Lord
of hosts*" (Mal. 3:1). This is the "Angel of the Covenant," the Christ who ushered in the New Dispensation.

The Son and the Spirit in the New Testament. It is to
the New Testament that we must turn for the full revelation of the Son as the Second Person of the Trinity; and
for the personality and deity of the Holy Ghost as the
adorable Third Person. Such is the wealth of expression found in the Scriptures that it will be impossible to
consider the full range of their teachings and we must
therefore confine our discussion to a few outstanding
proof texts.

The deity of Christ is sustained by the following
classes of scripture: (1) Those which refer to His pre-
existence. *He that cometh after me is preferred before
me, for he was before me* (John 1:15). *Verily, verily,
I say unto you, before Abraham was, I am* (John 8:58).
I am the living bread which came down from heaven
(John 6:51). *No man hath ascended up to heaven, but
he that came down from heaven, even the Son of man
which is in heaven* (John 3:13). *And now, O Father,
glorify thou me with thine own self, with the glory which
I had with thee before the world was* (John 17:5).

In considering these passages, Strong points out that no Jewish writer
before Christ had succeeded in constructing from them a doctrine of the
Trinity. Only in the light of the New Testament do they show their real
meaning. His conclusion is that they do not by themselves furnish a sufficient basis for the doctrine of the Trinity, but that they contain the germ
of it, and may be used in confirmation of it when its truth is substantially
proved from the New Testament.—STRONG, *Systematic Theology*, I, p. 322.

Here it is clear that Christ had an existence, not only before His incarnation but before the foundation of the world. (2) Divine names and titles are applied to Christ. He is called Lord (Κύριος), *Prepare ye the way of the Lord* (Matt. 3:3; Cf. Isa. 40:3). *Whosoever shall call upon the name of the Lord shall be saved* (Rom. 10:13; Cf. Joel 3:32 where the term *Jehovah* is used). Thomas addresses Him as *My Lord and my God* (John 20:28) and Peter calls Him *Lord of all* (Acts 10:36). He is called God. *In the beginning was the Word, and the Word was with God, and the Word was God* (John 1:1). *And of whom, as concerning the flesh, Christ came, who is over all, God blessed forever* (Rom. 9:5). *Looking for that blessed hope, and the glorious appearing of the great God and our Saviour Jesus Christ* (Titus 2:13). *And we are in him that is true, even in his Son Jesus Christ. This is the true God, and eternal life* (I John 5:20). (3) Divine attributes are ascribed to Christ, such as aseity or self-existence (John 2:19, 10:17, 18, John 5:26); eternity (John 1:1, 2, 17:5, 24, Heb. 1:8, 10-12, I John 1:2); omnipresence (Matt. 18:20, 28:30, John 3:13, Eph. 1:21); omniscience (Matt. 9:4, 12:25, Mark 2:8, Luke 6:8, 9:47, 10:22, John 1:48, 2:24, 25, 10:15, 16:30, 21:17, Col. 2:3, Rev. 2:23); omnipotence, (Matt. 28:18, Luke 21:15, John 1:3, 10:18, I Cor. 1:24, Eph. 1:22, Phil. 3:21, Col. 2:10, Rev. 1:18); immutability (Heb. 1:11, 12, 13:8). (4) Divine works are ascribed to Christ. Creation (John 1:3, 10, I Cor. 8:6, Col. 1:16, Heb. 1:10); He upholds and preserves all things (Col. 1:17, Heb. 1:3); He forgives sins (Mark 2:5-10, Luke 5:20-24, 7:47-49, Acts 5:31); He gives the Holy Spirit (Luke 24:40, John 16:7, 20:22, Acts 2:33). He gives peace (John 14:27, 16:33, Rom. 15:33, 16:20, II Cor. 13:11, Phil. 4:9, I Thess. 5:23, Heb. 13:30); light (John 1:4-9, 8:12, 9:5, 12:35, 46, I John 1:5-7, Rev. 21:23); eternal life (John 17:2) and confers spiritual gifts (Eph. 4:8-13); (5) Divine worship is offered to Christ. *They worshipped him, saying, Of a truth thou art the Son of God* (Matt. 14:33; Cf. also Luke 24:51,

52, Acts 1:24, 7:59, 60, Heb. 1:6, Rev. 5:13). Here may be mentioned also the doxologies, ascriptions of praise, and benedictions. *To him be glory, both now and forever. Amen* (II Peter 3:18). *Unto him that hath loved us, and washed us from our sins in his own blood, and hath made us kings and priests unto God and his Father, to him be glory and dominion for ever and ever. Amen* (Rev. 1:5, 6). *Grace to you, and peace from God our Father, and the Lord Jesus Christ* (Rom. 1:7). *The grace of the Lord Jesus Christ, and the love of God, and the communion of the Holy Ghost, be with you all* (II Cor. 13:14).

The personality and deity of the Holy Spirit does not require the same extended discussion, as that which has just been given to the deity of the Son, inasmuch as many of the principles involved have already been considered. That the Person of the Holy Spirit is distinct from that of the Father and the Son is clearly taught in the Scriptures. He is called "the Spirit," "the Spirit of God," "the Holy Spirit," "the Spirit of glory." He is spoken of by our Lord as "the Comforter" or "another Comforter." That the Holy Spirit is more than an attribute or an influence is brought out clearly in the words of our Lord, *I will pray the Father, and he shall give you another Comforter, that he may abide with you forever* (John 14:16). *But the Comforter, which is the Holy Ghost, whom the Father will send in my name, he shall teach you all things, and bring all things to your remembrance, whatsoever I have said unto you* (John 14:26). Here the Holy Spirit is expressly stated to be the Third Person, as the Father is the First and the Son the Second in the Holy Trinity. There are certain texts, also, where it would be mere redundancy to speak of the Holy Spirit as a power or influence from God. *God anointed Jesus of Nazareth with the Holy Ghost and with power* (Acts 10:38). *That ye may abound in hope, through the power of the Holy Ghost* (Rom. 15:13). Here it is evident that the Holy Spirit cannot be regarded as a power, but must be thought of as a person. Again, there are distinct symbolical representations of the Holy Ghost, as the dove at the baptism of Jesus and the rushing wind and the tongues of fire at Pentecost. But the highest evidence is the fact that the personal pronoun with a neuter noun is used in reference to the Holy Spirit. It is a departure from the ordinary rule to use a masculine pronoun with a neuter noun, says Dr. Charles Hodge, unless the masculine is warranted by the fact that the person referred to may be called "He." Hence the use of the masculine pronoun is strong evidence that the writers of Sacred Scripture intended to set forth the personality of the Holy Spirit.

The deity of the Holy Spirit may be proved scripturally, by a collation of texts as in the case of the Divine Sonship. The name of God, His attributes, His works and His worship are all applied to the Holy Spirit. We can give only a few instances of the many found in the scriptures: *Why hath Satan filled thine heart to lie to the Holy Ghost? Thou hast not lied unto man, but unto God* (Acts 5:3, 4). The Apostle Paul in his reference to spiritual gifts attributes them to *that self-same Spirit* and concludes with the statement that *it is the same God which worketh all in all* (I Cor. 12:6-11). He also applies the term "Lord" to the Holy Spirit, *Now the Lord is that Spirit: and where the Spirit of the Lord is, there is liberty* (II Cor. 3:17). The work of Inspiration, as has been pointed out, is peculiarly the office of the Spirit. Hence we read that *God spake unto the fathers by the prophets* (Heb. 1:1). St. Peter attributes this inspiration to the Spirit, *holy men of God spake as they were moved by the Holy Ghost* (II Peter 1:21) and further to *the Spirit of Christ which was in them* (I Peter 1:11).

THE DEVELOPMENT OF THE DOCTRINE IN THE CHURCH

During the apostolic and subapostolic period, the doctrine of the Trinity was held in an undogmatic form. There was no scientific or technical expression of it, nor was there any necessity, until heresies arose which demanded exact and guarded statements. The fact of this indefiniteness, however, has been pressed too far by the rationalists. The Apostolic and Primitive Fathers faithfully reproduce the spirit of the New Testament.

In creation we see Him moving upon the face of chaos, and reducing it to beauty and order; in providence, renewing the earth, garnishing the heavens, and giving life to man. In grace we behold Him expanding the prophetic scene to the vision of the seers of the Old Testament, and making a perfect revelation of the doctrines of Christ to the apostles of the New. He reproves the world of sin, working in the human heart a secret conviction of its evil and danger. He is "the spirit of grace and supplication"; and from Him are the softened heart, the yielding will, and all heavenly desires and tendencies. He hastens to the troubled spirit of penitent men, who are led by His influences to trust in Christ, with the news of pardon; bearing witness with their spirit that they are the children of God. He helps their infirmities; makes intercession for them; inspires thoughts of consolation and feelings of peace; plants and perfects in them whatever things are pure, lovely, honest, and of good report; dwells in the soul as in a temple; and, after having rendered the spirit to God, without *spot or wrinkle, or any such thing,* finishes his benevolent and glorious work by raising the bodies of the saints at the last day, to immortality and eternal life. So powerfully does the *Spirit of glory and of God* claim our love, our praise, our obedience! Hence, in the forms of the Christian Church he has been constantly associated with the Father and the Son in equal glory and blessing; and this recognition of the Holy Spirit ought to be made in every gratulatory act of devotion, that so equally to each person of the eternal Trinity glory may be given *in the church throughout all ages. Amen.*—WAKEFIELD, *Christian Theology,* p. 233.

For further study we give the following collation of Scriptures concerning the personality of the Holy Spirit: (1) It is stated that He proceeds from the Father (John 15:26) and that He is given or sent by the Father (John 14:16, 26; Acts 5:32) and by the Son, (John 15:26, 16:7, Acts 2:33). (2) He is called the Spirit of the Father (Eph. 3:16) and also the Spirit of Christ or of the Son (Rom. 8:9, Gal. 4:6). He is distinguished from the Father and the Son in such passages as the following; (Matt. 3:16, 17, 28:19, John 14:26, 16:13, Acts 2:33, Eph. 2:18, I Cor. 12:4-6, II Cor. 13:14, I Peter 1:2). (3) Proofs may be drawn also from his personal action and emotion. He is active (Gen. 1:2, Matt. 3:16, Acts 8:39); teaches and instructs, (Luke 12:12, John 14:26, 16:8, 13, 14, Acts 10:19, I Cor. 12:3); witnesses of Christ to the people, and to believers of their sonship, (John 15:26, Rom. 8:16, II Cor. 1:22, 5:5, Eph. 1:13, 14, 4:30); He is a Guide (Rom. 8:14) and dwells within the sons of God, to us revealing the Divine presence, (John 14:16, 17, Rom. 8:9-11, I Cor. 3:16, 17, 6:19); He may be grieved (Eph. 4:30); resisted, (Acts 7:51), and vexed (Isa. 63:10); He strives with men (Gen. 6:3), intercedes for them (Rom. 8:26, 27) and inspires them (Acts 2:4, 8:29, 13:2, 15:28, II Peter 1:21).

The deity of the Holy Spirit may be proved in the same manner as that of the Son. Creation is ascribed to Him (Gen. 1:2, Job 26:13, Psalm 104:30); divine attributes belong to Him (Psalm 139:7-10, 11, I Cor. 2:10); and He searches the deep things of God (I Cor: 2:10). The deity of the Holy Spirit is also clear from His relationship to Christ (birth, Matt. 1:18-20, Luke 1:31-35; baptism, Matt. 3:16, John 1:33; temptation, Matt. 4:1, Mark 1:12; ministry, Luke 4:14-21; power over evil spirits, Matt. 12:28). His spiritual influence is said to be without measure, John 3:34, and He is expressly called God by Peter in connection with Ananias and Sapphira.

They apply the term God (Θεός) to Jesus Christ whom they commonly conceive of as the God-man. Clement of Rome writes, "Brethren we ought to conceive of Jesus Christ as God, as of the judge of the living and the dead" (Ep. II, 1). Ignatius greets the church at Ephesus as "united and elected by a true passion, according to the will of the Father, and of Jesus Christ our God"; and to Rome as "illuminated by the will of Him who willeth all things that are according to the love of Jesus Christ our God"; and urges them "to mind invisible rather than earthly things," "for even our God Jesus Christ being in the Father is more glorified." The Primitive Fathers, Justin Martyr (c. 163), and Clement of Alexandria (c. 220), represent the Greek Trinitarianism; and Irenæus (c. 202), Hippolytus (c. 235) and Tertullian (c. 220) the Latin Trinitarianism. All of these held to the two fundamental catholic positions, a unity of essence and a distinction of persons as set forth in John 10: 30, *I and my Father are one*, that is, one being, not one person (ἐλὼ καὶ ὁ Πατὴρ ἕν [not ἐις] ἐσμεν).

It was not long after the close of the apostolic period, however, that the seeds of error began to germinate and various heresies arose in the Church. It should be borne in mind that the construction of the doctrine of the Trinity in its theological form did not so much grow out of a consideration of the three Persons, as from a belief in the deity of the Son. The highly metaphysical doctrine, therefore, sprang from a vital belief among primitive Christians, that Christ was the coequal Son of God.

Against those who would criticize the scientific statement of the Trinitarian doctrine, Dr. Shedd says, "Many a man in the very bosom of the church at this day cherishes a belief in the Triune God that involves a speculative definition of the three Persons and their mutual relations, which in his present lack of theological discipline he could no more give with exactness, and without deviation toward Sabellianism on the right hand and Arianism on the left, than he could specify the chemical elements of the air he breathes, or map the sky under whose dome he walks every day. The same fact meets us upon the wider arena of the universal Church. The Christian experience is one and the same in all ages and periods, but the ability to make scientific statement of those doctrines which are received by the believing soul, varies with the peculiar demands for such statements, and the intensity with which, in peculiar emergencies, the theological mind is directed toward them.— SHEDD, *History of Christian Doctrine*, I, pp. 246, 247.

Both Irenæus and Tertullian connected the Son and the Spirit with the Father to form a triad which tended toward either dytheism or tritheism accordingly as the Spirit was regarded as personal or impersonal. To safeguard against this, the idea of subordination was introduced which gave precedence to the Father and led immediately to what Tertullian first called Monarchism. "To be sure the plain people," he says, "not to call them ignorant and common—of whom the greater portion of believers is always composed . . . . shrink back from the economy. . . . . They are constantly throwing out the accusation that we preach two gods and three gods. . . . . We hold, they say, the monarchy" (Adv. Prax 3). Thus there arose the acute problem of attempting to relate Christ to God and yet preserve the belief in monotheism. Monarchism was a vain attempt to reconcile the Trinity with the essential unity of the Godhead, and took many forms. They all agreed in denying the deity of Christ and the Holy Spirit, and maintained that the Father alone is God. The first, or Dynamistic form, which regarded Christ as a creature, found its development in Origen's subordinationism and later in Arianism. The second form, known as Modalistic or Sabellian, identified Christ with the Father and regarded the Trinity solely as economic, that is, simply as three modes of manifestation. The Father, the Son and the Holy Spirit were therefore the same Divine Person manifesting Himself in different capacities.

Antitrinitarian Theories. Theologians usually classify the Antitrinitarian theories as (1) Monarchianism; (2) Nominal Trinitarianism; and (3) Humanitarianism. Dr. Shedd and Dr. Foster both use this classification. (1) *Monarchianism.* The Monarchians, through a misapprehension of the nature of divine unity, held that the Trinity was irreconcilable with it. God the Fa-

---

The earliest tradition not only spoke of Jesus as κύριος, σωτήρ and διδάσκαλος, but as ὁ υἱὸς τοῦ Θεοῦ, and this name was firmly adhered to in the Gentile Christian communities. It followed immediately from this that Jesus belongs to the sphere of God, and that, as is said in the earliest preaching known to us, one must think of Him ὡς περὶ Θεοῦ.— HARNACK, *Hist. of Dogma*, I, p. 186.

ther was the only Person, who becoming incarnate they called God the Son, or Logos. In this incarnate form, it was the Father himself who suffered for the sin of mankind. For this reason they were called Patripassionists or Father-sufferers. They denied a proper soul in the person of Jesus Christ, maintaining that He was God in alliance with a physical organization, but having no real human nature. The principal representatives of this form or Monarchianism were Praxeas (c. 200), who was opposed by Tertullian in his tract, *Adversus Praxean;* Nœtus (c. 230) opposed by Hippolytus in his *Contra Hœresin Nœti;* and Beryl (c. 250) an Arabian bishop who later was convinced of his error and renounced his Patripassionism. (2) *Nominal Trinitarianism.* This form of Monarchianism held that Christ was divine but not true Deity. The distinction between "divinity" and "deity" has held an important place in the history of Trinitarianism. The Logos was not regarded as a Person, but only the Divine Wisdom or Reason which emanated from Essential Deity, and united itself in a pre-eminent manner with the man Jesus at His birth. Because illuminated in a higher degree than any of the prophets before Him, the man Jesus was called the Son of God. The chief representative of Nominal Trinitarianism was Paul of Samosata, Bishop of Antioch (c. 260). He was pronounced heretical by two Antiochian synods, and after much delay was deposed from his office. Sabellius occupied a mediating position between this and the preceding forms of Monarchianism. His teachings will be presented in a later paragraph. (3) *Humanitarianism.* The Humanitarians asserted the mere and sole humanity of Christ and denied His divinity in any form. Some held to the ordinary humanity and others to an extraordinary humanity. Here we may class the Ebionites, Theodotians, Artemonites, Alogoi and Cerinthians. They were so far afield from the commonly accepted teachings of Scripture that the Church engaged in no conflict or controversy with them.

Sabellianism. This form of Monarchianism adopted the Modal Theory of the Trinity. It rejected the theory

of three hypostases or Persons, and substituted, instead
three *prosopa* or faces or semblances, corresponding to
the three dispensations of the Father, the Son and the
Holy Spirit. The doctrine was first taught by Praxeas
in Rome, Nœtus in Smyrna and Beryl in Arabia, but it
remained for Sabellius (c. 250-260) Presbyter of Ptole-
mais in Pentapolis to more fully develop the error which
has taken his name. He held that God manifested Himself in three personal modes. God as Father is Creator;
and manifested through the Incarnation the same God
is known as the Son and fulfills the office of redeemer;
and lastly, as the Holy Spirit, God carries on His spiritual ministry in the Church. The principle is pantheistic for it is the same God evolving Himself as Jehovah,
then more clearly to His creatures as the Son, and still
more fully and spiritually as the Holy Spirit. The only
point which satisfied the Christian faith was the deity
of the Son, but in asserting this, Sabellianism denied the
distinct personality of the Father and the Holy Spirit.
Its opposition to the scriptural position was clear, for
there the Father is constantly addressing the Son,
and the Son the Father. Dr. Shedd regards the position
of Sabellius as midway between Patripassionism and
Nominal Trinitarianism. He belongs to the first class
in that he denied that Christ was merely an ordinary
man upon whom the Divine Logos exerted a peculiar
influence, and affirmed that the Logos power belonged
to the proper personality of Christ. He approaches the
second class in that he regards the Logos and the Holy
Spirit as two powers ($\delta \upsilon \nu \acute{\alpha} \mu \epsilon \iota \varsigma$) streaming forth from
the Divine Essence, through which God works and re-
veals Himself (Cf. SHEDD, *History of Christian Doctrine*, I, p. 257). The decisive blow against Monarchianism was struck by Origen of the Alexandrian School,
in his *De Principiis* or First Principles, a work generally
acknowledged to be the first positive and systematic presentation of Christian doctrine.

Arianism. At the other extreme from Sabellianism is
Arianism, which takes its name from the Presbyter
Arius (256-336), who held an important position in the

Church of Alexandria at the time the controversy with Bishop Alexander began, about 318 A.D. There were two stages in the full development of Arianism, (1) that of subordinationism as advocated by Origen, but which assumed various forms as presented by different writers: and (2) Arianism proper, which found expression in the teachings of Arius himself.

1. The Subordinationism of Origen grew out of an attempt to explain the doctrine of the Trinity in the light of the current philosophy of his time. The Gnostics had upheld the Monarchian principle, by maintaining a series of emanations from what was known as Primal Being. The Neo-Platonists, especially Philo, had modified Platonism and applied this philosophy to the theology of the Old Testament. The Logos according to both Plato and Philo was the collective term for the ideal world. It was the Divine Reason, which containing in itself the ideas or types of all things, became in turn the living principles by which all actual existences are formed. In the development of the Philonic Logos, the term came to be used in a twofold manner: (1) as transcendent Reason, apart from its manifestation, to which the term *Logos endiathetos* (λόγος ἐνδιάθετος) was applied; and (2) as a personal existence begotten in the Divine Essence, and as such the Divine Archetype or Firstborn of Creation. To this term *Logos prosphorikos* (λόγος προσφορικός) was applied, although Philo used other terms, especially βιός or life, δόξα or glory (as used in the New Testament) and δεύτερος Θεός a second or other God. In the first or transcendent sense, the Logos was merely impersonal and eternal reason. It was the sum or total of all the ideas and types, which in an abstract sense, existed as the archetypal forms in which created existences were to appear. In the second or personal sense, especially in its later development, the

The writers during the first three centuries of the church may be classified as follows: (1) The catholic doctrine of the Trinity: Justin Martyr, Theophilus of Antioch, Athenagoras, Irenæus, Clement of Alexandria, Tertullian, Origen, Dionysius of Alexandria, Cyprian, Novatian and Dionysius of Rome. (II) Monarchians or Unitarians: Theodotus, Artemon and Paul of Samosata. (III) Patripassionists or Sabellians: Praxeas, Noetus, Beryllus of Bostra and Sabellius.

Logos was the self-manifestation of God, which in creation had its birth and was sent forth or projected, as giving form and life to all things. It was divine but subordinate, divinity but not deity, except in a limited and accommodated sense. Those who held to the Monarchian principle, attempted to explain the Trinity on the basis of the concealed or hidden God, revealing Himself by two Powers streaming forth like rays of light from the sun. The one was an illuminating Power, the Logos or Divine Reason, existing *first* as the reflective reason of the Deity by which He is capable of rational intelligence (λόγος ἐνδιάθετος), and *second*, the outworking of that self-expressive reason, whereby He creates and communicates with His creation, (λόγος προσφορικός). As the Logos was the illuminating Power, so the Holy Spirit was the enlivening Power, but neither were regarded as hypostases, only emanations. Justin Martyr, Tatian and Theophilus, on the other hand, applied the term Logos to Christ, but in the sense of hypostasis, and therefore asserted His personality. Justin in his *Apologia* (I, 13) declares, "We worship the Creator of this universe. . . . . Again we have learned that He who taught us these things, and who for this end was born, even Jesus Christ . . . . was the Son of Him who is truly called God; and we esteem Him the second place. And that we with reason honor the Prophetic Spirit in the third rank, we shall hereafter shew." While Christ was by this means exalted above all creatures, it did not meet the demands of the Christian consciousness, in that it made the divinity

The learned Christians of the second century confined their discussions of the Trinity largely to the Logos, a term applied in the New Testament to Christ. These philosophizing Christians connected in general the same idea with the term Logos as was done by Philo and the other Platonists, and consequently in many instances drifted far from the Johannine conception. The Neo-Platonists understood by the term Logos, the infinite understanding of God, which they conceived to be a substance which emanated with its functions from God. They supposed that it belonged from eternity to His nature as a power, but that agreeably to the divine will, as Justin expresses it, it began to exist out of the divine nature, and is therefore different from God its Creator and Father, and yet as begotten of Him, is entirely divine. The Holy Spirit was more rarely mentioned by these early Fathers, and their views respecting Him are far less clearly expressed than concerning the Son.—Cf. KNAPP, *Christian Theology*, p. 149.

of Christ essentially subordinate, and His generation antemundane, but not eternal. They saw that after all the distinction between the hidden God (ὁ Θεός) or God in Himself, and the Logos, (Θεός), or God in nature, was but a revamping of the pagan pantheism which makes the universe a manifestation of the existence of God.

It is at this point that the work of Origen begins, his deductions being of such importance that they mark an epoch in the history of Trinitarianism. Origen lifted the doctrine of the Logos to a higher plane, and introduced in his speculative thought, the idea of eternal generation. Tertullian had identified the Logos with the Son, and both he and Irenæus differed from Justin in that they employed the word "Son" more frequently than the term "Logos." They thereby brought more of the personal element into the doctrine. But Origen grasped more fully than his predecessors the idea of sonship and its importance. This led him to assert that the Son was as truly a hypostasis as the Father, and that to either, the personal pronouns could be strictly applied. He associated the Holy Spirit in dignity with the Father and the Son, but maintained that He had not the same immediate relation to the Father as did the Son, although He has direct knowledge and searches the deep things of God. Origen endeavored to harmonize the Trinity of Persons with the unity of essence by employing the idea of eternal generation. By this he meant, the eternal generation of the Son by the will of the Father. There are two momenta here, *first*, a subordination of the hypostasis of the Son to that of the Father in respect to essence, and *second*, creation as opposed to emanation. Origen opposed the idea that the Logos was merely antemundane and came into full expression through birth in creation, and asserted instead an eternal existence of the Logos. He objected to the position of the emanationists that the Son is generated out of the essence of the Father, and maintained that the generation of the Son proceeds eternally from the will of the Father. He was concerned primarily with the personality of the Son as over against Monarchianism, but he so interpreted this relationship as to make the Son subordinate in essence. Basing his discussion upon John 1:1 he makes a distinction between God (Θεός) as divinity, and the God (ὁ Θεός) as deity. He uses, therefore, the article in referring to the Father or God as unbegotten, and omits it when the Logos or Word is denominated God. This leads him to adopt that form of subordinationism which holds that the Son does not participate in the self-subsistent substance of the Deity and therefore it is not proper to use the term *homoousios* (ὁμοούσιος) of the Son as being consubstantial with the Father. This furnished the basis upon which Arius later developed his idea of the creaturehood of Christ. Yet at the same time, Origen denied that Christ was a creature, insisting that he is of a nature "midway between that of the Uncreated and that of all creatures." This distinction between the Son and the created universe, he maintains, lies in this, that the Son derives his divinity (Θεὸς) immediately from the Absolute Deity (ὁ Θεὸς), while the universe derives its being immediately through the Son who is the Logos or first ground and cause of all things. In proof of this he cites John 5:26, *For as the Father hath life in himself; so hath he given to the Son to have life in himself,* that is, God the Father (ὁ Θεός) has given to God the Son (Θεός) to have life in Himself; and therefore He becomes the Creator of the world, which in relationship to God, is one degree farther removed. In this sense He cannot be classed wholly with the creatures. Origen, therefore, denies "that there was a time when He was not," and on this ground was cited as an authority by the Athanasians in their opposition to the Arians.

2. Arianism proper was the most formidable enemy encountered in the development of the Trinitarian doctrine. Arius was from the school of Lucian of Antioch, where the dynamic Monarchianism of Paul Samosata was the dominating influence. This, conjoined with the Jewish idea of transcendency, prejudiced him in favor of the unity of God to the disparagement of the Trinitarian concept. Arius sought to find a place for Christ

above that of creation, and yet outside the Godhead. Beginning with the idea of subordinationism as advanced by Origen, the ultimate effect of his teaching was to make both Christ and the Holy Spirit created beings. God alone was eternal, and could not therefore communicate His substance to any created being. Furthermore, he regarded the unity of God in such a transcendent manner, that it not only excluded all distinctions within the Godhead, but also all contacts without it. When God would create the world, it was necessary for Him first to create the Son or "Word" as His Agent. The Son as a creature suggests that God was not always Father but became such only in the creation of the Son, who, therefore, was of a different essence from the Father. The Son, however, was different from other creatures by way of pre-eminence, so that we may speak of him as "God only Begotten." Arius explains his view in a letter addressed to Eusebius of Nicomedia as follows: "But we say and believe, and have taught and do teach, that the Son is not unbegotten, nor in any way unbegotten, even in part; and that He does not derive His subsistence from anything subjacent; but that by His own will and counsel He has subsisted before time, and before ages, as perfect God, only begotten and unchangeable, and that He existed not before He was begotten, or created, or determined, or established. For He was not unbegotten. We are persecuted because we say that the Son had a beginning, but that God was without beginning. We repeat it—for this we are persecuted, and also because we say that He is from nothing. And this we affirm, because He is neither part of God, nor of anything subjacent." According to Arius, Christ took only a human body in the incarnation, not a human soul; and the Holy Spirit bears the same relation to the Son that the Son does to the Father.

As the doctrine of the Trinity grew out of the devotional life of the Church and not out of philosophy, so it was its devotional consciousness and not its philosophy that rejected the Arian heresy. If Christ was not God, then to worship Him was idolatry. Again as

Athanasius pointed out, Arianism destroyed the ground of redemption in Christ. If He was neither God nor man, He could not be a mediator; and if He could not himself know the Father, how could He reveal Him to others. Thus the Church then, as since that time, has rejected every attempt to make Christ a mere creature. The chief value of the Arian controversy lay in the fact that it forced the Church to clarify its belief in the Trinity, and to so state this belief as to include Jesus Christ within the eternal being of God. This it has done in the Nicene Creed (325) and its later revision at Constantinople (381), sometimes known as the Nicæo-Constantinopolitan Creed. A more explicit statement is also given in the so-called Athanasian Creed of later date (449 A.D.). After a brief notice of the Trinitarian developments as found in the writings of the schoolmen and the Reformers, we shall give attention to the various forms in which the doctrine of the Trinity is stated, and summarize the results as generally held in the Church.

The Schoolmen and the Reformers. The Trinitarian doctrine underwent some change in the controversy over the single or double procession of the Holy Spirit, but otherwise the Nicene statement was generally accepted by the schoolmen. Through the influence of John of Damascus, the Eastern Church confirmed the creed and adopted the doctrine of a single procession, the Holy Spirit proceeding from the Father only. Following this the emperor Charlemagne called a synod at Aix-la-Chapelle in 809 A.D. which added the word *filioque* to the creed adopted at Constantinople, thus confirming the doctrine of the Western Church that the Spirit proceeded from the Father "and from the Son." Of necessity, therefore, the doctrine of the Trinity challenged the philosophical ingenuity of the scholastics and the imagination of the mystics. The dominant philosophy of the universals greatly influenced the thought of the schoolmen. John Scotus Erigena (c. 800-877) of Gnostic or Neo-Platonist tendencies, leaned toward Sabellianism. He declared that there were no distinctions in the divine essence corresponding to the names

Father, Son and Spirit. Roscelinus on the other hand was a nominalist in philosophy and therefore regarded the term *God* common to the three Persons as a mere name, the abstract idea of a genus under which the terms Father, Son and Holy Spirit are to be comprehended. By this position he laid himself open to the charge of tritheism. Abelard, also a nominalist (1079-1142) fell into Sabellian views by maintaining that Power, Wisdom and Love were the three persons of the Trinity and that any distinction was merely nominal. Gilbert de la Porree (1076-1154) was a realist in philosophy but reached the same results as Roscelinus. He was charged with separating the persons much as did Arius. The error of Sabellianism, according to Gilbert, was a failure to distinguish between the *quo est* and the *quod est*, that is, we may say that the Father, Son and Spirit *are* one, but not that God *is* Father, Son and Holy Spirit. He distinguished between *God* and the *Godhead* as between humanity and man, the former being the universal form in which man exists, but not man himself. This was an attempted compromise between the realist position in regard to the essence, and the nominalist position concerning the three persons. Gilbert was accused of reviving the error of Tetratheism held by Damian of Alexandria, but was not formally condemned. Anselm (1033-1109) was an extreme realist and defended the unity of God against the tritheistic position of Roscelinus.

The Reformers were faithful to the doctrine of the Trinity as set forth in the three Creeds. They were given to careful analysis, and carried to a higher degree of perfection the philosophical distinctions worked out with such ingenuity by the schoolmen. They maintained that the one essence subsisted in three Persons, the unity being numerical and the triunity hypostatical. They worked out minutely the distinctions between the properties and the processions, the acts *ab intra*, generation and spiration, and the acts *ab extra*, creation, redemption and sanctification. The circumcession is peculiarly a doctrine of the Reformation.

Following the Reformation the older errors reappeared from time to time, the principal heretical doctrine being that of Socinianism, which issued later in modern Unitarianism. This is a revival of the ancient Monarchianism, which recognizes the Father only as God, and denies the deity of Christ and the personality of the Holy Spirit.

THE TECHNICAL TERMS OF THE CREED

The technical terms in which the Church has set forth the doctrine of the Trinity demand special consideration. The terms "substance" and "essence" have already been discussed in connection with the philosophical conception of God. The terms which now demand attention are unity and trinity; person, subsistence and hypostasis; procession, generation and spiration; property and relation; mission and economy; circumcession and monarchy.

Unity and Trinity. Unity as applied to God is used in connection with substance or essence, trinity in connection with persons. Thus *Una substantia* and *Tres Personæ* first used by Tertullian came to be the accepted formula for expressing the unity and triunity of God. The term *Trias* was first used by Theophilus (c. 180) in connection with God, His Word and His Wisdom. Somewhat later than this the word *trinitas* was used by Tertullian. The formula *Una substantia* or "one substance" was used in a philosophical sense to denote a real entity. To Tertullian it was the underlying being by which things are what they are, and was, therefore, a deeper term than *natura* or "nature," which he used only to denote the sum-total of the properties of things.

Person, Subsistence and *Hypostasis.* The Latin word *persona* presupposes another term frequently used in theology, that of *suppositum,* by which is meant an individual in the concrete sense. A person is a *suppositum* with a rational nature or a rational individual. The term *persona* or "person" applies to the principle of unity, or to the center of that rational nature. In the modern use of the word, a person is the individual subject or self (αὐτός) of a rational nature, self-conscious and self-determining, and includes also the nature and properties of which it is the subject. This latter, however, is frequently termed personality in contradistinction to the individual subject. But in theology the word is never used in this sense. Here it must be clearly distinguished from the content of the nature of which it is the subject. It does not include the nature so united, nor the content or system of experience, nor is it the core or any part of this content. It is rather that by which the entire system of experience is united, a position of peculiar importance in Christology. The divine persons are not therefore separate individuals, but possess in common, one nature or substance, their distinction lying not in a separate substance, but in the manner in which they share the same substance. Since human persons are associated with bodies and are separated in space, it is difficult for us to conceive of persons without the idea of separateness. By subsistence is meant a distinction within ultimate substance rather than substance itself. The term is reserved for the distinctions of the Trinity, and as commonly used is the equivalent of person or hypostasis.

The term hypostasis (ὑπόστασις) is also used to express the distinctions of the Trinity, and as such is the equivalent of person or subsistence. The word originally meant simply *being* (οὐσία), and in this sense was the exact equivalent of the Latin word substance *(substantia)*. But it also conveyed another meaning, that of the abiding reality of a thing which persisted through all changes and experiences. In this sense it most nearly approaches the term "ego," and consequently came to be used in the sense of a subsistence or person. The use of the term in a twofold sense brought great confusion into the Church. The Latins used not only the word essence to translate *ousia* (οὐσία), but they used the word *substance (substantia)* to translate both *hypostasis* (ὑπόστασις) and *ousia* (οὐσία). The word *hypostasis* therefore became ambiguous. Augustine says, "That which must be understood of persons according to our usage, is to be understood of substances, according to Greek usage; for they say three substances (*hypostases*) one essence (*essentia*) in the same way as we say three persons, one essence or substance (*essentiam vel substantiam*)." Bicknell points out that those who used ὑπόστασις as a synonym for οὐσία and spoke of μία ὑπόστασις seemed Sabellians to those who distinguished between the terms. Conversely, those who distinguished between them and spoke of τρεῖς ὑποστάσεις seemed tritheists to those who regarded the two terms as synonymous. However at the Council of Alexandria (362) both uses of the word were recognized, and the formula τρεῖς ὑποστάσεις was approved as orthodox. After this the Eastern Church settled down to the formula μία οὐσία τρεῖς ὑποστάσεις and the West retained its *Una substantia, Tres Personæ* (Cf. BICKNELL, *Thirty-nine Articles*, p. 65).

Procession, Generation and Spiration. By procession is meant the origin of one person from another. It belongs to both Son and Spirit in a general way, but more specifically to the Holy Spirit alone. By generation is meant an eternal relation which always exists, and not merely an event which once happened and then ceased to happen. The generation of the Son is usually referred to in theology as eternal generation. This does not mean that the Father existed before the Son, or that the attributes of the former are greater than those of the latter, but that the Father has his nature from Himself, and the Son has His nature by the gift of the Father (Cf. John 5: 26). The term spiration is similar to that of generation and is the peculiar property of the Spirit. As the Son is said to be generated by the Father, so the Spirit is said to be spirated by the Father, and in a secondary sense by the Son.

Properties and Relations. By properties (*proprietates*) are meant the peculiar characteristics of the persons; by relation is meant the order in which one person stands toward another. The properties are paternity (which means "to be of none"), filiation and procession. Paternity is the property par excellence of the

Father, filiation is the property of the Son, and procession the property of the Holy Spirit. The relations are these:

1. The Father to the Son, paternity; the Father to the Spirit, spiration.

2. The Son to the Father, filiation; the Son to the Spirit, spiration (Western theology).

3. The Spirit to the Father, procession; the Spirit to the Son procession, but in a sense different from that of the procession from the Father.

The Missions and Economies. The relations just mentioned are eternal processions, sometimes known as *opera ad intra;* and from these the temporal processions or missions are derived. The working out of these missions constitutes the economies. They are not separate activities of the Persons since the activity of God is one, but relations to some temporal and external effect, or *opera ad extra.* It is evident that distinction must be made between the one who sends and the one who is sent (John 8: 42); and it must be further recognized that the Person sent stands in some new relation to that to which he is sent (or *terminus ad quem*). The change is not in the Person but in the economic relation. For this reason the Father is specially related to God's work in creation; the Son by incarnation is specially related to God's work in redemption; and the Holy Spirit by His indwelling is specially related to God's work in sanctification. The entire Trinity of Persons of course comes into the world (John 8: 42, 14: 23, 16: 7), but the Father does not proceed and therefore is not sent, while both the Son and the Spirit, though in different ways, proceed from the Father. The relation of each Person to the temporal effect is therefore different, and this accounts for the fact that acts are attributed to one Person rather than another. In this sense we may say (1)

Hall classifies the Trinitarian terms as follows: There are one Nature, two processions (Son from the Father, the Spirit from the Father through the Son); three Properties (Paternity, Filiation and Procession); four relations (Paternity, Filiation, Spiration and Procession); and five notions *(notiones)* (Innascibility, Paternity, Spiration belong to the Father, Filiation and Spiration to the Son, and Procession to the Spirit.)

the Father is God above us; (2) the Son is God with us; and (3) the Holy Spirit is God in us. Thus the religious values of the economies make the Christian religion the full expression of practical and spiritual values. St. Paul used the term economy (οἰκονομία) or "law of the house" in the sense of a dispensation or plan of God's government. It carries with it, however, the thought of truth as not having been fully revealed, and hence the apostle calls it a mystery (μυστήριον), incomprehensible in its fullness, but intelligible in so far as it has been revealed. The term "economical Trinity" has reference to the revelation of God progressively as Father, then as Son and finally as Spirit. In this sense it is true. It becomes false only when it is held to be merely aspects of one God, and not eternal distinctions in the divine essence itself. The twofold idea of the "essential Trinity" and the "economic Trinity" must be held in firm grasp, if there is to be any proper view of this fundamental doctrine of Christianity.

Circumcession and Monarchy. Having recognized the distinctness of the Persons of the Trinity and their religious value, it becomes necessary to emphasize the divine unity in a new and different manner, not now because of the unity of their substance, but over and above this in the sense of social unity. The doctrine of the Circumcession (περιχώρησις or coinherence συμπεριχώρησις) maintains that the three Persons permeate or dwell in each other by sharing the one nature, thereby giving social unity in the plurality of Persons. The Latin equivalents of *perichoresis* or mutual permeation are *Interactiio, Interexistentia* and *Intercommunio*. The *Monarchia* or Divine Monarchy further stresses the unity of the Godhead by maintaining one source of the Divine Persons, that is, the Father, and this in the sense of genetic unity or a kinship group.

THE EVANGELICAL DOCTRINE

The evangelical doctrine of the Trinity is best expressed in the ancient creeds and articles of faith. The Athanasian Creed has the most explicit statement. It says, "We worship one God in Trinity, and Trinity in Unity; neither confounding the Persons, nor dividing the substance. For there is one Person of the Father, another of the Son, and another of the Holy Ghost; but the Godhead of the Father, of the Son, and of the Holy Ghost is all one, the glory equal, the majesty coeternal." Article I of the *Thirty-nine Articles* as revised by John Wesley and the Methodist bishops of 1789 is as follows: "There is but one living and true God, everlasting, without body or parts; of infinite power, wisdom and goodness; the maker and preserver of all things, both visible and invisible. And in unity of this Godhead, there are three persons of one substance, power, and eternity— the Father, the Son, and the Holy Ghost." (Art. I of the *Twenty-five Articles of Methodism.*) We may say, therefore, that the evangelical doctrine affirms that the Godhead is of one substance, and that in the unity of this substance there are three subsistences or Persons; and further, that this must be held in such a manner as to not divide the substance or confuse the Persons. We shall therefore, summarize our statement of the doctrine under four heads as follows: (1) The Unity of the Essence; (2) The Trinity of Persons; (3) The Divine Monarchy and (4) The Circumcession.

The Unity of Essence. The term unity is applied to the essence or substance of God, trinity to His personality. It is sometimes asserted that unity and trinity are contradictory terms, but the Church has never used the one and the three in the same sense. It does not teach that the three Persons are one in the same sense that they are three; nor does it teach that the one substance is three in the same sense that it is one. There

While it is obvious, on the one hand, that no human language can utter this mystery, Theology, both scientific and practical, demands that the Trinitarian phraseology be ordered with careful precision as at least guarding the truth against the approach of error. After all that may be said as to the inadequacy of human words, and the absence of definitions from Scripture, it still remains true that many others besides those of the New Testament must be used both in teaching and in worship. As it regards the scientific terminology of the doctrine, it is well to be familiar with the terms that express the relations of the One to the Three-in-One. No thoughtful student will either discard or undervalue them.—POPE, *Compend. of Chr. Theology,* I, pp. 285, 286.

is not a trinity of essence or being, but a trinity of Persons, a plurality within the one being of God. This is the most simple conception possible. In affirming that the substance is numerically one and the same, the Church guards against the error of supposing this unity to be similar to that of human nature, which may be the same in two or more human individuals. In this case the human nature is generically the same, but not so numerically; whereas in the Godhead it is not only generically the same but numerically so—otherwise we should have three individuals or three Gods. This leads to Tritheism but not to the Christian conception of the Trinity. It was for this reason that the Church rejected not only Arianism but also semi-Arianism. The latter held that Christ or the Son was not a created being but a generation, in which the substance or essence of the Son was not that of the Father but only like it, that is *homoiousios* (ὁμοιούσιος) instead of *homoousios* (ὁμοούσιος). While unity belongs to God in the sense of the simplicity and indivisibility of His being, it implies more than this, for the unity of the Divine Being must transcend all necessity, all human limitations and finite conceptions. It is used, therefore, to express symbolically what otherwise is outside the range of human consideration. In the case of human persons previously cited, by virtue of a common generic nature they become a class, and the term unity is applied to each individual as a member of that class. But this is not applicable to God. He is not one of a class. Hence in this sense of the definition, God is not an individual, that is, unity cannot be thus applied to Him. But an individual may be defined otherwise, that is, in the sense of a Being who can exist independently or alone. Dorner uses the term "soleness" to express this independency. In this sense, God only has individuality, for He alone is absolute being. It is in this sense also that we apply the term unity to God. "Unity is not in any sense determinative of what God is in Himself," says Dr. Miley. "Just the reverse is the truth. God is the deepest unity because He only is absolute spirit, existing in eternal personality, with the infinite perfection of moral attributes. This deepest unity, is therefore, in no sense constitutive or determinative of what God is in Himself, but is purely consequent to the infinite perfections which are His sole possession. Unity is therefore in no proper sense an attribute of God."—MILEY, *Systematic Theology*, I, p. 217.

The Trinity of Persons. While the Scriptures associate the Divine Trinity chiefly with the historic redemptive process, this does not give us ground to suppose that it is, therefore, merely an "economic" Trinity or a Trinity of manifestations such as Sabellianism holds. The Church has always maintained that the Trinity expresses not only God's outward relation to man, but His inner relation to Himself; and therefore, that there is an "essential" as well as an "economic" Trinity. It does this on the ground of clear scriptural teaching. It believes that *In the beginning was the Word, and the Word was with God, and the Word was God* (John 1:1). In the divine declaration that the Word was *with* God, and that the Word was itself God, it finds inner distinctions in the Godhead, a distinction between God and God, and a relation of God to God. St. Paul unfolds the same truth in another scripture, *But God hath revealed them unto us by his Spirit: for the Spirit searcheth all things, yea, the deep things of God* (I Cor. 2:10). Here conjoined with a statement concerning the economic or revealing Trinity, is another of equal import concerning the essential Trinity. The Spirit is not, according to this scripture, merely an activity directed outwardly toward the world, but is directed inwardly also, the Spirit being God who searches God. Hence on the basis of both Scripture and reason, the Church has maintained a distinction between the economic Trinity or the revelation of God to the world *ad extra* (πρόπος ἀποκαλύψεως), and the essential Trinity

It is impossible to define the unity of God: the word unity in human language gives no adequate notion, barely serving to defend the doctrine from every opposite error. Hence it is our wisdom to study it in the light of its exhibition in Scripture: marking the uses to which the doctrine is applied, the scriptural method of stating it, and the confirmations of the truths which may everywhere be found in the one and uniform economy of nature.—POPE, *Compend. Chr. Theology*, I, p. 255.

or the revelation of God to Himself *ad intra* (πρόπος
ὑπάρξεως).

The earlier Fathers, both Greek and Latin, and later
the schoolmen and the Reformers, made use of analogies
to illustrate their teachings concerning the Trinity,
though not to explain it. The human *logos* or word,
they said, is spoken and thereby emitted from the human
soul without loss from its essence, so the eternal generation of the Son left the divine nature unimpaired. Likewise the reason or wisdom or God mediates the divine
essence without subtracting from it. The most common
illustration, however, was borrowed from the human
consciousness and has come down to us from the primitive Fathers. In modern times it has been given its
most perfect form by the mediating theologians, Nitzsch,
Wiesse, Dorner and Martensen. These writers have
sometimes been charged with being Hegelian in their

For if God be indeed Trinity in Unity, then there is every reason to
suppose that the works of His hands should, in some degree at least,
reflect His nature, and especially that man, who is created in the image
of God, should evince in his nature certain analogies which indicate a
triune Creator. And what an abundance of such indications meets our
eye, so long as we do not forget that we cannot expect to find within
the limits of created life analogies perfectly corresponding with that
which is incomparable and unique! Christian thinkers, even in olden
times, discovered traces of the Trinity in the life of the human spirit;
and hence Augustine and others speak of a human trinity, consisting in
the threefold function of feeling, thought and will. And indeed, these
principal faculties of the spirit present us, as it were, with a threefold
cord, the threads of which are distinct and yet one, and they give us
some idea of the united and harmonious co-operation of the three Divine
Persons. No single one of these functions of feeling, thought, and will
can be exercised without the simultaneous activity of the others. . . . .
In like manner, the process of our thought will explain to us in some
degree the pre-existence of the Son as the Logos or Word of the Father. In our human consciousness a certain thought always simultaneously produces the corresponding word; we can only think in conceptions and words, for our thought is inward speech. So, too, God's thought
of Himself necessitates the utterance of the Word which represents this
primal thought; but the divine utterance is at the same time a real act,
and hence this inner Word in God as a being equal to Him. True, in our
human self-consciousness we do not, by conceiving ourselves, produce a
second self: we all the time have only one ego. But we are only
creatures, not the creative source of life: and even our human consciousness is still imperfect. But the case is different with God, who is the
eternal and almighty source of life and power. His self-consciousness is
absolutely perfect, and hence the intellectual image of Himself, which He
has conceived, may become a real substantial antitype of the Father. In
any case, we have an analogy to the Trinity in the thought, its product the
word, and the unity of both, the spirit."—CHRISTLIEB, *Modern Doubt and
Christian Belief*, pp. 275, 276.

modes of thought, especially as it concerns the thesis, antithesis and synthesis. Hegel's philosophy makes God the thesis and the world the antithesis. This made the world necessary to the idea of God's existence and led to pantheism and agnosticism. The Trinitarian theologians, on the other hand, found the synthesis within the Trinity itself, God the Father being the subject, God the Son the object, and God the Spirit the bond of union or perfectness. "When, therefore, following in the footsteps of the Church," says Bishop Martensen, "we teach that not merely the Father, but also the Son and the Holy Spirit eternally pre-existed and are independent of creation, we say that God could not be the self-revealed, self-loving God, unless He had eternally distinguished Himself into an I and Thou (into Father and Son), and unless He had eternally comprehended Himself as the Spirit of love, who proceeds forth from that relation of antithesis in the divine essence" (MARTENSEN, *Chr. Dogm.*, p. 107). To this it is sometimes objected that the distinctions in the human mind are merely ideas, not real distinctions. The objection rests upon a failure to distinguish the difference between created and uncreated self-consciousness. The created mind is bound down by the antithesis between being and thought, and therefore its self-consciousness can develop only in connection with the world outside of itself. But in God, thought and being are one, and the movement by which the divine self-consciousness is completed, is not merely of the divine subject but also of the divine substance. The three ego centers, therefore, are not merely forms of consciousness but become hypostatic distinctions or forms of subsistence. This, then, is the first step in the argument from self-consciousness, *i.e.*, that the three focal centers in created self-consciousness must be regarded as hypostases or real subsistences in uncreated or Divine Self-consciousness.

The second step in the argument is concerned with the nature of the *Logos*. As in human consciousness the self becomes conscious of itself, the act of self-cognition furnishing both subject and object in one being or substance, so God the Father out of the depths of His own eternal nature, sees the image of His own Ego in a second subsistence, which is the eternal *Logos* or Son. It is for this reason that the author of the Epistle to the Hebrews speaks of the Son as *the brightness of his glory and the express image of his person* (Heb. 1:2, 3). Here the word "brightness" is the effulgence or outshining of the glory or *doxa* (ὧν ἀπαύγασμα τῆς δόξης); and the "express image" (χαρακτὴρ τῆς ὑποστάσεως αὐτοῦ), the exact image or impress of the substance (ὑποστάσεως) of Him; thus sustaining (or making manifest) all things by the word of His power. As in the prologue to the Fourth Gospel, the author of this Epistle identifies the *Logos* as the intermediary of creation with Jesus Christ, who as the incarnate Son of God becomes the Mediator of redemption. His statement concerning the glory of the Son is therefore followed immediately by another which relates to His redemptive purpose, declaring that *when he had by himself purged our sins* (having made purification for sins), He *sat down at the right hand of the Majesty on high* (or at the right hand of the Majesty in high places).

It is worthy of note, that there is in the Old Testament an intimation of this conception of the *Logos,* found more especially in the description of Wisdom as previously mentioned. God becomes manifest to Himself in Wisdom which was with Him in the beginning, and rejoiced always before His face. *Then was I by him, as one brought up with him: and I was daily his delight, rejoicing always before him; rejoicing in the habitable part of his earth; and my delights were with the sons of men* (Prov. 8:30, 31). The Jewish conception of wisdom, however, was impersonal. It was the eternal image of the world, the heavenly *pleroma,*

Nitzsch maintains that the Divine Ego, in order to have a living personality, must not only view its second "other self" as an object, but also revert to itself by a further act as a third subject, in that it comprehends its "alter ego" as the real image of itself. Thus if God be conceived as the Primal Ego, and from this basis begets an objective alter Ego, the thesis and antithesis would still remain severed or incomplete until a third Ego proceeds from the Divine essence through the medium of the second, and thus fully consummates the personality.

uncreated and supernatural, but as yet only personified. So also the Philonic *Logos* was a ($\kappa \acute{o} \sigma \mu o \varsigma \ \nu o \eta \tau \acute{o} \varsigma$) merely a term for the heavenly world, and though uncreated was likewise impersonal. St. John, therefore, struck a deep note when by the pen of inspiration he declared that the *Logos* was the Son, and that as such He was not only the spoken Word but the speaking Word, not only a revelation, but a Revealer, not only personified Wisdom, but the eternal Word, which was in the beginning with God, and was God (John 1:1). God therefore is not only the Father of the creature or the idea, but of the *Logos* who is the vehicle of the idea, without whom no single thought would present itself to the Father as an *object,* different from Himself. This is the true conception of eternal generation which has been so prominent in the controversies of the Church—not an event in time or even before time, but an eternal relationship without which personality is impossible. It was for this that the Arians were striving, but they failed in that they made generation so completely a birth out of the will of God instead of His essence, that the Son became a mere creature, of which they affirmed that there was a time when he was not.

The third step in the argument for the evangelical doctrine of the Holy Trinity is concerned with the nature of the Spirit and His relation to the Father and the Son. It is evident that if the revelation of the Father had terminated in the Son, this relation would have been one of necessity and not of freedom. It is the work of the Spirit proceeding from the Father and the Son, to glorify this necessary relation into one of freedom and love. The relationship existing between the Father and the Son is therefore ethical as well as metaphysical. God's relation to the world, then, is not merely one of contemplation, as the pantheists teach, but one of creation motivated by divine love.

The evangelical doctrine of the Trinity, therefore, perfectly satisfies the unifying principle of the human mind. The self-revealing energy of God is revealed also as personal activity in the *Logos,* manifested from the foundation of the world, and reaching its climax in the Word made flesh. The incarnation is then but the focussing of that personal Light which lighteth every man coming into the world. The pre-existence of Christ is not only a religious but a philosophical truth, in which man and God are conjoined, in both natural and moral relations. *For God, who commanded the light to shine out of darkness, hath shined in our hearts, to give the light of the knowledge of the glory of God in the face of Jesus Christ* (II Cor. 4:6). Thus in this second hypostasis we have the Word as the "exact image" or true revelation of the Father, and also the Word as the Revealer, the "effulgence" or outshining of His glory. The third hypostasis, or the Spirit, has reference, not to the self-revealing energy, but to the self-imparting energy of God, which likewise is a personal activity. As the self-revelation of God advances there is a constantly increasing display of the self-imparting energy of the Holy Spirit. For this reason the Divine Word must come to full expression in the incarnation, before the Holy Spirit could come in the fullness of pentecostal glory. As the self-revealing energy of God found its perfection in the unique personality of Jesus Christ the Son; so the self-imparting energy of God reached its highest expression in the personal presence of the Holy Spirit. Here is the deep and abiding significance of the words of our Lord, *It is expedient for you that I go away: for if I go not away, the Comforter will not come unto you; but if I depart, I will send him unto you* (John 16:7).

The Divine Monarchy. Our previous discussion of the Trinity has been concerned mainly with the metaphysical questions of unity and triunity, and we must now give some attention to the social and governmental

Dr. Sheldon thinks that an intelligible statement of the Trinity is essentially comprised in a formula like this: "Corresponding to the threefold manifestation of Father, Son, and Spirit, there subsist in the Godhead, in a certain logical order, eternal and necessary distinctions, which enter into the divine consciousness and determine the perfection of the divine life. To affirm less than this is to fail to do justice to the total data of the subject. To affirm much more is to resort to unintelligible categories, or to an unintelligible combination of categories" (Cf. SHELDON, *Syst. Chr. Doct.*, p. 227).

aspects of this important doctrine. What is termed the "Monarchia" of the Father has reference to His pre-eminence viewed, not from the standpoint of meta-physical essence, but from that of order and relation. It belongs to the offices of the persons and not to their substance. It is the principle of unity in the social aspect of the Trinity, not an inequality in the aspect of the essential Trinity. In the Nicene statement of the monarchy, the Father is not more divine than the Son, or the Son than the Holy Spirit. But in the order of subsistence in that one essence, the Father depends up-on Himself alone for His Godhead, the Son derives His Godhead from the Father (God of God $\Theta\epsilon\grave{o}\nu$ $\dot{\epsilon}\kappa$ $\Theta\epsilon o\hat{v}$), that is, He is the Word or self-revelation of the Father and therefore eternally dependent upon Him; and the Holy Spirit proceeds from ($\dot{\epsilon}\kappa$) the Father and the Son (Father through the Son $\delta\iota\acute{a}$ $\pi\alpha\rho\acute{a}$), and therefore in order and relation is eternally dependent upon both. As to nature and being, however, the Son does not be-long to a grade of divinity lower than that of the Father, but is "very God of very God, begotten not made, being of one substance with the Father." The filial relationship as Son to Father is second and therefore in this sense subordinate; but the filial essence is equal and co-ordin-ate with that of paternity, "the glory equal, the majesty coeternal." Furthermore, the order is not temporal or chronological, but grounded in the three distinctions or

The Trinity is the chief cornerstone of the Christian system. Elim-inate that, with what logically follows it, and nothing is left but what is common to all theistic systems of religion known among men. By so much as Christianity has any claims to consideration, by so much more as it contains excellencies confessedly superior to any other sys-tem of religion extant among men, by so much more is it authenticated by indubitable proofs as the revelation of God's will, by so much as man has reason to receive the Bible as his sole and authoritative rule of faith and practice, by so much more is it incumbent upon one who de-sires to know God and do His will to inquire diligently, honestly, without prejudice, without fear or favor, whether the Bible does or does not teach the Church doctrine of the Holy Trinity.—RAYMOND, *Systematic Theology*, I, p. 392.

From all this it follows, that the doctrine of the Trinity is the con-summation and the only perfect protection of Theism. We have already shown that the theistic conception of God is the only true one; and we may now add, that if this theistic conception is to be effectually guarded against Atheism, Pantheism, Dualism and Deism, it must be expanded into the Trinitarian idea.—CHRISTLIEB, *Mod. Doubt and Chr. Belief*, p. 271.

subsistences of the one essence, and therefore real and eternal. Hence we have the statement of the creed that "in this Trinity none is afore or after other, none is greater or less than another; but the whole Three Persons are co-eternal together and co-equal. So that in all things as is aforesaid, the Unity in Trinity and Trinity in Unity is to be worshiped." We have previously pointed out some of the errors which arose concerning monarchianism in the earlier or anti-Nicene period, such as the subordinationism of Origen, Arianism and Semi-Arianism. The Nicene statement of the Trinity marked a decided advance over the previous period in clarity of doctrine, but the theologians found it necessary to guard against two errors. The first was the confusion of essence or substance with personal distinctions. When these two were identified, or at least not clearly separated, the "generation" of a Person meant the generation of the essence, and the "procession" of a person meant the procession of the essence. This resulted in a difference of essence and as a consequence, the multiplication of deities, or tritheism. The second error was closely allied with the first, and consisted in a confusion of the ideas of generation and creation. Generation was regarded as creation from nothing; and the procession of a person from another, meant the creation of that person out of nothing by the former. This reduced the Son and the Holy Spirit to mere creatures. The Nicene theologians corrected the first error by making a sharp distinction between substance and subsistence, between essence and persons. They regarded these as two distinct and separate conceptions. To the first belonged the unity of the Godhead, to the second, the triunity. Hence it was possible to combine the unity of the essence with the trinality of persons. The generation or procession of one person from another did not, there-

Referring again to the Athanasian Creed we may say that "The catholic faith is this: that we worship one God in Trinity, and Trinity in Unity; neither confounding the Persons nor dividing the Substance. For there is one Person of the Father, another of the Son, and another of the Holy Ghost. But the Godhead of the Father, of the Son, and of the Holy Ghost is all one—the glory equal, the majesty coeternal."

fore, necessitate a difference of essence, and the two could be combined without any contradiction of terms. The second error was corrected by regarding the Father and Son as correlatives, so that the one could have no existence without the other, and the hypostasis of the one demanded the hypostasis of the other. In Origen's teaching, the Father was a Monad existing anterior to the Son in the order of nature, and the Holy Spirit subordinate to both, rather than being divine and coeternal hypostases. And while Origen held to eternal generation, he made this to lie more in the will of the Father

The Fathers illustrated their idea of this eternal and necessary act of communication by the example of a luminous body, which necessarily radiated light the whole period of its existence. Thus the Son is defined in the words of the Nicene Creed, "God of God, Light of Light." Thus the radiance of the sun is coeval with its existence, and of the same essence as its source. By this illustration they designed to signify their belief in the identity and consequent equality of the Divine Persons as to essence, and the relative subordination of the second to the first, and of the third to the first and second as to personal subsistence and consequent order of operation (Cf. A. A. HODGE, *Outlines of Theology*, p. 155).

Bishop Pearson maintains that the pre-eminence consists in this, "that He is God not of any other but of Himself, and that there is no other Person who is God, but is God of Himself. It is no diminution to the Son, to say that He is from another, for His very name imports as much; but it were a diminution to the Father to speak so of Him; and there must be some pre-eminence, where there is place for derogation. What the Father is, He is from none; what the Son is, He is from Him; what the first is, He giveth; what the second is, He receiveth. The first is Father indeed by reason of His Son, but He is not God by reason of Him; whereas the Son is not so only in regard to the Father, but also God by reason of the same."—PEARSON, *On the Creed*, p. 35.

The early Arian and Semi-Arian teachers laid so much stress on the Θειότης or divinity of the two subordinate Beings. They were regarded as the bond, or rather the intermediary links, between the Absolute and the conditioned, the Infinite and the finite: looking toward the creature they were firstborn or rather first created before the worlds; but looking Godward they were more directly emanations of the Monad than the creature. The doctrine was a speculative substitution for the Gnostic errors of æonic emanation. . . . . Early Arianism also has been sporadic. It has molded opinion very extensively in later Christendom: never shaping a formulary or founding a sect, but influencing the thoughts of many thinkers and coloring the sentiments of poetry, and infusing itself into the devotions of many who are almost unconscious of their error. The history of the Arian tendency in England is an important and instructive one: it brings in some great names in our philosophical and theological literature; but it shows that the healthy common sense of readers of Scripture never has and never will accept this compromise. Either the New Testament must be rejected as final authority and the Deistic Rationalism of Unitarianism accepted, or, the Scriptures being received as the rule of faith, the fullness of the Godhead must be adored in the incarnate Son.—*Pope, Compend. Christian Theology*, I, p. 283.

than in the necessity of His nature. The Arians, therefore, making a distinction in essence as well as persons, held to a higher and lower form of divinity a ὁ Θεὸς and a Θεὸς. Athanasius insisted upon the identity of essence and therefore maintained the *homo-ousia* as over against the difference in essence or *heter-ousia*, held by the Arians. The Semi-Arians in an attempt at mediation proposed the term *homoi-ousia* or like essence, but this was also rejected by the orthodox theologians. We may say, therefore, that the Nicene Trinitarianism harmonized the doctrine of the one substance with the three Persons, by insisting upon the necessity of this generation and procession, as over against the voluntary idea of the Arians. They inferred from their idea of voluntary generation that there was a time when the Son was not. Against this, the orthodox affirmed that the generation of the Son was a necessary consequence of the divine nature, and hence was as independent of the volitional action of the Father as was the existence of any of the Divine attributes. This was a long step forward. It needs now the doctrine of the Circumcession, to guard against too strong a tendency toward an undue separateness of the Persons and their divine missions.

The Circumcession or Perichoresis. The circumcession or perichoresis comes from the Greek word περι-χώρησις or συμπεριχώρησις as previously pointed out in our definition of terms. The Latin equivalents are

Dr. Shedd summarizes the teachings of the Nicene theologians as to generation and creation in these brief statements: (1) Eternal generation is an offspring out of the eternal essence of God; creation is an origination of a new essence from nothing. (2) Eternal generation is the communication of an eternal essence; creation is the origination of a temporal essence. (3) That which is eternally generated is of one essence with the generator; but that which is created is of another essence from that of the creator. The substance of God the Son is one and identical with that of the Creator. The Father and Son are one nature, and one Being, God and the world are two natures and two beings. (4) Eternal generation is necessary, but creation is optional. The filiation of the second Person in the Trinity is grounded in the nature of Deity; but the origination of the world depends entirely upon arbitrary will. It is as necessary that there should be Father and Son in the Godhead, as that the Godhead should be eternal, or self-existent; but there is no such necessity for creation. (5) Eternal generation is an immanent perpetual activity in an ever-existing essence; creation is an instantaneous act, and supposes no elements of the creature in existence.—SHEDD, *History of Christian Doctrine,* I, pp. 317, 318.

interactio, intercommunio or *interexistentia.* The term
signifies an intercoherence of the Persons of the Trinity,
or that property, which by reason of identity of essence,
they can communicate with each other without confusion of persons. It guards the unity of the Godhead, by
affirming that the three Persons do not exist alongside
of each other as separate individuals, but that they permeate and penetrate one another, and so exist not alongside but in and through one another. . . . . As the Divine
Monarchy stressed the social aspect of the Trinity, so
also does the perichoresis. It affirms that there is unity
of purpose and coinherence in action as well as essence.
As they were united in the work of creation, so also they
are each engaged in the work of redemption, and will
each share in the consummation of all things. The
divine essence is undivided and indivisible. The whole
Godhead is in the Father, in the Son and in the Holy
Spirit. In the Father as the origination of all things; in
the Son *(Logos)* as God's self-utterance and in the
Spirit as His self-consciousness. The circumcession is
especially necessary in guarding the religious unity of
God, or that approach to the Trinity through religious
experience. Reason is primarily concerned with the unity
of God, but religious experience with the distinction of
Persons. The danger of the one is abstraction, that of
the other anthropomorphism. The mind tends to think
of personality as that which distinguishes one individual
from another. Tritheism, therefore, is the practical outcome of the distinction of Persons, unless the perichoresis
be fully understood and kept constantly before the individual in his devotional life. And, further, the distinctness of persons tends to emphasize individuality and
minify the social aspects of personality, whether considered with reference to the human or the divine. That
there is a deep line of cleavage between the individual
and social aspects of personality may be allowed, and
this doubtless is intensified by sinful pride and selfishness. It is only as we realize that the higher goods of
life must be shared in order to be fully realized and en-
joyed, that we come to see that human personality is not

less but more truly social. This has its perfect prototype
in the perichoresis or circumcession, the mysterious indwelling and interpenetration of the three Persons of
the Godhead, the promise and potency of spiritual fellowship in the Church. *And the glory which thou gavest
me I have given them; that they may be one, even as we
are one: I in them, and thou in me, that they may be
made perfect in one: and that the world may know that
thou hast sent me, and hast loved them, as thou hast*

It is generally supposed that Augustine introduced the psychological
analogies of the Trinity, maintaining that the complexity of the Trinity
finds an image in our own being as memory, reason and will: or "I
exist, I am conscious, I love the existence and the consciousness." Thus
in the process of consciousness we discover three "I's" which form the
foci of consciousness. the self that thinks, the self which is thought of,
and the self which is conscious of the self thinking of self. This self is
at once, subject, object and consciousness of subject and object.—STUMP,
The Christian Faith, p. 55.

Liebner, Sartorius and others have drawn analogies from the standpoint of love rather than self-conscious reason. Love demands a process of self-communication which in its highest perfection must be
Trinitarian. Love is the transposition of oneself into another person
as an *alter ego* or second self. God who is Love, must therefore trans-
pose Himself into His second Self, which as such is of the same divine
nature, since otherwise the act of self-transposition would not be perfect. No less necessary, however, is the conception of a third homog-
enous Self, by which the infinite equality is mediated so as to produce
harmonious unity in distinctions. It is this which fixes the Divine
Personality, for mere self-transposition would be equal to infinite rest-
lessness. Thus Spirit is predicated of the whole nature for God is
Spirit (John 4:24), and the Lord is the Spirit (II Cor. 3:17). Thus God
is one person in three persons in the sense of the perichoresis, each of
which is only in and through the others. This apparent contradiction
that the several persons should be one and have their full personality
only in this unity, is solved by the principle of love (Liebner). Sartorius
distinguishes between the love which begets and the love which blesses
the Son—the love of the well-pleased Father and the answering love on
the Son's part. The breath of that blessing and answering love is the
Spirit. But were He only breath, and not a person, the glorification of
the Father and the Son would be egoistical. This egoistical element is
removed only if the Spirit who glorifies the Father and the Son is Himself a person. Christlieb gathers up the sentiment of the above as follows: "Love always includes delight in the object loved. If this object
be an entirely separate person, the purity of my love is not sullied by
my delight. But this is not the case with God. The object of His love
is not a Person outside of Him, but His second Self. Here, therefore,
the delight in another is at the same time delight in Himself. In order,
therefore, that this delight may not appear as self-seeking egoism, God
has committed this delight in Himself to a Third Person, which represents the mutual delight of Father and Son in each other; and this
Person is the Holy Spirit. When the Father uttered Himself, he begat
the Son, the eternal Word. But no speech can take place without
breathing, and the breath of that spoken Word was hypostatized in the
Spirit, which represents the delight of the Divine Love.—CHRISTLIEB,
Modern Doubt and Christian Belief, p. 273.

*loved me. . . . . And I have declared unto them thy name,
and will declare it: that the love wherewith thou hast
loved me may be in them, and I in them* (John 17:22,
23, 26).

Dr. Summers closes his discussion on this subject
with a quotation from the ever memorable John Hales,
who became professor of Greek in Oxford in 1612, and
whom Bishop Pearson mentions as a "man of as great
a sharpness, quickness, and subtility of wit as ever this
or perhaps any nation bred; . . . . a man of vast and
illimited knowledge, of a severe and profound judgment." Dr. Tigert in an attached note says that he went
to the Synod of Dort a Calvinist and left it an Arminian.
"At the well-pressing of John 3:16 by Episcopius there,"
he says, "I bid John Calvin good night, as he has often
told me." The following is from the *Golden Remains*
(London 1673) and is a "Confession of the Trinity" by
John Hales:

"God is one; numerically one; more one than any
single man if unity could *suscipere magis et minus:* yet
God is so one that He admits of distinction; and so admits of distinction that He still retains unity.

"As He is one, so we call Him God, the Deity, the
Divine Nature, and other names of the same significa-
tion; as He is distinguished, so we call Him Trinity:
Persons; Father, Son, and Holy Ghost.

"In this Trinity there is one essence; two emanations;
three persons or relations; four properties; five notions: a notion is that by which any person is known or
signified.

"The One essence is God with this relation, that it
doth generate or beget, maketh the Person of the Father: the same essence with this relation, that it is begotten, maketh the Person of the Son: the same essence
with this relation, that it proceedeth, maketh the Person of the Holy Ghost.

The two emanations are, to be begotten and to proceed or to be breathed out: the three persons are Father,
Son, and Holy Spirit: the three relations, to beget,
to be begotten, and to proceed, or to be breathed out.

The four properties are: the first inascibility and in emanability; the second is to generate—these belong to the Father: the third is to be begotten; and this belongs to the Son: the fourth is to proceed or be breathed out; and this belongs unto the Holy Spirit. The five notions are: the first, innascibility; the second is to beget; the third, to be begotten; the fourth *spiratio passiva*, to be breathed out; the fifth, *spiratio activa* or, to breathe: and this notion belongs to the Father and Son alike; for *Pater et Filius spirant Spiritum Sanctum.*"

The word emanation as used above is not the oriental concept of finiteness proceeding from infinity, but an accommodated use of the term in the Christian sense. But we are ever brought back to the thought that the Being of God is by St. Paul termed a *mystery* (μυστήριον), and we are commanded to worship the "Unity in Trinity and Trinity in Unity" not necessarily to understand it. "The Bible Doctrine of the Trinity," says Ralston, "is one of those sublime and glorious mysteries which the mind of man, at least while shrouded in clay, cannot penetrate. We may study and meditate until lost in thought, yet never can we comprehend the mode and nature of the divine being" (RALSTON, *Elements of Divinity*, p. 65). Dr. Pope cautions us concerning the scientific terminology of the doctrine that "it is well to be familiar with the terms that express the relation of the One to the Three-in-One. No thoughtful student will either discard or undervalue them. The Deity is the divine essence or substance or nature; the three are subsistences, hypostases and persons. . . . . Nowhere is precision more necessary than in the ordering of the phraseology of worship. The mind and the tongue must be so educated as to recoil from such language as is tinctured with either the Tritheistic, or the Sabellian, or the Arian error. One of the results of careful and reverent study will be the discipline that shall make every word faithful to the equal honor of each of the three adorable persons in the unity of the other two, and in the unity of the Godhead; adoring and praying to each with this sacred reservation. But, after all, we must remember what the ancient Church was never weary of enforcing in relation to this subject; the nature of God is ἄρρητος ineffable, unsearchable and unspeakable; the Godhead can be known only by him who is Θεοδίδακτος, taught of God; and that knowledge itself is and will eternally be only ἐκ μέρους in part" (POPE, *Compendium of Christian Theology*, I, p. 286). Is it any wonder, then, that the Church has not only given us a statement of the Trinity in the creed, but set its teaching to music in the matchless *Gloria*? Here is summarized all its teachings concerning the Trinity as they are to be used in the service of worship. "Glory be to the Father, and to the Son, and to the Holy Ghost; as it was in the beginning, is now, and ever shall be, world without end. Amen."

CHAPTER XVI

COSMOLOGY

The study of Cosmology may embrace the entire universe in its scope, or as commonly treated it may be divided into (1) Cosmology, as applying to the kingdom of nature apart from man; and (2) Anthropology, as dealing with the science of man. Even though man from the physical standpoint belongs to the animal kingdom, the wide divergence between personality and the non-personal orders is sufficient to warrant this division. Within the science of Anthropology as treated in theological study, a further division is made, Anthropology being limited to man in his original state, and Hamartiology treating of man in his fallen or sinful state.

The Meaning of the Term "World." By the term "world" in the philosophic sense, we mean everything which is extrinsic to God, whether animate or inanimate, whether rational or nonrational. Ancient peoples had little conception of the world as such, and in the dawn of the reflective period, generally regarded it as existing by chance or by necessity. There was no single term which could be used to express the universe. With the development of the period of reflection men first turned their attention to the earth upon which they lived, and to the heavens which they saw above them. Thus "the heavens and the earth" became the earliest expression for the created universe (Cf. Gen. 1:1, 2:1, Psalm 115:15). Those nations, however, which lived near the sea coast frequently spoke of "the heaven, earth and sea" (Cf. Psalm 146:6, also Acts 17:24 which is evidently a quotation and implies but does not mention the word sea). This was the dominant Greek conception also. Homer regarded the world as divided into three portions, heaven, earth and sea. In the process of time other words came into use. The

Hebrews, the Chaldeans and the Syrians used a term which corresponded to the Greek *aion* (αἰών) which referred more especially to the duration or age of the world rather than to its creative aspect. The Greeks later spoke of the world as *cosmos* (κόσμος) because of its beauty and orderliness. The Latin equivalent of this term is *mundus*.

The Eternity of Matter. The ancient people found difficulty in explaining the origin of the first material. This was due largely to the fact that they insisted on the principle *ex nihilo nihil fit,* or from nothing, nothing comes. They could not, therefore, admit that the world was created out of nothing. Consequently, they accepted almost universally, the belief in two eternal principles, God and self-existent matter, neither being dependent upon the other. The principle may indeed be true as it applies to material causes, but it is not applicable to an efficient cause of which omnipotence is predicated. Before this truth, materialism, whether ancient or modern, must of necessity vanish. Plato taught that God voluntarily united Himself with matter, and thereby produced the world; and while both God and matter were regarded as eternal, the world which resulted from the conjoining of the two might be said to be created. Aristotle on the other hand taught, as did also Zeno the Stoic, that the union of God with matter was necessary and therefore the world must be regarded as eternal. Epicurus at the other extreme held that God was entirely separate and apart from the world. Generally the ancients believed that primordial matter was of the nature of thin air, or an ether, fluid and movable. The word *chaos*, is derived from either χάω or χέω because of this fluidity. The Latin word for that which is confused and unarranged is *silva*. Plato's conception of matter 'ὕλη involved both *silva* and *materia*. The Greeks supposed that from this fluid and fermenting mass the earth was formed. The Hebrews, however, with a different temper of mind, regarded the universe more after the pattern of a building, of which God was the creator of the materials as well as the structure.

THEORIES OF CREATION

The Church was very early forced to attempt an explanation of the universe, in order to bridge the chasm between the finite and the Infinite. With the advance of modern science, many of its discoveries apparently, came into conflict with the scriptural account of creation. However, this conflict was only apparent, for as scientific theory has become more exact there has been a closer approach to the biblical positions. The subject demands only brief attention.

The Mechanical Theory. This theory holds that the world was formed in a purely external and formal manner. It stresses the thought of transcendence and wholly disregards the divine immanence. This was never the theory of the early Church. It arose only in modern times, and came as a protest against the extreme rationalism of the critico-historical movement. Irenæus speaks of creation in this manner. "But He himself after a fashion which we can never describe nor conceive predestinated all things and formed them as He pleased." "Thou createst heaven and earth," says Augustine, "things of two kinds; one near to Thee, the other near to nothing." Again he says, "Thou createst heaven and earth; not out of Thyself, for they should have been equal to Thine only begotten Son, and thereby equal to Thee also." Athanasius taught that creation was through the *Logos* or the Divine Word.

The Physical or Materialistic Theory of Creation. This theory is closely related to dualism in that it presupposes the eternity of matter. It rejects, however, the architectonic idea of a creator, in the sense of a demiurge or fashioner of this material into the created forms as we know them; and substitutes instead the theory of spontaneous generation. It holds that matter has in itself the power of taking on new functions, and under proper conditions of developing into organic forms. It therefore assumes that all things may be explained on the basis of material changes. The theory is merely an application of materialistic philosophy to the idea of creation, and arose out of the rationalism of the early nineteenth century. It was held by Feuerbach, Vogt, Moleschott, Buchner, Bastian and Owen. Closely related to this is the revival of ancient Greek *hylozoism* which acknowledges a formative principle in the world, but regards this principle as confined within matter itself and a characteristic of its true nature. Matter it regards as imbued with life as in a plant which unfolds from a seed, and intelligence pertains to it in at least some of its combinations. In so far as God is acknowledged, He is merely the universal life of nature. The theory must therefore end in either pantheism or materialistic atheism. "If the soul of the world is an unconscious one," says Van Oosterzee, "how is the order and design in creation to be explained? If it is a conscious one, wherefore not, at the same time a free Agent? and if a free Agent, how does it become and remain so inseparably bound to its gigantic material raiment?"

The Emanation or Pantheistic Theory. At the other extreme is the theory of emanation which holds that the world was neither created nor fashioned out of preexistent material, but is to be regarded as an extension of the divine substance. It flows from God as a stream from a fountain, or as rays of light from the sun. This was the theory held by the ancient Gnostics, and in modern times has been revived as a consequence of the renewed emphasis upon idealistic philosophy. Lotze distinguished between emanation and creation by saying that creation necessitates a Divine Will, while emanation flows by necessary consequences from the being or nature of God. On this theory the world would either become in nature like God, or the cleavage in the substance of God would destroy the divine unity. The objections to this theory were presented in our discussion of pantheism and need not be repeated here.

The Theory of Eternal Creation. This theory arose as an attempt to guard against dualism and yet preserve the emphasis upon the eternity of God. Origen held to creation by the will of God and yet taught the theory of eternal creation. According to him, this world was not the first world God created; there never was a first and

444   CHRISTIAN THEOLOGY

there never will be a last. The schoolmen revived the theory on the ground that the thoughts of God were necessarily creative. *For he spake, and it was done; he commanded, and it stood fast* (Psalm 33:9). But to say that God's word must of necessity issue in creation, would be to identify the purpose of God with the creative fiat. This would be but another form of pantheism. It did, in fact, take this form in the teachings of Scotus Erigina, but others of the mediæval schoolmen avoided the pantheistic tendencies by maintaining that the world was in essence different from God, though eternally dependent upon Him. In so far as creation is independent of time, and the "birth of time" is regarded as taking place in the creative fiat, we may hold that creation took place in eternity. By this, however, it is not meant that the world had no beginning but that time began with creation. It rejects the idea that time was pre-existent, and that the creation of the world occupied merely a moment in that time scheme.

The Theory of Natural Evolution. This theory is similar if not identical with that of spontaneous generation, but has assumed a more philosophical form. When presented by Darwin and his school the evolutionary hypothesis was received with great applause. However, it could hardly be expected to hold its ground against the Christian belief in creation. It does not solve the problem. It merely pushes it back into time and therefore must rest ultimately in either creation or emanation. Naturalistic evolution breaks down at three vital points: (1) it has not been able to bridge the chasm between the inanimate and the animate; (2) it cannot pass from the diffused life of the vegetable realm, to the conscious somatic life of the animal kingdom; and (3) it cannot pass from the irrational life of animals to the rational self-conscious life of man. Only the creative activity of God could have originated vegetable, animal and personal life. The theory of the differentiation of species breaks down further in the case of the sterility of hybrids. The declaration in the Genesis account that each shall bring forth after its kind is an acknowledged fact, both in the realm of science and in the world of experience.

The Theory of Continuous Creation. In recent times, the idea of creation as an event, immediate and complete, has been challenged in favor of creation as a continuous process. The theory is the outgrowth of the renewed emphasis upon the divine immanence, and due to the influence of the evolutionary hypothesis, took the form of theistic evolution. While closely related to the theory of spontaneous generation, it regards the divine immanence as the basic reality in contradistinction to the eternity of matter. It insists that organic development is due, not to the spontaneity of the materialistic or hylozoistic principle, but to divine power working within the organism. The divine activity is sometimes identified with the entire process, and sometimes limited to merely the points of crisis in development.

THE SCRIPTURAL DOCTRINE OF CREATION

The scriptural doctrine of creation maintains that the universe had a beginning, that it is not eternal in either matter or form, that it is not self-originated, and that it owes its origin to the omnipotent power and the unconditioned will of God. This is the Christian conception. It involves, *first,* a belief in the Almighty God, whereby the world once began to be out of nothing, solely through the divine will; *second,* the concept of God in the Trinity of His essence; *third,* a display of the attributes of God—omnipotence, wisdom and love; and *fourth,* belief in creation through the Divine Word as a Mediator, the *Logos* forming the connection between the finite and the Infinite, between God and the world.

Creation and the Trinity. The very idea of Fatherhood which constitutes the Christian conception of God, suggests creatorship. It is, however, the love and not the creatorship which forms the essence of the Divine Fatherhood. In the act of creation God brings forth that which before had no existence, and which is different in essence from Himself. While creation originates in the love of God and is made effective by the divine will, the Scriptures specifically state that in this work both the Son and the Spirit are associated with the Father. Hence we read, that *to us there is but one God, the Father, of whom are all things, and we in him; and one Lord Jesus Christ, by whom are all things, and we by him* (I Cor. 8:6). The Scriptures record also, that in the dawn of creation, *the Spirit moved upon* the waters, that is, brooded over the waters in the sense of bringing order and beauty out of chaos (Gen. 1:2); and the psalmist said, *Thou sendest forth thy spirit, they are created* (Psalm 104:30). The Trinity, therefore, is revealed in creation as it is revealed in redemption, is in fact, the ground of the whole redemptive process. Love as the originating cause of redemption has its source in the inner freedom of the Trinity, which, existing there in infinite perfection, is expressed by the term blessedness. The love existing between the Father and the Son is *ad intra*, expressed in the Holy Spirit as the "bond of perfectness"; while that same love *ad extra*, is the originating cause of both creation and redemption. The Son is the "exact" or "express" image of the Father, and therefore under one aspect, the *pleroma* or the infinite range of possibilities existing in the Father, the κόσμος νοητός or world of ideas which form the archetypes of creation. St. Paul sums up the relation of the Trinity to the created universe in these words, *For of him* [as the originating cause], *and through him* [as the mediating or efficient cause], *and to him* [as the final cause or purpose], *are all things: to whom be glory forever. Amen* (Rom. 11:36). But Christ as the *Logos* is more than the spoken word or revelation of God, He is the speaking Word or the efficient cause of creation. To the Word or *Logos* as the mediating cause of creation we must later direct our attention.

Creation and the Attributes of God. Creation as we have shown, has its origin in the love of God and not in mere metaphysical necessity. It is the consequence of the overflowing fullness of love which seeks new objects upon which to expend itself. If the fundamental principle of theology is the self-revelation of God as we have all along maintained that it is, then creation may be regarded primarily as designed to display the perfections of God. The world is what it is because God is what He is. It is the ground for the manifestation of those attributes which can arise only out of a relation existing between the Creator and the creature. By this means only can they be brought within the range of creaturely comprehension. Here love manifests itself most prominently in omnipotence and omniscience as connected with primary creation; and in wisdom and goodness as associated with secondary creation. It is the divine omnipotence which furnishes the ground of causality and efficiency, and the divine omniscience which gives reason, order and purpose to the universe. It is the wisdom and goodness of God which have adapted all things to the promotion of happiness and enjoyment on the part of His creatures. It has been aptly said that there are no devices in nature for the promotion of pain for its own sake, but the manifestations of design for the production of happiness are beyond computation. *O Lord, how manifold are thy works! in wisdom hast thou made them all: the earth is full of thy riches* (Psalm 104: 24).

Creation and the Logos. By what means did God create all things? To this the Scriptures give answer, "By the word of his power." *By the word of the Lord were the heavens made; and all the host of them by the breath of his mouth* (Psalm 33: 6). *He sendeth forth his commandment upon earth: his word runneth very swiftly* (Psalm 147: 15). But this word must not be thought of as impersonal. It is rather, the *Logos*, the word and wisdom of the Father. It is an essential element in Christian belief, that Christ as the *Logos* or Word is the Mediator in creation, without which He could not have been the Mediator of Redemption. This is clearly taught by both St. John and St. Paul. *In the beginning was the Word [Logos], and the Word was with God, and the Word was God. . . . . All things were*

*made by him; and without him was not anything made
that was made* (John 1: 1, 3). *But to us there is but
one God, the Father, of whom are all things, and we in
him; and one Lord Jesus Christ, by whom are all things,
and we by him* (I Cor. 8: 6). *For by him were all things
created, that are in heaven, and that are in earth, visible
and invisible, whether they be thrones, or dominions, or
principalities, or powers: all things were created by him,
and for him: and he is before all things, and by him all
things consist* (Col. 1: 16, 17). "That which many a
philosopher dimly conjectures," says Van Oosterzee,
"namely, that God did not produce the world in an absolutely immediate manner, but some way or other,
mediately, here presents itself to us as invested with the
luster of revelation, and exalts so much more, the claim
of the Son of God to our deep and reverential homage."

It is just here that the thought of the Logos is so com-
pelling. Without a mediating cause, the idea of creation must lead directly to dualism with its eternity of
matter, or to pantheism as a mere extension of the
divine essence. This would be an emanation rather
than a creation. There must be, both for thought and
for reality, an intermediate idea; and as the Christian
doctrine of creation maintains an essential difference between God and the world, so also it maintains a distinction between the eternal idea of creation, and the creative Word or Logos. It is by the latter as the efficient
Agent, that the idea of creation becomes a reality in
actual existence. Otherwise, to maintain that the divine
purpose and the execution of this purpose are necessarily
simultaneous, resolves the absoluteness of God into
physical necessity, and cannot therefore escape its logical
issue in pantheism. God is not merely the Father of the
idea of creation, but the Father of the *Logos* which is the
vehicle of the idea. Jewish thought as represented in the
Alexandrian school, regarded the Logos as merely a
cosmos nœtus (κόσμος νοητός) or world of ideas, as we
have previously indicated. St. John makes bold to affirm
that the *Logos* is not an idea only, but a Person, and as
such the vehicle of the idea by which the world is given

reality. Thus the *Logos* becomes the sole link between the Infinite and the finite, between the realm of ideas and the realm of actual existences. Here, then, is the mystery hid from the ages but made manifest in the incarnation, namely, that the *Logos* or creative Word is Himself God. The Word veiled in the Old Testament in the expressions "God said," and "Let there be" is now seen to be not only the spoken Word but the speaking Word. It is through Him that God's word of wisdom passes into created reality. Creation, therefore, demands a Mediator, both for thought and reality. It was because the *Logos* was the Mediator of both purpose and efficiency in the work of creation, that the *Logos* incarnate as the Son, became the Mediator of both the revealing and the enabling grace of redemption.

THE HYMN OF CREATION

The Book of Genesis opens with an inspired Psalm, sometimes known as the "Hymn of Creation," and sometimes as the "Poem of the Dawn." By this it is not meant that the account is an allegory or fiction, but a true historical description, poetically expressed. It is fitting that the harmony of creation, at which the morning stars sang together, and all the sons of God shouted for joy, should be revealed to us in the harmonies of poetical description. Dr. Miley denies the poetical form of the chapter, and quotes Dr. Terry as saying that "every thorough Hebrew scholar knows that in all the Old Testament there is not a more simple, straightforward prose narrative than this first chapter of Genesis" (MILEY, *Syst. Th.*, I, 298). We may admit that it is not cast in poetical form, but the balanced rhythm, the stately movement, the recurrent refrains and the blend of beauty and power, all indicate that it is of the nature of poetry. "The rhythmical character of the passage," says Dr. Whedon, "its stately style, its parallelisms, its refrains, its unity within itself all combine to show that it is a poem." Dr. Cocker holds that it contains the same unity as the 104th Psalm, or the Lord's

Prayer, or the Parable of the Laborers in the Vineyard.
Dr. Thomas C. Porter says that "to him who could
grasp the mighty idea and take in the whole at one view,
the entire creation would appear like a solemn hymn,
like some grand oratorio which, starting on a few low,
faint notes, gradually gains strength and fullness, and
swelling louder and louder, rolls on from harmony to
height of harmony until it reaches its loftiest outburst
and expression, the diapason closing full in man." Dr.
Pace maintains that the whole Book of Genesis has a
typical metrical octad style which he calls the metric
composition of the Holy Spirit.

Exordium

In the beginning God created the heavens and the earth.

I.

Now the earth had become waste and wild (or formless and
    empty)
And darkness was on the face of the abyss (or roaring deep)
But the Spirit of God was brooding upon the face of the deep
    (waters or vapors)
(I) And God said,
    Light be (or Light exist)
And light was.

    First Refrain: And Gow saw the light that it was good.

And God divided the light from the darkness,
And called the light, day
But the darkness, called he night.

    So there was evening and there was morning: one day.

II.

(II) And God said,
    Let there be an expanse in the midst of the waters,
    And let it be a division of waters from waters (or vapor)
And it was so.

And God made the expanse,
And it divided the waters which were below the expanse
From the waters which were above the expanse.

    So there was evening and there was morning: a second day.

It will be noticed that at the beginning of each work of creation there
is the formula "And God said." If we include the two providential formulas found in verses 28, 29, the expression occurs ten times, giving rise to
the Jewish dictum, "By ten sayings, the world was created" (ABOTH, v. 1).

III.

(III) And God said,
Let the waters under the heavens be gathered into one
place,
And let the dry ground appear.
And it was so.
And God called the dry ground, Land,
But the gathering together of the waters, called he, Seas.
Second Refrain: And God saw that it was good.

(IV) And God said,
Let the land put forth vegetation (shoot forth shoots)
Herb yielding seed after its kind,
And tree bearing fruit, after its kind,
Wherein is the seed thereof, upon the land.
And it was so.
And the earth brought forth vegetation (*desche,* tender grass)
Herb yielding seed after its kind,
And tree bearing fruit wherein is the seed thereof after its kind.
Third Refrain: And God saw that it was good.

So there was evening and there was morning: a third day.

IV.

(V) And God said,
Let there be luminaries in the expanse of the heavens,
To divide between the day and the night,
And let them be for signs and for seasons,
And for days and for years,
And let them be for luminaries in the expanse of the
heavens
To give light upon the earth.
And it was so.

And God made two great luminaries (places or instruments of
light)
The greater luminary to rule the day,
The lesser luminary to rule the night.
(He made) also the stars.

The three terms used to express the idea of vegetation cover the
broad divisions. (1) The term *desche* is rendered tender grass (II Sam.
23:4) and tender herb (Job 38:27) (2) "Herbs" refer to the larger plants
(Gen. 3:18) and (3) fruit trees with seed-enclosed fruit, this expression
intending to convey the idea of self-propagation.

The words "And it was so" found in Verse 7 are misplaced and
should be placed at the end of Verse 6 as in the Septuagint translation.
We have so placed them in the above Hymn of Creation.

There are seven refrains in the Hebrew text, but the Septuagint
translation has an additional refrain, "And God saw that it was good"
at the end of verse 8. The refrains found in the Hebrew text are in
verses 4, 10, 12, 18, 21, 25, 31. Those in vs. 28, 29 are usually regarded
as providential rather than creative refrains.

And God set them in the firmament of the heaven (or expanse)
To give light upon the earth,
And to rule over the day and over the night,
And to divide the light from the darkness.
   Fourth Refrain: And God saw that it was good.

   So there was evening and there was morning: a fourth day.

V.

(VI) And God said,
   Let the waters swarm forth swarming things, living souls
   And let birds fly over the earth,
   Over the face of the expanse of the heavens.
And it was so (Septuagint translation)

And God created the great leviathans (sea-monsters)
And every living soul that moveth,
Which the waters swarmed forth after their kind,
And every winged bird after its kind.
   Fifth Refrain: And God saw that it was good.
And God blessed them, saying,
   Be fruitful and multiply, and fill the waters in the seas,
   And let the birds multiply in the land.

   So there was evening and there was morning: a fifth day.

VI.

(VII) And God said,
   Let the land bring forth living soul after its kind,
   Cattle (dumb or tame beasts) and creeping things,
   And land-animals after their kind. (Wild as opposed to
      tame on account of vital energy.)
And it was so.

   And God made the beast of the land after its kind,
   And the cattle after their kind.

The writer states the threefold purpose of the luminaries as follows: (1) to divide day from night, or the light from the darkness (v. 18). (2) For signs and for seasons, and for days and years. Signs refer to the cardinal points of the compass and the help which the stars give in finding these points. Seasons refer to the fixed times for migration of the birds (Jer. 8:7), seedtime, flowering and harvest—practically what we mean by the four seasons. It refers also to fixed religious festivals. The "days and years" are fixed as to their length by the heavenly bodies. (3) To give light upon the earth, the expression doubtless having reference to the furnishing of the necessary conditions for the existence and progress of the race.

Living souls is an expression which has reference to individualized somatic life. The term soul (*nephesh*) in Hebrew psychology is not peculiar to man, but represents the principle of life and sensibility in any animal organism. It is therefore, frequently transferred to the sentient organism itself (Cf. Ezek. 47:9, Lev. 24:18).

And everything that creepeth upon the ground after its
   kind.
Sixth Refrain: And God saw that it was good.
(VIII) And God said,

Let us make man in our image, after our likeness,
And let them have dominion over the fish of the sea,
And over the fowl (or birds) of the air,
And over all the land (W. Syriac, wild beasts of the land)
And over every creeping thing that creepeth upon the land.

And God created man in his own image,
In the image of God created he them.
Male and female created he them.

And God blessed them.

(IX) And God said unto them,
   Be fruitful, and multiply, and replenish the earth, and sub-
      due it,
   And have dominion over the fish of the sea,
   And over the fowl of the air,
   And over every living thing that moveth upon the earth.

(X) And God said,
   Behold, I have given you every herb yielding seed, which
      is upon the face of all the earth,
   And every tree wherein is seed-inclosed fruit.
   To you it shall be for food
   And to every living thing of the land,
   And to every bird of the heavens,
   And to every thing that moveth upon the land, wherein is
      a living soul,
   (I have given) every green herb for food.
And it was so.

   Seventh Refrain: And God saw everything that he had
      made, and behold it was very good.

   So there was evening and there was morning: a sixth day.

Epode

Thus were finished the heavens and the earth,
And all the hosts of them.
And on the seventh day, God finished (put period to) his work
   which he had made,

The expression "Let the earth bring forth" is not intended to convey the idea of spontaneous generation, but represents merely the adaptation necessary to the next stage of development. It emphasizes the
fact that all life originated at the command of God, whether immediate
or mediate.

And he rested on the seventh day from all his work which he
    had made;
And God blessed the seventh day, and hallowed it:
Because that therein he rest from all his work,
Which God by creating had made.

THE MOSAIC COSMOGONY

The Hymn of Creation which furnishes the basis of
the Mosaic cosmogony has been interpreted in various
ways. (1) *The Mythological Interpretation.* Modern
critics regard the first chapter of Genesis as a mythological account written by a highly cultured Israelite
who gives his reflections concerning the origin of all
things. But neither the tone nor the contents warrant
this construction. Both Jesus and the apostles treat
the chapter as sacred history. (Cf. Matt. 19:4). (2) *The
Allegorical Interpretation.* Due to the influence of the
Alexandrian School, many of the earlier Christian writers adopted the allegorical method of interpretation. To
modern thought, however, with its scientific background, this method is scarcely less objectionable than
the mythological interpretation. As late as the nineteenth century, Herder defended the method, regarding
the creation account as an optical representation of the
beginning of all things which reappears every morning
at sunrise. (3) *The Vision Hypothesis.* This theory was
advocated by Kurtz, Keerl and others, who regarded
the account as being made known in a series of retrospective visions, given in such a manner that the objective truth of revelation blended with the subjective
conception of the seer. While this form of revelation is
of course possible, it finds no support by other instances
of retrospective vision, and has never been an accepted
theory in the Church. (4) *The Historical Interpretation.* This account was a portion of the Scriptures which
existed in the time of our Lord, which He pronounced
holy and appealed to as divine. It is therefore authoritative. Interpretations may vary, but for us, this account is the truth concerning the origin of the world.

The Days of Creation. The Genesis account of creation is primarily a religious document. It cannot be

considered a scientific statement, and yet it must not
be regarded as contradictory to science. It is rather, a
supreme illustration of the manner in which revealed
truth indirectly sheds light upon scientific fields. The
Hebrew word *yom* which is translated "day" occurs
no less than 1,480 times in the Old Testament, and is
translated by something over fifty different words, including such terms as *time, life, today, age, forever, continually* and *perpetually*. With such a flexible use of
the original term, it is impossible to either dogmatize
or to demand unswerving restriction to one only of
those meanings. It is frequently assumed that originally
orthodox belief held to a solar day of twenty-four hours,
and that the church altered her exegesis under the pressure of modern geological discoveries. This as Dr.
Shedd points out is one of the errors of ignorance."
The best Hebrew exegesis has never regarded the days
of Genesis as solar days, but as day-periods of indefinite
duration. The doctrine of an immense time prior to
the six days of creation was a common view among the
earlier fathers and the schoolmen. Only with the scholastics of the middle ages and the evangelical writers of
the seventeenth and eighteenth centuries was this idea
current. Previous to this a profounder view was taught
by the acknowledged leaders of the Church. Thus
Augustine says, "Our seven days resemble the seven
days of the Genesis account in being a series, and in
having the vicissitudes of morning and evening, but they
are *multum in pares*." He calls them *naturæ* (natures
or birth), and *moræ* (delays or solemn pauses). Hence
they are God-divided days in contradistinction to sun-
divided days; they are ineffable days (*dies ineffabiles*)
as in their true nature transcendent, while the sun-
divided days (*vicissitudines cœli*) are due merely to
changes in planetary movements. He affirms, therefore, that the word day does not apply to the duration
of time, but to the boundaries of great periods. Nor is
this a metaphorical meaning of the word, but the original, which signifies "to put period to" or to denote a
self-completed time. Origen, Irenæus, Basil and Greg-

ory Nazianzen taught the same doctrine during the patristic period, as did also many of the learned Jewish doctors outside the Christian Church. Later writers holding this view are Hahn, Hensler, Knapp, Lee, Henry More, Burnett and others. Of the more recent writers we may mention Hodge, Pope, Miley, Cocker, and Stearns. Some writers, recognizing that the word for "day" as found in the Hebrew text may mean either a definite or indefinite period of time, leave the question open. Dr. Wakefield holds to the theory of solar days, while a number of theologians regard the subject of creation as belonging to the field of science rather than theology, and mention it but briefly or omit it altogether.

Creation and Cosmogony. The Genesis account of creation establishes a distinction between the first production of matter in the sense of origination, and secondary creation, or the formation of that matter by subsequent elaboration into a cosmos. These distinctions are usually known as primary and secondary, or as immediate and mediate creation. While primary creation is a direct origination, secondary creation is always indirect, that is it is accomplished by means of a Law behind other laws. The term mediate creation better expresses the thought, and conveys the idea that God creates through creation itself. Bishop Martensen points out that it is involved in creation that God brings forth not something dead, but something alive, and consequently able to reproduce itself. There is therefore a certain autonomy in the created universe, derived and dependent, indeed, but nevertheless an autonomy, with the capacity of being set up in opposition to God himself. St. Paul recognizes this limited creaturehood when he says, that *the creature itself also shall be delivered from the bondage of corruption into the glorious liberty of the children of God. For we know that the whole creation groaneth and travaileth in pain together until now* (Rom. 8:21, 22). When, therefore, God created the vegetation He did not say, "Let there be vegetation" but "Let the earth put forth vegetation"; when He created somatic life He said, "Let the waters swarm forth swarming things," and again, "Let the land bring forth living soul after its kind." This is mediate creation. As previously pointed out in a note on the Hymn of Creation, these expressions are not intended to convey the idea of spontaneous generation, but to emphasize a truth that all things either immediately or mediately were created at the command of God. Each of the new days was ushered in solely by virtue of the omnipotent word spoken by the Creator, and was therefore *creatura;* but each new day dawned only when the time was full and the conditions perfect, and was therefore, *natura.* There is here, also, a suggestion that the progress of the entire creation depends upon the progress made by the creatures in their natural development. The idea of creation dominant among the Hebrews was that of *creatura;* that among the Greeks, *natura.* The former was a direct creative act, an origination; the latter an unfolding or development in time. It is evident that the tendency of the former is toward Deism, while that of the latter is toward Pantheism. It is the glory of Christianity that it presents both the transcendent and the immanent aspects of creation in their balanced harmony. Thus St. John in his teaching concerning the Logos, regards the world (1) as a production through the Word, an origination of that which before had no being; and (2) as a transition from not-being to being through the *Logos. Through it everything was done* [γέγονεν]; *and without it not even one thing was done, which has been done* (John 1: 3, Emphatic Diaglot). The word *ginomai* (γίνομαι) occurs in the New Testament more than seven hundred times, and fifty-three times in this Gospel; and as the Emphatic Diaglot points out, is never translated create, but signifies to be, to become, to come to pass; also to be done or transacted. It is translated "made" in the sense of "to be born" in Romans 1: 3 and Galatians 4: 4 which gives the true import of the word as a birth or a becoming. The word for create is *ktizo* (κτίζω). It is clear then that according to the teachings of the Scriptures there has been both a creative and a cosmogonic beginning—the one supernatural and infinite, the other relative and finite, both being comprehended in any true Christian concept of the origin of the world.

THE ORDER OF CREATION

In considering the order of creation as given in the Genesis account, three things demand attention, *first,* Primary Creation or Origination; *second,* Secondary Creation or Formation; and *third,* Gradual and Cumulative Creation.

Primary Creation or Origination. The word "created" is used three times in the Genesis account, and is a translation of the word *bara,* which signifies origination, or creation *de novo.* This word occurs in the three following verses: *In the beginning God created the heavens and the earth* (Genesis 1:1). *And God created great whales* (leviathans or sea monsters) (Gen. 1:21). *So God created man in his own image, in the image of God created he him* (Gen.·1:27). Dr. Cocker makes the statement that a careful study of this and the following chapter led him to the conclusion that there was something fundamental and distinctive in the word *bara* which did not attach to the words *yetsar* and *aysah.* "It is in reality," he says, "the distinction between origination *de novo,* and formation out of pre-existing materials. There are three instances in which *bara* occurs in Genesis 1. We are fully convinced that in each case it denotes the origination of a new entity—a real addition to the sum of existence (COCKER, *Theistic Conception of the World,* p. 157). Dr. Miley questions this position and cites Isaiah 43:7 where all three words occur and are applied to the same divine act. It is not that he denies that the primitive act of creation was the origination of matter itself, but insists that there is no conclusive proof of it on purely philological grounds (Cf. MILEY, *Systematic Theology,* I, p. 283). Dr. Adam Clarke throws the weight of his authority on the side of the former position. He interprets the word *bara* as causing that to exist which, previous to this moment, had no being. He says, "The rabbins, who are the legitimate judges in a case of verbal criticism of their own language, are unanimous in asserting that the word *bara* expresses commencement of the existence of a thing: or its egression from nonentity to entity. It does not in its primary meaning, denote the preserving or new forming things that had previously existed, as some imagine: but creation, in the proper sense of the term, though it has some other acceptations in other places (CLARKE, *Commentary*, Gen. 1:1). If then we examine the three instances where this word occurs, we shall find each of them an origination of a new entity.

The first origination was that of material substance, or the *prima materia* of all physical existences. Dr. Adam Clarke's rendering of this verse is, *God in the beginning created the substance of the heavens, and the substance of the earth, i.e.,* the *prima materia,* or first element out of which the heavens and the earth were successively formed. He substantiates his position by referring to the Hebrew word *eth* which is usually regarded as a particle denoting that the word following is in the accusative or oblique case, but which the rabbinical literature uses in a more extensive sense. "The particle *eth,*" says Eben Ezra, "signifies the substance of a thing." Kimchi, in his *Book of Roots,* gives a like definition. It is used by the Cabbalists to signify the beginning and the end as the words *alpha* and *omega* are used in the Apocalypse. Dr. Clarke states further that "it argues a wonderful philosophic accuracy in the statement of Moses, which brings before us, not a finished heavens and earth as every other translation appears to do, though afterward the process of their formation is given in detail, but merely the materials out of which God built the whole system in the six following days" (ADAM CLARKE, *Commentary*, Gen. 1:1). The first origination therefore, was that of matter in its chaotic or unformed state.

The second origination was that of somatic or soul life. *And God created the great leviathans* [or sea monsters], *and every living soul* [*nephesh* or soul of life] *that moveth* (Gen. 1:21). Here is the appearance of a new entity. The diffused life found in the vegetable realm is individualized and separated from the universal life of nature. It is called somatic life (from *soma,* a body), in that the individualized life is given a body separate and distinct from diffused life; and it is a *nephesh* or soul of life, in that the soul is the individualized center of force and the body is immediate field of activity. This soul is an immaterial entity, having sensation, feeling and will. It is therefore properly expressed by the word *bara,* in that a new power or principle was infused into the then existing nature.

The third origination was that of spirit or personal being. *And God created man in his own image, in the image of God created he him; male and female created he them* (Gen. 1:27). As the second origination was that of individualized life characterized by consciousness, so the third origination is a further individualization which may be characterized as self-consciousness. If then we understand by the soul, that principle which individualizes life, the soul must take on the character of the life thus individualized. We may regard the soul of an animal, therefore, as consciousness dominating a field of instinct; while the soul of man, is a self dominating a field of consciousness. Man not only knows, but he knows that he knows, and thus becomes responsible for his actions. It is this quality which constitutes man a free moral agent and thus makes him Godlike. This is the image of God in man.

We may say, then, that the three created entities expressed by the word *bara* are matter, soul and spirit, or matter, life and mind. They may be equally well expressed by the words matter, consciousness and self.

Secondary Creation or Formation. Deep as is the mystery of creation in the primary sense, it is no less so in the secondary sense of formation. God does not originate the material of creation, and then in an external manner form it into individual objects with no relation to each other, except that of a common fashioner or architect. He creates through creation itself. He creates that which has life in itself and consequently the power of self-propagation. Thus the world has both a supernatural and a natural beginning. It is a cosmos in which all the parts which compose one whole are arranged in order and beauty. They are not disconnected, but one emerges out of the other at the command of God so that all things are related both in nature and as a consequence of their supernatural origin. There is no place in the account for the theory of spontaneous generation. This is the fallacy of the evolutionary hypothesis. If now we note the various stages which are introduced by the creative fiat, *Let there be,* and concluded with the refrain, *And God saw that it was good,* we shall have before us the seven formative acts of God as found in Genesis account. These will constitute the sevenfold series of natural beginnings or births out of pre-existent and prepared material which through the Divine Word or *Logos* transformed the world from chaos to cosmos and united the universe in a true cosmogony.

(1) *Let there be light* (Gen. 1:3). This is the formation of cosmic light, sometimes regarded as radiant heat and light. The Hebrew word is *aur* and is translated "fire" in Isaiah 31:9 and Ezekiel 5:2; it is translated "sun" in Job 31:23 and "lightning" in Job 37:3. (2) *Let there be an expanse* (or firmament) (Gen. 1:6), and *Let the waters under the heaven be gathered into one place, and let the dry land appear* (Gen. 1:9). It will be noted that here there are two fiats included in the one refrain. In the Septuagint a refrain follows verse 6, but the best Hebrew exegesis holds that this formative period was not completed on the second day, and therefore the refrain was added only after the creation of the seas and land which began with the formation of the firmament. Dr. Cocker holds that the firmament represents a mechanical combination of chemical elements, while the sea and land represent chemical compounds and their molar aggregation. (3) *Let the land put forth vegetation* (Gen. 1:11). Here there is an introduction of a new force within matter, a vital element giving rise to vitalized germinal matter, and making possible the organic realm. (4) *Let there be luminaries in the expanse of the heavens* (Gen. 1:14). It is a significant

fact that the organic realms as well as the inorganic begin with the introduction of light. Here the light is an adjustment of the cosmical relations, furnishing the conditions for the further development of the organic realm. (5) *Let the waters swarm forth swarming things, living souls, and let birds fly over the earth* (Gen. 1:20). This fifth formative act or birth out of the waters and the atmosphere can refer only to the material organisms which embody the living souls, for conjoined with this formative act there is the use of the word *bara* as the origination of living soul which forms the second entity. (6) *Let the land bring forth living soul after its kind* (Gen. 1:24). The sixth formation is the emergence out of the earth of the material organisms of the animal, by the fiat of God. This appears to be the last of the purely emergent acts of God's mediate creation, for the next following combines with it the introduction of a new formative as well as a new creative element. (7) *Let us make man* (Gen. 1:26). Of the creative statement, this portion only refers to the formation of the material organism of man. But the formative act is not entirely mediate as in the former instances, for the word is not "Let the earth bring forth man," but *Let us make man.* Hence in the word "made," we find the formative act which relates man's body to the cosmos, while in the word "create" *(bara)* as previously indicated, we find the origination of man's spiritual being in the image and likeness of God. Thus each stage of development is the condition for each succeeding stage in orderly arrangement, until all are gathered up in a final refrain, *And God saw everything that he had made, and, behold, it was very good* (Gen. 1:31).

The Creative Periods. Perhaps the most outstanding feature of the Mosaic cosmogony is the orderly arrangement in stages and periods known as creative days. In the sense of origination, creation is instantaneous; but as

Whether St. Paul meant only to summarize the various orders of the animal creation, or whether he meant to teach distinctions in kind, the following verse is worthy of study. *All flesh,* he says, *is not the same flesh: but there is one kind of flesh of men, another flesh of beasts, another of fishes, another of birds* (I Cor. 15:39).

formation it is gradual and cumulative. There is a progressive revelation in an ascending scale of creative acts. Each stage is preparatory to that which succeeds it, as well as a prophecy of that which shall follow. The study of the Genesis account reveals certain facts which take on added significance with each new scientific discovery. *First,* there are two great eras mentioned, each with three creative days—the Inorganic and the Organic. *Second,* each of these great eras begins with the appearance of light—the one with the creation of cosmic light, the other with light emanating from created luminaries. *Third,* each of these eras ends with a day in which a twofold work is accomplished, the first the completing or perfecting act of that which precedes it, and the second a prophecy of that which is to be. This arrangement may be set forth in schematic form as follows:

The Inorganic Era

1st Day—Cosmical Light
2nd Day—The Firmament—water and atmosphere
3rd Day—Dry Land (or the outlining of land and seas)
    Creation of Vegetation (*transitional and prophetic*)

The Organic Era

4th Day—The Luminaries
5th Day—The lower animals—fishes and birds
6th Day—Land animals
    Creation of Man (*transitional and prophetic*)

The creation of vegetation which for physical reasons belongs to the third day, is the culmination of the Inorganic Era and the prophecy of the Organic Era which immediately follows. We may say also that man, the culmination of the work of the sixth day, is likewise prophetic of another æon, the new age in which the will of God shall be done on earth as it is in heaven.

With the rapidly increasing discoveries of science, the Genesis account was soon called in question by men who appeared to be authorities in their fields of investigation. But Christian men, eminent in science also, after prolonged study and research declared that not only is there no conflict between Genesis and modern science but that there is a remarkable parallel between them. Hugh Miller, eminent in geology, found no misplacement of facts in the Genesis account. Professors Winchell, Dana, Guyot and Dawson, among the earlier men of science, maintained that the order of events in the Scripture cosmogony corresponds essentially with the discoveries of modern science. One of the earlier parallels between Genesis and geology is that of Professor Dana who gives the following geological order (Cf. DANA, *Manual of Geology*, HODGE, *Syst. Th.*, I, p. 571):

1. Light.

2. The dividing of the waters below from the waters above the earth.

3. The dividing of the land and water on the earth.

4. Vegetation, which Moses, appreciating the philosophical characteristics of the new creation, distinguishes from previous inorganic substances, and defines as that which has seed in itself.

5. The sun, moon and stars.

6. The lower animals, those that swarm in the waters and the creeping and flying species of the land.

7. Beasts of prey.

8. Man.

Later discoveries in science demand new statements of these parallels, but we may believe, with James Ward, that there is not and never can be any opposition between science and religion, any more than there can be between grammar and religion. Sir William Ramsey once said, "Between the essential truth of Christianity and the established facts of science there is no real antagonism." We are indebted to Dr. L. A. Reed for the following parallels between the Genesis account of creation, and the more recent discoveries of modern science.

"When the Nebular Hypothesis was advocated in the early part of the nineteenth century by Pierre Simon

Laplace, French mathematician and astronomer, it was quite universally received by the scientific world. Almost any one of Laplace's original researches is alone sufficient to stamp him as one of the greatest of mathematicians. Some of his accomplishments are the discovery of the invariability of the major axes of the planetary orbits; the explanation of the great inequality in the motions of Jupiter and Saturn; the solution of the problem of the acceleration of the mean motion of the moon; the theory of Jupiter's satellites and many other important laws including this Nebular Theory, which was an attempt to explain the development of the solar system. 'This theory supposes that the bodies composing the solar system once existed in the form of nebulæ; that these had a revolution on their own axis from west to east; that the temperature gradually diminishing, and the nebulæ contracting by refrigeration, the rotation increased in rapidity, and zones of nebulosity were successively thrown off in consequence of the centrifugal force overpowering the central attraction. These zones being condensed, and partaking of the primary rotation, constituted the planets, some of which in turn threw off zones which now form their satellites. The main body being condensed toward the center, formed the sun. The theory afterward was extended so as to include a cosmogony of the whole universe' (Cf. WINSTON, *Encyl.*, Vol. VII, Neb. Hypoth.).

"Many objections were raised to this hypothesis, because it did not satisfy the demands of the interpretation of the first chapter of Genesis. With the discovery of the spectroscope, much in the above hypothesis was proved fact, for now nebulous matter is recognized to be in existence all through the universe. It was also discovered that much of the nebulæ is black and dark, and it was further discovered that the spiral nebulæ have a planetesimal organization. This brought forth the theory that the solar system was formed from nebulæ consisting of planetesimals. These formations still may be found in the universe. Hence, quite a change is noted from the old Nebular Hypothesis and instead of the blazing nebulous mass of 'Laplace,' we have the dark nebulæ building up a universe of planets, planetoids, asteroids* and meteors. As formally stated, this building process may still be discovered going on in the universe. Thousands of meteors fall on the earth each year and the magnetism of the various spheres builds them up by attracting the planetesimals to them. All this fits in beautifully with the second verse of the first chapter of Genesis, which says, *And the earth was without form and void; and darkness was upon the face of the deep.* And so the planets were formed from these shapeless masses. The smaller the nebulæ the quicker the contraction, hence this would explain why the earth is mentioned as being created before the sun, for it would not have begun to function until the earth was fairly well formed as a sphere. The earth also preceded the moon, for satellites were supposed to have come into existence through centrifugal force and it was mentioned in relation with the sun as being a 'lighter of the earth.' Thus in the first day this nebulous light was the universal illumination. The character of this light is somewhat of a mystery, but astronomers think it was electrical and phosphorescent. Suffice it to say that in the treatment of the planetesimal explanation (or hypothesis), the account of light being given before the mention of the sun and the moon, substantiates scientifically the claim of the creation story."

When one orients himself as to the first day of creation, then the other days follow in exact scientific order. These periods of time have never been arranged by scientists in any other manner than the first chapter of Genesis arranges them. Palæontological evidence substantiates the order and arrangement of life as laid down in Genesis. The creative fiat, in its triple expression in the first chapter of Genesis, is sufficient explanation for being, both inanimate and animate, and with the increasing discoveries of science is being verified each day by earth's greatest minds.

* About six hundred asteroids have their orbits between Mars and Jupiter, the largest of them, Ceres, having a diameter of not more than 500 miles.

The Restoration Theory. In order to account for the great geological periods, it has been held more or less extensively in the church, that the first verse of the creative account is an introductory statement without reference to a time order; and that between this and the following verses an immense interval of time elapsed. Thus Dr. Shedd makes the assertion that between the single comprehensive act of the creation of the angels and of the chaotic matter mentioned in Genesis 1:1 an interval of time elapsed; and he further declares that this was a common view among the fathers and the schoolmen. In this way the long creative periods which geology demands are accounted for without regarding the days of Genesis as other than solar days of twenty-four hours each. Modern writers such as John W. McGarvey and G. Campbell Morgan take this position, setting aside the two introductory verses as expressive of an immeasurably long period of time. This was followed by a great catastrophe in which everything upon the earth was destroyed. After this God re-created the earth and revivified it in a week of six solar days. In substantiation of this the words of Isaiah are cited, *God himself that formed the earth and made it; he hath established it, he created it not in vain* [*i.e.,* He created it not a waste], *he formed it to be inhabited* (Isaiah 45:18). Dr. Coggins calls attention to the Hebrew words *tohu wabohu* as implying such a catastrophe, the former meaning "wasteness" and the latter "voidness" or "emptiness."

THE PURPOSE OF CREATION

We have considered the world as *cosmos*, it remains now to direct our attention to the world as *æon*. By this we mean that succession of epochs and periods running throughout the course of the ages, and involving both the physical and ethical aspects of the world. One such æon is past, the second æon is the present age, and we have the promise of an age to come. What is beyond this we cannot know, although St. Paul refers to *the ages to come* (Eph. 2:7). The first æon on the physical plane is that indefinite formative age which antedates the present heavens and earth (Gen. 1:1). The second æon is the present economy. As the prehistoric æon was superseded by the action of persistent forces, which at the command of God issued in the current æon, so both the observations of naturalists and the words of divine revelation teach, that there are now mighty agencies held in check, which anticipate tremendous convulsions, and which when the fullness of time shall have come, will break forth into a new heavens and a new earth. *But the day of the Lord will come as a thief in the night; in the which the heavens shall pass away with a great noise, and the elements shall melt with fervent heat, the earth also and the works that are therein shall be burned up. Seeing then that all these things shall be dissolved* [λυθήσονται], *what manner of persons ought ye to be in all holy conversation and godliness, looking for and hasting unto the coming of the day of God, wherein the heavens being on fire shall be dissolved* [λυθήσονται], *and the elements shall melt with fervent heat? Nevertheless we, according to his promise, look for new heavens and a new earth, wherein dwelleth righteousness* (II Peter 3:10-13). In one sense therefore the present world will come to an end and pass away to make room for a different organization; but in another sense it will not come to an end, for at the command of God, all that hinders its progress, all that links it with the curse of man, will be melted away or dissolved, and it will then emerge into the heavens and the earth which are to be. *For, behold, I create new heavens and a new earth: and the former shall not be remembered, nor come into mind* (Isa. 65:17). *And I saw a new heaven and a new earth: for the first heaven and the first earth were passed away* (Rev. 21:1).

But the æons cannot be understood on the physical plane alone. There are ethical and spiritual realms which closely parallel them, and reveal in clearer light the purpose of God in creation. (1) The first æon on this plane is the prehuman realm of created spirits which is given only brief mention in the sacred Scriptures. A part of this world of spirits apostasized, thus bringing moral disorder and spiritual confusion into the universe. What the chaos of the geological ages was to the present material universe, that the prehistoric spiritual disorder is to the present moral and spiritual economy. The one answers to the other. (2) The second æon opens with the creation of man as an ethical and spiritual being and will extend to the final consummation of the present world order. Two decisive epochs may be observed. *First,* the fall of man into sin, which the Scriptures seem to indicate was the direct consequence of the defection of angels; and *second,* the incarnation or advent of the Second Man as the Lord from heaven. The first man was of the earth, earthy, by which we are to understand that he was the full complement of all the subhuman kingdoms. The Second Man was a quickening spirit which marked a new beginning in the human race—a beginning which can come to its perfection only with the return of the Son of man in His glory. While conditioned by the first Adam, the last Adam will be the full spiritual complement of all the essential demands implicit in the original constitution of the Adamic race, and of all the accidental demands due to man's depravity and sin. We may say, then, that the physical universe came to its triumph in the resurrection of Jesus Christ, and its ethical and spiritual triumph in the return of the Holy Spirit. Thus the physical universe finds its meaning in the ethical, the ethical in the spiritual, and the spiritual in the glory of God. (3) The third æon will open with the advent of Christ and usher in the new age which is to be. Then the world-idea which had been struggling through the ages will come to its perfection. This is the mystery, which according to St. Paul has been hidden from the ages and generations, but which is now made manifest. Christ is both the mystery and the manifestation. The new æon from the physical aspect will find its expression in a new heaven and a new earth; on the ethical and moral plane, it will be an age in which righteousness dwells—an age free from sin and all moral disorder.

The Kingdom of God. We may say then, that theology finds the purpose of creation in the kingdom of God. This kingdom is at once a present possession and a future hope. Jesus was Himself the Perfect embodiment of the principles upon which the kingdom rests. Through His redemptive work men may now be delivered from sin; with the full fruition of this work, His people will be delivered from the consequences of sin. The complete realization of this ideal requires other conditions than those which obtain during the present æon. Here there is an inner redemptive experience of *righteousness, and peace, and joy in the Holy Ghost* (Rom. 14:17); then at the appearance of the Lord in glory, the kingdom shall be ushered in as the full realization of man's highest ethical and spiritual ideals, and the perfect medium for the realization of all his aspirations and hopes.

There are three historical interpretations of the kingdom of God, each of which contains some truth which should be conserved. These concepts of the kingdom are, first, the Millennial; *second,* the Ecclesiastical; and *third,* the Individualistic. They demand only brief mention at this time.

The Millennial Concept of the Kingdom. This is a term used to describe that class of theories which look for the kingdom to be ushered in by a sudden transformation of the present order, at the coming of Christ. Since according to this theory the advent precedes the millennium, believers in this theory are commonly known as premillennialists. The term used in the early Church to express this concept was "Chiliasm." The Latin equivalent of the Greek χιλιάς is *mille,* or a thousand, from which our word millennium is derived. The beginnings of this doctrine lie far back in the eschatological ideal of later Judaism, and were revived and strengthened in the early Church through a study of the Jewish apocalyptical literature. While this teaching was not universal in the early Church, it was nevertheless the dominant theory, as may be confirmed by a study of the ante-Nicene Fathers.

The Ecclesiastical Concept of the Kingdom. With Augustine thought was diverted into different channels. The dying out of the expectation of the immediate return of Christ led to a reinterpretation of the teachings of our Lord. Augustine interpreted the millennium to mean the spiritual reign of the Church, and therefore, in large measure identified the kingdom with the visible Church. The extension of the Church meant the extension of the kingdom. The term, therefore, is applied to those theories which seek by social and ecclesiastical organization to mold the social structure after a Christian pattern. The theory finds its clearest expression, for the Roman Catholic Church at least, in Augustine's *City of God.*

The Individualistic Concept of the Kingdom. Against the social organization of the Roman Catholic Church, Protestantism reacted, and consequently developed the individualistic conception of the kingdom. According to this theory, the kingdom is an inner spiritual kingdom—the rule of Christ over His people through the indwelling presence of the Holy Spirit. It has taken different forms, as for instance, the elective grace of Calvinism and the individual probation of Arminianism. Luther stressed the idea of justification by faith, and John Wesley pressed the matter still further, insisting that as we are justified by faith, so also we are sanctified by faith. But whether Lutheran, Reformed or Arminian all agreed in denying the mediatorial offices of the Church, and insisted upon a direct relation of man to God through the Spirit.

The element to be conserved in the first theory is the necessity of a new order as a ground for the full expression of the Christian ideal. In the second theory, we must insist that the inner spiritual principles have their counterpart in an outward social structure; while the necessity of grace in the transformed lives of individual persons must ever give character and quality to the ideals of the kingdom.

ANGELS AND SPIRITS

The Scriptures clearly teach that there is an order of intelligences higher than that of men; and further asserts that these intelligences are connected with man both in providence and in the redemptive economy. These intelligences are called *Spirits* to denote their specific nature; they are called *Angels* to denote their mission. Nothing can be known of them other than that which is revealed in the Scriptures. They are created spirits but the time of their creation is not indicated. Dr. Miley holds that such creation must have been included in the statement found in Genesis 1:1, and therefore preceding the six days' formative period. Dr. Stump, on the other hand, states that this creative act must have followed the formative period, for at its close God pronounced everything that He had made as "very good."

The Nature and Attributes of Angels. Angels are frequently described as pure spirits, *i.e.*, incorporeal and immaterial beings. The Scriptures do not attribute bodies to them; but on the assumption that a world of spirits could not function in the material realm apart from the media of bodies, a council held at Nicea (A.D. 784) decided that angels had ethereal bodies, composed of either light or ether. In substantiation of this they quoted such verses as Matthew 28:3 and Luke 2:9, as well as other passages which spoke of their luminous presence. The Lateran Council (A.D. 1215) reversed the former decision and declared that angels were incorporeal. This has been the general opinion of the Church since that time. Dr. Pope, however, takes a different position. He holds that the angels, while less closely connected with the material universe than man, must not be regarded as pure spirits. "God alone," he says, "is pure, essential Spirit; these created spirits are clothed with ethereal vestures, such as Paul describes when he says, *There is a spiritual body* (I Cor. 15:44). Thus our Lord tells us that the *children of the resurrection are* [ἰσάγγελοι], *equal unto the angels* (Luke 20:36). Having a more subtle organization than man, they are at present higher in their range of faculties; greater in power and might (II Peter 2: 11), and angels that excel in strength (Psalm 103: 20). But what their faculties are, what organs they use, and what is the bond between their psychology and our own, we know not" (POPE, *Compend. Chr. Th.*, I, p. 409). That angels have assumed human bodies, either in appearance or reality, in order to converse with men is evident from the Scriptures. (Cf. Gen. 18: 2 the appearance to Abraham, and Gen. 19: 1, 10 the appearance to Lot.)

Bishop Martensen maintains that the angels or spirits represent general rather than specific powers, and therefore bear the same relation to man that the universal bears to the microcosmical. While the angel is the more powerful spirit, man's spirit is nevertheless the richer and more comprehensive. "For the angel in all his power," he says, "is only the expression of a single one of all those phases which man in the inward nature of his soul, and the richness of his own individuality, is intended to combine into a complete and perfect microcosm." He further asserts that "it is precisely because the angels are only spirits, but not souls, that they cannot possess the same rich existence as man, whose soul is the point of union in which spirit and nature meet. The high privilege, which man enjoys above the angels, finds expression in the Scriptures, where it is said that the Son of God was made not an angel, but a man (Heb. 2: 16). "He was willing to unite Himself with nature alone, which is the central point of creation. . . . . As man is that point in which the spiritual and corporeal worlds are united, and as humanity is the particular form in which the Incarnation has taken place, it follows that men are capable of entering into the fullest and most perfect union with God, while angels, on account of their pure spirituality, can be made only partakers of the majesty of God, but cannot, in the same immediate manner as man, be made partakers of His revelation of love, the mystery of the Incarnation, and the sacramental union connected with it" (Cf. MARTENSEN, *Chr. Dogm.*, p. 132ff). It is for this reason that

St. Peter speaks of those *that have preached the gos-*
pel unto you with the Holy Ghost sent down from
heaven; which things the angels desire to look into
(I Peter 1:12); while St. Paul speaks of *the fellowship*
of the mystery, which from the beginning of the world
hath been hid in God, who created all things by Jesus
Christ: to the intent that now unto the principalities and
powers in heavenly places might be known by the church
the manifold wisdom of God (Eph. 3:9, 10). Here it
is expressly stated that the angels and spirits in heavenly places are merely witnesses to the redemptive glory
of man, but that they themselves cannot partake of
Christ in the same real manner. Hence St. John in the
Apocalypse hears redeemed men singing a new song,
saying, *Thou art worthy to take the book, and to open*
the seals thereof: for thou wast slain, and hast redeemed
us to God by thy blood out of every kindred, and tongue,
and people, and nation. The angels, however, say with
a loud voice, *Worthy is the Lamb that was slain to re-*
ceive power, and riches, and wisdom, and strength, and
honour, and glory, and blessing; while the created universe was heard to say, *Blessing, and honour, and glory,*
and power, be unto him that sitteth upon the throne, and
unto the Lamb for ever and ever (Rev. 5:9, 12, 13).

The attributes ascribed to angels usually include indivisibility, immutability, illocality and agility. Being
indivisible and immutable, angels may be described as
invisible, incorruptible and immortal. Their relation to
space is that of *illocalitas, i.e.,* they are not omnipresent,
but always somewhere present. The attribute of agility
refers more especially to the power of angels to move
with the greatest celerity. Angels must also be regarded as individuals and not as composing a race. It is expressly stated that they are not male and female and do
not propagate their kind (Matt. 22:30). However there
appear to be grades or ranks among the angels, such as
cherubim (Gen. 3:24) seraphim (Isaiah 6:2), thrones,
dominions, principalities, powers (Col. 1:16, Eph. 3:10,
Rom. 8:38), and archangels (I Thess. 4:16, Jude 9).
It is interesting to note that in the lower orders of cre-

ation, the species predominates and the individual is nothing, in man the species and the individual are blended, while in the upper world the species is lost and the individual is alone before God. Whether in church or state, the social structure is divinely intended to care for and preserve the individual, but ultimately the individual must himself appear before God to answer for the deeds done in the body.

The Ministry of Angels. The highest exercise of angels is to wait upon God. The expression, "Lord of hosts," refers to the Lord attended by His angels. When it is said that *all the sons of God shouted for joy* (Job 38: 7) the reference is to the angels as sons. Their chief duty is to minister to the heirs of salvation. They were present at creation, at the giving of the law, at the birth of Christ, after the temptation in the wilderness, in Gethsemane, at the resurrection and the ascension. Hence the author of Hebrews inquires, *Are they not all ministering spirits, sent forth to minister for them who shall be heirs of salvation?* (Heb. 1: 14). For this free service they were prepared by a probationary period. Both Dr. Adam Clarke and Dr. Pope regard the cherubim as symbolical rather than descriptive forms, and signify the forces of the created universe as attendant upon God. The seraphim likewise represent the creature before God and are the watchers, burning with divine love. The schoolmen divided the angels into three hierarchies; (1) Thrones, cherubim and seraphim which attended immediately upon God; (2) Dominions, virtues and powers, which operated in nature and in warfare; and (3) Principalities, archangels and angels, which fulfilled special missions and ministered to the heirs of salvation.

Good and Evil Angels. The angels in their original estate were holy beings, endowed with freedom of will and subjected to a period of probation. They were meant

Four archangels are named in the Scripture: Michael (Dan. 10:13, 12:1; Jude 9, Rev. 12:7); Gabriel (Dan. 8:16, 9:21, Luke 1:19, 26); Raphiel (Apocrypha, Tobit 3:17, 12:15) and Uriel (2 Esdras 4:1). Three others are named in Jewish tradition: Chamuel, Jophiel and Zadkiel.

to choose voluntarily the service of God, and thus be prepared for the free service of ministering to the heirs of salvation. They did not all keep their first estate, but some fell into sin and rebellion against God. Hence we read of the *condemnation of the devil* (I Tim. 3:6) who we gather from the Scriptures was at the head of that portion of the angels which fell away. Satan for this reason is called the *prince of the power of the air* (Eph. 2:2), and his hosts are referred to as *spiritual wickedness in high places* (Eph. 6:12). We may believe also that following their probationary period, the good angels were confirmed in holiness and admitted to a state of glory—a state of indefectibility wherein they always behold the face of God (Matt. 18:10). The wicked likewise were confirmed in their state of misery. Their fall was not due to any necessity from within, or any compulsion from without, but may be regarded as voluntary apostasy. It is surmised that their sin was pride (I Tim. 3:6). As a consequence of their sin they have been brought under the condemnation of God (II Peter 2:4), and shall be punished eternally (Matt. 25:41). Since God is a God of love, we may infer that the angels were not salvable, or He would have made provision for their salvation. Their disposition toward God is one of enmity, this malignant purpose being centered in Satan who stands at their head.

Satan. Satan is a personal being, the head of the kingdom of evil spirits. He is the essential anti-Christ. Two names chiefly, are applied to him, both of which express his character. He is Satan, or adversary, and devil (*diabolus*) or calumniator. Our Lord describes him as sowing the seeds of error and doubt in the Church (Matt. 13:39), and as being both a liar and a murderer (John 8:44). He is able also to transform himself into an angel of light. The rationalists have always denied a personal devil, regarding Satan as a personification of the principles of evil. Even Schleiermacher combatted the idea of a personal Satan. The later mediating theologians, however, such as Martensen, Dorner, Nitsch and Twesten held firmly to the view of Satan as a personal being. This subject must be given further attention in connection with the origin of evil.

PROVIDENCE

The God of creation is also the God of providence. He sustains and cares for the world which He has made, and His tender mercies are over all His works. Providence involves the attributes of God, His goodness, wisdom and power being the most prominent. It involves the Trinity with its various missions and economies. Providence is ascribed to the Father (John 5:17), to the Son (John 5:17, Col. 1:17, Heb. 1:3), and to the Holy Spirit (Psalm 104:30). As Father, God rested from His work of creation but continues it in providence. The Divine Sabbath is therefore a perfect rest filled with perfect activity—not in a new creative work, not even in continuous creation, but in the preservation and upholding of all things by the word of His power. There is also a special economy of providence which belongs to the Son in the administration of redemption—that of the kingly office of the mediatorial economy (Matt. 28:18, Eph. 1:22, Heb. 1:2, 3). There is a further economy of the Holy Spirit as the Lord and Giver of life. He is especially the God of Christian providence in the administration of redemption. Providence, however, is conventionally ascribed to the Father. Since God as Creator is both transcendent and immanent in His relation to the world, we are under the necessity of guarding against the errors of Deism and Pantheism in any discussion of the subject. These positions have been previously discussed and need only brief mention here.

Providence may be defined as that activity of the Triune God by which He conserves, cares for and governs the world which He has made. The subject may be broadly divided into *General Providence* by which is meant God's care for the world as a whole and everything in it; and *Special Providence* which refers more particularly to His care for the human race. In the strictest sense of the term, providence can be revealed only in history, and is concerned with the exigencies arising from the freedom of man's will. Since the subject of creation in the sense of the æon necessitated a discussion of God's purpose in creation, we need now to direct our attention only to a consideration of the administrative phases of this subject. Here we find another classification, that of *Ordinary Providence,* by which is meant the general exercise of God's care through established principles and laws; and *Extraordinary Providence,* or God's miraculous intervention in the ordinary course of nature or history. It is with the former that we are now specially concerned. Providence further involves the twofold idea of a conserving and a ruling Agency, but in its application to the objects of providence, the threefold division is more comprehensive and appropriate. We shall, therefore, treat the subject of Providence under the following main divisions, *first,* Conservation as referring to inanimate nature; *second,* Preservation as referring to animate nature and the creaturely wants of the subhuman kingdoms; and *third,* Government in its application to man in his probationary state.

Conservation. Conservation is God's preserving providence in the realm of the physical universe. It is

You say, you allow a general providence, but deny a particular one. And what is a general, of whatever kind it be, that includes no particulars? Is not every general necessarily made up of its several particulars? Can you instance me any general that is not? Tell me any genus, if you can, that contains no species? What is it that constitutes a genus, but so many species added together? What, I pray, is a whole that contains no parts? Mere nonsense and contradiction. Every whole must, in the nature of things, be made up of its several parts; insomuch that if there be no parts, there can be no whole.—JOHN WESLEY, *Sermon on Providence.*

A general and a special providence cannot be two different modes of divine operation. The same providential administration is necessarily at the same time general and special, for the same reason, because it reaches without exception equally to every event and creation in the world. A general providence is special because it secures general results by the control of every event, great and small leading to that result. A special providence is general because it specially controls all individual beings and actions. All events are so related together as a concatenated system of causes and effects and conditions, that a general providence that is not at the same time special is as inconceivable as a whole which has no parts or a chain which has no links.—A. A. HODGE, *Outlines of Theology,* p. 266.

concerned with the relation of God to the world. The question immediately arises, Is there no further relation of God to the world than the primary fact of creative causality? Have the laws of God as found in nature a real efficiency, so that His immediate presence and agency are no longer required? Or, is God still immanent in nature, upholding all things with the word of His power? (Heb. 1:3). The Scriptures are explicit in their statements: *He giveth to all life, and breath, and all things* (Acts 17:25); *For in him we live, and move, and have our being* (Acts 17:28); *And he is before all things, and by him all things consist* (Col. 1:17); *For of him, and through him, and to him, are all things* (Rom. 11:36). Mr. Wesley sums up the evangelical belief concerning conservation in the following clear and concise statement. He says, "God is also the supporter of all the things which He has made. He beareth, upholdeth, sustaineth all created things by the word of His power; by the same powerful word which brought them out of nothing. As this was absolutely necessary for the beginning of their existence, it is equally so for the continuance of it; were His almighty influence withdrawn, they could not subsist a moment longer" *(Sermon on Providence)*.

As to the mode of this relation existing between God and the world, three theories have been advanced. (1) *Continuous Creation.* Admitting that creation is by the power of God, and that continued existence is due to

"It follows from what has been observed," says Edwards, "that God's upholding created substance, or causing its existence in each successive moment, is altogether equivalent to an immediate production out of nothing, at each moment; because its existence at this moment is not merely in part from God, but wholly from Him, and not in any part or degree from its antecedent existence. For the supposing that its antecedent existence concurs with God in efficiency, to produce some part of the effect, is attended with all the very same absurdities which have been shown to attend the supposition of its producing it wholly. Therefore the antecedent existence is nothing, as to any proper influence or assistance in the affairs; and consequently God produces the effect as much from nothing as if there had been nothing before. So that this effect differs not at all from the first creation, but only circumstantially; as in first creation there had been no such act and effect of God's power before; whereas, His giving existence afterward follows preceding acts and effects of the same kind in an established order.—EDWARDS, *Works*, II, p. 489.

the unceasing conservation of His Power, the notion of constant dependence easily passes over into the error of continuous creation. If conservation requires momentarily the same divine energizing as was required for its original existence, the transition is easy. In this form the doctrine appeared early in the Church. Augustine taught that the created universe is ceaselessly and absolutely dependent upon the omnipotent power of God, and were He to withdraw from the world His creative power, it would straightway lapse into nothingness (Cf. *De Civitate Dei,* xii, 25). So also, Thomas Aquinas held that preservation is an ever-renewed creation, and that all creaturely causes derive their efficiency directly and continually from the First Cause (AQUINAS, *Summa Theologica,* pt. 1, ¶ 104, art. i; pt. 1, ¶ 105, art. 5). This theory of continuous creation, however, as it relates to conservation, is essentially different from the theory of continuous creation as a theory of origination. The former insists upon a creative act and a continuation of these creative acts in conservation; the latter, as previously discussed would supersede any creative act and substitute in its place an emergence or continuous becoming. Among modern theologians, Jonathan Edwards is the best representative of this position.

Another theory is (2) *Concurrence.* By this is meant that activity of God which concurs in second causes, and co-operates with living creatures. The term came into prominence with the Lutheran theologian Quentedt (1617-1680), and was used by the earlier theologians to express what, in more recent theology, is known as divine immanence. The theory, however, must be understood to mean, not merely that God conserves certain powers in nature as second causes, but that there is an immediate co-operation of God with the action and effects of these second causes. Dr. Pope rejects the theory, stating that it disguises "under the term concursus the idea of such co-operation between the First Cause and second causes as makes the resultant action equally that of God and that of the immediate agent." He admits, however, that outside the sphere of moral action, we may adopt Quentedt's position. Dr. Stump admits also that the doctrine of concurrence raises some difficulties in connection with the sinful acts of men, but points out that the older dogmaticians solved this problem by declaring that God concurs in the *effect* but not in the *defect* of a sinful act. Dr. Strong holds that God concurs with the evil acts of His creatures, but only in so far as they are natural acts and not evil (Cf. STUMP, *Christian Faith*, p. 80, STRONG, *Syst. Th.*, II, p. 418). The theory of concurrence appears to be closely related to what is known in philosophy as the Occasionalism of the Cartesians, and is so treated by Dr. Miley.

There is still another theory, that of (3) *Absolute Dependence,* which makes all things depend upon the immediate agency of God to the exclusion of second causes. This theory shows the influence of an idealistic philosophy of the Berkeleyan type, and tends directly towards pantheism in theology. In the moral realm it has had the same effect as the Fatalism of the ancient Stoics, and by Dr. Pope is considered the ground of rigid predestinarianism in modern theology (Cf. POPE, *Compend. Chr. Th.*, I, p. 447).

In the scientific realm, certain theories have also been advanced as solutions of this perplexing problem. Here may be mentioned: (1) *The Hypothesis of Natural Law,* which holds the inseparability of matter and force, from which spring all forms of energy in nature, whether inorganic or organic. The theory denies the necessity of the Divine Will and is atheistic in its tendencies. Its chief representative was Tyndall. (2) *The Theory of a Supramaterial Physis or Nature.* Another school of scientists of which Owen and Huxley were representatives denied likewise the distinction between matter and force but held that both were phenomenal manifestations of an underlying substratum. This Divine Substance was in some sense identical with the *natura naturans* of Spinoza. The whole theory tended toward pantheism of the Spinozan type, but was in another sense the ground of the modern Evolutionary Hypothe-

sis. (3) *The Theory of a Plastic Nature.* This theory
holds that there is an intermediate nature between God
and the world, as does the former, but instead of regarding this as an unknown substratum, it regards it as an
unconscious organizing intelligence. This appears to
differ in name only, from the world-soul or *anima-mundi*
of Platonic physics. All these theories are attempts to
explain the world by means of secondary causes and to
dispense with the immediate agency of God. Attempts
have been made by later theologians to Christianize at
least one of these theories under the name of Theistic
Evolution. The scientific discoveries of the present are
becoming more and more an apologetic for the biblical
teaching concerning creation and conservation.

We may then, summarize the theological position
concerning Conservation as follows, (1) Divine Co-
operation *(concursus Dei generalis)* which is a concursus amounting almost if not entirely to continuous creation. This theory was held by Augustine, Thomas
Aquinas, Jonathan Edwards and in an accommodated
sense by Hopkins and Emmons. (2) The Divine Intermediate Impulse *(impulsus non cogens)* as advanced
by Luther; (3) The Divine Sustentation *(sustentatio
Dei)* as held by the Arminians; and (4) The Theory of
Divine Superintendence and Control—a theory which
Dr. Cocker approved in a measure, as approximating
the ever-present and pervading energy which he advocated (Cf. COCKER, *Theistic Conception of the World,*
p. 176). It is evident that the truth of conservation lies
somewhere between the extremes of thought, which on
the one hand would eliminate all second causes, and on
the other deny the necessity of a First Cause. Not only
the theological writers, but the religious life of the
Church generally, has ever maintained a belief in the
immediate presence of God in the conservation of the
material universe, and has likewise regarded the laws of
nature as the observed principles of the divine activity.
Dr. Miley admits that this is the position commonly held
in the Church, but questions the application of Conservation to anything but mediate or secondary creation. It

does not, he thinks, apply to original or primary creation. The doctrine, however, was held by John Wesley who declares that "all matter of whatever kind is absolutely and totally inert. It does not, cannot in any case, move itself. . . . . Neither the sun, moon, nor stars move themselves. They are moved every moment by the Almighty hand that made them" (Cf. WESLEY, *Sermons*, II, pp. 178, 179). Other writers which have defended this view are Dr. Samuel Clarke, Dugald Stewart, Nitzsch, Mueller, Chalmers, Harris, Young, Whedon, Channing, Martineau, Hodge, Whewell, Bascom, Tullock, Herschel, Wallace, Proctor and Cocker (Cf. CROOKS and HURST, *Cyclopædia, Art. Providence*). However, all of these recognized laws, principles, and secondary causes in the conservation of the world, but they did not hypostasize them into active agencies which would supersede God and banish Him from the universe.

Preservation. As we use the term preservation, we do not identify it with conservation, but employ it in an accommodated sense to designate the work of providence in the animate realm. Its scope includes all animate nature, whether impersonal or personal. It may be difficult to tell when the line between the inorganic and organic realm is passed, such is the mystery of life; but we may be sure that down to the lowest cell structure, there is need for providential care if the organism is to expand into its predetermined forms. Plant life has many ingenious ways of providing for its propagation or seeking its nourishment from the soil. God governs the lower orders of the animal kingdom principally by appetites and instincts. *The ants are a people not strong, yet they prepare their meat in the summer* (Prov. 30:25); *The stork in the heaven knoweth her appointed times; and the turtle and the crane and the swallow observe the time of their coming; but my people know not the judgment of the Lord* (Jer. 8:7). *The eyes of all wait upon thee; and thou givest them their meat in due season. Thou openest thine hand, and satisfiest the desire of every living thing* (Psalm 145:15, 16). *He giveth to the beast his food, and to the young ravens which cry* (Psalm 147:9). This providential care extends to man also as a creature of God, although as a free moral agent man must be considered as under the providential government of God. In this broader division of providential care, we have the words of our Lord who declared that the Father *maketh his sun to rise on the evil and on the good, and sendeth rain on the just and on the unjust* (Matt. 5:45).

Government. When we pass to the realm of responsible, voluntary action, there is a new relation which subsists between the purpose of God and the manner in which this purpose is realized. Here God's relation is not properly causative as in Conservation and Preservation, but moral, that is, it must be exerted in the form of a motive, and not in the sense of compulsion. The finite will is interposed between the will of God and the consequences of that will in free activity, so that the resulting action is not properly the work of God, but that of the creature to whom the act belongs. Hence while God has given the power of freedom to the creature and permitted its exercise, a sinful action on the part of the creature cannot be said to be God's act. The older theologians distinguished four different modes of the divine government. (1) *Permissio* or Permissive. "When we say that God permits any event," says Wakefield, "we are not to understand the term to indicate that He allows it, or consents to it; but rather that He does not exert His power to prevent it. God permits sin but he does not approve of it; for as He is infinitely holy, sin must always be the object of His abhorrence. Accordingly, He testifies against the very sins into which He permits men to fall, denouncing His threatenings against them, and actually punishing them for their crimes" (WAKEFIELD, *Chr. Th.*, p. 266). (Cf. II Chron.

Dr. Miley states that it is the sense of Scripture that life was to be perpetuated through a law of propagation, but it does not mean that life itself as thus initiated should be sufficient for all the future of this realm. We should rather find in the facts the proof of a divine agency than the intrinsic sufficiency of life itself for such a marvelous outcome.— MILEY, *Syst. Th.*, I, p. 326.

32: 31, Psalm 81: 12, 13, Hosea 4: 17, Acts 14: 16, and Rom. 1: 24, 28.) (2) *Impeditio,* or Preventive. This is the restraining act of God by which He prevents men from committing sin. There are many instances of this grace in the Scriptures: *Behold, I will hedge up thy way with thorns, and make a wall, that she shall not find her paths* (Hos. 2: 6). The thorns and the wall evidently refer to the restraining grace of God (Cf. Gen. 20: 6, Gen. 31: 24, Psalm 19: 13). (3) *Directio,* or Directive. God overrules the evil acts of man, and brings out of them consequences which were unintended by the evil agencies. This is sometimes referred to as an overruling providence. *As for you,* said Joseph to his brethren, *ye thought evil against me; but God meant it unto good, to bring to pass, as it is this day, to save much people alive* (Gen. 50: 20). (Cf. also Psalm 76: 10, Isaiah 10: 5, John 13: 27, Acts 4: 27, 28, Rom. 9: 17, 18.) (4) *Determinatio,* or Determinative. By this is meant the control which God exercises over the bounds of sin and wickedness. *And the Lord said unto Satan, Behold, all that he hath is in thy power; only upon himself put not forth thine hand* (Job 1: 12). (Cf. also Job 2: 6, Psalm 124: 2, II Thess. 2: 7.) One of the best known and most frequently quoted passages of Scripture comes under this general head. *God is faithful, who will not suffer you to be tempted above that ye are able; but will with the temptation also make a way to escape, that ye may be able to bear it* (I Cor. 10: 13).

The root idea of the Christian doctrine of Divine Providence in this sphere is, that God rules over all in love. This reaches its triumphant expression in St. Paul who declares that *we know that all things work together for good to them that love God, to them who are the called according to his purpose* (Rom. 8: 28). As to the mode of Providence, its events are as supernatural as the miracles but have no open manifestation. Miracles have a distinct office in attesting the authority of prophets or apostles, but as Dr. Miley points out, providential events have no such office and therefore need no such manifestation. It is evident that the question of Divine Providence is far-reaching in its scope, involving as it does, not only the government of the world generally, but also such questions as the existence of evil in the world, the place and importance of miracles, the efficacy of prayer, and the whole problem of theodicy. These subjects will be considered in their proper place.

One of the best summaries of this subject of Divine Providence is that found in Dr. Pope's *Compendium of Christian Theology* (Vol. I, p. 456). He says, "A few general observations are still necessary to complete this view of Providence. It is obviously the most comprehensive term in the language of theology; the background, mysterious in its brightness or darkness, of all the several departments of religious truth. Rather, it penetrates and fills the whole compass of the relations of man with his Maker. It connects the Unseen God with the visible creation, and the visible creation with the work of redemption, and redemption with personal salvation, and personal salvation with the end of all things. There is no topic which has already been discussed, none which awaits discussion, that does not pay its tribute to the all-embracing, all-surrounding doctrine of Providence. The word itself—let it be once more impressed—in one aspect of it carries our thoughts up to that supreme purpose which was in the beginning with God, and in another carries our thoughts down to the foreseen end or consummation of all things; while it includes between these the whole infinite variety of the dealings of God with man. It silently accompanies theology, therefore, into all its regions of study and meditation; touches it literally at every point, and sheds its glory, oppressive to reason but invigorating to faith, over all the branches of its investigation. It ought to be the grand reconciler of the contending advocates of predestination and conditional election. The former claim must have all the legitimate rights of the *prothesis* (πρόθεσις); the latter should not be defrauded of the rights of the *prognosis* (πρόγνωσις); while both must rejoice in the *pronoia* (πρόνοια) that comes between.

All theological truths are rounded out by this unfathomable word. But for the very reason that it is, in its widest compass, so literally boundless and universal, we find it necessary to give it only a scanty treatment as one distinct department."